IMISCOE (International Migration, Integration and Social Cohesion)

IMISCOE is a Network of Excellence uniting over 500 researchers from various institutes that specialise in migration studies across Europe. Networks of Excellence are cooperative research ventures that were created by the European Commission to help overcome the fragmentation of international studies. They amass a crucial source of knowledge and expertise to help inform European leadership today.

Since its foundation in 2004, IMISCOE has advanced an integrated, multi-disciplinary and globally comparative research programme to address the themes specified in its name, short for: International Migration, Integration and Social Cohesion in Europe. IMISCOE members come from all branches of the economic and social sciences, the humanities and law. The Network draws from existing studies and advances innovative lines of inquiry key to European policymaking and governance. Priority is placed on developing a theoretical design to promote new research and offer practical alternatives for sound policy.

The IMISCOE-Amsterdam University Press Series was created to make the Network's findings and results available to researchers, policymakers, the media and the public at large. High-quality manuscripts authored by IMISCOE members and cooperating partners are published in one of four distinct series.
   Research
   Reports
   Dissertations
   Textbooks

The RESEARCH series presents empirical and theoretical scholarship addressing issues of international migration, integration and social cohesion in Europe. Authored by experts in the field, the works provide a rich reference source for researchers and other concerned parties.

The REPORTS series responds to needs for knowledge within IMISCOE's mandated fields of migration research. Compiled by leading specialists, the works disseminate succinct and timely information for European policymakers, practitioners and other stakeholders.

The DISSERTATIONS series showcases select PhD monographs written by IMISCOE doctoral candidates. The works span an array of fields within studies of international migration, integration and social cohesion in Europe.

The TEXTBOOKS series produces manuals, handbooks and other didactic tools developed by specialists in migration studies. The works are used within the IMISCOE training programme and for educational purposes by academic institutes worldwide.

IMISCOE Policy Briefs and more information on the Network can be found at www.imiscoe.org.

The Family in Question

Immigrant and Ethnic Minorities in Multicultural Europe

edited by
Ralph Grillo

IMISCOE Research

AMSTERDAM UNIVERSITY PRESS

Cover photo: © Meghann Ormond (Agacan Kebab House, Dundee, Scotland)

Cover design: Studio Jan de Boer BNO, Amsterdam
Layout: The DocWorkers, Almere

ISBN   978 90 5356 869 9
e-ISBN   978 90 4850 153 3
NUR   741 / 763

© Ralph Grillo / Amsterdam University Press, 2008

Table of Contents

Acknowledgments

The chapters included in this collection were selected from papers presented to a workshop on 'Debating Cultural Difference: The Family', held at the University of Sussex in April 2006, funded by a generous grant from IMISCOE Cluster B6. Dr. Ruba Salih (University of Exeter) and Professor Steven Vertovec (Director, Max Planck Institute for the Study of Religious and Ethnic Diversity, Göttingen) chaired the sessions. The workshop was followed by an IMISCOE-funded training session for doctoral students. During the workshop, the trainees acted as discussants and, in some cases, presented papers. I would like to thank the following for their contributions: Anna Arnone, Kristine Krause, Paulien Muller, Marianne Pedersen, Radha Rajkotia, Roberta Ricucci, Marta Rosales, Anna Stepien, Femke Stock and Susanne Wessendorf.

Preface

Ralph Grillo

Families of immigrants and settled populations of immigrant origin have become central to arguments about the rights and wrongs of ways of living in multicultural societies in Europe and elsewhere. The cultural practices believed to be characteristic of such families are central to the current intense, acrimonious debate about difference and its limits. Such (often imagined) practices are frequently the object of policy initiatives and much media comment, and on a daily basis preoccupy social service practitioners, teachers and others. At the same time, immigrants and ethnic minorities are themselves reflecting on how to manage their family relationships in a changing world in which migration is transnational, societies are increasingly pluralised, and relations ever more complex and less clear-cut.

This politicisation of the family, as it may be called, which touches not only immigrants, occurs on many levels, and in different interconnected locations in Europe and across the globe. It may be observed at the United Nations and in the array of international organisations concerned with human rights, especially the rights of women and children (born and unborn), as well as in transnational religious organisations such as the Catholic Church or (in a different way) the Muslim ummah. It is apparent in debates within the European Union and its constituent nation-states, and within local states and their institutions (health, social services, housing, etc.). The contested nature of families and everyday familial practices also appears in arguments (sometimes their resolution) in migrant and minority ethnic communities, associations, and neighbourhoods, and within households and networks of relations which may, in an era of transnational migration, be widely dispersed across geographical and socio-cultural space, linking members perhaps located – and this would not be especially unusual among Sikhs, for example – in Punjab, the United Kingdom, Canada, Australia, and East Africa. Views on the nature of the 'Turkish family' may be aired in Germany as much as in Turkey.

Within this plurality of multi-sited, multi-vocal representations, discourses, narratives and reflections, the family is, crucially, seen as a moral order, a set of beliefs, values, ideas and practices by reference to which family members and their relationships are identified, organised and bound together. Sometimes idealised, sometimes vilified, there are many doubts, hesitations, and disputes about what the family is, and how familial relations should be defined and practiced. Following the first introductory chapter, which reflects on such issues, the multiplicity of representations and their interaction is explored in this volume in a series of case studies focusing on immigrant and minority ethnic families in selected European countries, including Austria, the Netherlands, Norway, Portugal, Spain, Switzerland, and the UK, with one chapter casting a wider, comparative net, reminding us that these processes are evident in the management of migrants' transnational relationships, and in debates about how to manage such relationships, which criss-cross the globe.

Each case study is specific as to time and place, but has wider implications and, through diverse methodological and theoretical approaches, deals with the complex relationship between what may be called 'external' (or 'outsider') and 'internal' perspectives on migrant families. In many Western societies, public discourse typically represents immigrant and minority ethnic families as 'problematic', their cultural practices reckoned unacceptable for pragmatic or ideological reasons. This external perspective, which may be observed in many of the institutions seeking to influence familial relations within minority ethnic communities, can be compared with one from the standpoint of migrants themselves, though as the first chapter shows, such a simplistic contrast, while a useful heuristic device, is ultimately inadequate for describing the various subject positions of those engaged in these debates.

Concern about the commitment of immigrants to kinship conventions different from those of the receiving society has a lengthy history – some 40 years in the case of the UK – but in contemporary Britain this concern is central to a debate which is no less heated than that surrounding religious affiliation. Arguing that migratory processes are to a large extent kinship-driven, Roger Ballard shows that, in the face of criticism of their ways of life, most settlers of South Asian origin and their locally born offspring are resolved to maintain distinctive domestic lifestyles, involving complex networks of individual and collective reciprocities, which have formed the basis of thriving ethnic colonies. Despite the efforts of migration managers, the transnational extension of kinship networks has reinforced this tendency, with both positive and negative consequences. The result is a complex stand-off, in which marriage has become a central bone of contention.

Anniken Hagelund, writing about Norway, notes that the immigrant family has become a key site of conflict in debates about integration, multiculturalism and ethnic relations. In public discourse, immigrant families, and particularly transnational arranged marriages, have been

linked to a wider integration problematic, and public debate has focused on the need to use immigration controls to manage familial relations. This has led to changes in the regulation of family immigration,
partly in order to produce behavioural changes among families living
in Norway.

Maria Lucinda Fonseca and Meghann Ormond show how the legal
and administrative framework in receiving countries affects immigrant
families, with specific reference to the Portuguese experience. While family reunification is the main immigration gateway into the European
Union, in 2004 only a fifth of non-EU citizens applied for a Portuguese residence permit via this official route, and the chapter considers
why the percentage was so low. Data from a major survey ('Family Reunification and Immigration in Portugal') documents how the concept
of family has been defined and put into practice by the authorities, and
the official barriers that must be overcome for sponsors and family
members to qualify for reunification in Portugal. Paradoxically, say
Fonseca and Ormond, imposing a traditional nuclear family model on
immigrants inadequately reflects the fluid nature of contemporary
non-immigrant families.

Erik Snel and Femke Stock explore some of the attitudes underlying
these approaches to immigrant families by analysing the views on the
'Muslim family' found in the writing and speeches of Ayaan Hirsi Ali.
Hirsi Ali is a controversial public figure in the Netherlands, with
strong opinions about Islam and the place of women and the family in
Muslim communities. In her estimation, the nature of the 'Muslim family' is constituted by the patriarchal relations between men and women which are embedded in, and emblematic of, the cultures of the regions from which immigrants come, and which make their bearers un-
suitable for integration. For her, Islam legitimates the cultural values
and social organisation characteristic of those regions. Snel and Stock,
however, criticise Hirsi Ali for her generalising statements about the
position of women in Islam and her implicit essentialist notion of culture.

Snel and Stock lead us into a series of chapters which look more closely at the perspectives of migrants themselves and the debates taking
place among them, and how these relate to outsider perspectives within societies of immigration. Susana and José Bastos compare three different 'family dynamics' – modes of articulating the relationship between genders and generations – present within six migrant groups in
Portugal, and examine the different views and practices to which they
give rise. But they also consider these dynamics from the perspective
of Portuguese society and discover that for social, cultural and historical reasons they seem to pose fewer problems than might be expected
from research findings in other parts of Europe. This raises the ques-

tion whether this is unique to Portugal and/or reflects socio-historical differences between countries like Portugal and other countries in Europe, such as Norway.

Two of the groups studied by Bastos and Bastos (Ismailis and Sunnis of Indian origin) are Muslim, and Anna Stepien provides a further opportunity for reconsidering the representation of the Muslim family as found in the writing of Hirsi Ali, and indeed widely in the European imagination. She does so by documenting the reflections of Muslim migrants on familial relations in their everyday lives in Austria, and in relation to the contemporary integration debate in that country, offering a detailed account of their aspirations, their 'dream of a family', and their perception of what it means to live as a Muslim in a Western country. She shows that in Austria, as in Germany, public discourse is complex, inconsistent and constantly changing, but both within migrant families and within the public sphere there seems to be a general agreement that Austrian families are to be equated with 'modernity' and Muslim families with 'tradition', though there is no clear agreement on the evaluation of these associations.

While Stepien is concerned with the views of young Muslim men and women, Kanwal Mand reflects on the situation of the elderly, and documents alternative perspectives on migrants of various South Asian background in Britain. She presents a case study of a voluntary organisation (Ekta) dedicated to the welfare of the elderly in a borough of London, and finds three sets of actors with different perceptions and needs: local council staff (who in London may well come from ethnic minorities) concerned to implement national policies; Asian women and their families who draw on local facilities for support; and the staff of the voluntary organisation (themselves Asian) who mediate between these two. Such organisations, she argues, can be interpreted as holding an intermediate position, whereby they are involved in a form of translation between one voice (the public) and the internal voice (of migrant families).

The chapters by Bastos and Bastos and by Mand remind us that, although Islam figures prominently in contemporary debates in Europe, the 'Muslim family' – or what is imagined to be the 'Muslim family – is not the only family in question. Susanne Wessendorf, for example, writes about alternative perceptions of the family among second-generation Italians in Switzerland. While some see the family as a valuable resource, others experience it as 'golden cage' which restricts them in shaping their lives. These views emerged from the context of post-war Italian labour migration to Switzerland when, as a consequence of repeated separation, Italian migrants developed idealised notions of the 'united family'. A similar idealisation of the Italian family appears in Swiss public discourse, and contrasts with the perception of other migrants, such as Muslims, whose familial relations are thought to make their integration impossible.

Radha Rajkotia also explores young people's concerns about familial relations which they confront through migration. She focuses on their views on a controversial practice, female circumcision, illegal in much of Europe but traditionally important in defining the role of women in the family in Sierra Leone. She does not argue its legitimacy, but examines its meaning within the institution of *Bondo*, the women's initiation association, and the changing perspective of teenage girls on *Bondo* in Sierra Leone and in England, where they sought refuge from civil conflict. Rajkotia highlights the transformation of the institution through migration, arguing that *Bondo* is central to girls' identities as women in Sierra Leone, and as Sierra Leoneans in England. In migration between these two contexts, not only does the meaning of *Bondo* change, but at the same time the girls find freedom to voice alternative views, opening the possibility for an internal debate different from that possible in Sierra Leone.

The two concluding chapters widen the discussion in a number of ways. Dan Rodríguez-García, in exploring the situation of Senegalese and Gambian (male) immigrants living in mixed unions with Spanish nationals in Catalonia, Spain, shows how cultural debates (including, for example, about circumcision) may be observed within the conjugal relationship itself. Intermarriage, involving the formation of transcultural and transnational families, constitutes a complex socio-cultural space, encompassing both the local and the global, in which social actors, rather than cultures as whole, fixed entities, are protagonists. Their responses are very diverse and Rodríguez-García illustrates the dialogic aspect of family life as a negotiated intercultural order.

Mixed marriages of the kind discussed by Rodríguez-García have an important transnational dimension, and indeed most of the families with which the present volume is concerned live transnationally, with transnationalism shaping their lives and the debates with which they are engaged. Indeed, transnationalism and the transnational family figures more or less prominently, and in various ways, in several of the chapters (e.g. those by Ballard, Fonseca and Ormond, Bastos and Bastos, Stepien, Mand, Wessendorf, Rajkotia, Rodríguez-García). Loretta Baldassar brings that dimension to the fore by focusing on migrants and refugees whose families are scattered across different parts of the world and who are engaged in caring 'at a distance', a phenomenon which is commanding increasing scholarly attention. She is concerned centrally with the family as a moral order, and with the negotiation of that order by people who are constrained by a multiplicity of circumstances at micro, meso and macro levels. She reminds us that the obligation on kin to provide care and support, and the practical difficulties of so doing while living transnationally, entail great emotional stress, and the debates in which informants engage, are, she says, 'heartfelt'.

The chapters show that instead of recognising the complex changes now taking place, which are earnestly debated by migrants as much as anyone, those concerned with public policy are often in danger of un-thinkingly reflecting popular imagination, thus contributing to what has become a dangerous xenophobic stereotyping and essentialising of immigrants and their descendants. Indeed, if there is a single lesson of these case studies, it is that social actors in multicultural societies are all too often talking past each other. Those who debate immigrant and minority ethnic families from an external perspective tend to focus on the rights and wrongs of their social and cultural beliefs and practices from the point of view of how far they clash with values sanctioned by the dominant receiving society or with assumed universal rights. Inter-nal debates also address such issues, but at the same time many immi-grants are more likely to be concerned with the reciprocal obligations, including obligations to care and support, which define their familial relations and underpin the moral order which the family represents.

1 The Family in Dispute: Insiders and Outsiders

Ralph Grillo

Introduction

With the movement to the European Union of increasing numbers of migrants and refugees originating from outside Europe, 'migrant families (and their composition, their way of life) have become a true obsession for migration policies and public opinion' (Balibar 2004: 123). Traditional migration models (first came men, then families) are rightly criticised for omitting economically active, independent females, and representing women as 'passive followers' (Kofman 1999: 273). Yet although many migrants (women and men) have indeed been 'single', coming from Africa or Latin America, and more recently Eastern Europe, and eventually returning to countries of origin, many others, unintentionally or perforce, have become settlers, bringing or sending for partners and children or establishing new families *in situ*.[1] The population of migrant or refugee origin is thus now substantially a family population, with implications for housing, health and educational systems in receiving countries which in varying degrees are implementing neoliberal economic and social agendas, running down provision for welfare.

Although many so-called migrants are long-term settlers, or have been born and brought up in receiving countries, relationships with sending countries have not diminished. As a huge literature has shown, information and communication technologies, and cheap air travel, enable many to maintain significant transnational social, economic and cultural ties with countries of origin, and with fellow migrants elsewhere. Their transnationalism, especially after 9/11, fed an increasingly influential view, apparent by the beginning of the new millennium, that immigration had led to an 'excess of alterity' (Sartori 2002), with European countries becoming 'too diverse' (Goodhart 2004), and migrant 'communities' (quotes hereafter understood) with values at odds with those of Western secular society threatening social cohesion. At the same time, rapid changes in morality and in the structure and form of cohabitation, have led, across Europe, to a more general uncertainty about the family, the nexus of relations of *kinship* (understood biologically and/or socially), and *affinity* (relations through spouses or partners). In this context, the immigrant or minority ethnic family is at issue in several senses.

The Family at Issue

As Pine points out, in the social sciences, the family 'has come to be seen less and less as a "natural" form of human social organization, and more and more as a culturally and historically specific symbolic system, or ideology' (1996: 223), and she emphasises the way in which in 'Euro-American discourse', the idea of the family is 'ideologically "loaded"', or imbued with sets of politically and culturally contested ideas about the correct or moral ways in which people should conduct their lives, and the people with whom they should conduct them' (ibid.) The family is a social construct which entails beliefs and values defining family members and relationships with them. It thus constitutes a moral order, albeit with widely diverse understandings of what that order should be. At the same time, certain conceptions of what the family is, and how relations within it should be conducted, are likely to be hegemonic in a particular national formation. This has two implications.

First, migrants arriving from different cultural backgrounds, often with very different 'premigration cultural frameworks', as Foner calls them (1997: 961), confront policymakers who may persist in employing an ideal (European) model of the nuclear family to judge qualification for entry, for example, even though such a model fails to acknowledge alternative constructions of familial relations. Thus, while the right to live in a family is recognised in international conventions, immigration policies may circumscribe that right by defining what a family is or should be. Kofman (1999: 279), for instance, argues that conditions set for family reunification, which since restrictions on migration implemented in the 1970s have become the principal official means of entering the EU,

> exemplify the construction of family norms and the role of the state in shaping gender relations, in particular in setting the conditions of marriage and social reproduction, and sustaining female dependency ... conformity to a model of the traditional family is imposed in order to gain entry, cohabiting not being recognized for purposes of family reunification by most European states (see also Moch 2005; Nauck & Settles 2001)

Secondly, the tenor of public discourse on immigration and integration not only poses questions about administrative ethnocentrism, but also about the application of apparently universal but outmoded definitions of familial relations. As Fonseca and Ormond comment (*infra*):

> imposing a traditional nuclear family model on immigrants by allowing only for certain members that can fit in the stereotypical, traditional nuclear family unit may not adequately reflect the reality of the modern Western family structure.

In reviewing research on family migration, Bailey and Boyle point to the rapid diversification of family and household structures in Europe at large. The traditional, mainstream idea of the nuclear family, they say, is 'becoming increasingly redundant in an era when cohabitation, separation, divorce and "reconstituted families" are becoming increasingly common' (2004: 236; see also Kofman 2004). But immigration managers, while refusing to recognise other cultural modes of constructing familial relations, also ignore the changing contemporary world of 'single-parents families, same-sex unions, serial monogamy, and households based on friendship rather than sexual partnerships' (Pine 1996: 227), to say nothing of dramatic changes in the nature of kinship made possible by new reproductive technologies,

The migrant family has also been at issue when, during the 1990s, entry criteria were tightened at a time of growing concern in policy circles about integration, and against the background of a 'backlash' or 'cultural-diversity skeptical turn' (Grillo 2003; Vertovec & Wessendorf 2006). 'Integration' – the word appears in numerous European languages – is a 'controversial and hotly debated' term (Castles, Korac & Vasta 2002: 3.1.1). Sometimes it connotes assimilation, but the more generally accepted view is that integration refers to 'a long lasting process of inclusion and acceptance of migrants in the core institutions, relations and statuses of the receiving society' (Heckmann 2005: 15). A question much debated in contemporary accounts of immigration in Western Europe is whether a lack of integration (in the sense defined) is the result of migrants' self-exclusion from mainstream society (Bracalenti & Benini 2005), and immigrant and minority ethnic families are 'at issue' because they are suspected of playing an important role in this 'failure' to integrate.

Within the public sphere of Western societies such families are for these and other reasons often represented as problematic, sometimes practically (what should be done about accommodation for extended households, for example), sometimes ideologically, because their practices and the collectivist beliefs thought to underpin them (e.g. arranged marriages) are deemed unacceptable in contemporary societies which espouse liberal, democratic, individualistic values. This viewpoint, which may be grounded, consciously or unconsciously, in essen-

tialist idealisations of the 'Western' family by comparison with the families of 'others', permeates much (often polemical) journalism and
popular and political discourse. It may also be observed in the interventions of institutions such as social services which, nationally or locally,
engage with, and seek to mould familial relations within minority ethnic communities. This perspective on their families may be contrasted
with one which takes the viewpoint of migrants themselves, among
whom the family is equally at issue.

Immigration regulations (e.g. in Norway or Portugal; see Hagelund,
and Fonseca & Ormond *infra*) influence family structures and practices
at the point of entry, affecting how families present themselves to the
authorities. *Inter alia*, this shows how 'the act and circumstances of migration itself ... produce variants in the practice and meaning of family
and household' (King, Thomson, Fielding & Warnes 2006: 260). What
happens to the family under conditions of transnational migration provides another illustration. Bryceson and Vuorela (2002: 6) demonstrate
how transnational migrants continue to 'enact their sense of being part
of the same family', and they coin the term 'relativizing' to describe
how members of transnational families 'work out the nature of their
relationships to other family members', as well as engaging in the 'construction and continual revision of one's role and family identity
through the individual's life cycle' (2002: 15).

Transnational migration means that new questions are posed, and
new solutions sought, for example through the demands of distant
care, largely ignored in official, traditional, conceptions of the family
(Kofman 2004: 246). This is an important theme in the work of Baldassar and her co-researchers in their studies of transnational migrants
from Europe and Asia living in Australia (Baldassar *infra*, and Baldassar, Baldock & Wilding 2007), and has been taken up in research on
transnational mothering and more generally the transnationalisation of
the sphere of socialisation. Baldassar's account of transnational caring
documents debates among transnational family members about what
their migration (voluntary or forced) has done to values and practices
which may previously have been taken for granted, *inter alia* reminding
us of the great hardship this may involve for both caregivers and those
receiving care. More generally, she reminds us that debating the family
is not simply a matter of sitting in a coffee shop, à la Habermas, discussing the rights and wrongs of this or that practice, but involves difficult questions and decisions which cause much anxiety and distress,
guilt and shame (see also Chamberlain & Leydesdorf 2004).

Finally, the family is at issue methodologically and theoretically.
While recognising the dangers of ethnocentric assumptions about the
universal character (or value) of hegemonic, 'Western' models of the family which often underlie policy in Europe, Bjerén (1997) rightly in-

sists that migration takes place within a framework of familial relations, in the broad sense, even if the nature of those relations (their structure and content) is very varied, and continuously changing; as King et al. affirm, migration itself 'destabilis[es] notions of household and family' (2006: 260). The focus in this volume on the family as unit of analysis probably reproduces migrants' own lived experience, and how they conceive their lives, hopefully without privileging a particular conceptualisation. But analysing the family involves deconstruction, reconstruction, and perhaps deconstruction again (King et al. 2006: 253). The family is at once a social construct, a conceptual entity, a moral order, and a set of real social and cultural practices. Its investigation requires examining both the trope of family (including implicit or explicit definitions offered by informants, policymakers included), and the relationships (moral and practical) which it is thought to entail. Nonetheless, under that examination it dissolves into a bundle of more specific (and related) institutions. As both imagined and real, it consists of internal relations which are sometimes antagonistic, with multiple (actual or potential) points of fission along lines of gender and generation.

Perspectives from the point of view of gender or intergenerational relations are essential, but while 'family' may imply gender and generation, the reverse is not necessarily true. Dissolving the family into 'gender' and 'generation', while important for placing familial relations in wider social and historical contexts, may entail the loss of a sense of location, of an iconic cultural, social and ideological 'site' in which such relations are enacted. Bastos and Bastos's conception of 'family dynamics' (*infra*), defined as 'specific modes of articulation' between gender and other relations is highly pertinent here. As Wessendorf says (*infra*), referring to Italian immigrants in Switzerland:

> Disagreements between parents and children mainly evolved around issues of control in the realm of gender relations, sexual orientation, obligations towards kin and ideas of care and responsibilities *within the family*. (my emphasis)

Reinstating the family at the centre of analysis is not to revert to an older model of migration and the place of families in its historical development, which Kofman and others rightly criticise, nor is it to deny the validity of arguments about the marginalisation of gender and the prevalence of the 'dependent female' model in migration studies. A holistic approach, treating the family as an entity, albeit one which is not a 'thing in itself' (to echo a classic anthropological perspective on kinship), foregrounds an important site in which relations of gender and generation are articulated and/or in terms of which they are conceptualised, and around which debates circulate.

Internal and External Cultural Debates

In analysing the controversies surrounding immigrant and minority ethnic families, a starting point is to describe some perspectives as 'external' (from the viewpoint of 'outsiders'), others as 'internal' (from the viewpoint of 'insiders').[2] The first encompasses (but is not confined to) the public policy perspective which addresses the real or imagined familial relations within immigrant and minority ethnic communities (e.g. arranged marriages again) from the viewpoint of the society of immigration. It is concerned with how those relations and attendant practices appear to fit (or not) the hegemonic (real or imagined) practices of the receiving society. The second includes what happens 'inside' minority ethnic and immigrant families, and the communities claiming their allegiance, and may be observed in many different locations, local, national and international: the world of Islam provides many compelling examples.

This approach may be linked to what Parkin (1978), in a dense and sophisticated study of the control of meaning among Luo-speaking migrants in Nairobi, Kenya, has called 'internal cultural debate'. Parkin describes how the views of younger Luo (men) about abandoning traditional ideas and values concerning polygyny, large families, bridewealth and the role of women, in favour of monogamy, small families and children's education, were 'stifled' by Luo elders. Drawing on linguistic anthropology, Parkin (1978: 291) comments that 'much of the conversation we call culture goes on within and not between socio-cultural groups', and concerns threats to group values 'often seen by those in authority to come from the enemy or sinner within'. 'Represented' is perhaps more accurate than 'seen', as in the Luo case (and indeed elsewhere), much effort is devoted to preventing these 'conversations' escaping control. 'Attempts to turn the long conversation between generations into an open debate' (1978: 292), Parkin contends, are 'muzzled', 'and so there is no debate'. Yet conversation-cum-debate does occur and change does take place with rhetorical support for 'traditional' values in public, new practices in private.[3] Thus, 'under the compelling cover of unchanging word and thought, significant changes of action are taking place' (1978: 22), and 'external forces of radical change can be "smuggled" in and create internal discontinuities and contradictions in the logic of [a] culture' (1978: 284). New ideas and practices become possible despite apparently intensive semantic control (Goodman 2002) and 'every culture or cultural complex contain[s] within itself the seeds of its transformation' (Parkin 1978: 290).

This idea has considerable resonance for the present discussion, albeit translating it from the context of a post-colonial society in Africa shortly after independence to that of contemporary multicultural Europe is hazardous, particularly problematic being the identification of participants as from 'inside' a culture. Nonetheless, Parkin's study underlines the value of treating the family as a much-debated moral and practical order. Migration (like other forms of social change, and indeed along with them) puts a great strain on this order, forcing people to think about what they should do, to interpret and reinterpret beliefs and practices in the light of alternatives that migration has opened up or foreclosed (Ewing 2006: 267). Typical are tensions surrounding relations between spouses or partners and between parents and children, especially as these pertain to changing gender relations and the influences of school, work, the media and so on, in the context of immigration. These are the staple of novels, plays, and films which often depict the (changing) situation of what is still often called the 'second generation' (the term is less appropriate than it was), once characterised as falling 'between two cultures' (now an outmoded perception). It, too, may involve ethnocentric and essentialist idealisations (or their opposite) of a past or present (minority ethnic) family, perhaps located in an imaginary homeland or defined by religious ideal, e.g. the 'Muslim' or 'Asian' family, seen from 'within'.

While a useful starting point, the external/internal, outsider/insider distinction is too simplistic in the context of contemporary Europe. It may once have had some validity (see Grillo 1985), but matters are now more complex, with the growing significance of global and transnational influences, and the multiplicity and range of voices involved. Like the distinction between micro/meso/macro levels of analysis it should not be taken too literally. One problem is that it suggests two sets of relatively homogeneous 'parallel worlds'. Such reification is inadequate because, neither among insiders, within migrant and minority ethnic communities, nor among outsiders, in debates taking place in the public sphere, is there a single, homogenous voice. Moreover, while some actors may have a clear-cut vision, many more will, consciously or not, be sifting through alternatives, uncertain about what to do for the best, shifting from one to another as circumstances, personal and collective, change. As chapters in this volume illustrate, this is apparent in the multitude of negotiations and compromises that occur in dialogues between spouses, parents and offspring, and extended family members, about who should care for elderly and distant relatives, for example, or what kind of lives young men and women should lead, how children should be raised, or, often most contentiously, who might marry whom.

Thirdly, these viewpoints (internal or external) are never static. Images (idealisations and other) of the family are constantly changing, for example in the perception of individuals as they move through the developmental cycle, or in a society or community's perception of self and other.

Fourthly, if voices are multiple they are also interactive: insider/outsider perspectives are not discrete, autonomous discourses. There is a dialectical, if usually asymmetrical, relationship between them; in varying degrees the 'external' perspective informs and shapes the 'internal', as in debates about female circumcision (Rajkotia *infra*). Likewise, what happens at one level (e.g. internationally) influences what happens at another (e.g. within particular families).

Fifthly, it is increasingly difficult to assign voices to one perspective or the other, to identify them as 'inside' or 'outside'. This might have been possible in Britain or France in the 1960s or 1970s, but among immigrant and minority ethnic populations in Europe there are now many who are both 'inside' and 'outside'. Some of these are public intellectuals who see themselves, or are seen as, critical insiders: Ayaan Hirsi Ali is a well-known international example, and the British Sikh writer Gurpreet Bhatti, author of the controversial play *Behzti*, a lesser-known British one (Grillo 2007). Both write against the grain of 'their' communities/cultures, and suffer for their pains. In both cases, too, their insider status and perspective has been co-opted by those outside. The history of Hirsi Ali, herself of Muslim background, illustrates how an 'insider' perspective, in this instance one which censures Islam, crosses over into external perspectives, and is taken up by opponents of multiculturalism and the immigrant presence in Europe. As Snel and Stock observe (*infra*):

> [Hirsi Ali's] argument gains much power from the fact that she herself is of Somalian descent and was raised as a Muslim. This immunises her against reproaches of being prejudiced or even racist. After all, she can claim to know the cultural practices she condemns from first hand.

There are others, intellectuals in academia and in the media, who, as in the Rushdie Affair, reject hegemonic representations, insider or outsider, and seek to define their own ground. As Pnina Werbner puts it, they participate in a 'resistant and yet complicit public arena ... that tells a story of cultural hybridity and cosmopolitanism' (Werbner 2004: 897). Tariq Ramadan is one example of this heteroglossia, of how individuals may give voice to a multiplicity of cultural references. Another is represented by minority ethnic activists such as the feminist Southall Black Sisters (2004), based in Britain, concerned with domestic violence and forced marriage.

Sixthly, the 'insider' perspective may appear to be the viewpoint of someone able to speak authoritatively, or who claims to speak authoritatively, on behalf of a minority ethnic or religious community (quotes again understood). This begs the question of representativeness. 'Representation' encompasses two related things (Grillo 1985). It may refer to how immigrants and their families are conceptualised by themselves or by members of the receiving society especially those with certain institutional responsibilities (social workers, teachers, police, etc.). But it may also refer to how such representations are 'represented' and become hegemonic, and instrumental, in public arenas. The politicisation of the family involves a contest of representations and raises issues such as who has the power to define the situation of immigrants and their families, to 'represent' them, in a political sense, in the institutional order? How are immigrant voices incorporated in this process? What space is available for alternative discourses (counter-narratives) which challenge dominant ones?

Finally, even when voices unambiguously represent those who conceive of themselves as belonging to a specific and distinct (different) culture or society from an ethnic and/or religious point of view, rarely do their representations omit any reference to other worlds. The internal is invariably defined at some point by reference to the external spectre at the feast. Contemporary debates about 'Asian' or 'Muslim' families reveal some of these complexities.

The 'Asian' or 'Muslim' Family

> These brainwashed young men threatening us are not coming from liberal, Westernised homes full of moral relativism and then suddenly turning psycho. If they come from observant Muslim families – which the 7/7 bombers all did despite all the nonsense about them being 'ordinary Westernised boys' – then the priming started long ago. They would have been brought up to genuinely believe that Allah intended women to have a single purpose in life as subservient wives and mothers; gay people are perverts; freedom of speech does not apply to any kind of criticism of their belief; democracy is a man-made sham; and the values of the West are inferior. (Muriel Gray, *Sunday Herald*, 24 September 2006)

The above quotation, from an article by a journalist, represents a viewpoint more widespread than one might care to think. In public discourse in Britain and elsewhere in Europe, a commonly held stereotype of the 'Asian' population is that 'all families are extended, children respect their elders, religious faith is total and unquestioning, and women are veiled creatures living in the shadows' (Ali 1992: 109). The position of 'the Asian woman' is central in this, and popular representations of the 'Asian family' emphasise the presumed plight of young women, for example in respect of marriage (Gardner 2002: 6).

This is especially noticeable with regard to the 'Muslim' family (Snel & Stock *infra*). Ansari (2004: 252-297) draws attention to the predominant Western view of Muslim women as 'passive and docile, subject to patriarchal traditions, and lacking any active agency to change their condition; also as exotic, ruthlessly oppressed victims of religion', and Western feminists (for instance), sometimes argue that it is the Muslim family which is the 'key element' in their oppression (Ansari ibid.), with the Islamic faith underpinning conceptions of the family and legitimating violence against women. In German public discourse, says Ewing, the Muslim woman is 'cast as the embodiment of the "other" ... oppressed by her "culture" and in need of liberation by enlightened Western saviors' (Ewing 2006: 267; see also Moch 2005: 104), with the trope of the rebellious adolescent girl constrained by her 'traditional Turkish family' 'replayed over and over in media accounts, in cinema and literature, and in social science scholarship' (Ewing 2006: 270). Similarly in France, Rassiguier (2003: 12) shows that it is women who, while 'robbed of any real agency, are conjured up to capture the cultural distance between the French and their post-colonial others'. There is a perception of the unintegrable African family (predominantly Muslim) built around images of alien customary practices (polygyny, female circumcision, endless children, patriarchy) through which the African woman is constituted. Consequently the African woman – the iconic alien – is discursively seen only in the context of the family and male dependency (the existence of the autonomous woman is effectively denied), and this is reinforced through legal practice. Women stand metonymically for the family, and in Germany, as in France, the assumed obligatory wearing of the hijab is taken as a sign of the Muslim family's oppressive character (Ewing 2006: 270).

'Never', says Timera (2002: 153), referring to France, 'have arranged marriages excited so much interest not only among the general public, parents, student associations, and so forth, but also among French government ministers and African presidents'. Debates across Europe about arranged or forced marriages (the two not always distinguished) constantly give voice to concerns about oppression. 'Many parents,' says Ewing (2006: 277):

> continue to arrange the marriages of their children with relatives back in Turkey. However, these are precisely the practices that are taken by the media as evidence that Turks are backward, traditional, and do not allow their children free choice in marriage.

She adds that these marriages 'violate the Western model of a marriage based on "love," and the Muslim preference for marriage between cousins is often regarded by Westerners as incest' (Ewing 2006: 289). 'Ironically', she continues, German policies of family reunification have in fact encouraged such marriages which became 'an important economic strategy for migrant families'. Yet, as Ansari points out, there is a wide spectrum of practices, and among South Asian Muslims in Britain, arranged marriages are 'increasingly a halfway house between the "forced" variety, in which the children had no say at all, and "love" marriage, where parents have been completely excluded from decision-making' (Ansari 2004: 281).[4]

In Germany, stereotypical views of the Turkish family were heavily influenced by a social work study published in 1978 (Ewing 2006) whose representations were adopted by film makers. Social workers also influenced representations of the North African family in France (Grillo 1985). This is not to deny that terrible things may occur in Turkish as in any families, but as Ewing (2006: 283) points out, German public discourse on Turkish women and *the* Turkish family confuse 'explanations based on "culture"' with those which would refer to the 'dynamics of particular families'. In a similar way, in Scandinavia certain celebrated cases (e.g. 'Nadia's case', discussed by Wikan 2002) have come to stand for the values and practices of Muslim families as a whole. Yet, as Erel (2002: 128) points out, discourses on the Turkish/ Muslim family are 'contradictory, complex and multifaceted' with numerous alternative perspectives, ranging from what Ewing (2006) calls 'rural Turkish discourse', through to a 'renewed and purified' Islamic point of view (represented by the views of the Milli Görüs).

Consonant with the first ('rural Turkish') perspective is the view widely expressed by male Muslims in Britain that the family is, as Ansari reports, a 'source of emotional strength and a haven of spiritual and moral safety from the perceived assault of British society and its unwelcome values' (2004: 253). One informant interviewed by Beishon, Modood and Virdee (1998: 56) contrasted the close-knit Muslim families with (white) British families:

> Their thinking is different. We think in terms of holding our family together. We are always thinking about what is good for our families, they always think of themselves and their personal freedom. We always consider our family reputation/name before we act. Like that, they are more free thinking. The women are more liberal than our women. (Beishon et al. 1998: 56)

Underpinning such views is a conception of what Husain and O'Brien (2000: 6) call the 'traditional idealized' (Muslim) patriarchal extended family, grounded in sharia principles, and bound by notions of honour and shame. While acknowledging the variety of practice to be found across the Islamic world, Mai Yamani (1998), like Stepien (*infra*), shows how these principles provide a framework for the ideal Islamic marriage (from the point of view of Sunni Islam as practiced in Saudi Arabia). At the same time, Beishon et al. (1998) emphasise the differences among minority ethnic families (in Britain) as much as those that exist between them and majority families, documenting their varied attitudes towards marriage, cohabitation, parenthood, gender, domestic responsibilities, intergenerational relations, religion, as well as perceptions of where they stand in relation to majority (and indeed minority) others. There is also, in the immigration context, and perhaps more widely, a tendency for practices to become more 'European'-like, with single-family units, fewer children, more single-person households etc, and shifts in intergenerational relations in which disputes about religious adherence are prominent (Husain & O'Brien 2000). All of this generates intense reflection, generally, and with respect to the personal relationships in which people are engaged.

Migrant families, says Foner, are sites of negotiation and creolisation, processes in which migrants are active participants, reconciling 'premigration' cultural practices and beliefs, for example Vietnamese conceptions of family collectivism, with 'dominant American cultural beliefs and values concerning marriage, family, and kinship that are disseminated by the mass media, schools, and other institutions' (1997: 970). 'Mixed' marriages (i.e. across culture and religion or both), which are increasing throughout Europe, provide a good illustration. Such marriages, says Kofman (2004: 252), pose questions about family definition, gender relations, communication, and the 'creation of spaces of intercultural social contacts'. Breger and Hill comment on how those engaged in mixed marriages 'perceive and cope with mismatched expectations and cultural diversity' (1998: 3), which may include different (cultural) understandings of what constitutes a 'good' marriage, and Alex-Assensoh and Assensoh optimistically claim that 'the politics of mixed or cross-cultural marriages augur well for a healthy dose of compromises' (1998: 105).

For Pakistani/Bangladeshi (Muslim) informants interviewed by Beishon et al., mixed marriages create special problems, the principal obstacle being religious difference. There is no formal objection to marrying another Muslim whatever their background, though cultural differences were believed to be important and difficult to overcome. On the other hand, Rodríguez-García's study (*infra*) of mixed unions between African (male) Muslim immigrants and Spanish (female) nationals shows that in their case cultural factors are ultimately more significant than religion per se. What influences family values and practices and the debates surrounding them, and what gives rise to the kind of different responses to mixed marriages described by Rodríguez-García on the one hand and Beishon et al. on the other?

What Influences the Debates?

One factor is the legal system,

> making certain premigration customs and practices illegal or giving legal support to challenges to these practices ... The legal system and government agencies can affect family relations by defining family membership and rules, like those pertaining to inheritance, in terms of American cultural assumptions. (Foner 2004: 971)

Foner's observation points us in a number of directions, and suggests that the factors shaping or influencing debates may be observed at a number of different levels.

In broadest terms, the family is a *global* site of debate. The UN, for example, has long been concerned with what has been happening to the family. International declarations have emphasised the rights of families since 1948, and of women and children within families, and these have increasing purchase, at the very least discursive purchase, across the globe. Sometimes, internationally sanctioned rights may conflict with claims based on culture or religion, and choices may have to be made. At the European level, there is much disagreement about whether the EU could and should have a family policy and in what areas it might intervene. In general, following the principal of subsidiarity, the EU eschews such interventions, nonetheless, as the Commission of the Bishops' Conferences of the European Community (COMECE), which favours an EU family strategy, points out:

> family ties and family life become a subject of European interest each time they come into play in a sphere of social life which is covered by EU legislation. When this occurs, they become so important as to alter the existing norms, either by widening or restricting their application, or by creating special provisions adapting the general framework to the specificity of family life. (COMECE 2004: 19)

Areas in which the EU has an influence include employment and social legislation and judicial cooperation. However, it is in the context of the nation-state that macro influences on migrant and minority ethnic families are felt most strongly.

As indicated, one important strand in the literature on migration and the family has been concerned with how governments, through the regulation and management of migration and integration, operationalise policies which define families and appropriate family values and practices for migrants and minority ethnic groups. Less well studied is the influence of different political and cultural ideologies and hegemonic ideas about the family prevalent (historically) in a particular national formation. Bastos and Bastos (*infra*) discuss the case of Portugal, and Norway and Italy provide other examples.

As Gullestad (2002) has pointed out, Norway, like other Scandinavian countries, has historically favoured a strong egalitarian ideology, and the 'vocabulary of humanitarianism, justice, equality and decency' (Hagelund 2003: 12) has traditionally been of great import.[5] In reflecting on this tradition in the context of contemporary immigration, Gullestad coins the term 'imagined sameness' as 'a culturally specific way of resolving tensions between the community and the individual' (2002: 46). 'Imagined sameness' points to ambiguity in the Norwegian concept of *likhet* which can be translated as both equality and sameness. Gullestad's argument is that historically there has been a perception in Norwegian society that equality must entail sameness and that the search for sameness means, *inter alia*, that social and cultural differences (for example in family practices) pose great problems for an egalitarian ideology and threaten social democratic principles.

Italy provides an interesting contrast (Eriksen 2002). Andall's study (2000) is principally concerned with the interaction of class, race and gender in the Italian context specifically with respect to 'black', especially African women migrants. It does not directly cover the ground addressed here, but it raises many issues which are highly pertinent to the themes discussed in this volume. These include the way in which the family is seen in a particular national (Italian) ideology, how this is reflected in and reinforced by the way the family is constituted in law and in religious and political representations. Not surprisingly, of particular significance has been the way the Catholic Church has defined family values and practices and the appropriate role of women (Andall 2000: 26). At the same time, the Church, or an element of it, has been influential in promoting opposition towards Islam and Muslim values which it perceives as inimical towards the Christian faith.

National values, perhaps of long duration, though also subject to change (sometimes quite abrupt)[6] help to explain how and why certain issues appear in some contexts and not in others, or have greater salience in one location rather than another – for example why honour killings, by no means absent from debates elsewhere, have had such prominence in Scandinavia, or the headscarf, again important across Europe in debates about Islam and women, has assumed such an iconic character in France (Bowen 2006). Nonetheless, for a variety of reasons, an explanation which relies on the influence of long-standing (national) cultural values cannot tell the whole story. Although there may be historically hegemonic models of family values and practices, it would be a mistake to assume that these are universally held and always authoritative. Concerning Italy, for example, Andall documents the views of the Catholic organisation Caritas, which often represents a different perspective (e.g. on immigration) to that promoted by the hierarchy. She also illustrates the impact of the feminist movement on the understanding of, and actions concerning, migrant/ethnic minority families. There are other alternatives, too, such as that represented by the contemporary policies of the *Front National* in France (Le Pen 2007), or by the earlier French, Catholic, corporatist conceptions of the family and gender relations and their place in society, summarised in the Vichy slogan: *Travail, Famille, Patrie*.

While understanding the national framework remains crucial, the transnational character of much contemporary migration means migrants are brought within the orbit of not just one, but two, or more, nation-states and national ideologies of the family, for example in the case of the 'Turkish family'. For this reason, among others, Salih (2003) employs the term 'plurinational' to refer to the situation of her Moroccan informants who have to negotiate multiple national and cultural norms. Families engaged in caregiving across nation-state boundaries are similarly affected. Other more localised influences may also be identified. Baldassar (*infra*) argues the methodological point that a focus on

> internal debates concerning migration and care within the transnational domestic sphere provide[s] a link between micro, meso and macro levels of analysis locating the practices of individuals and families in the context of local and transnational communities and states.

The meso level, for example, points to what happens in particular localities (cities and neighbourhoods), including the local institutional complexes (e.g. in Lyon, France [Grillo 1985]). This is where the local state comes in, and it is well to remember that the influence of the state often comes down to the acts of its agents, often at a quite lowly administrative levels, and operating in a local institutional context.

The meso level also encompasses many local voluntary organisations of the kind studied by Mand (*infra*), as well as ethnic/migrant communities and their associations and networks. Anthropologists studying migrants have typically focused on urban neighbourhoods with their mosques, temples and churches, schools, social centres, clubs and societies, and the networks of families which link them together. The African Pentecostal churches in European cities provide a good illustration, with research showing how they intervene in migrant families, seeking to exert a moral authority. They are, says van Dijk, 'particularly concerned with the creation of monogamous, conjugal, but not necessarily equal relations between husband and wife' (2002: 181). It is within such contexts that one can often best observe the interplay of forces which frame/influence internal cultural debates, though these are also readily apparent at the micro level where men, women and children engage with their personal dilemmas, for example, the circumstances of a particular marriage or partnership, and negotiate (or not) a modus vivendi.

Conclusion

This chapter, indeed this volume as a whole, focuses on the immigrant and minority ethnic family, or familial relations, as trope or ideological construct – the family imagined. In this sense the family is a discursive terrain, a site of conversation, debate, dialogue and negotiation, on many different levels and from many different perspectives. We say much less about familial relations as practised, and Anniken Hagelund (personal communication) points out that emphasising the way in which families are constructed as sites of oppression, for example, may delegitimise accounts of oppressive behaviour that actually occur. This is not the intention; to analyse stereotypes and their problematic effects is not to deny that real abuses exist which policy interventions may have to address.

The exploration of the discursive terrain began with the observation that what is said about such families may reflect two perspectives: the internal view of the communities to which the families might be said to belong, and the external view of those belonging to what historically are (or were) the dominant populations of the receiving society. Although a valuable heuristic device, perhaps close to the viewpoint often held by social actors themselves, the formulation breaks down in the face of the complexities of the contemporary, globalised, world, characterised by individual and collective social and cultural mobility and change. It is overly simplistic, too, given the multiplicity of voices engaged in these debates, and the overlapping subject positions they represent.

Complexity and change is in fact the point, though this probably does not accord with the 'common sense' perception of migrant and minority ethnic families to be found in the popular press or in the speeches of politicians. Ansari, for example, has observed that 'by the end of the twentieth century the pattern of gender relations among younger Muslim women seemed neither to follow parental norms nor to amount to a wholesale adoption of Western standards' (2004: 296). Yet instead of recognising such complex changes (earnestly debated by Muslims as much as anyone), all too often those concerned with public policy unthinkingly reflect the popular imagination, and resort to simplistic assumptions of unchanging 'otherness'. This was certainly true in the past (for example in Britain or France at the end of the nineteenth century, Grillo 1998), but perhaps at no time has it been more apparent than in the context of contemporary concerns in the European public sphere about integration, and more generally of increasing scepticism about the value of multicultural diversity. As Hagelund notes (infra), in Scandinavia, as elsewhere in Europe,

> the debates have increasingly turned to the limits of choice and tolerance, and to the potential tensions between cultural diversity on the one hand and the need for a shared 'glue' to keep society together on the other.

There is a perceived 'failure' on the part of immigrants to integrate, which is often laid at the door of their families, or rather their practices of familial relations, and the (collectivist) principles (cultural, religious) which underpin them. The immigrant (i.e. non-Western, non-European) family, the principles and practices it espouses, are constantly seen as a threat to the values of the individuated (neo)liberal (or Christian) worldview.

Such perceptions are often grounded not just in a particular model of the family, but in a certain conception of culture as a way of life attached to an identifiable collectivity, static, finite and bounded. This 'fundamentalist' (Stolcke 1995) or 'essentialist' view (Grillo 2003) may be contrasted with the dynamic, dialogic account of culture, stressing a multiplicity of voices rather than homogeneous (customary) practices, which dominates contemporary social science (Rodríguez-García, infra). Culture is more akin to an ideology (Bjerén 1997), and it is the family's perceived moral imperatives and cultural practices which are fundamentally at issue.

It is easy enough to see how and why the family (the fons et origo of socialisation) is treated as iconic (Ballard infra). As Wessendorf says (infra) it is a 'powerful category with which some migrants are idealised as warm-hearted people who contribute to the good of the majority society, while others are essentialised as violent and oppressive', it can construct cultural differences in both negative and positive terms. It is

much harder to know what to do about it. Nonetheless, what this volume shows is the importance of recognising and distinguishing between the rhetorics and representations of immigrant families, conjured often powerfully by both outsiders and insiders (depending on
various contexts), and the messier, more complex lived experiences, the
outcome of interplay between external and internal disagreement and
contest at many levels. It provides a timely reminder of the danger of
losing sight of these lived realities and seeing the world too readily in
terms of a 'clash of civilisations' or cultures. The question of culture is
at the heart of both the particular issue of the migrant family and the
broader issue of immigrant integration in general. The chapters in the
volume eschew homogeneous, reified, static and unchanging notions
of culture and emphasise its dynamic, heterogeneous, changing, contested and transformative nature. If the social sciences can deliver this
message then they may provide a much-needed check on what in recent times has become a dangerous 'othering' of immigrants and their
descendants.[7]

Notes

1   Kofman (2004) discusses a number of ways in which migrant/minority ethnic
    families form in receiving societies: family migration, family reunification, marriage
    migration, e.g. importing spouses from places of origin, a controversial matter for
    many countries, and 'mixed' marriages.
2   This is different from the contrast between 'etic' and 'emic', the perspectives of
    (scientific) observers and subjects. Internal/insider and external/outsider perspectives
    are both 'emic', i.e. attached to certain subject positions, though actors themselves
    might think otherwise, and may be the product of cultural debate among those
    sharing that position. As Ballard (*infra*) puts it: 'concepts of inside and outside are ...
    mutually interchangeable'. The distinction is also different from that between what
    Baumann calls 'dominant' and 'demotic' discourses, as may be judged from his
    comment (1996: 115) that '[The] demotic discourse disengages the equation between
    culture and *community* that the dominant one assumes *a priori*' (his emphases). Thus
    a particular representation, for example that of an anthropologist such as Baumann
    himself, might be characterised as 'external'/(or 'outsider'), 'demotic', and 'etic'.
3   That is, among the Luo. Elsewhere the reverse might be the case.
4   Grillo (forthcoming) reviews these and related issues more fully.
5   Thanks to Marianne Holm Pedersen and Anniken Hagelund for these observations.
6   Why certain perspectives on the family become hegemonic, or traditional hegemonic
    values suddenly shift, as for instance in the contemporary 'backlash' against difference
    in a countries such as the Netherlands or Denmark, cannot be addressed here.
7   I am indebted to Loretta Baldassar for her suggestions for this concluding paragraph.

References

Alex-Assensoh, Y. & A.B. Assensoh (1998), 'The Politics of Cross-Cultural Marriage: An Examination of a Ghanaian/African-American Case', in R. Breger & R. Hill (eds.), *Cross-Cultural Marriage: Identity and Choice*, 101-12. Oxford: Berg.

Ali, Y. (1992), 'Muslim Women and the Politics of Ethnicity and Culture in Northern England', in G. Sahgal & N. Yuval-Davis (eds.), *Refusing Holy Orders*, 101-23. London: Virago Press.

Andall, J. (2000), *Gender, Migration and Domestic Service: The Politics of Black Women in Italy.* Aldershot: Ashgate.

Ansari, H. (2004), *The 'Infidel Within': Muslims in Britain since 1800.* London: Hurst.

Bailey, A. & P. Boyle (2004), 'Untying and Retying Family Migration in the New Europe', *Journal of Ethnic and Migration Studies* 30 (2): 229-241.

Baldassar, L., C.V. Baldock, & R. Wilding (2007), *Families Caring Across Borders: Migration, Ageing and Transnational Caregiving.* New York: Palgrave Macmillan.

Balibar, E. (2004), *We, The People of Europe? Reflections on Transnational Citizenship.* Princeton University Press: Princeton.

Baumann, G. (1996), *Contesting Culture: Ethnicity and Community in West London.* Cambridge: Cambridge University Press.

Beishon, S., T. Modood, & S. Virdee (1998), *Ethnic Minority Families.* London: Policy Studies Institute.

Bjerén, G. (1997), 'Gender and Reproduction', in T. Hammar (ed.), *International Migration, Immobility, and Development: Multidisciplinary Perspectives*, 219-246. Oxford: Oxford University Press.

Bowen, J.R. (2006), *Why the French Don't Like Headscarves: Islam, the State, and Public Space.* Princeton: Princeton University Press.

Bracalenti, R. & M. Benini (2005), 'The Role of Families in the Migrant Integration Process', in J. Pflegerl & S. Trnka (eds.), *Migration and the Family in the European Union*, 59-79. Vienna: Austrian Institute for Family Studies.

Breger, R. & R. Hill (1998), 'Introducing Mixed Marriages', in R. Breger & R. Hill (eds.), *Cross-Cultural Marriage: Identity and Choice*, 1-32. Oxford: Berg.

Bryceson, D. & U. Vuorela (2002), 'Transnational Families in the Twenty-first Century', in D. Bryceson & U. Vuorela (eds.), *The Transnational Family: New European Frontiers and Global Networks*, 3-30. Oxford: Berg.

Castles, S., M. Korac, & E. Vasta (2003), *Integration: Mapping the Field.* Oxford: COMPAS.

Chamberlain, M. & S. Leydesdorf (2004), 'Transnational Families: Memories and Narratives', *Global Networks* 4 (3): 227-241.

COMECE (2004), *A Family Strategy for the European Union.* Brussels: Commission of the Bishops' Conferences of the European Community.

Dijk, R. van (2002), 'Religion, Reciprocity and Restructuring Family Responsibility in the Ghanaian Pentecostal Diaspora', in D. Bryceson & U. Vuorela (eds.), *The Transnational Family: New European Frontiers and Global Networks*, 173-96. Oxford: Berg.

Erel, U. (2002), 'Reconceptualizing Motherhood: Experiences of Migrant Women from Turkey Living in Germany', in D. Bryceson & U. Vuorela (eds.), *The Transnational Family: New European Frontiers and Global Networks*, 127-46. Oxford: Berg.

Eriksen, T.H. (2002), 'The Colonial and the Post-Colonial: A View from Scandinavia on Italian Minority Issues', in R.D. Grillo & J.C. Pratt (eds.), *The Politics of Recognizing Difference: Multiculturalism Italian Style*, 219-236. Basingstoke: Ashgate.

Ewing, K.P. (2006), 'Between Cinema and Social Work: Diasporic Turkish Women and the (Dis)Pleasures of Hybridity', *Cultural Anthropology* 21 (2): 265-294.

Foner, N. (1997), 'The Immigrant Family: Cultural Legacies and Cultural Changes', *International Migration Review* 31 (4): 961-974.

Gardner, K. (2002), *Age, Narrative and Migration: The Life Course and Life Histories amongst Bengali Elders in London*. Oxford: Berg.

Goodhart, D. (2004), 'Too Diverse?', *Prospect Magazine* 95.

Goodman, R. (ed.) (2002), *Family and Social Policy in Japan: Anthropological Approaches*. Cambridge: Cambridge University Press.

Grillo, R.D. (1985), *Ideologies and Institutions in Urban France: The Representation of Immigrants*. Cambridge: Cambridge University Press.

Grillo, R.D. (2003), 'Cultural Essentialism and Cultural Anxiety', *Anthropological Theory* 3 (2): 157-173.

Grillo, R.D. (2007), 'Licence to Offend? The Behzti Affair', *Ethnicities* 7 (1): 5-29.

Grillo, R.D. (forthcoming), 'Marriages, Arranged and Forced: The UK Debate', in E. Kofman, M. Kohli, A. Kraler & C. Scholl (eds.), *Gender, Generations and the Family in International Migration*.

Gullestad, M. (2002), 'Invisible Fences: Egalitarianism, Nationalism and Racism', *Journal of the Royal Anthropological Institute* 8 (1): 45-63.

Hagelund, A. (2003), *The Importance of Being Decent: Political Discourse on Immigration in Norway, 1970-2002*. Oslo: Unipax.

Heckmann, F. (ed.) (2005), *Integration and Integration Policies: IMISCOE Network Feasibility Study*. Bamberg: EFMS INTPOL Team.

Husain, F. & O'Brien, M. (2000), 'Muslim Communities in Europe: Reconstruction and Transformation', *Current Sociology* 48 (4): 1-13.

King, R., M. Thomson, T. Fielding, & T. Warnes (2006), 'Time, Generations and Gender in Migration and Settlement', in R. Penninx, M. Berger & K. Kraal (eds.), *The Dynamics of International Migration and Settlement in Europe: A State of the Art*, 233-268. Amsterdam: Amsterdam University Press.

Kofman, E. (1999), 'Female "Birds of Passage" a Decade Later: Gender and Immigration in the European Union', *International Migration Review* 33: 269-299.

Kofman, E. (2004), 'Family-related Migration: A Critical Review of European Studies', *Journal of Ethnic and Migration Studies* 30(2): 243-262.

Le Pen, J.-M. (2007), *Discours à Paris sur le thème de la démographie*, www.frontnational.com/docinterventionsdetail.php?idinter=57.

Moch, L.P. (2005), 'Gender and Migration Research', in M. Bommes & E. Morawska (eds.), *International Migration Research: Constructions, Omissions and the Promises of Interdisciplinarity*, 95-108. Aldershot: Ashgate.

Nauck, B. & B. Settles (2001), 'Immigrant and Ethnic Minority Families: An Introduction', *Journal of Comparative Family Studies* 32 (4): 461-463.

Parkin, D.J. (1978), *The Cultural Definition of Political Response: Lineal Destiny among the Luo*. London: Academic Press.

Pine, F. (1996), 'Family', in A. Barnard & J. Spencer (eds.), *Encyclopedia of Social and Cultural Anthropology*, 223-228. London: Routledge.

Rassiguier, C. (2003), 'Troubling Mothers: Immigrant Women from Africa in France', *Jenda* 4 (1): 1-15.

Salih, R. (2003), *Gender in Transnationalism: Home, Longing and Belonging Among Moroccan Migrant Women*. London: Routledge.

Sartori, G. (2002), *Pluralismo, Multiculturalismo e Estranei*. Milan: Rizzoli.

Southall Black Sisters (2004), *Domestic Violence, Immigration and No Recourse to Public Funds*. London: Southall Black Sisters.

Stolcke, V. (1995), 'Talking Culture: New Boundaries, New Rhetorics of Exclusion in Europe', *Current Anthropology* 36 (1): 1-24.

Timera, M. (2002), 'Righteous or Rebellious? Social Trajectory of Sahelian Youth in France', in D. Bryceson & U. Vuorela (eds.), *The Transnational Family: New European Frontiers and Global Networks*, 147-154. Oxford: Berg.

Vertovec, S. & S. Wessendorf (2006), 'Cultural, Religious and Linguistic Diversity in Europe: An Overview of Issues and Trends', in R. Penninx, M. Berger & K, Kraal (eds.), *The Dynamics of International Migration and Settlement in Europe: A State of the Art*, 171-200. Amsterdam: Amsterdam University Press.

Werbner, P. (2004), 'Theorising Complex Diasporas: Purity and Hybridity in the South Asian Public Sphere in Britain', *Journal of Ethnic and Migration Studies* 30 (5): 895-911.

Wikan, U. (2002), *Generous Betrayal: Politics of Culture in the New Europe*. Chicago: University of Chicago Press.

Yamani, M. (1998), 'Cross-Cultural Marriage within Islam: Ideals and Reality', in R. Breger & R. Hill (eds.), *Cross-Cultural Marriage: Identity and Choice*, 153-169. Oxford: Berg.

2 Inside and Outside: Contrasting Perspectives on the Dynamics of Kinship and Marriage in Contemporary South Asian Transnational Networks[1]

Roger Ballard

Introduction

In much of the Euro-American world, the possibility that family life might be reaching a point of collapse has emerged as a regular focus of an increasingly anxious public debate. It is easy to see why. Besides steadily eroding the range and intensity of networks of extra-familial kinship reciprocity so that such relationships are but a shadow of their former selves, the ever-more active pursuit of personal freedom has now begun to have a similar impact on the integrity of the nuclear family itself. The results are plain to see. In the face of the apparently inexorable rise in the frequency of divorce, even the institution of marriage is falling steadily out of favour. But in contrast to the way in which these developments have precipitated urgent public discussions about the prospect of reinforcing shrinking levels of familial solidarity, this chapter explores a set of issues lying right at the other end of the spectrum: those in which a perceived degree of over-commitment to familial solidarity is alleged to be precipitating such serious challenges to human and personal rights that urgent legislative efforts are now required to contain their pathogenic consequences.

Such developments might seem bewildering but for the context within which they have erupted. The underlying contradictions which have driven these arguments forward have little, if anything to do with kinship, *per se*, or even with human rights, though this provides the legitimising framework within which the debate is set. Instead they are better understood as the outcome of contradictions generated by the rapid growth in the scale of the non-European presence precipitated by processes of mass-migration and globalisation during the course of the past half century.

Why, though, should family and kinship have become such a serious battleground in this context? On the face of it such matters would appear to be peripheral, since public concern in this sphere is primarily directed at the competitive threat which the inflow of immigrants is

perceived as offering to the material interests of the indigenous majority. Hence, popular concern was initially articulated in terms of fears
about the extent to which newcomers would steal jobs, lower wages,
precipitate a shortage of housing and place an unreasonable burden on
scarce public services. By contrast, the current debate with respect to
non-European settlers' preferred patterns of kinship solidarity has a different focus. Given wider concerns about the declining resilience of family ties amongst the indigenous population, one might expect that in
this respect, at least, the consequences of the settlers' commitment to
kinship solidarity might be regarded as welcome. That expectation may
have had some substance when they first arrived, but now popular opinion towards this dimension of their presence is no more positive in
than it is in any other.

The reasons for this deserve careful examination. Critiques of the
settlers' practices largely ignore the manifold benefits which the maintenance of extended networks of kinship reciprocity routinely precipitate. Instead they are primarily concerned with the relative weight that
should be given to the right of every individual to determine his or her
own futures on a wholly autonomous basis, as opposed to the freedom-
limiting duties and obligations to which participants in networks of
mutual reciprocity amongst kinsfolk are required to subordinate themselves. Debates about such matters swiftly precipitate much argument
about the legitimacy of specific forms of practice – most especially in
terms of marriage, family and household formation – to which such
corporately oriented values give rise. In exploring the logic of the resultant arguments, this chapter will swing back and forth between policy
as opposed to practice, between ideological norms and their behavioural implementation, and above all between the often radically different
insiders' and outsiders' perspectives on, and interests in, what is happening.

The social and cultural landscape of most of Europe's major towns
and cities has been transformed during the course of past half century.
Thanks to the arrival of substantial numbers of non-European settlers,
each has been rendered markedly more plural in character. As a result,
cross-cultural communication has become the locus of increasingly
salient socio-political contradictions. Where those on either side of an
ethnic disjunction are unfamiliar with each other's conceptual vocabulary, those making efforts to communicate across the disjunction can
all too easily find themselves talking past each other. In such contexts
of mutual miscommunication, the linked concepts of 'inside' and 'outside' assume of crucial analytical significance. But in adopting such a
terminology it is vital to remember that the contending perspectives
are rarely, if ever, of equal socio-political weight. One of the most salient features of our current context is that members of the dominant

majority (who we can more explicitly identify as the indigenes, the whites, the hosts, the natives, perhaps most comfortably of all as the Europeans) routinely conceive of themselves as legitimate insiders vis-à-vis members of more recently arrived immigrant, alien, non-European minorities who have settled in their midst. Having thus defined themselves as insiders in contra-distinction to such 'immigrant' outsiders, the indigenes routinely assume that their own conventions and expectations about the ways in which one should organise kinship and marriage are normal, natural and proper. And having established their own taken-for-granted, and hence necessarily parochial, conceptual vision as the yardstick of normality, if newcomers deploy conventions which differ significantly from their own, their behaviours are marked out as alien, artificial, improper, and at worst as *illegitimate,* by comparison with those enshrined within the established socio-cultural order (Ballard 2006).

Of course, within the safety of the settlers' own self-constructed worlds, this evaluation is frequently stood on its head. From the 'outsiders' insider perspective, it is the 'alien' ways which they have brought with them from their distant homelands which are deemed to be normal and natural, whilst those routinely deployed by the indigenes amongst whom they have settled will be perceived as alien, artificial and unnatural. Concepts of inside and outside are by definition mutually interchangeable.

Issues of relative power further condition these perceptions. Those fortunate enough to occupy a position of hegemonic advantage tend to be blissfully unaware of the parochial character of the conceptual schema within which they operate. Hence, they routinely view their own perspectives as so intrinsically superior to those of all others as to be of universal applicability. Those entrenched within such a condition of ethnocentric myopia have access to ready means of turning any complaints which 'outsiders' might make about the difficulties they have encountered back on the complainants themselves. From their position of unacknowledged hegemony, it seems self-evident that if only settlers had made greater efforts to assimilate to established European norms, rather than clustering mindlessly together, they would have won a much higher level of acceptance. As a result, the newcomers' bizarre and baffling commitment to the maintenance of alterity has become a focus of ever-more vigorous criticism as time has passed; and, as 'insider' demands that the 'outsiders' should assimilate have become steadily more intense, popular representations of the outsiders' preferred lifestyles have become steadily more hostile. No longer are they merely viewed as exotically oriental, but are represented as being inherently oppressive, immoral, barbaric and terroristic, the very antithesis of the

civilised European traditions which comfortably established insiders insist they have every right to sustain and defend (Ballard 2007).

In seeking to explore the dynamics of an increasingly fervent debate,
the central focus of this chapter is the role which issues of kinship and
marriage have come to play as those standing on both sides of the disjunction have sought both to advance their interests, and to legitimise
their strategic efforts to do so, in the midst of sharpening levels of ethnic polarisation.

Migration and Its Consequences: A View from Above

Since the collapse of the Soviet Union and, subsequently, of the Twin
Towers, Euro-America has discovered a new threat to its integrity:
Islamic Fundamentalism has slipped neatly into the space once occu-
pied by the Red Menace. But whilst the American perspective has largely settled on the view that the principle threat to its integrity is external, such that its freedoms are best preserved by waging a 'war on terror' beyond its borders, the prism through which Europeans have
perceived these self-same issues is of a different order. It is easy to see
why. In the US, the vast majority of migrant workers who arrived during the course of the past half century were overwhelmingly Hispanic
in origin; by contrast, their counterparts in Western Europe were overwhelmingly Muslim. Hence, whilst the principal American response to
the events of 9/11 was to engage in external military adventures (Afghanistan, Iraq), the European response to the attack on the Twin Towers
and subsequent outrages in Madrid and London was quite different.
The outrages served to reinforce a trope that had been gathering
strength for several decades, namely that the most pressing threat to
the integrity of Europe's many nations arose from the presence of the
Muslim minorities whose members had stealthily insinuated themselves within their borders. This chapter is not, however, concerned
with Europe's anti-terrorist initiatives, but rather with a similarly
grounded debate which runs in parallel to those developments, and
which suggests that the cultural commitments of the new minorities,
and especially the ways in which they have begun to utilise their distinctive conventions of kinship, marriage and family organisation to
their own advantage, offer just as serious a challenge to the integrity of
Western Europe's established socio-cultural order.

Whilst paranoid concerns about the rising influence of religious fundamentalism are very largely a post-9/11 phenomenon, debates about
the prospective significance of non-European settlers' commitment to
distinctive kinship conventions have a much longer history. As is invariably the case in the initial stages of migration, the early pioneers of

the non-European inflow were young men in their twenties and early thirties who were content, at least at the outset, to leave their families back home, and then to take lengthy furloughs in their company to enjoy the fruits of hard-earned savings. However the personal costs associated with such a strategy of trans-continental commuting were substantial, so it was not long before an ever-increasing number of non-European sojourners took the next step and began to call their wives and children to join them, and hence transformed themselves into more permanently rooted settlers (Ballard 1994, 2003).

As their settlements grew steadily in scale, it soon became apparent that the social and cultural conventions which the newcomers' preferred to deploy in organising their domestic and personal lives were a matter of substantial socio-political consequence. In sharp contradiction to indigenous hopes and expectations, the settlers showed little sign of assimilating into the mass of the surrounding population; instead they rapidly set about constructing ethnic colonies, within which all the most significant social, cultural and religious institutions of their homelands began to reappear. Indigenous reactions varied markedly by social class, especially at the outset. Since, in the UK for example, the vast majority of migrants settled in impoverished inner-city areas, their presence, and the deep-seated alterity of their domestic lifestyles, was largely unnoticed by anyone other than their immediate working-class neighbours. Hence, no matter how alarmed and challenged their neighbours may have been by their alterity, the vast majority of more affluent outsiders took the view that the white working-class response was simply a product of ignorant racism. Hence, they were able to reassure themselves that behavioural oddities, of which the settlers' inner city neighbours so insistently complained, would soon be swept away by the inevitable process of assimilation.

Those days have long since passed. Whilst the settlers and their locally born offspring are still largely concentrated in the same localities in which they first put down roots, such that there is still a substantial social distance between them and more prosperous members of the indigenous majority, public awareness of the existence of such ethnic colonies and their pluralising impact on the local social order is much more widespread. It is equally apparent that these developments are in no sense temporary. It is not just the older generation of settlers who remain committed to the maintenance of their own distinctive lifestyles; so, too, do their locally born offspring. To be sure, the second generation are far more familiar with the ways of the indigenous majority than their parents, such that they have acquired the navigational skills which enable them to order their presentation of themselves in terms of majority conventions and expectations as and when they choose. Nevertheless, most still quietly signal their alterity even in the most public arenas, whilst maintaining those commitments far more actively in personal, domestic and leisure contexts (Ballard 1994; Shaw 2000).

As the minorities' ethnic colonies have continued to burgeon, so majoritarian outsiders have come to view their vitality with ever-greater levels of concern. Feelings of hostility and alarm with respect to their presence is no longer confined to the white working class population of the inner city where most, although by no means all, of these colonies remain spatially grounded. Certainly, those feelings remain most intense amongst those whose interests have been most directly challenged by the presence of the new minorities, but the range of those affected by such concerns has expanded way beyond the inner cities, to encompass ever-wider swathes of the population at large. Suggestions that the heightened levels of plurality precipitated by the minority presence add a welcome touch of spice to the humdrum patterns of established practice have by now lost virtually all the traction they once had. Instead these developments are now routinely viewed as an unwelcome and indigestible threat to the integrity of the established socio-cultural order (Ali, Kalra & Sayyid 2006; Ballard 2007).

Alterity in the Headlines

Whilst it was to be expected that such developments would attract the attention of the popular press, the extensive, but unremittingly sensationalist, coverage they have received over the years have done little more than mirror, and hence exacerbate, the underlying contradictions. Stories revealing 'the shocking truth' about one aspect or another of 'immigrants' (it has long been unnecessary to specify their colour), and their lifestyles, have been a regular source of dramatic headlines for the best part of half a century. At the outset most such accounts focused on the squalid conditions in which the settlers lived, together with their willingness to work for next to nothing, so enabling unscrupulous employers to undermine all the achievements of the trades union movement. Following the introduction of immigration controls – themselves introduced to assuage such fears – attention began to switch to the ever-more inventive strategies which would-be settlers began to deploy in their efforts to evade them. Whilst reports on these themes continue to appear, they have since been supplemented by stories highlighting the 'excessive' rates of fertility displayed by migrant mothers, as well as the marked proclivity of settlers to arrange the marriages of their offspring with spouses from back home, so comprehensively undermining the authorities' efforts to bring 'primary migration' to an end.

This has led to the most recent chapter of much-headlined revelations: lurid accounts of forced marriages and honour killings, of ways in which international gangs of 'people-smugglers' have forced their victims into servitude as prostitutes and cockle pickers, and of mysterious underground *Hawala* operations by means of which huge sums of 'dirty' money have been filtered through transnational networks to unknown destinations overseas. In highlighting these developments, I would in no way wish to suggest that incidents and processes to which these stories refer are fictitious. To be sure, they are invariably sensationalised, but nevertheless they are largely grounded in reality. Rather, my concern here is with the perspective from which they have been prepared. Driven by the priorities of their readers no less than their editors, few journalists have sought to step across the ethnic disjunction on whose significance they have sought to comment. As a result their stories, together with the public discussion which such accounts have generated, have remained relentlessly externalist and problem focused. Such perspectives have rarely been challenged. When allegedly authentic accounts of the experiences of those standing on the far side of the fence do emerge as a focus of public discussion, they are all too often framed in such a way as to confirm, rather than to contest, the normative expectations of the hegemonic majority. The attention paid to the experiences of Ayaan Hirsi Ali (Snel & Stock, *infra*) provides a spectacular example of just that tendency.

What then, has been the shape of the normative expectations precipitated by these processes? So far as most members of Europe's indigenous majority are concerned, the intensifying socio-political contradictions which have been precipitated by the settlers' arrival are largely the fault of the settlers themselves. The emergent consensus has coalesced around the view that if only the settlers had made more urgent efforts to adjust, and better still to abandon, their ancestral heritage, they would have received a far warmer welcome. If they have found themselves confronted by escalating displays of hostility as a result of their dogged pursuit of perverse and unwelcome strategies of non-assimilation, the settlers and still more their offspring have only themselves to blame. Had they been prepared to behave more cooperatively and hence less transgressively, thereby displaying a greater degree of respect for the underlying principles of European civilisation, the current impasse would not have arisen.

Not surprisingly, the view from the other side of the fence stands most of these arguments on the settlers' head. From the settlers' perspective the principal cause of their shift of residence was economic. Without the input of their labour, and their willingness to perform all manner of dirty, heavy and unpleasant tasks from which members of the indigenous population had withdrawn, Europe's economy would be in dire straights. But their alternative vision of their position in the global economy goes much further than that. Even though the role which they were initially required to perform was to act as the low-paid collectors of their hegemons' garbage, they had no intention of staying there. Their central objective in moving into the transnational labour market was not to reproduce their role as helots, but to transcend it, and to build a better material future for themselves and their families. By invading the territory of their former colonial masters, few could fail to be aware that in doing so they were engaging in a transgressive initiative of global, no less than parochial, significance. Moreover, as former colonial subjects, they were well aware their former masters had little interest in, or respect for, the cultural and religious practices of those over whom they had imposed their rule, and no interest whatsoever in adopting those practices as a significant component of their own colonial lifestyles.

Hence, despite the fact that post-war migrant entrepreneurs were transgressors 'from below' rather than 'from above', the circumstances in which they found themselves were far from unfamiliar. No matter how disappointed they may have been to discover that the European evaluation of their status and capabilities was no more positive in the metropolis than in the colonies, their experience of being so treated was hardly novel. Moreover, however much the Europeans might urge them to adopt indigenous cultural conventions and assimilate, they were well aware that European settlers had in no way behaved in such a manner when they themselves engaged in transnational migration from above.

The Emergence of Ethnic Colonies

This is not to suggest that the settlers remained untouched by the context in which they found themselves. Interaction with the hegemonic order which surrounded them was unavoidable, not least in the most essential task which faced them when they arrived at their destination, making a living. And as they rapidly discovered, the natives were rarely, if ever, prepared to go out of their way to help them find their feet. Hence, it swiftly became self-evident that by far the best means of finding a roof beneath which to shelter, a job by means of which to support themselves, was through the good offices of those in the same boat, and especially those with whom they shared some degree of linguistic and cultural commonality. Thus the processes of ethnic crystallisation – driven by the need to build a resilient, mutually supportive and emotionally comfortable 'inside' world, the better to cope with, and to survive in the alien universe into which they had inserted themselves – began almost from the moment when pioneer migrants first stepped ashore. And since the networks of mutual reciprocity so generated provided such effective sources of material and psychological support, successive waves of settlers tapped into them at the earliest possible opportunity.

From this perspective, ethnic aggregations were in no sense the outcome of a mindless commitment to traditionalism. Rather they were precipitated by settlers' creative utilisation of the resources embedded in their ancestral cultural traditions as they set about devising adaptive strategies better to cope with the multitude of practical challenges with which they found themselves confronted. These initiatives in no sense represented a withdrawal from the wider social order in which they found themselves. On the contrary, they are better understood as a vital component of the way in which they *engaged* with the world around them, and which in no way excluded parallel efforts to acquire the social, linguistic and cultural skills which would also enable them to handle face-to-face interactions with members of the indigenous majority as and when required. They were well aware that if they were ever to move away from the positions at the bottom of the socio-economic order to which they had been so humiliatingly ascribed, it was essential to acquire such skills.

But by the same token it was equally clear that mere conformity was an insufficient basis for everyday survival, let alone for achieving their more distant dreams of upward mobility. The natives were manifestly far too hostile, and their strategies of exclusion far too effective, for them to achieve those goals without extensive and determined 'insider' activity on their own account. Hence, whilst by no means averse to acquiring the linguistic and cultural capital required to participate in arenas where conformity with indigenous conventions was a necessity, most settlers put much more energy into the construction of their own alternative networks of mutual support. In doing so the reciprocities that could readily be generated on the basis of ideologies of kinship proved to be particularly helpful, not least because of their inherent flexibility. At least at the outset, pioneers whose prior connections ranged from tenuous to non-existent could readily utilise idioms of quasi-kinship, so enabling them to construct binding relationships of reciprocity between themselves by acting *as though* they were brothers. However it was not long before chain-migration hastened the emergence of ever-more coherent ethnic colonies ground in reciprocities of real rather than fictive kinship, precipitating the outcomes to which head-line-writers subsequently reacted with such alarm.

Kinship and the Construction and Maintenance of Transnational Networks

Analysts of migration have paid remarkably little attention to matters of kinship. Whilst textbook accounts routinely point to the way in which transnational migrants have been 'pulled' by the insatiable demand for cheap and willing labour in the world's most prosperous economies, and 'pushed' by sharpening levels of relative poverty experienced by the inhabitants of much of Asia, Africa and Latin America, much less attention has yet been paid to the human processes which have sustained the internal dynamics of each of these many separate population flows. As a result there is still only a dawning recognition that the success with which migrants are continuing to sweep across ever more heavily defended borders is to a large extent a consequence of a further factor: the extent to which these processes are *kinship driven*.

It is now extremely rare for long-distance migrants to set off with no knowledge of their final destination. Once examined from within, virtually all contemporary migratory flows turn out to be grounded in processes of chain migration, such that earlier settlers encourage the passage of their kinsfolk to the particular destination at which they have established themselves, who in turn provide similar assistance to further kinsfolk. Such processes rapidly develop their own near-exponential dynamic, most especially when those involved are in a position to draw on extended networks of kinship reciprocity within which to further their collective entrepreneurial exercise. As immigration authorities around the world have discovered, once such chain-migratory escalators are in full flow, such that a substantial number of settlers are strategically located overseas, bringing them to a halt is a well-nigh impossible task (Bhagwati 2003). The dynamics of these powerful engines of socio-economic change deserve far closer examination than they have hitherto received.

Viewed from above, the internal driving forces which have sustained these developments were entirely unexpected. It is easy to see why. Whilst it was common knowledge that the dynamics of twentieth-century globalisation have reinforced the unequal distribution of material assets between Euro-America and the inhabitants of most parts of Asia, Africa and Latin America, it seemed apparent that those standing on the losing side of the global division of resources for the most part lacked the educational, economic and political resources which would allow them effectively to compete with the global hegemons. However, what such gloomy perspectives overlooked is the extent to which the cultural capital available to those who find themselves in such a position can, when suitably mobilised, provide some highly effective strategies by means of which those involved can begin to extract themselves from the positions of hopeless disadvantage to which they might otherwise be condemned. Seen from this perspective, it is now quite clear that by taking advantage of the dramatic falls in the cost of long-distance travel and communications, and given the often-unacknowledged scale of demand for unskilled labour in most of the world's developed economies, the entrepreneurial potentiality embedded in networks of extended kinship reciprocity has been unleashed with dramatic success. The result has been the construction of innumerable transnational 'escalators' which have emerged to facilitate the transfer of hundreds of millions of people from a host of specific localities in the developing world to equally specific destinations in Euro-America, as well as a number of other prosperous economic hot spots.

Such developments are best understood as one of the most significant countervailing responses to established patterns of Euro-American global hegemony to have emerged during the course of the past half century. From that perspective these self-generated entrepreneurial initiatives reaching upwards 'from below' have achieved much more than mere population-transfer. Besides facilitating the growth of ever-more prosperous ethnic colonies, the remittances which such settlers transfer through those self-same networks to their kinsfolk back home are now estimated to exceed US$ 250 billion per annum, greater than the global flow of development aid. They now form a stable, counter-cyclical source of development aid, transferred directly into the pockets of the poor (Ratha & Maimbo 2005).

No less than their counterparts operating 'from above', the transnational networks which have recently emerged from below are strongly corporate in character: that is the key to their success. But in contrast to the formal bureaucratic structures on which multinational corporations rely, those deployed by the countervailing entrepreneurs operating from below have been implemented on a much more 'informal' basis. By making the most of the potential for corporate activity embedded in their kinship systems, they have found themselves able to redistribute people, ideas and capital within their global networks with just as much facility, but with much lower overheads than those incurred by more formally organised multinational corporations (Ballard 2005). Given this, it should be apparent why European expectations about the prospect of settlers rapidly abandoning their prior cultural commitments have proved to be so wide of the mark. Far from falling into abeyance as a consequence of their transnational extension, the utility of networks of reciprocity has for the most part been actively enhanced in such contexts, so precipitating precisely the opposite outcome. Whilst the results were by no means a carbon-copy replica of what went on back home – for the adaptations made to cope with the demands of new transnational environments were nothing if not far reaching – the institutions around which ethnic colonies crystallised actively facilitated the circulation of information, ideas, financial assets and (of course) people within a myriad of diasporic networks, so promoting their members' economic, educational and spatial mobility (Ballard 2003a,b; Shaw 2000).

As these intrinsically transgressive developments have begun to gather strength, so the very structure of the global order is gradually being transformed. By devising strategies to beat their former hegemons at their own game, the outsiders have begun to topple the insiders from their former positions of unchallenged hegemony. But in so doing, the upstarts are by no means always choosing to play by the established rules of the game. The strategic initiatives of transnational migrants provide numerous examples of the effectiveness of discarding conventional practices in favour of the creative deployment of one's alterity, the better to circumvent the obstacles lying in one's path, and in so doing to devise yet more efficient and effective solutions to the remaining problems at hand.

Family and Kinship

In these circumstances it should come as no surprise that preferred kinship conventions of members of Europe's non-European minorities have become the focus of such heated debate. The challenge which their presence offers to the established social order is real, not fictional.

Kinship conventions do much more than generate distinctive patterns of interpersonal behaviour; they also have a far-reaching impact on demographic developments, on innumerable aspects of their users' everyday social, personal and strategic practices, and hence on the structure of the wider socio-political order.

How far do migrants' assumptions about family, kinship and marriage differ from those of the indigenous majority? Thanks to the influence of the Church, European (and especially northern European) kinship conventions have traditionally assumed that the institution of marriage stands *ipso facto* at the core of family life. Marriage, it is routinely assumed, is, or at least should be, a monogamous and life-long heterosexual partnership, established on the basis of a personal choice, and contracted as a necessary precursor to sexual cohabitation. It is also assumed that marriage will precipitate the establishment of an independent nuclear household, within which the offspring of the union will be raised to adulthood. Having reached that condition, it is further expected that these free and autonomous individuals will select partners, marry, and set up similarly structured autonomous conjugal families of their own. To be sure, members of these autonomous households still expect to keep in contact with their parents and siblings, but such relationships are sustained by far weaker bonds of reciprocity than those associated with conjugality. Hence, for example, they are only expected to be associated with co-residence in contexts of exceptional economic hardship. Such is the overwhelming salience of the conjugal tie that the use of wider relationships of kinship reciprocity as a means of constructing the corporately organised descent and lineage structures is virtually unknown.

The priority assigned to conjugality in European kinship conventions has been reinforced by a strengthening commitment to individualism, with far-reaching consequences; the strength of both inter- and intragenerational kinship bonds was subject to further erosion. Furthermore, conjugal units have not only been rendered steadily more autonomous, but ties of conjugality themselves have now begun to weaken. As obstacles in the way of divorce have been progressively discarded, the frequency of its incidence has increased by leaps and bounds. Likewise, marriage has lost its sacramental status. It has ceased to be a regarded as necessary precursor to sexual intercourse, to the production of offspring, or even to the establishment of socially acceptable conjugal partnerships; and most recently of all, legislative changes have sought formally to confirm that homosexual partnerships should be regarded as having the same level of social and legal acceptability as those constructed on a heterosexual basis. The resulting behavioural changes, accompanied by unprecedented levels of prosperity and spatial mobility, steady increases in life expectancy, and a rapid decline in fertility rates with the introduction of reliable means of birth control, have precipitated far-reaching socio-demographic changes. Family units are steadily shrinking in size, in some cases almost to the point of disappearance, whilst single-person households are becoming increasingly commonplace, especially amongst young and affluent members of Europe's indigenous majority.

By contrast, the vast majority of non-European settlers continue to operate within the context of ideologies which bind them into all-consuming networks of mutual reciprocity with a far wider range of kinsfolk. Restricting attention to the conventions deployed in that part of the world from which the great majority of settlers have arrived – the swath of territory which runs from North Africa through the Eastern Mediterranean and the Middle East to South Asia – one common feature stands out. Despite much local and national variation, the conjugal tie is by is far from being the principal foundation of family life. To be sure, marriage is a crucial component of the kinship system, but it is nevertheless set within, and to a large extent over-shadowed by, a much

wider network of inter- and intra-generational ties of mutual reciprocity, largely ordered within the priority given to ties of patrilineal descent (Ballard 1973, 1982).

In such contexts, family life is grounded not so much in the conjugal tie between husband and wife, but rather in the more demanding
links of mutuality which bind parents, patrilineal offspring and offspring's offspring into all-consuming corporate networks. When ties of
reciprocity within the extended family assume such salience, the significance of marriage differs strikingly from that generated by contemporary Western European ideological expectations. Rather than being the
very foundation of personal and family life, it is reduced to the status
of an appurtenance, albeit one of great significance. Moreover, in more
corporately oriented contexts, marriage gains additional functions
which are almost entirely absent in more individualistically oriented
systems. Hence, besides giving rise to a conjugal partnership between
husband and wife, marriage also brings additional domestic partnerships into being, such that in the early days of marriage a newly arrived bride can often find that her relationship with her mother-in-law,
and beyond that with her newly acquired sisters-in-law, is of more
pressing concern than that with her husband. Nor is that all. When families are corporately constructed, each new marriage sets up a long-
term affinal alliance between the two corporations, whilst also providing the wife-receiving family with its most valuable asset of all, a
means whereby the descent group can reproduce itself through time,
provided that the wife so acquired proves to be fertile.

Within the context of such conventions, each successive marriage
marks a crucial step in the development of the corporate family. Carefully selected wives not only add to the group's resources of domestic
labour, but are a prospective source of the children whose arrival will
ensure that the family's honour and prosperity can be sustained for a
further generation. Moreover, the arrival of their offspring's offspring
marks the point at which parents can begin to feel that having fulfilled
their obligation to ensure the continuity of the corporate whole, they
can legitimately step sideways into retirement, and receive the respect
and support they deserve as a result of having fulfilled their duties. But
whilst the strength of the mutual reciprocities so generated may attract
some grudging respect, in the eyes of more individualistically minded
observers such positive evaluations are swiftly to be overwhelmed by
other features of the system. From their perspective there is nothing
admirable in cultural traditions in which parents claim the right to
superimpose their own priorities over those of their offspring in the
choice of their marital partners, where polygamy is accepted as permissible, and where notions of honour and modesty lead to the imposition
of such tight constraints on personal freedom that homicidal retribu-

tion can be precipitated when conventional expectations are seriously contravened. To those whose normative outlook is as individualistic as it is libertarian, behaviours of this kind are nothing less than barbaric.

A Clash of Cultures?

All this has precipitated much talk of the inevitability of a clash of cultures. External observers regularly suggest that as the locally raised offspring of migrants reach adulthood they are bound to encounter severe contradictions as they struggle to negotiate the competing demands of their authoritarian and traditionally minded parents and the opportunities for personal freedom to which they have gained access as a result of their participation in the more liberal and progressive cultural order which surrounds them. But although the contradictions between the conceptual premises used to underpin the logic of interpersonal relationships within the two arenas are real enough, are the consequences really so unbridgeable, as external commentators routinely suggest must be the case? And perhaps most importantly of all, how sound is their assumption that the prospect of access to unlimited personal freedom, regardless of one's responsibilities to others, will of necessity trump the emotional and material benefits to which membership of a tight-knit network of mutual reciprocity offers its participants?

Current debates about the legitimacy or otherwise of the everyday lifestyles of members of the new minorities must be approached with caution. Given the extent to which a commitment to individualism and personal freedom is so entrenched in all the contemporary manifestations of Western Europe's indigenous cultural traditions, let alone the strength of the contradictions between the indigenes and settlers outlined earlier, the ideological arena within which debates with respect to such issues are currently being played out is anything but level. In such circumstances it is unsurprising that the practices of minority communities, within which a more corporately oriented set of kinship conventions are utilised as a means of organising their domestic affairs, is routinely perceived not just as bizarre, but as morally and socially unacceptable. In making such negative judgements, external observers invariably focus their critical gaze on the binding obligations, or rather what are seen as excessively authoritarian demands, which superordinates place on more junior members of the family, thereby substantially compromising their rights to personal freedom. More informed outsiders may well acknowledge that there is much to be said for mutuality and cooperation – after all, relationships of mutuality may well have provided a valuable source of solidarity in the adverse material conditions in which such settlers' ancestors once lived. But,

they ask, for how long can these archaic structures be expected to survive in the midst of contemporary conditions of affluence? From this
perspective it seems self-evident that restrictive practices associated
with such authoritarian, and indeed anachronistic, forms of family organisation are everywhere being swept away by irresistible forces of
modernity, liberty and personal freedom sweeping the globe.

If the forces of globalisation were indeed destined to have such an effect, efforts by members of the anachronistically oriented older generation mindlessly to preserve their ancient traditions would soon be overcome by the impact of the rising tide of modernity on their locally born
offspring. But how accurate are such prognostications proving to be?
To be sure, the *material* aspects of all settlers' lifestyles have changed
dramatically since their arrival in Europe; and no matter how much
they may have striven to sustain more traditional behavioural practices
in domestic contexts, their offspring have by now had sufficient contact
with the indigenes and their institutions to act in a wholly 'English',
'French', 'German', 'Dutch' or 'Italian' manner when and as they
choose. Yet despite their acquisition of the navigational skills that enable them to participate with ease in virtually all the arenas in which
the linguistic, social and cultural conventions of the indigenous majority hold sway, it is equally clear that the vast majority of young people
of minority descent still stubbornly maintain a strong sense of their
own distinctiveness in more personal, domestic and leisure contexts.
How is this 'stubbornness' best accounted for? Is it merely a consequence of authoritarian parents imposing traditionalist restrictions on
gullible and long-suffering offspring, or of charismatic preachers
managing successfully to seduce naïve young Muslims into accepting
the premises of immoderate Islam? Or is it, to the contrary, that the
parallel strategies of non-assimilation, most especially in personal, domestic and leisure spheres, which so many members of the younger
generation turn out on close inspection to have adopted, are better understood as an adaptive, and from that perspective a *positive*, response
to the manifold challenges with which they have found themselves
confronted?

That those subjected to systematic patterns of racial and ethnic denigration and exclusion should not only have closed ranks, but deployed
all the other characteristic 'weapons of the weak' (Scott 1985, 1990)
should come as no surprise. In doing so they have followed a multitude of predecessors by quietly elaborating their sense of alterity, the
better to extend the range of strategic resources with which to confront
and confound their excluders. In this sense at least, the ways in which
members of all the various components of the minority communities,
young and old, female and male, are making creative use of the resources of their ancestral heritages in conjunction with all manner of

ideas and perspectives quietly borrowed from their hegemons, the better to resist, to circumvent and ultimately to overcome and obliterate the forces of exclusion with which they find themselves confronted, is anything but unprecedented, even in a European context. After all, innumerable local minorities have pursued the same tactic, though their deeper local roots have enabled them to legitimate their ethnic consolidation as patriotic nationalism. Whilst the new minorities' strategies of resistance may indeed be stubborn, they are anything but a manifestation of inherent social pathology: rather they are prerequisite for the achievement of more equitable outcomes. By just the same token those responsible for their marginalisation have just as much interest in sustaining the opposite view. Efforts to demonstrate that all manifestations of ethnic alterity are as unhelpful as they are pathogenic have always been one of the one of the most favoured weapons in the armoury of the strong.

The Costs and Benefits of Collective Solidarity

Whatever outsiders might suggest, those who order their domestic lives on a corporate basis are for the most part acutely aware of the most salient benefit of collective solidarity. In the face of the vicissitudes of an uncertain world, mutual cooperation provides a highly effective bastion against the prospect of personal insecurity. However, such outcomes only occur if certain conditions are fulfilled. One of the most important is the willingness of those involved to sacrifice their own personal interests in favour of those of the collectivity as and when the need arises. The unbounded pursuit of personal interests and/or individual freedom is of necessity inimical to collective solidarity. That said, however beneficial to others such behaviour may be, it is by no means necessarily an unmitigated good as far as those required to make such sacrifices are concerned. In principle, at least, their willingness to put their personal interests to one side in the short term should guarantee that they will at some point reap benefits which are at least proportionate to those which they had previously foregone. That is what the principle of reciprocity is all about. But what if the promised returns begin to look far smaller than the sacrifice made, and the prospect of their fulfilment becomes so distant as to be rendered meaningless?

Such queries are far from hypothetical. No matter how strongly committed to the principles of cooperation and mutuality members of corporately constituted families may be, most also keep a wary eye on the demands which have been placed on them by others. They are rarely so stupid as to assume that, in the absence of regular reminders, those who have gained from their sacrifices will of necessity fulfil their reci-

procal obligations without having their memories jogged. Contrary to
the assumptions of libertarian outsiders whose personal experience has
been limited to that of an egalitarian/individualistic conceptual universe, all my experience suggests that those who have grown up within
collectively ordered families are rarely so naïve as to assume that the
ideology of reciprocity will of itself be sufficient to guarantee their personal interests as against the self-interested machinations of others
members of the group. Indeed, as anyone with personal experience of
the dynamics of interpersonal interactions within such extended families can readily testify, the broad framework of mutuality is simultaneously accompanied, and indeed underpinned, by endless competitive
efforts by those involved to scheme and manoeuvre their way to positions of advantage with respect to their personal rivals. Hence, even
though such groups may close ranks in comprehensive unity in the
face of external threats, at a more everyday level the centrifugal forces
precipitated by the processes of mutual competition are only margin-
ally trumped by the centripetal forces of mutuality holding the group
together.

Once extended families are viewed as processual arenas whose organisational stability is the outcome of a constantly renegotiated condition of dynamic equilibrium, it becomes much easier to gain a better
appreciation of the actual operation of what might otherwise appear to
be static and authoritarian hierarchical structures. Once this kind of
perspective is adopted, it is immediately apparent that the female
members of such families are relatively rarely reduced to the position
of helpless pawns which ill-informed external observers so often assume they must of necessity occupy. On the contrary, all my experience
suggests that women have an exceptionally keen appreciation of the
distribution of costs and benefits within the family, and consequently
spend much time and effort executing complex manoeuvres whose
principle objective is to advance the interests of both themselves and
their offspring. Moreover, their husbands are by no means the only 'al-
ters' whose interests they seek to oppose in so doing. Once one taps
into these processes it soon becomes apparent that whilst wives invariably take great care not to topple their husbands from their positions
of nominal authority, such that their partner's ability to determine the
course of events within the family is often far more limited than public
appearances might suggest. Given the simultaneous presence of
mothers-in-law and any resident sisters-in-law within such networks,
by far the most explosive contradictions within such extended families
tend to be those which periodically erupt between powerful women.

The Dynamics of Constantly Contested Equilibrium

With such considerations in mind, corporate families relatively rarely take the form of the authoritarian monoliths which haunt the imaginations of external observers. Much changes when they are understood as arenas of mutual interaction where kinsfolk of varying ranks and statuses, bound together by mutually advantageous bonds of mutual reciprocity, constantly engage in a complex set of interpersonal manoeuvres aimed at least at much at advancing the manoeuvrer's own interests (and countering those devised by his or her many rivals) as they are at advancing the interests of the corporation as a whole. From this perspective a vision of happy families is just as misleading as that depicting them as living in constant terror of the untrammelled and arbitrary power of a coldly authoritarian patriarch. Instead, such families are best understood as being grounded in a condition of dynamic equilibrium where the centrifugal forces of interpersonal competition are more or less consistently held in check by the commitment to cohesion generated by the manifest benefits of mutual cooperation.

In such circumstances the quotidian distribution of power and authority within such families is more the outcome of endless processes of interpersonal manoeuvring than of the ideological commitments around which they are formally constituted. Nevertheless those remain of crucial importance, not least because they provide the yardstick against which participants routinely seek to measure the extent to which others have fulfilled their responsibilities, or failed to do so. From this perspective, the overall ideological framework is far less prescriptive than it might seem at first sight. On the one hand, it leaves plentiful scope for individual members of the family to establish alliances with others in an effort to advance their own interests, which will very often include those of their immediate dependents; meanwhile it simultaneously provides an equally effective means of seeking to counter and undermine their rivals' parallel manoeuvres, not least by accusing them of failing to live up to those prescriptive ideals. Moreover, if the conflicts precipitated by these manoeuvres reach such a degree of intensity as to begin to threaten the integrity of the group as a whole, a further remedy is readily available: the family meeting. Most usually chaired by a respected elder who stands above the fray, the central objective of such an exercise is to facilitate the renegotiation of strained relationships, and on that basis reach a compromise which serves to satisfy the pragmatic interests of all concerned.

Nevertheless, family meetings do not always produce the desired outcome. When contradictions have become sufficiently deeply entrenched, and the contending parties so stubbornly committed to their respective positions, such that successive attempts to broker compromise have all collapsed, it eventually becomes clear that no viable means of resolving the underlying contradiction is available. Such an impasse invariably precipitates a change in the very structure of the collectivity itself, as when marriages are recognised as being in a condition of irretrievable collapse, when brothers who have hitherto organised their affairs jointly decide they are no longer able to live together under the same roof, or when no agreement can be reached about a suitable spouse for a son or daughter. When both sides have entirely lost confidence in the others' commitment to mutuality, only one solution is possible, an irretrievable split in the structure of the corporate whole. In such circumstances the elders are likely to change course, and to seek to broker an amicable division of corporate assets and responsibilities. But if the elders fail to calm the hurt feelings which are often harboured by the party which feels itself most aggrieved, violence can all too easily ensue. In such circumstances the bitterness generated when close kin fall out – such that relationships of comprehensive reciprocity are replaced by those of equally comprehensive feud – must be seen to be believed.

To observers raised in societies where networks are shallow and individualism is the order of the day, such outcomes seem quite bewildering. In their world, similar breakdowns are unlikely to precipitate anything more than a short period of anger and resentment before normality is restored. But the larger and more corporate the kinship networks within which such breakdowns occur, the more explosive the consequences of such a collapse in relationships of reciprocity tend to become. It is in these kind of circumstances that so-called 'honour crimes' tend to occur.

The Consequences of Transnational Extension

The transnational extension of networks of kinship reciprocity has powerfully reinforced all aspects of these tendencies, both positive and negative. As the settlers themselves are well aware, it is because of their success in sustaining such links of mutual reciprocity amongst themselves, together with their equally substantial success in socialising their overseas-born offspring into these self-same modes of behaviour, that they have been able to achieve such a dramatic degree of socio-economic mobility, no less in spatial than in vertical terms. However, these successes have not been without their downsides. As ever, such exercises demand that all concerned make substantial sacrifices of their immediate interests in the expectation this will provide even more substantial future benefits. But by just the same token there is as much, if not more, danger that those less fortunately placed will find the bulk of the benefits falling into the hands of those better placed than themselves, whilst the established means whereby those so marginalised have hitherto been able to flag their distress have been attenuated by the transnational extension of formerly parochial networks.

If so, it is hardly surprising that the diminished effectiveness of internal modes of reconciliation should have been accompanied by an increase in the scale and severity of contradictions within extended families, and hence in the frequency of violent interpersonal confrontations amongst kinsfolk. But if so, how should such developments be read? Viewed through the prism of contemporary European liberal/egalitarian conceptual expectations, the answer seems obvious. The kinship structures which such migrants have brought with them were inherently patriarchal and authoritarian in character, and led to the imposition of wholly unjustifiable limits on the personal freedom of those who consequently found themselves at the bottom of the resultant hierarchy. But as a result of the transfer of such families to a more open and progressive environment, the underlying contradictions have grown unsustainably wide. Hence the oppressed victims of these processes have at long last begun to challenge their subordination, and husbands, fathers and brothers have sought to reassert their traditional authority by violent means, so precipitating the gruesome outcomes so regularly reported in the media.

However satisfied with such explanations external observers may be, not least because they are both congruent with and serve yet further to reinforce their prior assumptions, a view from within invariably throws up far more complex representations of what is going on, albeit of a kind which external observers regularly regard as close to incomprehensible. Why should this be so? In my experience the problem starts with such observers' difficulty in gaining an appreciation of just what the concept of *reciprocity* might mean in these circumstances, most especially in the sense of the long-lasting patterns of duty and obligation to which relationships ordered in this way are expected to give rise. Likewise the concept of *personal sacrifice* which arises in such contexts, and especially the suggestion that this might be a noble and honourable way of behaving, is one which most contemporary European observers find as bizarre as it is alien. From their perspective, behaviour which contravenes deeply held assumptions about the way in which personal dignity arises from the freely expressed exercise of personal choice – as the notion of sacrifice necessarily demands – is wholly unacceptable. Hence, the prospect that such behaviour should be evaluated so positively is by definition incomprehensible.

This in turn serves to highlight the immensity of the conceptual gulf between the cognitive universe in which contemporary Euro-American thinking and action is routinely set, and the social and conceptual uni-

verses within which most of the world's non-European populations order their daily activities and mutual interactions. Amongst the latter,
corporately organised kin groups, rather than free-standing, autonomous personal-contract-making individuals are the building blocks of
the social universe. Within such a universe, personal freedom in the
contemporary Euro-American sense stands at a discount, not a pre-
mium. Indeed those who occupy such a position of 'freedom' stand, by
definition, in lonely isolation, excluded from the world of mutual obligations around which the social order is constructed. From the perspective of those operating within such collectively ordered systems it
is the fulfilment of obligations, as opposed to the exercise of rights,
which is assumed to provide the foundation of the social order. From
that perspective, the notion that individuals might have free-standing
personal rights vis-à-vis others which can legitimately be exercised on
an a priori basis is regarded as entirely alien. Instead, human rights in
the Euro-American sense are perceived as a *dependent* variable, in the
sense that they arise as a consequence of the fulfilment of one's obligations to others, and not least to the members of the family into which
one has had the good fortune to be born. Hence, just as parents sacrificed their own interests, and thereby fulfilled their own necessary obligations, by raising their children to adulthood, so those children are regarded as having a consequent obligation to respect and obey their parents, and to repay them for all their efforts by offering them unstinting
support when in due course they become elderly and infirm. In such a
world, rights of all kinds are not given, but earned on the basis of the
fulfilment of the many obligations due to the group of which one is a
member, in the confident expectation that one's sacrifices will in due
course be repaid (Ballard 1982, 1973).

Transnational Marriages

Marriage plays a key role in these long-term processes. Marriage facilitates the ongoing continuity of corporate families, since it is a necessary prerequisite for the production of the heirs who will carry the
group forward into the next generation. It also plays an equally significant role in building strategically advantageous interfamilial ties of affinal reciprocity which supplement, or provide a counterpoint to, the
less malleable patterns of alliance and differentiation precipitated by
patrilineal descent. Whilst the strategic use of marital manoeuvres to
achieve such objectives may now have fallen into abeyance in Euro-
American contexts, they were once of pressing concern to the aristoc-
racy and landed gentry of medieval and early modern Europe, and continue to be the very stuff of village politics in those parts of world

where extended kinships networks, and through them the hereditary distribution of rights in land, provide the foundations of the local socio-economic order. It is of course from societies of the latter kind from which the vast majority of the settlers with whom we are concerned here have been drawn.

Had those who implemented such practices stayed in their villages, it might have been possible to dismiss such matchmaking manoeuvres, and the competitive quests for strategic advantage which underpin them, as arcane matters of little concern to anyone but kinship-besotted anthropologists. But given the key role played by kinship reciprocities in the construction and maintenance of escalators of chain migration, there is no way in which such judgements can be sustained. Instead, concern with such matters has become a substantial focus of social policy throughout Western Europe. It is not difficult to see why. Migrants have been no less entrepreneurial in circumventing immigration controls than they have in any other sphere, so causing many migration managers to conclude that they have been saddled with a wholly impossible task. In the face of directions from on high to bring the inflow of non-European immigration under control, they found their targets deploying what they perceive as being every trick imaginable in their efforts to evade the controls they are required to enforce. Moreover, their attempts to plug the resultant gaps are regularly rendered nugatory by 'unhelpful' restrictions such as those arising from the European Convention on Human Rights, or from the provisions of asylum law. In consequence, immigration law has everywhere been transformed into an arcane game of cat and mouse.

The result is a complex stand-off, in which marriage has become a central bone of contention. It is now nearly 40 years since the UK authorities took their first steps towards closing off unlimited primary migration, or in other words the entry of young unmarried adults who had not been granted work permits. However, one of the central consequences of their efforts has been to divert the inflow of what was once expected to be a self-limiting source of future arrivals, the immediate kinsfolk of established settlers. But 'secondary migration', as this inflow was initially described, has not followed the expected pattern, remaining as vigorous as it was when immigration controls were introduced. As marriage emerged as the weakest link in the authorities' exclusionary provisions, so it has become an ever-more contentious battleground.

In the early days of settlement, the vast majority of 'secondary' applicants were the wives and children of men who had already established themselves in the UK. In an effort to curb their inflow, the authorities queried the legitimacy of the applicant's marriage, and/or whether all the children accompanying her were indeed the offspring of the spon-

sor. That strategy temporarily served to curb the inflow, until the introduction of DNA tests provided an incontestable means of identifying
parentage. When the great majority of contested claims proved to be
valid, the inflow resumed with a vengeance, precipitating ever more intense pressures to bar the door once again. Further initiatives were introduced, but none proved more effective than the 'primary purpose'
rule, which was by now directed at excluding not so much the wives of
men who had entered the UK as adults, but rather the spouses of those
of their UK-based offspring who had reached marriageable age.

In this respect the dilemma facing the immigration authorities was
even more challenging. If members of the rising generation chose (or
rather responded positively to their parents' suggestions that they
should choose) a spouse from back home, how could the couple be pre-
vented from taking up residence in the UK? The obvious answer was
to challenge the legitimacy of the marriage itself. This led to the construction of the notorious 'primary purpose' rule (Sachdeva 1993)
which targeted couples whose relationship was not preceded by a period of courtship, in other words whose marriage had been arranged. By
demanding that the overseas-resident partner seeking entry into the
UK should demonstrate that achieving that goal was *not* the primary
purpose of their marriage, all such applicants were required to prove a
negative before they could be granted a right of entry into the UK.
Whilst this rule served its purpose for a while, such was the wave of
criticism that its continued application became indefensible, and it was
abandoned by the 1997 Labour Government. Nevertheless the underlying contradictions remained as vigorous as ever, and no effort has since
been spared in the search for a viable alternative.

In doing so, an approach initially developed in Norway has begun to
attract increasing attention in many other parts of the EU, including
the UK. It is easy to see why. Just like the 'primary purpose' rule it
seeks to de-legitimise a whole category of marriages. The Norwegian
approach was grounded in the vocabulary of human rights, and the
proposition that 'forced' marriages were thereby inherently illegitimate.
It was further argued that those forced to contract such marriages were
typically cousins, and/or spouses aged under the age of 25 (Bredal
2005). Since marriages where those conditions were fulfilled were
most unlikely to have been based on personal choice, and therefore
compromised the human rights of one or both partners, it was entirely
legitimate to remove the exemption of spouses who had married on
that basis from immigration controls. By adopting such an approach,
migration managers clearly hope they have at long last found secure
ground on which to base their arguments. They may well be right. So
far at least, legislative initiatives grounded in appeals to human rights,
to individual freedom and to the necessity of curbing the evils of patri-

archy, have attracted widespread support. No one denies that such measures also provide a strategically convenient means of reinforcing the effectiveness of Europe's carefully constructed barriers of immigration control, but the justification of such measures on human rights grounds provides an excellent means of assuaging both legal criticism and liberal consciences.

That said, it is no part of my argument that marriages of the kind which such measures seek to target are necessarily problem-free, far from it. But if such matches do indeed display an alarming tendency to be beset by personal contradictions, I would argue that such problems are best addressed on a basis which is a good deal more sensitive to the perspectives of the actual participants. Why, then, might insiders choose to contract such transnational marriages? That question can be answered at a number of different levels. The first and most obvious answer is that if one's personal social arena is transnationally extended, and if one also expects to find a spouse 'of one's own kind' within such an arena, then the process of spouse-choosing is also likely to conducted on a transnational basis. Hence, for example, a young Sikh who has grown up in Birmingham is as likely to meet a potential spouse whilst visiting Leeds to attend a marriage as when he (or she) attends a similar event in Vancouver or Phagwara. Likewise if such spouse-hunters turn to the Internet to expand their range of choices, they may well use a religious, and indeed caste-specific, website of global scope. In this, as in many other spheres, transnational networks progressively render national boundaries irrelevant, widening the opportunities for exercising strategic choice and developing entrepreneurial opportunities, and simultaneously enabling one to exploit and reinforce the resources of the network to which one is affiliated.

There are a several more specific reasons why members of the older generation find the prospect of locating spouses for their offspring from back home particularly attractive. Amongst the most straightforward is the wish to recruit a daughter-in-law who is comprehensively steeped in the values of one's ancestral tradition, such that she will be able to pass those traditions on to one's grandchildren on a far more effective basis than an overseas-born and raised daughter-in-law could ever hope to achieve. At the other end of the scale, such a match is also widely regarded as a convenient backstop when all else fails – as, for example, when some aspect of a son's or a daughter's behaviour, experience, appearance or health is such that the prospect of finding an appropriate spouse in the local marriage market has been virtually eliminated. However the pressure to migrate – as migration managers have come to describe it – arising from this source is relatively limited. The situations which have caused them a great deal more concern are those in which transnational spouse recruitment appeared (at least from their perspective) to have been deployed in deliberate efforts to exploit loopholes in their carefully constructed system of immigration control. These fall into two main classes. Firstly those marriages in which parents of overseas-based spouses paid large dowries in return for the privilege of being able to see their son or daughter reach the preferred destination; secondly, and much more frequently, those in which the spouse in question was a close relative, most usually a cousin, of his or her UK-based spouse, and whose primary purpose appeared to be to enable an additional member of the *biraderi* (descent group) to join the otherwise halted escalator. It is with such concerns in mind that cousin-marriage has come figure so largely in current efforts to block what has come to be regarded as the family-reunion loophole in the bastion of Fortress Europe.

Marriage Rules and Their Consequences

As I argued in a paper published nearly two decades ago (Ballard 1990), the conventions deployed within any given community with respect to just what categories of kinsfolk one may and may not marry can have a far-reaching impact on the precise way in which transnational escalators of chain migration develop over time. In an analysis which appears to have helped to have spark off the subsequent debate in Norway, I explored the comparative impact of the conventions deployed by Muslim emigrants from Pakistani Punjab, which are largely derived from the incest taboos set out in Leviticus, with those deployed by Sikh and Hindu neighbours from Indian Punjab who follow complex rules of *gotra* (lineage) exogamy.

The central consequence of these conventions is that, whilst Hindus and Sikhs are effectively barred from contracting marriages into families with whom they have any prior links of kinship, Punjabi Muslims are subjected to no such restrictions, such that marriage between cousins is regarded as entirely permissible. These differences have far-reaching consequences when parents set about choosing partners for their offspring. Thanks to the rules of exogamy, every Sikh and Hindu marriage has to be negotiated afresh with 'strangers', or more precisely, with non-kin. Revealingly, the term *rista* means both marriage and relationship, so highlighting the extent to which every marriage also generates a vigorous link of affinal reciprocity between the givers and the recipients of the bride. But although *riste* have exactly the same relationship-building consequences in Muslim contexts as they do for Sikhs and Hindus, the absence of exogamous restrictions has strategic implications. Hence, whilst Punjabi Muslims are well aware of the benefits of using carefully negotiated marriages as a means of building alliances with non-kin, their much more usual practice is to deploy their *riste* as a means of reinforcing existing ties within the agnatic *biraderi*. Similar choices are also exercised across the length and breadth of the Islamic world, but nowhere does the option appear to be more actively pursued than in the Punjab, where more than half of all marriages are arranged between first cousins.

Why, though, do Punjabi Muslims exercise this choice so frequently? One of the most important factors behind this preference in the exceptional intensity of the bonds of emotional reciprocity between siblings, such that siblings expect to be able to exercise a right of first refusal when it come to arranging the *riste* of each others' children. In these circumstances, to refuse such an offer of *rista* without good cause is regarded as a repudiation of one of the key obligations of sibling solidarity, not a step to take lightly. Nevertheless there is a further counterpoint to this. If the sibling group in question is of any size, there will be a large number of potential permutations as to how the marriages of the cousins in the next generation might be arranged. Moreover, those choices are multiplied yet further by the fact that the offspring of a wife's siblings, no less than those of her husband's, are all in play when it comes to the negotiation of *riste*. In these circumstances a preference for cousin marriage is normally far from being narrowly prescriptive. Nevertheless, let alone the fact that wives, no less than husbands are actively engaged, and in consequence frequently in competition with one another, in an effort to ensure that the *riste* constructed for each of their offspring fall as far as possible to their own strategic advantage, this practice does have two obvious outcomes. When a high proportion of all *riste* are arranged between cousins, descent groups (*biraderi*) become much more tightly knit and in-turned than in communities in which marriages are expected to conform to rules of exogamy. Secondly, and just as significantly, no matter how tightly knit such *biraderi* might seem when viewed from an external perspective, their internal processes of internecine micro-politics whose roots are more often than not generated by squabbles both between siblings and between husbands and wives over exactly where such *riste* alliances should be placed, are also exceptionally vigorous, even if they are largely inaccessible to external observers.

In no way did the establishment of transnational escalators interfere with these practices; all they did was to extend the spatial dimensions of the arena within which these manoeuvres took place. Hence, as soon as their overseas-raised offspring began to reach marriageable age, Muslim parents, no less than their Sikh and Hindu counterparts, began to explore where their *riste* could be most suitably placed, and in like manner began to receive offers of *riste* for their offspring from back home. Whilst the settlers' initial response was to continue to deal with

these offers on the basis of their established priorities, and hence to
make their choices as if they had never left home, it was not long before
significant differences began to emerge as between the out-marrying
Sikhs and Hindus and the in-marrying Muslims, largely as a result of
pressure from their offspring. Even though the principles around which
their domestic lifestyles were organised differed little from those with
which the spouses their parents were likely to select for them expected
to operate, other dimensions of their everyday lifestyles had been much
more heavily influenced by the wider British context within which they
had been brought up. Moreover, it soon became apparent that many
couples found the resultant contradictions difficult to negotiate, so
much so that the very stability of their marriage could be compromised.
However, the reaction of Sikh and Hindu parents to these developments differed significantly from those of their Muslim counterparts.

Faced by ever-more insistent protests from their offspring that
matches ordered according to their own established priorities were in
considerable danger of collapsing as a result of the impact of these contradictions, Sikh and Hindu parents began to revise their priorities.
Whilst insisting that all such *riste* should still be arranged in conformity to the rules of caste endogamy and *gotra* exogamy, they nevertheless agreed that those conditions could still be satisfied by looking for
matches with other families who had already made a similar move into
the diaspora, no matter how socially well-connected the source of the
offer from India might be. After all, they were under no obligation to
make a positive response to such offers. By contrast, parents belonging
to communities in which cousin marriage was the norm found themselves in a very different position. When similar offers of *riste* on behalf
of their offspring arrived, the proponents were not strangers, but their
own siblings. Such offers could not be lightly refused. Doing so would
not only be read as a denial of their obligations of siblingship, but a deliberate effort to repudiate their nephews' and nieces' efforts to gain access to all the many benefits which they had themselves, by great good
fortune, acquired.

Such pressures became even more intense as migration managers
progressively tightened entry criteria, such that marriage became virtually the only legitimate basis on which kinsfolk of established settlers
could gain a permanent right of abode in an affluent and highly developed European environment. Hence, whilst the young people whose
domestic and personal futures were being determined by their parents'
choices were for the most just as concerned about their likely prospects
as were their Hindu and Sikh counterparts, any protests they might
make met with much more adamant opposition from their parents.
The dilemma they faced was acute. However reasonable they might
consider the appeals of their offspring, they had to weigh them against

the prospect of compromising the fundamental principles of sibling so-lidarity. Could they bring themselves to repudiate the interests of close kinsfolk by denying them assistance in attaining, like themselves, the benefits associated with residence in a far more affluent and opportu-nity-ridden society? Many could not bring themselves to treat their kinsfolk in such a heartless fashion. The impact of their decisions is immediately apparent in the immigration statistics. Close to 50 per cent of young UK-based Pakistanis still contract marriages with spouses from back home. By contrast, the percentage of Hindus and Sikhs contracting such marriages has long been in single figures.

That said, what are we to make of the likely emotional impact, let alone the personal consequences, for young British-born spouses who find themselves despatched to a rural corner of the subcontinent to fetch their future life partner? Or, for that matter, for his or her partner-to-be, for whom marriage will likewise entail a transfer to a physical and material environment wholly unlike anything she or he has hither-to experienced? Such prospects routinely precipitate reactions of intense alarm amongst external observers. To those whose normative expecta-tions are individualistically oriented, the prospect of being required to enter such a transnational conjugal partnership in the absence of any significant degree of personal choice, let alone a period of prior court-ship, appears to be quite unconscionable. Moreover, every news item re-porting the collapse of such marriages reinforces their belief in the soundness of such a judgement. If, however, we switch to an insider's perspective, a rather different picture emerges. This is in no way to dis-count the potentially pathogenic consequences of the underlying contra-dictions already identified, but rather to set them within wider continu-ities. Over and above those associated with the transnational arena to which the wider network has itself given rise, brides who marry their cousins do not enter their in-laws' households as total strangers, as is the case in those communities where marriages are construed by rules of exogamy. Not only will such spouses have been well aware of each other's existence long before the marriage took place, but the bride will enter a household in which either her mother-in-law or her father-in-law will be a sibling of one of her parents, and will consequently have an active interest in the *rista*'s successful implementation. So it is that for emotional reasons no less than in response to their parents' strategic concerns, British-based spouses frequently actively look forward to mar-rying their overseas-raised cousins (Shaw & Charsley 2006).

Likewise the absence of courtship prior to marriage must also be placed in its appropriate context. Although the UK-resident spouse will be well aware of, and will in all probability have dabbled in, alternative modes of pre-marital engagement with members of the opposite sex, both will also have been brought up in domestic arenas in which normative conventions suggest that such behaviour is not only intrinsically shameful, but also in no way a necessary precursor to a successful marriage. At the same time Punjabi parents are far from naïve on this score. They are well aware, not least on the basis of personal experience, that once the rush of hormonal activity precipitated by puberty is in full flow, their offspring can only be expected to develop an acute interest in the prospect of sexual activity, no matter how carefully they have been brought up. In consequence they take a pragmatic view of temptations with which their offspring are likely to find themselves confronted unless those natural urges are suitably assuaged. At the same time their concerns are powerfully conditioned by considerations of *izzat* (honour) and *sharam* (modesty), both of which have a far-reaching impact on the standing of the family within the *biraderi*. Such concerns are also strongly gendered. As in many other cultural traditions, few parents are greatly concerned about the prospect of their sons sowing wild oats, always provided they take care to distribute them well beyond the bounds of their own immediate community. By contrast, the prospect of one of their daughters emulating such behaviour, even to the mildest possible degree, can have disastrous consequences. Besides severely compromising her own personal reputation, her actions will lead to humiliating shame being poured on the *izzat* of every other member of the corporate family.

Many members of the older generation take the view that marriage provides a sovereign remedy to – and indeed a prophylactic against – problems of this kind. If sexual activity is a necessary and natural function, it makes much better sense to facilitate its exercise in a legitimate rather than an illegitimate context, and to provide one's offspring with the opportunity to do so as soon as is reasonably possible. Nor has the passage to Britain undermined that view. Having observed that their indigenous neighbours appear to be wholly unable to prevent their children engaging in what appears to be unbridled sexual activity, many Punjabi parents find themselves becoming yet further committed to what is for them a well-established remedy: early marriage. On the grounds that the mutual affection which is the necessary foundation of a sound conjugal relationship is much better rooted in marriage, rather than in the purely animal passions let loose in an unregulated period of nominally pre-marital courtship, they take the view that exposing children to the prospect of legitimate sexual activity just as their biological urges are reaching their peak, provides by far the most effective foundation for a life-long partnership. Of course, most will also readily acknowledge that such strategies by no means always produce the desired result, but in doing so also note that if divorce rates are used as a yardstick of success, their own preferred solutions fare extremely well in comparison with those championed by their critics.

The moment one adds the dimension of gender further complexities arise. Whilst arguments of the kind rehearsed above become urgent once daughters reach their late teens, Punjabi parents give every appearance of being far more relaxed about the behaviour of their sons. However, most are merely biding their time. Once sons reach their mid-20s, and all the more so if there appears to be any danger of their becoming inextricably involved with a girlfriend who would in their view would be incapable of adequately fulfilling the role of daughter-in-law, parents rapidly step in to take remedial action. Having begun by reminding their errant heir of the debt of loyalty he owes to his progenitors, they will swiftly set about bringing a series of potentially attractive *riste* to his attention. If he should reject all such suggestions that will by no means be the end of the matter. Support will be called in from ever-more distant depths of the *biraderi*, and before long the errant son will find himself under ever-greater pressure to return to the Punjab with the entire family in search of a suitable bride. Nor are such strategies reserved solely for sons. Daughters who are perceived to have 'gone off the rails' regularly find themselves subjected to exactly the same treatment. In such circumstances, the pressure to conform to established expectations invariably becomes intense. Some resist for all they are worth. Many, however, eventually succumb, and accept one of the proposals put before them.

Should the outcome of such exercises be described as a 'forced marriages'? That is certainly the case as far as most newspaper editors and sub-editors are concerned. Moreover, there can be little doubt that there is usually considerable substance to the lurid accounts of distress and personal exploitation beneath the dramatic headlines with which even serious publications seek to titillate their readers when they print such stories. But could it be that such accounts serve to conceal as much as they reveal? How far do the journalists who prepare such stories explore the wider context within which the events in question occurred? Or are their accounts unreservedly partial? Is it indeed the case that all such marriages contracted on this basis necessarily end in disaster? Or could it be that in many, perhaps even in most, such cases, the combination of emotions generated by sexual engagement, the birth of offspring, and above all the unstinted support of family and kinsfolk, can lead to outcomes very different from those which the headlines so regularly suggest? And above all are draconian – although nominally libertarian – legislative initiatives whose subtext is firmly grounded in considerations of immigration control the most appropriate way to deliver lessons in marriage guidance, let alone to disentangle and renegotiate the tangled contradictions which may have arisen in such circumstances?

Conclusion

To those who have been socialised into assuming that individual rights, and consequently the capacity to exercise largely unfettered personal choice, provide the necessary foundation of any kind of reasonable and equitable social order, many of the values, practices and manoeuvres highlighted in this chapter will doubtless appear to be as unconscionable as they are barbaric. But to those socialised into a conceptual order which accords greater priority to the fulfilment of obligations to others than it does to the exercise of personal choice, it appears entirely reasonable that every effort should be made to facilitate both corporate coherence and the ongoing process of family development. From that perspective it makes just as much sense that every possible effort should be made to ensure that those who might otherwise go astray are firmly reincorporated into the networks of familial reciprocity, within which their prospects for personal security would be far greater than if they were to drop out into a world of chaotic individualism. Moreover, such claims are far from idle; by and large such strategies work. In an unstable world, corporate families deploying strategies of this kind continue to enjoy a remarkable degree of coherence and stability, as the global success of the transnational networks of which they are the building blocks amply demonstrates.

That said, no set of kinship conventions yet constructed is a model of perfection: all have their downsides. If contemporary Euro-American conventions offer almost unlimited freedom of choice, they do so at the cost of rapidly attenuating levels of personal security; and while more corporately oriented systems offer high levels of personal security to those willing to submit themselves to the obligations required to the maintenance of networks of reciprocity, they do so at an equally necessary cost: the attenuation of personal freedoms of choice.

With such contradictions in mind, it is worth remembering that the expression of acute concern for the helpless victims of barbarian gynophobic practices as a strategic means of establishing the legitimacy of European hegemony is in no way unprecedented. Could it be that current initiatives to suppress forced marriage, cousin marriage and honour killing are merely a replication of those which led the East India Company to celebrate its efforts to suppress Suttee and Thugee? A recent study highlights the way in which missionary arguments supporting such initiatives

> hinged on the assertion that the victims were British subjects and due all the respect and protection accorded to British subjects at home: 'Yes, it is in *British* India, where these agonizing shrieks are heard, where the blood of these Widows flows into a

torrent, and where these cries of miserable Orphans are heard'.
(Pennington 2005: 98)

It seems that we have been here before.

Note

1   This chapter is a product of 40 years of close observation of processes of
    interpersonal interaction in South Asian families. This began when I conducted
    fieldwork in Himachal Pradesh for my doctoral thesis at Delhi University, and was
    powerfully reinforced when I was subsequently appointed to one of the earliest
    research posts directed at exploring developments within the South Asian
    community in Britain. Hence, the principal source on which I have drawn in
    constructing the arguments and analyses set out in this chapter is my own personal
    observations of patterns of behaviour within Hindu, Sikh and Muslim families based
    in the Pennine region of northern England, and from extended periods of
    ethnographic fieldwork in Punjab and Azad Kashmir. In recent years I have been
    able to supplement these ethnographic observations with the analysis of statements
    on which I have been instructed to reflect in the course of preparing more than four
    hundred expert reports for use in proceedings in the civil, criminal, family and
    immigration courts in which South Asian settlers and their offspring have been
    involved.

References

Ali, N., V. Kalra & S. Sayyid (eds.) (2005), *A Postcolonial People: South Asians in Britain*.
    London: Hurst & Co.
Ballard, Roger (1973), 'Family Organisation amongst the Sikhs in Britain', *New Commu-
    nity* 2: 12-23.
Ballard, Roger (1982), 'South Asian Families: Structure and Process', in R. Rapaport &
    M. Fogarty (eds.), *Families in Britain*, 179-204. London: Routledge.
Ballard, Roger (1990), 'Migration and Kinship: The Differential Effect of Marriage Rules
    on the Process of Punjabi Migration to Britain', in C. Clarke, C. Peach & S. Vertovec
    (eds.), *South Asians Overseas: Contexts and Communities*, 219-249. Cambridge: Cam-
    bridge University Press.
Ballard, Roger (2003a), 'The South Asian Presence in Britain and its Transnational Con-
    nections' in H. Singh & S. Vertovec (eds.), *Culture and Economy in the Indian Dia-
    spora*, 197-222. London: Routledge.
Ballard, Roger (2003b), 'A Case of Capital-Rich Under-Development: The Paradoxical
    Consequences of Successful Transnational Entrepreneurship from Mirpur', *Contribu-
    tions to Indian Sociology* (n.s.) 37 (1&2): 49-81.
Ballard, Roger (2005), 'Coalitions of Reciprocity and the Maintenance of Financial Integ-
    rity within Informal Value Transmission Systems: The Operational Dynamics of Con-
    temporary Hawala Networks', *Journal of Banking Regulation* 6 (4): 319-352.
Ballard, Roger (2006), 'Ethnic Diversity and the Delivery of Justice: The Challenge of
    Plurality', in Prakash Shah (ed.), *Migrations, Diasporas and Legal Systems in Europe*,
    29-56. London: Routledge Cavendish.

Ballard, Roger (2007), 'Living with Difference: A Forgotten Art in Urgent Need of Revival?', in J. Hinnells (ed.), *Religious Reconstruction in the South Asian Diasporas: From One Generation to Another*, 265-301. London: Palgrave Macmillan.

Ballard, Roger (ed.) (1994), *Desh Pardesh: The South Asian Presence in Britain*. London: Hurst .

Bhagwati, Jagdish (2003), 'Borders Beyond Control', *Foreign Affairs* 98 (1): 98-106.

Bredal, Anja (2005), 'Tackling Forced Marriages in the Nordic Countries: Between Women's Rights and Immigration Control', in N. Welchman & S. Hossain (eds.), *"Honour" Crimes, Paradigms and Violence Against Women*, 332-369. London: Zed.

Pennington, Brian (2005), *Was Hinduism Invented? Britons, Indians and the Colonial Construction of Religion*. New York: Oxford University Press.

Ratha, D. & S.M. Maimbo (2005), *Remittances: Development Impact and Future Prospects*. Washington, D.C.: The World Bank.

Sachdeva, Sanjiv (1993). *The Primary Purpose Rule in British Immigration Law*. Stoke-on-Trent: Trentham Books and School of Oriental & African Studies.

Scott, James (1985). *Weapons of the Weak: Everyday Forms of Peasant Resistance*. New Haven: Yale University Press.

Scott, James (1990), *Domination and the Arts of Resistance: Hidden Transcripts*. New Haven: Yale University Press.

Shaw, Alison (2000), *Kinship and Community: Pakistani Families in Britain*. London: Routledge.

Shaw, Alison & K. Charsley (2006), 'Rishtas: Adding Emotion to Strategy in Understanding British Pakistani Transnational Marriages', *Global Networks* 64 (3): 405-421.

3 'For Women and Children!' The Family and Immigration Politics in Scandinavia

Anniken Hagelund

Introduction

The immigrant family has become a key site of conflict in Scandinavian debates about integration, multiculturalism and ethnic relations. Much-publicised instances of forced marriages, genital mutilation and honour killings have created moral panics where patriarchal immigrant cultures and family structures appear as the major culprits. One popular response is to make claims for more demands on immigrants to acculturate, with less tolerance of cultural diversity. Phenomena such as forced marriage, genital mutilation and, obviously, honour killings are all illegal, and few, if any, have defended them publicly. But also technically legal practices associated with immigrants' familial relations are attracting public attention and generating heated debates. The very institution of arranged marriage, which in many immigrant communities has largely become a transnational practice, is the most prominent example, but also gender and generational relations within the migrant family in general have been placed in the public searchlight. One such example is the issue of parents who are sending children to their country of origin for extended periods of time – should the authorities intervene in such practices in order to secure the continuity of these children's schooling and integration process in Scandinavia? At a more reflective level, gender and generational relations within the immigrant family have become turning points for discussions about the limits of tolerance and the art of balancing between recognition of difference and equality of rights. For many debaters and opinion leaders, it is precisely this set of issues related to the immigrant family which have brought to the fore the *dilemmas* of liberal diverse societies, and questions are arising about the compatibility of individualised liberal societies and the more collectively orientated dispositions many immigrants are thought to bring with them.

Such issues are breaking down the comfortable distinction between the public and the private which underlies much policy thinking about integration. If publicly sanctioned rights are being breached and undermined within and by families, governments cannot stand back and respect privacy. Of course, opinions differ widely and little solid knowledge exists about the precise extent of, for example, forced marriages or genital mutilation. However, as long as there is a general consensus that these things do happen and that they are related to particular ethnic groups, policymakers have a need to respond. Furthermore, another viewpoint which seems to be gaining ground is the one that construes linkages between aspects of immigrants' family structures and the problems that can be observed in relation to non-Western immigrants' integration into the labour market and civil society. As all Scandinavian governments over the past 30 years have professed their dedication to integration in the sense of equal participation in work, education and political life, this kind of causal explanation of the failure to reach such equality is bound to raise concern. Meanwhile, statistics continue to demonstrate considerable inequalities between non-Western immigrants and the native majority on most conventional welfare indicators. For policymakers the question is becoming uncomfortably urgent: What do we do about it?

It is precisely the linkage between the emerging problematisation of the immigrant family in political discourse *and* policymaking that interests me in this paper. What kinds of policies and proposals are now being launched in order to solve the 'problems' attached to immigrant families? How are these problems constructed in the first place? And how do they affect immigration politics at large in these countries? In particular I want to focus on how the problematisation of the immigrant family has worked to establish a stronger connection between the internal (integration) and external (entry) aspects of immigration policy. In other words, immigration control policies are now in the process of being changed, partly in order to produce behavioural changes within immigrant families living in Scandinavia. This is primarily done through modifications in the policies that are regulating family migration, but also by attaching new conditions to the receipt of benefits, as well as to the right to permanent residency and citizenship.

In the next section I offer some general background information on immigration to Scandinavia and to the particular political context constituted by Sweden, Norway and Denmark. Then I present some aspects of the public discourse on immigrants' familial relations with particular emphasis on some of the explanatory accounts that have worked to establish linkages between family structure, integration and immigration control. In the subsequent section I present some of the concrete policy changes that have been introduced and/or proposed in response to the concerns raised. Throughout the paper, my primary empirical focus will be on Norway, but I will also make references to Denmark and, to a lesser extent, Sweden.

The Scandinavian Context

The three Scandinavian countries have all experienced considerable immigration, first in the shape of labour migrants, and later as family and refugee migration. Today, nearly one in five Swedish residents are immigrants or children of immigrants, while around eight per cent of the populations of Denmark and Norway have some kind of immigrant background.

In a general sense, the linkage between the internal and external aspects of immigration politics – integration and entry control – is not recent. Ambitious aims of socio-economic and cultural equality between newcomers and natives have been defined as dependent on limited immigration; if the influx became too large, welfare policies would not be able to cope with the pressure. This was an important part of the rationale behind the restrictions placed on labour immigration in the 1970s. However, the turn from labour to family and refugee immigration has also changed the state's role as regulator of immigration. While it has been considered relatively unproblematic to regulate labour immigration according to the state's need for labour and its capacity to offer housing and other welfare services, such regulation is, at least potentially, more controversial and morally problematic when it comes to refugees and family members. These are more easily conceived of in terms of their own needs and rights. International conventions protect the right to family life as well as the right to seek protection. In public discourse, arguments about the rich country's moral obligation towards people in need carry considerable weight. Accordingly, Scandinavian authorities have placed relatively few restrictions on the immigration of close family members (partners and children). Given the barriers erected against labour immigration, a family connection has in practice been the only route open into Scandinavia for many prospective immigrants. Family unification schemes have thus become a major immigration channel to these countries. For example, in 2003 more than 10,000 residence permits were obtained through the family unification scheme in Norway, compared to only 1,100 labour immigrants and 5,200 refugees (NOU 2004: 202).

With respect to integration policies, all countries have been through a process of reassessing their views on multiculturalism and diversity. While the 1970s were marked by enthusiasm for the protection of immigrants' cultural identities and emphasis on immigrants' freedom to choose how to adapt to their new countries of residence, the debates have increasingly turned to the limits of choice and tolerance, and to the potential tensions between cultural diversity on the one hand and the need for a shared 'glue' to keep society together on the other. The concern with the cultural needs of particular ethnic groups has been replaced by a concern about the host society's need for participation and civic commitment from all residents. Significant socio-economic inequalities between natives and immigrants are manifest in all three countries. Ethnic minorities' higher unemployment rates and greater degrees of social welfare dependency make the question of integration urgent. Finally, issues of gender and generational relations are coming to the fore of the debate.

There are significant differences between the three countries' policies and debate climates. Following the election of a Liberal-Conservative government in 2001, Denmark has introduced significant restrictions both in its family unification and asylum policies. Norway and particularly Sweden have less restrictive regimes. Norway seems to be positioned somewhere in the middle, introducing greater restrictions than Sweden, but hardly venturing as far as Denmark. The linkage between familial relations and immigration control has not been made to the same extent in Sweden as in Denmark and Norway. Similar issues have been discussed, but under the headline of patriarchal and/or honour-related violence against women, and without linking it to cultural difference and the management of migration as has been the case in Denmark and, to some extent, in Norway. For this reason I will concentrate on Denmark and Norway in the remainder of the paper.

Highlighting the Family – Glimpses from Public Discourse

It is well established that gender and sexuality play a crucial part in the construction of ethnic identities and in the maintenance of ethnic boundaries. Differences in the ways women are socially constructed are used as markers of difference (Anthias & Yuval-Davis 1996; Necef 2000). As vehicles of reproduction, women's sexuality forms a decisive part in a group's concern with its own survival through maintenance of boundaries and recruitment of new members (Borchgrevink 2004; Taylor 1994). In this paper, however, I am reversing the perspective as I want to call attention to how the state, in countries of immigration, is being mobilised in attempts to transform gender relations and reproductive practices within minority groups. Below, I will present three rather extensive explanatory accounts that have quite successfully linked immigrants' familial relations to the wider integration problematic in ways that also point towards a need to use immigration control to manage familial relations. I use the term successful, not because they are necessarily true or have been universally accepted as such – indeed they have all been controversial – but because accounts such as these have received massive attention and, in my view, are gaining increasing legitimacy among politicians and policymakers. Their effects can be seen in the proposals and legislation that I outline in the latter part of the paper.

The Anthropologist

In 1995 Unni Wikan, a professor in social anthropology, sent shock-waves through the Norwegian public when she published a book named *Mot en ny norsk underklasse* (*Toward a New Norwegian Underclass*) (1995), later elaborated in English under the title *Generous Betrayal* (2002). She claimed that immigrants were becoming an ethnic under-class, thus radically transforming the relatively egalitarian Norwegian welfare society. Furthermore, Norwegian authorities were to blame. A misconceived 'respect for culture' had made authorities shy away from intervening in and making claims on immigrant families, resulting in poor language skills, high unemployment and social welfare depen-dency. The losers were foremost women and children. Subjected to pa-triarchal familial relations and without the means to find their own way in Norwegian society, they were effectively cut off from the relative gender equality enjoyed by Norwegian women. This will have grave consequences for the social integration of future generations, warned Wikan. In many immigrant families it is the mother who carries the main responsibility for child rearing. Without language and knowledge of Norwegian society, education systems and labour market, these mothers will be unable to provide their children with the knowledge and skills necessary to succeed in Norway, and subsequently pass on their own social marginalisation to the next generation.

The summary of Wikan's argument is that, despite the very best in-tentions, the Norwegian welfare state has favoured the interests of im-migrant men over those of immigrant women and children by refrain-ing from active intervention in immigrants' familial relations (Wikan 2002: 207). Dramatic stories of individual women and their vulnerable position both in the family and in the Nordic welfare state work to sub-stantiate the claim: Aisha was forcibly removed from her Norwegian foster parents and returned to her own family so that she could grow up in her 'own culture'. The result was that her parents brought her back to their country of origin in the Middle East, where a marriage she did not want awaited her. Sara was killed by her own brother be-cause she had become 'too Swedish'. Anna escaped from her parents to avoid forced marriage and abuse. Noreen was nearly killed by her rela-tives in Pakistan because she refused to marry a Pakistani relative. Na-dia was abducted to Morocco by her parents. The recurring theme is the authorities' lack of ability, or will, to recognise and do something about these kinds of female life histories – an impotence which in practice means that their rights as Norwegian (or Swedish) citizens are undermined. The explanation given is twofold. Partly it has to do with the ideological currents of multiculturalism that values the inviolability of cultural collectives higher than individual freedoms; partly with a more idiosyncratic Norwegian or Scandinavian eagerness to do good, where the fear of appearing racist has made authorities shy away from confronting what would otherwise be considered as breaches of women's and children's rights.

The threat of forced marriage is a common thread through most of Wikan's case stories and this is also the thread which is providing the linkage from her analysis of immigrants' familial relations to immigration policy. 'It is family unification that provides the impetus whereby many young people of both sexes are compelled to marry against their will' (Wikan 2002: 214). In short, young people are forced to marry because it is the only way their relatives can gain access to the benefits of residing within a Scandinavian welfare state. Wikan (mostly) refrains from spelling out the consequences of this point for future immigration policies. As we will see below, such implications have been much more forcibly formulated from other quarters.

The Activist

Hege Storhaug has produced numerous articles, books and television documentaries about forced marriages, female genital mutilation and more generally about the vulnerable position of young minority ethnic women in Norway and in their own transnational families. With the establishment of the foundation *Human Rights Service* (HRS) in 2001, Storhaug made a definite move from journalism to a political activism performed through active media participation, documentation and lobbyism. In the report *Feminine Integration* (Storhaug & Human Rights Service 2003), the organisation sets out to document the particular problems faced by women in immigrant communities, linking this to patriarchal family structures and, in particular, to ongoing family migration through transnational marriages. The main message is twofold: firstly, this is a humanitarian problem where women's human rights are violated. Secondly, this is an integration problem endangering the state of welfare in Scandinavian societies.

Through the use of statistics and case stories the report establishes a widespread and growing tendency among non-Western immigrants (and their children) to marry transnationally with a partner from their own countries of origin. These statistical findings are interpreted as indicators of a negative integration trend. The 'import' of foreign spouses means that a genuine second or third generation will not develop, but that the first generation is continually reproduced (ibid. 96). Moreover, this is considered a humanitarian problem in light of the 'broad set of experiences' which, allegedly, indicate that a large proportion of these marriages are entered into by force. Furthermore, it is problematic because the ethnic segregation that is constituted by such endogamous marriage patterns in themselves is judged 'undesirable in light of human rights and fundamental democratic values' (ibid.). Statistical findings are thus incorporated into a much broader narrative about fundamental issues in Norwegian democracy.

As in Wikan's books, case stories are repeatedly used to substantiate the analyses. *Feminine Integration* presents Mina's story. She is the daughter of a labour migrant, Ahmed, who arrived in 1973 and who later brought in one wife, eight children and two adoptive sons through family unification. Each of these children has married cousins from their countries of origin, and their children are now also beginning to marry cousins from abroad. Mina lives in an abusive marriage, and the report details her destructive round dance between a violent husband, abusive in-laws, unsympathetic relatives and hospital emergency rooms, while child authorities and police both appear powerless in the face of a manipulative extended family and impotent legislation. Mina's destiny is obviously appalling, but is it representative? And does it represent a deviant case or a symptom of deeper pathologies? Although the report is careful to insist that such behaviours are not universal among minority ethnic families, it does go quite far in linking the violence and sexual abuse prevalent in Mina's family to the very institution of the extended family as it operates when transferred into a Western society. It clearly establishes that 'the family pattern with import marriages and lack of integration into human rights and democratic values, and the extent of illegal acts (particularly forced marriages and loss of liberty)' (ibid. 118) are widespread. The problem is, firstly, a conflict between traditional notions of honour and shame revolving around the control of female sexuality and Western gender equality and individualism. The preoccupation with the former may even become more pronounced as it encounters its apparent opposite. Secondly, strict immigration regulations in Europe mean that marriage in practice is the only way to emigrate there. The combined result is that the continuance of transnational, and thus by definition arranged and potentially enforced, marriage practices becomes of utmost importance to many extended families. Again, a singular finding – Mina's sad story – is transferred into a larger narrative about fundamental structural problems in the encounter between immigrants' familial relations and Western liberal democracies.

HRS and Wikan share the fundamental concerns about minority ethnic women's and children's rights and welfare prospects in situations where they are drawn between the interests of the transnational extended family and the ideals and possibilities of a liberal welfare state.

Their respective problem analyses, emphasising male power and identity politics on the one side and liberal weakness and legal impotence on the other, also overlap. But HRS goes much further than Wikan in drawing immigration political consequences from its analysis, and it is the regulation of family migration that comes under particular scrutiny.

Feminine Integration launches a number of proposals aimed at preventing forced marriages, violence and abuse within marriage, and the use of marriage for immigration purposes. Just to mention some:

- A ban on marriages between cousins (which are common in some minority ethnic communities, see Ballard *supra*);
- A limit on the number of family unifications through marriage one person can obtain, set at once every ten years (to counteract repeated circles of marriage and subsequent divorce, either through *pro forma* marriages for immigration purposes or to establish polygamous families in Norway);
- A ban on family unification for those with a history of marital violence;
- An age limit of 24 years and affiliation requirement for family unification through marriage, in line with Danish regulations (see the section on 'Immigration Law and the Family', below);
- To make only those foreign marriage contracts which contain a clause about equal divorce rights valid as a basis for subsequent family unification with the spouse residing in Norway (to secure equal divorce rights for Muslim women).

The various proposals and policies in this field will be discussed in more detail below. Note however, firstly, how ethnic minorities' marriage practices are being emphasised in a wider analysis of gender inequality and oppression, and, secondly, how the proposed Norwegian Alien Act (see below) is turned into a major tool for combating them. A third account from Denmark can serve to elaborate the rationale behind such linkages between marriage and immigration and immigration control.

The Politician

The Danish Liberal-Conservative government which came to power in November 2001 has introduced some of the most radical changes in family unification regulations in Europe. Karen Jespersen belongs to the defeated Social Democratic Party and was a cabinet minister with special responsibility for integration and immigration policies. Jespersen became a controversial figure in her own party due to her views on immigration and integration, but received considerable popular support and saw her own government lose an election perhaps precisely over immigration issues. In *In Support of Fatima* (English title), she elaborates the position that made her so controversial, a position where she explicitly rejects the ideal of a multicultural Denmark in the sense of a society where all cultures are given equal status (Jespersen 2003: 228).

This book is written out of love for the Danish welfare society, she states by way of introduction, defining this as a society characterised by equality, security, personal freedom and community (Jespersen 2003: 9). And one of the greatest challenges this welfare society is faced with is how to handle 'immigration from societies that are economically, culturally and politically very different to ours' (p. 9). The analysis is, in brief, as follows. Many immigrants come from societies that are dramatically different from the Danish one. This background from 'premodern cultures' (p. 11) makes it hard to adapt to life in Denmark; many fail to find work, they rely on welfare and live spatially apart from Danes. The result is an 'underclass' (p. 10) of immigrants, and a society divided into 'ethnic parallel societies' (ibid.) This development may in the long run weaken social cohesion and solidarity, thus also eroding the very basis of the welfare society. The more immigration, the harder it will be to achieve a good process of integration. Thus, it is necessary to control and limit the influx. Finally, integration does not mean that there should be no cultural differences, but there needs to be a shared basic culture founded in 'the values of a modern humanistic society' (p. 12).

Apart from some of the blunter characterisations of cultural distance, these are well-known arguments in European politics. The point here is how Jespersen places familial relations and the need to control family migration at the heart of her analysis. Firstly, familial relations, gender relations in particular, form the basis for her claim that a multicultural society is not desirable. Cultures are not of equal value, she argues, some are better adapted to life in a modern welfare society than others. Many immigrants come from societies where the constitutional state and the welfare state are poorly, if at all, developed. Instead, the extended family achieves a crucial position that provides individuals with protection, but which also constitutes strong barriers on their personal freedom. These family structures are generally highly patriarchal and status is founded in notions of honour dependent on the control of women's sexuality. It is this background which, according to Jespersen, makes many immigrants ill equipped to understand the workings of the liberal Danish society. To them it appears boundless and immoral, and one response is to remain on the outside in 'parallel societies'. Marriage traditions – where families arrange marriages for their sons and daughters, preferably with someone from their own country of origin – are another key factor in maintaining these boundaries. Arranged marriages are part and parcel of an oppressive patriarchal culture and

through these transnational alliances, such cultural attitudes and values are kept alive. Furthermore, because these marriages are arranged
transnationally, generous family unification schemes will mean that
immigration flows remain high. For Jespersen the conclusion is that
the freedom to maintain such marriage traditions, even when no force
is involved, must yield to the interests of the wider Danish welfare society, a welfare state that cannot handle large-scale immigration as long
as newcomers fail to integrate.

Controversy and New Dilemmas – The Wider Debate

There are important common denominators between these three accounts. They are all written by women. The authors have all been extremely controversial, but have also been praised for their courage to
'speak up', and they have profoundly affected the state of public discourse. None of the authors has any kind of formal relations to the
anti-immigrant right. They may be accused of playing into the hands
of the populist right, they may receive praise and support from that
side, but this is certainly not how they want to present themselves. Jespersen was a Social Democratic cabinet minister; Wikan gives special
thanks to the former Social Democratic mayor of Oslo, Rune Gerhard-
sen, in her foreword; and HRS insists on their party-political neutrality.
In fact, many of the proposals that have been made by the right-popu-
list Norwegian Progress Party in Parliament regarding immigrant women were originally launched by Storhaug and HRS. The Progress
Party has also been instrumental in securing direct funding for HRS
in the national budget, while other NGOs must apply to the relevant
ministries for funds (Bredal 2005). Lately Storhaug has also given explicit praise to Progress Party policies.

The three accounts all focus on women and children, and explicitly
link their position in the family – epitomised through the institution of
arranged marriage – to an analysis of failed integration and emerging
ethnic underclasses in Scandinavian societies. The stories of individual
women, named but anonymised, play a vital part in all the narratives –
Aisha, Mina, Fatima and many more – and are treated as indicative of
wider patterns and fundamental issues. Force and violence against women and children within the framework of the transnational migrant
family are thus entered into a wider narrative of integration problems
and liberal challenges in the multicultural society. Their fear is that
multiculturalism will imply an unintentional break with the egalitarianism they see as the basis of the Scandinavian welfare state. Against
this they promote strong normative ideals for the future development
of these societies in a time of population movement and growing diver-

sity, namely to protect the welfare state and citizens' human rights. To achieve this, they all, some more strongly than others, point towards the regulation of family unification.

It would be misleading to present these three accounts as representative of public discourse in general in their respective countries. But they have to a large extent raised issues that now constitute the fundamental agenda for much public debate about the multicultural society. There are certainly deep disagreements, but issues have been raised that cannot legitimately be ignored by anyone in the field. Particularly with respect to marriage practices, the debates have been plentiful and difficult. While it is generally accepted that arranged marriages are widespread in many immigrant communities, the extent to which force and violence are part of such processes has been contested; while some claim that force is integral to any arranged marriage, others argue that force is deviant. There is universal agreement that practices such as forced marriages, female genital mutilation and honour killings are both illegitimate and illegal; the debates rather concern the appropriate means to combat them. Policy proposals range from encouraging dialogue and providing information to increased levels of policing, prosecution and punishment. There is also a debate on how such phenomena should be represented. Some will insist that it is imperative to avoid unfortunate and unfair generalising that stigmatises ethnic minorities; others claim that the main problem is political correctness and under-communication of real problems. Related to this is the debate on whether phenomena such as forced marriages or honour killings can be linked to deeper cultural patterns or must be considered as plainly criminal deviances. Accounts about young people as victims of the extended family coexist and clash with stories that allow greater scope for seeing individual agency. There are also debaters who issue reminders that the freedom to marry whom one wants should also apply to those who do not conform to the marriage patterns and ideals of the majority population. The right to diverse family lives stands against claims for increased control in order to safeguard other rights and concerns.

While much blame has been placed on immigrants themselves for maintaining patriarchal relations and resisting integration, the agent which is ultimately called upon to *do something* is the state. There is a historical logic to this, as the Scandinavian welfare state has a long history of active intervention in the family in order to modify both gender and generational relations (Sejersted 2005). The immigrant family is being recognised now as a site where policy interventions are called for. What does this mean in terms of specific policies?

Immigration Law and the Family

Denmark is one of the European countries that have gone furthest in changing its legislation on family unification in a restrictive direction. The Danish case has become a reference point in the debate both in Norway and Sweden – for some debaters it represents an ideal for future policy making, for others it is quite the opposite. Mona Sahlin, then Swedish integration minister, criticised her Danish counterpart in such strong words that commentators described a new 'war' between the two. In contrast, the Norwegian Progress Party has made several proposals in parliament that explicitly seek to replicate the Danish rules. Let us start by looking at the Danish rules.

A Liberal-Conservative government came to power in November 2001, after an election fought largely on the issue of immigration, an issue that continues to be crucial to its popular backing (Hedetoft 2006). It soon went to work on immigration legislation. In the amended Alien Act that came into force in 2002, the reduction of immigration was a primary aim; secondary goals included the prevention of forced marriages and ensuring the 'best possible base for a successful integration' (Bredal 2005). In the government's status report on integration and immigration policy from 2003, it also states clearly that the combat of *both* forced *and* arranged marriages is a main motivation for its amendments to the Alien Act.

Most prominent among these changes was the age threshold set at 24 years for transnational marriages, which specifies that family unification between youth settled in Denmark and foreign residents can only take place if both parties have reached 24 years of age. The idea is that people will be more vulnerable to possible pressure from parents and family to marry, and thus more susceptible to accepting an arranged transnational marriage, when they are younger. As they grow older and gain more education as well as financial and emotional independence, they will be more able to resist such pressure. In a later memorandum to the Council of Europe's commissioner for human rights, the government also states that the rule promotes 'better integration, because it contributes to improved educational and work opportunities for young people' (Ministry of Refugee, Integration and Integration Affairs, Ministry of Justice and Ministry of Foreign Affairs (2004: 11)). Several other requirements also apply to those who seek family unification with a foreign spouse. It must be established that the marriage is entered into voluntarily. The resident spouse must meet housing and maintenance requirements and must have managed without social assistance for at least a year. Finally, there is an affiliation requirement, meaning that both spouses considered together must have ties with Denmark that are stronger than the couple's combined ties to any other country. In practice this means that if a Danish resident or citizen has lived in Turkey for extended periods and then marries a Turk, the couple's combined affiliation may be judged to be stronger to Turkey than to Denmark, and the foreign partner will be denied residence.

As these rules apply universally, the affiliation requirement caused considerable protests when it emerged that also native Danes who had lived abroad for longer periods faced problems when wanting to bring their foreign-born spouses to live in Denmark. As a consequence, the Act was amended so that those with 28 years or longer history of citizenship or continuous residency were exempted (Bredal 2005). Apart from making transnational marriages considerably more difficult for those wishing to live in Denmark, the affiliation requirement is also intended as a disincentive for those families who consider sending their children to their country of origin for longer periods, but yet foresee a future transnational marriage based in Denmark.

In Norway there have been few signs of a universal endorsement of the Danish policies by mainstream parties, though similar, if weaker, proposals have been gaining ground. However, the arguments employed have often differed. The Progress Party has, not unexpectedly, been the political party which has gone furthest in a restrictive direction. With respect to marriage, the party has expressed an explicit scepticism towards transnational marriage practices, as they are seen to impede integration processes and to be an expression of 'contempt for the Norwegian'. It has also suggested that no legal distinction should be made between arranged and enforced marriages. More specifically, it has proposed a number of restrictions in line with the Danish policies, including higher maintenance requirements, an age requirement of 24 years and an affiliation requirement. Also in line with the Danish rules, it has proposed a ban on marriages between cousins, thus targeting the immigrant communities that tend to practice transnational marriages between such relatives. The Progress Party has rarely gained much support for its immigration policies from other political parties (Hagelund 2003a). What is remarkable about this set of issues is that representatives from mainstream parties have also supported some of the proposals. Karita Bekkemellem for example, later a Labour Party minister of equality, has argued strongly for a ban on cousin marriages. The argument for protecting young people, especially women, from unwanted enforced marriages is hard to refute, no matter what the immigration political implications may be.

The committee appointed to make recommendations for a new Norwegian Alien Act also presented a number of proposals aimed at transnational marriage practices. It proposed to establish a legal distinction between reunification of existing families and the establishment of new families through marriage, with stronger rights to family immigration in the former case than for the latter. The committee stated clearly that neither concerns about integration nor about possible abuse of immigration law can legitimate the establishment of legal measures in the Alien Act directed against the very tradition of arranged marriages. It is however both legitimate and requisite that the state establishes measures against the use of force and undue pressure towards marriage (NOU 2004: 241-3). It thus proposed to include a clause in the new Alien Act which explicitly allows the refusal of residence permits for new spouses on the ground that the marriage is established against the wishes of one partner. Additionally, the committee proposed to raise the age limit for family unification, but rejected the Danish limit of 24 years because it is too invasive with potentially extensive effects also for marriages that are contracted voluntarily. Instead it proposed an age limit of 21 years that will 'imply a greater probability that the partners have reached a stage of maturity and independence vis-à-vis their own families which better enable them to claim their own interests and wishes also against the family's will' (ibid. 247), at the same time fewer serious and voluntary marriages will be affected. A trade-off is thus being set up between the need to attack forced marriages on the one hand, and the freedom to marry in diverse ways on the other.

Some changes directed at family immigration have been implemented. A maintenance requirement has been introduced for groups that had hitherto been able to bring in spouses independently of financial standing. One such category was marriages where one of the spouses is under the age of 23. Again the rationale provided was that measures serving to raise the age of marriage would reduce familial pressure on the youngest and most vulnerable potential victims of forced marriages. By the spring of 2008, however, the Act had still not been passed. In the earlier stages of the government's work on the bill, the responsible cabinet minister indicated that, in order to combat forced marriages, he considered measures quite similar to those established in Denmark, including an age requirement of twenty, an affiliation requirement and stronger maintenance requirements. In the end, the government chose to drop the age requirement, opting instead for higher maintenance requirements to ensure that the Norwegian party to a transnational marriage would be financially independent from his/her family.

A notable difference between the Danish rules and the similar proposals that are emerging in Norway is in the objectives that are expressed for the changes. While the Danish government has been clear on wanting to reduce family immigration and to counteract arranged marriages in general, their Norwegian counterparts seem to limit their

goals to combat forced marriages, protect young people's personal freedom against unwarranted family interference and promote integration.
The expressed intention is not to restrict immigration as such. Ironically, this may lead the Norwegians into greater dilemmas. While the
Danish policy changes are explicitly motivated as measures to reduce
family immigration and, particularly, to reduce the number of marriages between minority ethnic youth living in Denmark and foreigners, the Norwegian proposals primarily aim at reducing the number of
forced marriages. Thus, the introduction of restrictions carries a much
higher risk of affecting types of migrations and marriages that policymakers insist that they do not want to affect. The Norwegians also have
to deal with the ambiguous grey zones between illegitimate force and
legitimate family involvement, where it can be hard to make precise
distinctions between required advice and undue pressure. By declaring
transnational arranged marriages in general as undesirable, the Danish
authorities have bypassed the need to make such distinctions.

I have concentrated on the use of immigration legislation in changing and counteracting aspects of immigrants' familial relations, but
also other measures are mobilised for this purpose. The Marriage Act
has been amended so that bride and groom now have to declare explicitly that the marriage is contracted voluntarily and that they acknowledge each other's equal right to divorce (Asland 2005). This was introduced in order to secure genuine divorce rights for Muslim women,
but has generated unexpectedly strong reactions from other religious
communities which do not allow divorce (Thorbjørnsrud 2005). For
newly arrived refugees and immigrants, compulsory training programmes have been introduced that primarily aim at improving Norwegian language skills and labour market participation, but which also
address the family. A wide range of immigrant categories now have to
take 300 hours of Norwegian language and social issues classes in order to qualify for permanent residency – and the family is on the curriculum. In one such class I observed, we discussed issues such as marriage, divorce, gay rights, adoption, the role of religion in marriage, un-
derage sex, abuse, respect for the elderly and child rearing. Newly
settled refugees and their families are enrolled in an introduction programme requiring full-time participation over two years. Women are
entitled to one year maternity leave, but are otherwise required to participate in the programme also when they have small children. Motivat-
ing families to place their children in kindergarten thus becomes an
important part of the programme (Nygård 2006). Finally, locally one
will find a range of measures targeting immigrant families that provide
advice on, guidance with and monitoring of child rearing to ensure integration from an early age. In summary, while Wikan accused the welfare state of ignoring the immigrant family in the mid-1990s, a range

of initiatives can be observed that are aimed at the family as a site of culturally founded abuse and potential barrier to integration. The background for such a change in policy cannot be reduced to the selection of texts I have reviewed. However, I would argue that the changes in how immigration is being debated publicly, of which such contributions are part, have been instrumental in generating a new sense of urgency that have both incited and enabled politicians to look for new policy measures that are intervening in family lives in previously unheard of ways.

Concluding Remarks

Stories of forced marriages, genital mutilations and honour killings could not be accommodated within the established ways of talking about immigration politics (Hagelund 2003b). In this sense they appeared as moments of dislocation (Torfing 1999: 53), events that destabilised the dominant discourse where mainstream politicians had tended to take for granted the right to family reunification, and where it was assumed that the rights of women and children were rarely in conflict with cultural recognition. The stories about women's suffering in the multicultural society, at times also hinting at a deeper incompatibility between 'our' culture and 'theirs', were dislocations that enabled new connections to be made between immigration control, integration and immigrants' familial relations. New and troublesome elements call for changes, and it is these first attempts at such policy reform I have addressed in this paper. The common denominator between these policies is that they have been presented with the purpose of protecting the rights of women and children by transforming aspects of immigrants' familial relations through immigration control regulations.

Immigration policies that target the family inevitably run into a number of dilemmas, and Scandinavian authorities have chosen different strategies in tackling these. Firstly, there are dilemmas concerning different types of rights. Rights to family life and rights to organise familial relations in different ways encounter the nation-state's right to make immigration a political consideration as well as its obligation to protect the rights of women and children. Secondly, from a somewhat different perspective we may consider this as a matter where the state's aspiration to protect and take responsibility for its citizens' interests risks overstepping the boundary to paternalism, where it is instructing citizens (or potential citizens) about what is good for them. This is not least visible in some of the other amendments that have been proposed to the Norwegian Alien Act that enable the authorities to reject family unification if there is a risk that the foreign partner or his or her children will be exposed to domestic violence or abuse (Lidén 2005). Finally, there are dilemmas related to how policy and legislation function as communicative events vis-à-vis their target groups. The intention may be to give a clear message that force is both illegal and unacceptable, but by targeting minorities with special laws and measures there is also a risk that the message received is one of stigmatisation. On the other hand, while this risk is real, so is the risk of underestimating what may undoubtedly be serious issues of force and abuse in some families.

There are indeed significant variations in how the immigrant family and the problems it allegedly represents are assessed. In some versions, the very institutions of arranged marriage, extended families and collective orientations are considered problematic in the context of the Scandinavian welfare state. In others, there is still space for more diverse ways of organising familial relations, and it is primarily the occurrence of force and violence within the extended transnational family that is problematic. This approach, however, opens up a wide grey zone where the authorities acquire a responsibility for monitoring familial relations that are, explicitly or implicitly, defined as suspicious. The immigrant family, then, runs the risk of becoming a site of benevolent surveillance, always under scrutiny for potential abuse.

This is perhaps the most difficult dilemma for ambitious welfare states that seek – or, at least, are expected to seek – to protect the rights of its most vulnerable members: Interventions can create new problems both for specific families and for ethnic relations in general, but so can the lack of engagement. There are no easy solutions here. What is certain is that at the moment it seems that the trend in Scandinavia goes towards increased policy intervention in the immigrant family. Careful discussion of the consequences of such interventions is imperative.

References

Anthias, F. & N. Yuval-Davis (1996), *Racialized Boundaries*. London: Routledge.

Asland, J. (2005), 'Norske rettsregler om ekteskap, samboerskap og partnerskap', in B. Thorbjørnsrud (ed.), *Evig din? Ekteskaps- og samlivstradisjoner id et flerreligiøse Norge*, 37-59. Oslo: abstrakt forlag.

Borchgrevink, T. (2004), 'Dishonourable Integration: Between Honour and Shame', *AMID Working Paper Series 36/2004*. www.amid.dk/pub/papers.

Bredal, A. (2005), 'Tackling Forced Marriages in the Nordic Countries: Between Women's Rights and Immigration Control', in L. Welchman & S. Hossain (eds.), *'Honour' – Crimes. Paradigms and Violence Against Women*, 332-353. London: Zed Books Ltd.

Hagelund, A. (2003a), 'A Matter of Decency? The Progress Party in Norwegian Immigration Politics', *Journal of Ethnic and Migration Studies* 29 (1): 47-66.

Hagelund, A. (2003b), *The Importance of Being Decent. Immigration Political Discourse in Norway 1970-2002*. Oslo: UNIPAX.

Hedetoft, U. (2006), 'More than Kin and Less than Kind: The Danish Politics of Ethnic Consensus and the Pluricultural Challenge', in J. Campbell, J. Hall & O.K. Pedersen (eds.), *National Identity and the Varieties of Capitalism: The State of Denmark*, 398-430. Montreal: McGill-Queen's University Press.

Jespersen, K. (2003), *Til støtte for Fatima. Indvandrernes omstilling til Danmark*. Copenhagen: People's Press.

Lidén, H. (2005), *Transnasjonale serieekteskap. Art, omfang og kompleksitet*, ISF-report 2005:11. Oslo: Institute for Social Research.

Ministry of Refugee, Integration and Integration Affairs, Ministry of Justice & Ministry of Foreign Affairs (2004), *Memorandum on the Report of 8 July 2004 by Mr. Alvaro Gil-Robles, Council of Europe Commissioner of Human rights, As Regards the Part of the Report Concerning Foreigners*, Copenhagen.

Necef, M.Ü. (2000), 'Den seksualiserede integration – seksualitetens rolle i indvandrernes modernisering og integration', *Sosiologi i dag* 30 (4): 25-42.

NOU (2004), *Ny Utlendingslov, Norges Offentlige Utredninger 2004: 20*. Oslo: Statens forvaltningstjeneste.

Nygård, O. (2006), 'Between Care and Control: Interaction Between Refugees and Caseworkers within the Norwegian Refugee Integration Programme', Sussex Migration Working Paper No. 32. www.sussex.ac.uk/migration/1-3-3.html.

Sejersted, F. (2005), *Sosialdemokratiets tidsalder. Norge og Sverige i det 20. århundre*. Oslo: Pax.

Storhaug, H. & Human Rights Service (2003), *Feminin integrering – utfordringer i et fleretnisk samfunn*. Oslo: Kolofon.

Taylor, C. (1994), 'The Politics of Recognition', in A. Gutman (ed.), *Multiculturalism. Examining the Politics of Recognition*, 25-73. Princeton: Princeton University Press.

Thorbjørnsrud, B.S. (2005), 'Innledning', in B.S. Thorbjørnsrud (ed.), *Evig din? Ekteskaps- og samlivstradisjoner i et flerreligiøse Norge*, 7-34. Oslo: abstrakt forlag.

Torfing, J. (1999), *New Theories of Discourse. Laclau, Mouffe and Zizek*. Oxford: Blackwell.

Wikan, U. (1995), *Mot en ny norsk underklasse. Innvandrere, kultur og integrasjon*. Oslo: Gyldendal.

Wikan, U. (2002), *Generous Betrayal. Politics of Culture in the New Europe*, Chicago: University of Chicago Press.

4 Defining 'Family' and Bringing It Together: The Ins and Outs of Family Reunification in Portugal

Maria Lucinda Fonseca and Meghann Ormond

Introduction

The family is widely accepted as a basic unit of cultural, social and economic production and reproduction which plays a fundamental role in the successful integration of its members, and functions as a support network for them. Many immigrants arriving in Portugal are at first deprived of this support structure, having left their families behind in their country of origin. While some will return to their families and countries of origin after temporarily living abroad, others will reunite with their families in Portugal and still others will start new ones.

As a consequence of the legal restrictions imposed by EU member states following the 1973 oil crisis, family reunification and asylum-seeking became the main immigration gateways into the EU-15 for third-country nationals. By contrast, in Portugal, in 2004, only 22.2 per cent of non-EU citizens applied for a residence permit in Portugal via the official family reunification route.[1] Clearly, reuniting with one's family through official family reunification provisions is but one of many ways to bring family members together in Portugal. Yet the question remains, why is the percentage of immigrants entering the country via official family reunification provisions so low?

Qualitative and quantitative data gathered in the scope of the 2005 'Family Reunification and Immigration in Portugal' research project commissioned by the Portuguese High Commissariat for Immigration and Ethnic Minorities (ACIME) has been used to suggest a response to this question by highlighting the relatively recent character of immigration to Portugal, the significance of uncontrolled irregular migration, the way in which the concept of 'family' has been defined and put into practice by authorities, the fluid nature of contemporary families, and the barriers that must be surpassed in order for sponsors and their family members to qualify for official family reunification in the country.

Family Reunification Provisions

Though more than three-quarters of the EU's annual inflow is based on family reunification for labour migrants and asylum seekers, policies on the right to family reunification have been created in a more or less ad hoc manner by receiving countries, sometimes with the input of the more important countries of origin by means of bilateral agreements drawn up between them.

In the more heavily industrialised Western European countries, family reunification initially played an important role in maintaining the health and well-being of labour migrants who arrived in these countries in the wake of the Second World War. While labour migration was initially meant to be temporary, in order to resolve post-war labour shortages and rebuild the countries, it eventually became more permanent as immigration policies favouring settlement and integration were developed in the face of recognition that immigrants were a 'structural necessity' (IGC 1997: 15) for the economies of the more heavily industrialised Western European countries. Foreign labourers who had been living in these countries – sometimes for decades – had already started to establish their lives and start families there. The new policies allowed spouses and children remaining in the countries of origin to join their families legally. Massive family reunification evolved out of new labour migration restrictions that were brought into force as a response to the industrial decline and consequent global economic crisis of the 1970s. These restrictions, in effect, barred most types of legal immigration, resulting in rising numbers of family reunification immigrants[2] and illegal and clandestine immigrants – a reality that continues today throughout Europe due to increasingly tight immigration controls.

Regularisation campaigns throughout the 1980s and 1990s in Western European countries – both those with a longer immigration history and newcomers (like Portugal and other Southern European countries) – show that migration has not only continued but, in fact, grown increasingly clandestine and diversified. In these countries, non-Western European immigration accounts for a highly significant percentage of the population of foreign origin. At the same time, as birth rates have fallen for the autochthonous populations and the replacement rate has significantly declined, migration into Western Europe has come to play a central role in the region's demographic and economic stability.

Since the 1990s, more attention has been paid to the issue of family reunification in Western Europe as social and political stakeholders have examined it as a possible way to replace high rates of clandestine immigration with a legal way to enter for family members of already legalised and sometimes naturalised workers of immigrant origin.

While immigration via family reunification provisions may not be the solution to receiving countries' labour market problems and for rejuvenating their ageing populations and social security schemes, it may provide greater stability among already present immigrant populations and serve to help mitigate the abovementioned socio-economic issues. In fact, the traditional immigration countries have usually favoured family reunification on the grounds that it benefits receiving countries' societies in the medium- and long-term (IGC 1997), given immigrant families' 'inherent geographical and social stability' (Inglis 2003) once they are united. Against this, however, there is currently renewed interest in controlling family reunification more strictly in Western European countries, such as France, given renewed interest also in temporary labour migration programmes and greater concerns about managing and integrating the 'second generation', or children of migrants born in the receiving countries. France's June 2006 approval of the Entry and Stay of Foreigners and Right of Asylum Code (Code de l'entrée et du séjour des étrangers et du droit d'asile) (CESEDA) made it more difficult to be eligible for family reunification. Migrants now must be legally residing in the country for eighteen months (up from twelve) before they can sponsor their families, though migrants with 'Skill and Talent' stay permits can sponsor relatives after just six months. Currently, of the EU-27, only Denmark, Greece and Cyprus have less favourable eligibility provisions. The CESEDA also made families less secure under the law, by giving the state new grounds to refuse their applications or later withdraw their status (Niessen et al. 2007: 70).

Marriage or a recognised legal partnership is the centre of the traditional nuclear family unit enshrined in family reunification provisions. It is therefore the fundamental manner in which spouses and partners may join immigrants in a receiving country via family reunification. The EU Directive on the Right to Family Reunification (Council Directive 2003/86/EC of 22 September 2003) recognises the principle of the reunification of spouses. However, member states may require the sponsor and his/her spouse to be of a minimum age, and at maximum 21 years, before the spouse is able to join him/her. In the UK, the joining spouse must be eighteen years of age or older; in Belgium, under certain circumstances, the spouse must be 21 or older; and in Denmark, both the applicant and the joining spouse must be 24 or older (Ensor & Shah 2005; Niessen et al. 2007; Stenum 2005).

Some countries, like Portugal, may define family reunification more as a 'right', while others, like Denmark, refer to it simply as an 'opportunity'. Spouses and partners arriving under family reunification provisions are subject to a variety of restrictions and sometimes direct surveillance in certain countries during probationary periods lasting between several months and years during which time receiving countries may restrict their access to the labour market, social benefits, permanent residency permits, etc., in order to prevent marriage/partnership fraud. As a result, because non-European immigrants' countries of origin allow for marriage and partnership situations different from those sanctioned within Europe, conflict may arise between immigration authorities responsible for family reunification and immigrants (including those who have been naturalised) trying to bring their spouses and partners to the country in which they live. Immigrant marriages are often considered from the very start to be suspect and prone to take advantage of the receiving country's resources and its openness to foreigners. Fiancés and future arranged marriage partners, for example, undergo extra scrutiny in order to prove the legitimacy of their relationship with the sponsor. Other types of marriage and partnership are not recognised at all, such as polygamy and marriage involving undocumented immigrants.

Undocumented migrants may not marry legal foreign residents or nationals. As such, they are confined to their illegal status if they choose to stay in the receiving country with their partner. Similarly, undocumented immigrants may not petition for reunification with their spouses and children still living in their country of origin. It is not surprising, then, that sometimes entire families may be undocumented so that they may be together. Possessing fewer rights than documented migrants, undocumented migrants living with their families in the host country must rely more heavily on the beneficence of their family members and employers. It is perfectly plausible for immigrant households to include family members with different legal statuses under one roof (e.g. one family member holding citizenship of the host country, another holding a temporary visa, another with undocumented status, etc.) Families often come together over time by means of different visas and provisions, sometimes overstaying the legal limit and becoming undocumented.

The EU Directive on the Right to Family Reunification also allows for the minor children of the couple, including adopted children and minors under the custody of either or both, to join them. One should note that, by way of derogation, when a child is over twelve years of age and arrives independently of the rest of his/her family, the member state may, before authorising entry and residence under this directive, verify whether he/she meets the conditions for integration set forth by legislation in force on the date of implementation of this directive. In general, as in the case of Portugal, children under eighteen years of age, provided that they are not married, have not established a separate household independent from that of their parents and are not dependent upon someone else, are eligible for family reunification.[3]

Disabled and fully dependent children regardless of age are also able to join their parents in receiving countries.

Yet, in practice, restrictions are placed on children by receiving countries that challenge the suitability of children's very presence in their new country.

> Although it is generally assumed that children ought to remain with their parents, the trauma associated with relocation, language shifts, unfamiliar surroundings, and the generally difficult circumstances in which the migrant parent lives may make it better for children to remain in the home country, at least until their parents can provide them with a reasonable standard of living. (Bracalenti 2001: 18-19)

Furthermore, whether or not children over twelve years of age can be reasonably integrated into the receiving society is a serious consideration for some EU/EFTA countries and in some, such as Switzerland, children over twelve must undergo an 'integration test' in order to be granted the right to join their parents under family reunification provisions. In the same vein, in March 2006, the Netherlands' Civic Integration Examination Abroad, entered into force, introducing an obligatory integration test that must be taken by family reunification applicants in their countries of origin. Applicants are required to pass a test on Dutch culture and a telephone test on Dutch language skills at Dutch embassies and consulates around the world (Marinelli 2005; Nielson et al. 2007).

Family reunification policies in the EU member states do not tend to recognise the right for family members other than spouses and offspring to reunite with their families living in a receiving country. Rules tend to be very restrictive when policies do allow for them at all. Relatives must typically prove that they are financially dependent upon their sponsoring family member living abroad or have been left alone in their country of origin, as is the case with Portugal. Although they may be legally restricted from financially providing for their families due to their dependent status, extended family members sponsored by family reunification provisions do provide valuable support that may be very difficult to supplant with public social service programmes and other types of assistance.

Family Strategies and Migration

There has been increasing recognition among those studying migration that 'households and families are the principle agents of decision-making and that migration should be viewed as part of broader group strategies for sustenance and socio-economic improvement' (Massey 1990: 4; see also Baker & Benjamin 1997; Boyd & Grieco 2003; De Jong 2002; Satzewich 1993). The unit of analysis has been extended beyond the traditional focus on individual actors to include the family or household, where families can be considered to make up an internal production unit that can be analysed in terms of costs and benefits.

> Household resources are combined productively in a variety of ways to meet the requirements of family maintenance and improvement, and migration is a very effective way of capitalising the household's labour power. A household's behaviour in allocating workers to different productive pursuits may be viewed as a series of dynamic, flexible strategies that shift as needs and economic conditions change. (Massey 1990: 9)

International migration can thus be understood as a collective decision, made as part of a strategy actively to sustain and benefit a family, to maximise earnings and minimise risk in relation to continuously changing social, economic and political conditions at different scales. Family strategies play a dynamic role in defining both the manner in which international migration occurs and those who will migrate. Households may choose to separate temporarily, sending their members abroad where earnings are better and, in return, possibly receiving remittances and other benefits that may sustain them or better their situation in the country of origin (De Jong 2002; Massey 1990; Parrenas 2001). In other cases, when the benefits – financial, political, emotional or a combination of these – of a united family outweigh those of a transnationally divided one, family members may reunite in their countries of origin or, alternatively, join those already living abroad, given the chance and the means to do so.

Choosing to reunite a family physically in a receiving country is generally part of a specific migratory logic – a project – developed by families themselves. They must decide who migrates, who joins them abroad (and who does not), at what point in time they should migrate, the roles and responsibilities of each family member abroad and in the country of origin, etc. This migratory logic involves the interplay between individual and collective access to resources and timing. While decision-making may occur within a family, however,

> family/household decisions and actions do not represent unified and equally beneficial outcomes for all members. This is because families and households, as units where production and redistribution take place, represent centres of struggle where people

with different activities and interests can come into conflict with
one another. (Boyd & Grieco 2003)

Families, especially those whose members may be separated, are 'fluid
and constantly being negotiated and reconstituted both spatially and
temporally' (Creese et al. 1999: 3; Satzewich 1993). Whether having
migrated alone or in the company of their family members, immigrants may be in constant contact with family members both in their
countries of origin and of destination. As such, families remain 'unified' in spite of physical distance throughout the migratory process, at
times, over generations. This contact has been increasingly facilitated
by developments in communication technologies, allowing immigrants
to call home more often and increasing their awareness of events in
their country of origin; in banking and financial transactions, enabling
greater ease and security in sending remittances; and in reduced trans-
portation costs, allowing for more frequent visits to the country of origin and visits by family and friends to the receiving country. In this
sense, families come together in multiple ways, be they physical or
mediated, temporary or permanent.

Families do not always migrate together nor do they always have the
intention to reunite their members at any given moment. Numerous
combinations of family members may migrate together (e.g. a husband
and wife may migrate together to work, leaving minor-aged children
with their grandparents or ex-spouses in the country of origin; a father
and son may migrate, leaving their wife/mother and other children/
siblings behind, etc.) or join one another over time and in phases (e.g.
a labour migrant may migrate to work and later be joined by his/her
spouse, their children, or dependent parents; a student may have extended family in the receiving country and choose to study there, living
with his/her extended family members who have lived there for more
than a generation, etc.). Family members wishing to be together can
avoid taking the official family reunification route by entering the
country independently with their own individual work, student, tourist
or Schengen visas (real or falsified) or as undocumented migrants.
Thus, reuniting with one's family via the route of official family reunification is but one of many ways to come together.

According to the Migrant Integration Policy Index (MIPEX), Portugal
ranks only behind Sweden with regard to best policy practices on family reunification. However, in 2004, the percentage of immigrants
entering Portugal via family reunification provisions was much lower
than many other EU member states (table 4.1).

Table 4.1 shows that in 2004, family migration (including family reunification or formation and accompanying family members) dominated in Sweden, France, Austria, Italy, Finland, Germany, the Nether-

Table 4.1 *Long-term migration inflows (foreigners) by type: work and family (including accompanying family), %*

	Family	Work
Austria	63.5	20.5
Denmark	39.7	43.6
Finland	52.1	34.1
France	64.3	11.9
Germany	44.7	19.1
Italy	61.7	31.9
The Netherlands	49.8	27.5
Portugal	36.2	56.7
Sweden	67.8	17.1
UK	37.8	35.5

Source: OECD 2006

lands and the UK. On the contrary, in Portugal, work-related migration exceeded 50 per cent. In Denmark, in contrast to the rise in labour migration because of the restrictions on family reunification introduced in recent years, the percentage of family migration in long-term migration inflows has been in continuous decline since 2001 (OECD 2006).

Family Reunification and Foreign Demographics in the Portuguese Case

Like its Southern European neighbours, Portugal was once a migrant-sending country and became a receiving country only in the last quarter of the twentieth century, rapidly becoming a home for Africans hailing from Portugal's former colonies (PALOP), Brazilians and Eastern Europeans who today comprise roughly 5 per cent of Portugal's population.

At the end of 2004 there were approximately 500,000 legal foreign residents in Portugal, with 265,361 'residence permit' (*autorização de residência*) holders, around 184,000 'stay permit'[4] (*autorização de permanência*) holders, with the rest holding student, work and short-stay visas (mainly family members of stay permit holders in the latter case) and other types of visas. A residence permit is in principle attributed to long-term immigrants, entitling them to the broadest range of rights (e.g. easier permit renewal, slightly broader conditions for family reunification, access to the labour market and to long-term vocational training, etc.) A stay permit, on the other hand, was originally meant for temporary forms of labour. This permit was attributed to 183,833 regularised workers, under the provisions of the 2001 Decree-Law No. 4/2001. The range of rights to which stay permit holders were entitled was more restricted, similar to that of a work visa (Fonseca, Malheiros & Silva 2005a). It has since been discontinued and replaced by the work visa; only original stay permit holders can apply for its renewal.

Immigration to Portugal remains dominated by flows of unskilled workers arriving on a non-family basis. However, as time goes by, family reunification processes and irregular migration (overstaying and/or irregular entry) have increased with tighter control over the entry of new immigrants. In 2004, Africans comprised the largest group of foreign residents in Portugal, constituting 46.4 per cent of all foreign residents holding residence permits. The number of European Union citizens continued to rise, making up the second largest group (28.1 per cent). Latin America ranks third (13.2 per cent). While the number of Asians is quite small (4.7 per cent), this group – particularly the Chinese, Indian and Pakistani communities – has grown quite rapidly in recent years. North Americans, comprising only 3.8 per cent of all foreign residents, reflect the counter-current generated by past emigration flows from Portugal and the immigration of skilled professionals connected to American investment in Portugal. More recently, flows from Eastern Europe have marked a new phase in the country's short history as a receiving country. The distribution of stay permits issued between 2001-2004 in order to regularise the presence of undocumented workers employed in Portugal illustrates the importance of this flow, particularly from Ukraine, Moldova, Romania and Russia, with these four countries comprising 51.9 per cent of all stay permits issued during the abovementioned period (table 4.2).

Because different groups of immigrants have settled in Portugal at different times and at varying paces over the last decades, and in light of their diverse demographic, socio-economic and cultural backgrounds, each group tends to have a distinct relationship to the way in which they have (or have not) reunited with their families in Portugal, corresponding with where they are in the time-sensitive migratory process. Within the scope of Fonseca et al.'s study 'Immigration and Family Reunification in Portugal' (2005b), a survey undertaken between December 2004 and January 2005 of 1,588 immigrants aged eighteen and over from Africa, Latin America, Eastern Europe and Asia living in Portugal found that family migration becomes more important the longer and larger the settled immigrant community is. For instance, the proportion of Cape Verdeans whose migration to Portugal took place following that of other family members (80.1 per cent) is somewhat higher than that of other Portuguese-speaking African communities and far higher than that of Brazilian and Eastern European communities (table 4.3).

However, reflecting the EU Council Directive on Family Reunification, Portuguese legislation on the right to family reunification under-

Table 4.2 Stay permits issued between 1 January 2001 and 31 December 2004, by nationality

Nationality	No.	%	Nationality	No.	%	Nationality	No.	%
Total	183,833	100.00	Africa	29,808	16.2	Latin America	39,054	21.2
Europe	101,106	55.00	PALOP	24,475	13.3	Brazil	37,951	20.6
Central & Eastern Europe	101,050	54.90	Angola	8,562	4.70	Colombia	194	0.1
Belarus	1,101	0.60	Cape Verde	8,574	4.70	Cuba	183	0.1
Bulgaria	2,849	1.50	Guinea Bissau	4,323	2.40	Ecuador	162	0.1
Latvia	233	0.10	Mozambique	461	0.30	Venezuela	126	0.1
Lithuania	926	0.50	Sao Tome & Principe	2,555	1.40	Others	438	0.2
Moldova	12,647	6.90	Other African countries	5,333	2.90	Asia	13,724	7.5
Poland	221	0.10	Algeria	141	0.10	Bangladesh	871	0.5
Romania	10,944	6.00	Egypt	660	0.40	China	3913	2.1
Russia	7,053	3.80	Mauritania	37	0.00	Georgia	957	0.5
Ukraine	64,730	35.20	Morocco	1,395	0.80	India	3,389	1.8
Others	346	0.20	Tunisia	136	0.10	Kazakhstan	795	0.4
Oceania	19	0.01	Ghana	214	0.10	Nepal	224	0.1
Australia	10	0.01	Guinea-Conakry	1,304	0.70	Pakistan	2,854	1.6
New Zealand	5	0.00	Nigeria	211	0.10	Uzbekistan	434	0.2
Others	4	0.00	Senegal	654	0.40	Others	287	0.2
Unknown nationality	83	0.05	Others	581	0.30	Stateless persons	39	0.02

Source: Serviço de Estrangeiros e Fronteiras (SEF) 2005

Table 4.3   *Surveyed immigrants aged eighteen and over whose migration to Portugal took place following that of other family members, by nationality (%)*

Country/Region of origin	Male	Female	Total	Country/Region of origin	Male	Female	Total
PALOP	68.5	78.1	72.5	Asia	18.2	55.6	29.0
Angola	64.9	79.0	70.2	Brazil	32.9	43.6	37.0
Cape Verde	79.1	81.3	80.1	Central & Eastern Europe	21.7	58.7	33.6
Guinea-Bissau	62.9	67.9	63.3	Ukraine	14.0	61.7	30.8
Mozambique	35.7	57.9	48.5	Total surveyed	47.6	67.1	55.0
Sao Tome & Principe	68.0	88.0	78.0				
Other African countries	33.3	50.0	35.4				

Source: Fonseca et al. 2005b: 142

went changes in 2003 with a new law (Decree-Law No. 34/2003 of 25 February) regulating the entry, exit, stay and expulsion of foreigners in Portugal that made it possible for legal immigrants to apply for family reunification after residing and working in Portugal for one year. This has effectively facilitated family reunification for stay permit holders whose permits must be renewed annually. Unsurprisingly then, recent figures point to the rising use of family reunification provisions among migrant groups holding stay permits and other temporary visas that have more recently arrived in Portugal, particularly Eastern European immigrants. On the one hand only 22.2 per cent of non-EU citizens issued a residence (long-term) permit in Portugal in 2004 received this via family reunification provisions, and within the period of 2002 to 2004 the number of family reunification-based residence permits actually declined from 3,104 to 2,457. On the other, an additional 3,631 new requests for short-stay visas were made in 2004, mostly by family members of workers with stay (short-term) permits. In the same year, of a total of 40,741 stay permits renewed, 39.9 per cent of them were given to family members of holders of stay permits and work, student and short-stay visas. Indeed, some 76.9 per cent of short-stay visas in 2004 were requested by family members of stay permit holders from Eastern Europe.

Three types of group-specific family reunification practices currently emerge when considering the amount of time migrant groups have been living in Portugal. Portuguese-speaking African immigrants, already at a later migratory phase, experienced significant growth in the number of immigrant entries associated with family reunification from 1999 to 2004. In this group, approximately one-third of new arrivals entered Portugal due to family reunification, indicating that, given the more advanced migratory process, the group is increasingly less dominated by pioneering male labour migrants and is more gender- and age-balanced. Asians, particularly the Chinese and Indian communities, statistically made significant use of family reunification provisions, which illustrates their longer, more established presence (most evident in the case of the small Indian community) and their migratory strategies that appear to make it so that adult members of the nuclear family move to Portugal within a relatively short period of time. Eastern Europeans and Brazilians until very recently have had much lower levels of immigration induced by family reunification than the two examples immediately above. This situation stems from the recent character of the presence of these groups in Portugal and serves to accentuate the importance of labour migration for them. In spite of some similarities in their migration processes, each group is distinct. Eastern Europeans generally display a greater conformity with the traditional migration model, with a predominantly male population, while Brazilians display a more balanced gender distribution. The greater presence of women in the Brazilian case indicates that they enter Portugal outside of the family context and more traditional reunification processes. Things are changing, however. As noted above, the number of Eastern Europeans entering Portugal via family reunion provisions has risen sharply, indicating that this group is beginning to settle down more permanently.

Along with the size of each migrant group and the length of time they have lived in Portugal, a variety of decisive elements such as the various phases in life in which each migrant group generally finds itself, the atmosphere at the moment in which they arrived in Portugal and cultural and religious specificities that determine social and gender roles and responsibilities also affect migrants' interests in and ability to reunify their families. Eastern European migrants, for example, are on average older than their Brazilian counterparts and most are married or in civil unions (65.8 per cent of those surveyed), with children. This effectively contributes toward a delay in the migration of women. Brazilians, on the other hand, are on average much younger (45.7 per cent of those surveyed were single) and many young women migrate to Portugal alone (table 4.4).

An overwhelming percentage of immigrants entering under family reunification provisions enter as spouses, most of them women. In Portugal, in 2004, 66.5 per cent of residence permit applications by non-EU citizens under family reunification provisions were women. Women also made 68.2 per cent of all requests for the renewal of short-stay visas, the visa granted to family members of foreign stay permit holders. In the Portuguese case, the gender differences also illustrate that the percentage of all foreign women surveyed having migrated after other members of their family were in Portugal is significantly higher than that of their male counterparts (67.1 per cent and 47.6 per cent, respectively) (table 4.4). However, one should note that this trend is not as marked in all immigrant groups; while it is the case

Table 4.4 *Immigrants surveyed, by marital status and place of origin (%)*

Country/Region of origin	Single	Married	Civil union	Separated	Divorced	Widowed	Total
PALOP	59.9	23.1	11.7	1.5	1.2	2.5	100.0
Angola	63.6	17.5	14.7	0.9	1.8	1.4	100.0
Cape Verde	60.2	24.0	9.8	1.6	1.2	3.3	100.0
Guinea-Bissau	46.9	36.7	11.2	3.1	0.0	2.0	100.0
Mozambique	58.8	32.4	2.9	2.9	0.0	2.9	100.0
Sao Tome & Principe	67.9	11.3	15.1	0.0	1.9	3.8	100.0
Other African countries	62.0	36.0	0.0	0.0	2.0	0.0	100.0
Asia	46.9	53.1	0.0	0.0	0.0	0.0	100.0
Brazil	45.7	37.7	6.5	1.6	6.9	1.6	100.0
Central & Eastern Europe	29.3	61.8	4.0	0.4	4.0	0.4	100.0
Ukraine	23.4	66.4	3.9	0.8	4.7	0.8	100.0
Moldova	31.8	63.6	0.0	0.0	4.5	0.0	100.0
Romania	38.1	54.8	2.4	0.0	4.8	0.0	100.0
Total surveyed	50.8	34.9	8.3	1.2	2.9	1.8	100.0

Source: Fonseca et al. 2005b: 143

for Asians and Eastern Europeans, it is rather less the case for Brazilians and Africans. Unlike the Brazilian case, women from South Asia and the 'other African countries' category tend to enter the country only after their spouses and other family members have established themselves there, if they migrate at all. This strategy is clearly related to the more recent character of migration from these areas but possibly also partly defined by cultural and religious norms in the countries of origin, and rings most true for families of Muslim origin from non-Portuguese-speaking African countries and Pakistan and India. In the case of Chinese migrants, women also tend to come after their spouses who have already established themselves in Portugal and use family reunification provisions as a springboard for starting up or re-establishing small family-owned enterprises (Oliveira & Costa 2008).

Each migrant group's distinct time-sensitive position within the migratory cycle and the age structure of each group are also visible when looking at the percentage of immigrants surveyed that live in the country with their parents and siblings. Longer-established communities have a higher number of reunified families, and families created following arrival in Portugal, tending to live with their spouses/partners and minor-aged children. This difference is particularly evident when comparing Eastern Europeans and Portuguese-speaking Africans (figure 4.1). Those from Portuguese-speaking African countries, on the other hand, have been living in Portugal for a greater length of time than other migrant groups and subsequent generations have been born in the country, thus on average they tend to live in households with at least three or four family members, with parents, siblings and extended family members. At the other extreme, 41.7 per cent of Asians

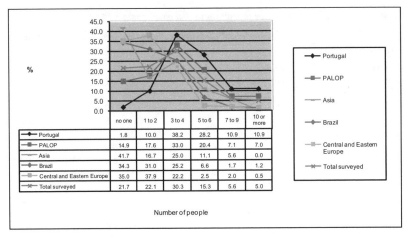

	no one	1 to 2	3 to 4	5 to 6	7 to 9	10 or more
Portugal	1.8	10.0	38.2	28.2	10.9	10.9
PALOP	14.9	17.6	33.0	20.4	7.1	7.0
Asia	41.7	16.7	25.0	11.1	5.6	0.0
Brazil	34.3	31.0	25.2	6.6	1.7	1.2
Central and Eastern Europe	35.0	37.9	22.2	2.5	2.0	0.5
Total surveyed	21.7	22.1	30.3	15.3	5.6	5.0

Number of people

Figure 4.1 *Immigrants surveyed, by place of birth and number of family members with whom they live in Portugal*
Source: Fonseca et al. 2005b: 153
Note: 'Portugal' refers to children of migrant parents surveyed that have Portuguese citizenship.

and 34.7 per cent of Brazilians surveyed live alone. Unlike the Eastern Europeans surveyed, Brazilians tend to be younger on average and live in Portugal before starting families of their own.

Structural Challenges to Family Reunification in Portugal: Getting into the Country

In addition to the age of the immigrants and their family members and the phases of life in which they find themselves, access to adequate social integration structures, employment opportunities, job stability, the ability to save money, furnish a home and provide for family members, etc., are also significant factors that determine the type and extent of family reunification. Immigrant families wishing to reunite under official family reunification provisions have run up against some barriers in Portugal to date. These include not being able to provide official evidence of family ties due to not having officially registered marriage, birth or adoption documents; the ineligibility of children over the age of eighteen for family reunification and the barriers to successfully sponsoring older parents because they may still work in their country of origin or benefit from help from other family members. To surpass these obstacles, children over the age of eighteen will at times apply for student visas or enter Portugal with work and tourist visas; older parents may also do the latter. This can lead to family members overstaying their visas and, from that point on, illegally residing in Portugal. Families will creatively seek out ways to be together, though their rights as individuals and members of family units may significantly vary and be compromised as a result.

To make use of official family reunification provisions, migrants must have lived in Portugal for at least one year with proof of a stable job and adequate housing. While some find this period to be too long, wishing to reunite with their families as soon as they possibly can, in practice, it tends to take immigrants more than one year to achieve the economic stability and acquire the material conditions necessary for re-uniting with their families. Many wait until they and their families have decided if they would like to settle for some time in Portugal or return to their country of origin. Interviews in the scope of the 'Immi-gration and Family Reunification in Portugal' project (Fonseca et al. 2005b) revealed that this decision is often made between two and four years after coming to Portugal. Choosing to reunite correlates with a choice to stay in the country for at least a few years and is based upon an evaluation of the socio-economic opportunities available to the fa-mily once they are together again. For this reason, many lone migrants may opt to return to their families in their countries of origin instead of staying in Portugal. This has particularly been the case among East-ern Europeans who arrived during the construction boom of the late 1990s but plan to return, or already have returned, to their countries of origin because of job instability created by the economic crisis in which Portugal finds itself.

The official family reunification process in Portugal calls for a genu-ine commitment to reuniting one's family because it is an investment of time, energy and resources on behalf of both the sponsor and the sponsored family members. Furthermore, prior to 3 August 2007, the date upon which Portugal's new immigration law (Law No. 23/2007 of 4 July) entered into force, those holding a residence (long-term) permit were required to submit less proof of their ability to sponsor family members than immigrants holding stay (short-term) permits and work, student and short-stay visas. Interviews in the scope of the 'Immigra-tion and Family Reunification in Portugal' project revealed several cases in which immigrants grew frustrated with the impossibility of gathering all the necessary documents and simply gave up. Across the board, migrants generally encountered some difficulty in obtaining documents required from both the country of origin and Portugal. As regards relations with the country of origin, migrants generally tend to encounter problems in obtaining documents because of bureaucratic issues, corruption and other difficulties as they are not in the country of origin in person. Criminal records appeared to be particularly diffi-cult to obtain. Interviewees representing all of the main migrant groups noted the great financial investments they had to make in the scope of the family reunification application process. For those whose remaining family members or friends live far from the Portuguese embassies in their country of origin, many immigrants hired a third party located near the Portuguese embassy in question to take care of the necessary paperwork (i.e. gathering documents, notarising them, translating them if necessary). Ukrainian and Moldovan immigrants faced even greater obstacles because, until recently, there was no Portuguese embassy in Ukraine and there is still no embassy in Moldova. Portuguese-speaking African immigrants also often complained about their countries' embassies in Portugal, describing their bureaucracy and overall unhelpfulness as real obstacles to their attempts to gather necessary information for the family reunification process.

A migrant applying for family reunification must prove his/her financial ability to support family members coming to live in the receiving country and, in some cases, he/she must produce a work contract and prove that he/she holds a steady job. It proved very difficult for many migrants to acquire documentary proof of their financial and housing stability because of high levels of job and housing informality and instability experienced by many immigrants. Sometimes putting together a successful family reunification application takes several attempts over many years to gather what is needed, as it may imply significant life changes, such as moving to an apartment where the landlord is willing to sign a rental contract or changing jobs to get a boss willing to issue a work contract. Many immigrants interviewed confirmed that the helpfulness of their employers in particular had a lot to do with their ability to sponsor their family members. While in some cases this simply meant that their employers agreed to issue a work contract, in other cases, especially in rural areas, it meant that employers went out of their way to help the process along by assisting with the translation of required documents into Portuguese, by helping to find work for their spouses once they arrived or by providing household goods.

The housing stock available to immigrants – its condition, location and cost – is at times severely limited, with people having to settle for poor quality, sometimes overcrowded rented flats that they typically share with people from the same country of origin. While generally an uncomfortable set-up, lone migrants sometimes temporarily prefer this type of housing situation because it allows them to save money more quickly and send it to their families. Once families are reunited or before family members arrive, a concerted effort is made to find a home that is more suitable to their needs. However, some immigrants' 'temporary migrant' status makes it nearly impossible to secure a bank loan for home repairs or a mortgage, thus complicating attempts to obtain better living conditions, restricting them to the rental market. In urban areas, reunited families will at times seek to share a home with another family because of financial limitations and/or prohibitive housing costs.

Interviewees appeared generally frustrated with the length and opacity of the application process. They were unable to check on their application status and never knew when they would receive a response, positive or negative, from the Foreigners and Borders Service (SEF) or the Portuguese embassies abroad. In extreme cases, it took between six months and a couple of years to receive a response. This uncertainty makes it very difficult for families to make plans, with their decision-making capacity suspended during the time it takes to receive a response as they cannot be sure as to the country in which they will be living in the near future. Many families discovered an alternative approach to this often lengthy process; most immigrants interviewed believed that it is far easier to petition for family reunification once family members are already on Portuguese soil than if they are still in their countries of origin. For this reason, many family members come to Portugal with legal tourist visas and then initiate the petition process from within the country. A clear advantage of this approach is that the family is already *de facto* reunited and does not have to remain separated from one another throughout the application process.

Because immigrant families – like their non-immigrant counterparts – encompass a broad range of family types, their compositions sometimes also pose a challenge to the applicability of the Western nuclear family model that has been employed more or less across the board as the typical family model in which to fit in order to qualify to live in Western European receiving countries under family reunification provisions. Paradoxically, however, imposing a traditional nuclear family model on immigrants by allowing only for certain members that can fit in the stereotypical, traditional nuclear family unit may not adequately reflect the reality of the modern Western family structure, given rising levels of divorce, single parenting, unmarried partnerships, openly recognised same-sex partnerships and the subsequent gradual dissolution of the nuclear family model in Western receiving countries. In enforcing a policy that does not realistically reflect the contemporary transformations within the modern Western family but rather a particular socio-cultural ideal, family reunification provisions effectively play a fundamental role in discriminating against functional alternative, non-nuclear and non-Western family structures and keeping families apart.

Given the weakened welfare state in Portugal and the lack of (and difficulty in accessing) social support structures developed by civil society, there are few alternatives beyond relying on family for assistance. Some find that Portuguese family reunification provisions do not suffi-

ciently recognise the often pivotal role of the extended family unit residing in Portugal that are particularly valued by African and Asian immigrant communities. Coming from cultures in which the extended family and community have played a significant role in their lives, there
is concern about the reduction (or even absence) of parental and community supervision of and guidance for their children. Yet, because
many Portuguese-speaking Africans and ethnic Indians have been established in Portugal for generations, chances are higher that older parents and members of their extended families live near them and actively participate in the daily management of their lives and the upbringing of their children. The proximity of grandparents and other
extended family members at times serves to increase family stability –
particularly in the case of single mothers – because, in addition to taking care of children and household duties when parents are working,
they are also are able to pass on cultural practices and traditional values
to grandchildren who may be little familiar with their families' culture
of origin. In doing so, they may soften the possibly radical changes in
family structure and the responsibilities of family members, as wives/
mothers assume new roles in Portugal that may include working outside of the home (more) and husbands/fathers must work more jobs to
make ends meet.

Structural Challenges to Family Reunification in Portugal: Staying in the Country

Families that do succeed in reuniting under family reunification provisions are subject not only to the receiving country's definition of what
an immigrant family looks like but also to its influence in redefining
roles within the family once it is together again following arrival. Once
reunited with their families in Portugal, the challenges immigrants
face assume new dimensions as their family members' roles and responsibilities change and they adapt to a new set of financial, legal and
social resources. Some families cannot overcome these challenges and
will end up separating once more or returning to their countries of origin.
    Boyd and Grieco (2003) find that family members' integration is pri-
marily influenced by three factors:

> the impact of entry status on the ability to integrate and settle –
> as entry status often determines residency and employment and
> social welfare rights, as well as other social rights and entitle-
> ments like access to faster citizenship, language classes, job
> training, etc.; patterns of incorporation into the labour market;

and the impact of migration on the status of women and men, altering marital power, decision-making, family care and household responsibilities.

Receiving countries, depending on several factors such as the strength of their national labour markets, the openness of social assistance and benefits coverage, and their immigration policies, play an essential role in defining how these three factors mentioned above are realised. Here, we shall restrict ourselves to a brief look at the pivotal role of labour market access in keeping migrant families in Portugal.

While most EU countries allow for spouses' and partners' direct access to the labour market via family reunification provisions, before the transposition of the EU Directive on the right to family reunification,[5] access was sometimes delayed for several months or years (e.g. Germany, France and Denmark), restricted to those whose sponsoring spouses have residence permits (e.g. Portugal) or fully restricted (e.g. Ireland). Restrictions in the labour market for spouses having entered by means of family reunification effectively mean that they are entirely financially dependent upon their spouses, as they are not able to legally contribute to the household income. Family members coming to a receiving country, however, are often vital economic players for their households. In contrast to many countries' concerns with the immigrant sponsor being able to financially provide fully for his/her family members and the potential burden of immigrant family members on receiving countries' social systems, law in Switzerland finds that, 'in considering the financial situation of the family, regard must be had to the willingness of other family members to contribute to the upkeep of the family. The possible contribution of all family members in the long run must be taken into account' (IGC 1997: 267-268).

A family living together tends to pool its resources in order to survive economically. Immigrants are affected by precarious employment conditions that, in addition to being more vulnerable to exploitation by their employers, suffer job instability and are often poorly remunerated. More often than not, when families reunite in Portugal, both spouses look for work. This is evidenced in the fact that, in 2001, more foreign women (65.3 per cent) were actively employed in Portugal than in any other of the EU-15 countries (where the average was 55.1 per cent) (OECD 2003: 61). Two incomes provide the family with more money to offset their newly increased costs of living. Furthermore, interviewees from Fonseca et al. (2005b) noted that both spouses will often work in order to remain afloat in unstable economic periods, thus ensuring a stable household income. Furthermore, because a single earner risks not getting his/her visa renewed if unemployed or not receiving unemployment benefits (as he/she is deemed unfit to take care of his or herself), a two-earner household also serves to secure a fa-mily's legal residence in Portugal over time.

In Portugal, until recently, the main economic obstacle to functional family life for immigrant families had involved impediments to em-ployment and economic stability, particularly in the case of families re-unifying under family reunion provisions. Sponsors with a stay permit, a temporary work visa, student visa or short-stay visa were eligible to apply for family reunion after residing and/or working in Portugal for one year. 'Family reunion' (*reunião familiar*) differs from 'family re-grouping' (*reagrupamento familiar*) because family members coming to Portugal under 'family reunion' provisions received a short-stay visa while those coming under the heading of 'family regrouping' were is-sued a residence permit. Unlike family members sponsored under fa-mily regrouping provisions that were issued a residence permit equal to that of their sponsor and thus enjoyed legal access to the labour mar-ket, short-stay visa holders were considered to be fully financially de-pendent upon their sponsors. In order be able to work legally, short-stay visa holders had to leap several barriers that involved proving to the Foreigners and Borders Service (SEF) the family's economic neces-sity. In practice, these hurdles presented a serious obstacle to many im-migrant families benefiting from family reunion. Because of the diffi-culty in qualifying for employment privileges, more often than not holders of this visa would resort to working informally, serving to further exacerbate their overall vulnerability to labour exploitation and encourage the development of the informal sector. It effectively ren-dered them doubly dependent, both legally and financially, on their fa-milies and their employers. Such obstacles might effectively contribute to the generally low use of family reunion provisions in Portugal, with migrants choosing to reunite with their families by acquiring indepen-dent permits allowing them to work or by entering the country illegally.

Conclusions

This paper has sought to respond to the question: why is the percen-tage of immigrants entering Portugal via official family reunification provisions so low? In doing so, it was necessary to consider a variety of aspects, both particular to the Portuguese case and more overarching in nature. Because different groups of immigrants have settled in Por-tugal at different times and at varying pace over the last decades and in light of their diverse demographic, socio-economic and cultural back-grounds, each group has a distinct relationship to the way in which they have (or have not) reunited with their families in Portugal that corresponds with where they are in the time-sensitive migratory process. Each migrant group's use of official family reunification provisions is also very distinct, evidence of their varying abilities to fulfil official requirements and fit into the official nuclear family model. Along with the size of each migrant group and the length of time they have lived in Portugal, a variety of decisive elements such as the various phases in life in which each migrant group generally finds itself, the atmosphere at the moment in which they arrived in Portugal and cultural and religious specificities that determine social and gender roles and responsibilities also affect migrants' interests in and ability to reunify their families.

Yet while families' own migratory strategies play a dynamic role in defining the manner in which international migration occurs and those who will migrate, they face a host of challenges in reassembling and re-establishing themselves both as a family unit and as individuals within a family in Portugal. Both the country of origin and the receiving country's cultural and socio-economic characteristics, values and predispositions play fundamental roles in defining their ability to migrate in the first place and, later on, their level of integration wherever they may choose to settle. We are particularly heartened by the new immigration law approved by the Portuguese Parliament on 10 August 2006 which came into force on 3 August 2007. It made significant strides towards improving family reunification in Portugal by doing away with the distinction between *reagrupamento familiar* (family regrouping) and *reunião familiar* (family reunion); issuing independent residence permits to spouses and civil union partners (together for five or more years), minor-aged children and dependent parents abroad or legally residing in Portugal that will enable them to work and study without restriction; eliminating the one-year waiting period for applying for family reunification; and ensuring that decisions on reunification are made and communicated within six months.

Notes

1 However, one should note that, of a total of 40,741 stay permits granted in 2004, some 39.9 per cent were issued to family members of holders of stay permits and work, student and short-stay visas.
2 For example, 76 per cent of all immigrants coming into France in 1999 came as a result of family reunification (Hamilton, Simon & Veniard 2002).
3 Some countries are experimenting with DNA tests to ensure that children coming to join their families are genuinely theirs.
4 A 'stay permit' (*autorização de permanência*) was a permit created in 2001 (Decree-Law No. 4/2001 of 10 January) that allowed undocumented foreign workers in Portugal to stay in the country for one year, if they could produce a valid work contract registered at the General-Inspectorate of Labour (IGT). This system was suspended in November 2001 and removed from the revised law on entry, stay and

exit of non-EU foreigners from Portuguese territory (Decree-Law No. 34/2003 of 25 February).
5   The Directive entered into force on 3 October 2003, and member states had to comply with it no later than 3 October 2005. However, this Directive does not apply in the United Kingdom, Ireland or Denmark.

References

Baker, Michael & Dwayne Benjamin (1997), 'The Role of the Family in Immigrants' Labor-Market Activity: An Evaluation of Alternative Explanations', *The American Economic Review* 87 (4): 705-727.

Baldaccini, Annaliese (2003), 'UK Country Report on Immigration Management', in J. Niessen, J. Schibel & C. Thompson (eds.), *EU and US Approaches to the Management of Immigration*, Migration Policy Group.
www.migpolgroup.com/multiattachments/2094/DocumentName/UKMigration.pdf/.

Boyd, Monica & Elizabeth Grieco (2003), 'Women and Migration: Incorporating Gender into International Migration Theory'.
www.migrationinformation.org/feature/display.cfm?ID=106.

Bracalenti, Raffaele (coord) (2002), 'Family Reunification Evaluation Project (FARE): Final Report', European Union Research Contract ERBSOE2-CT98-3081. Rome: Institute for Social Research.

Cohen, Steve (2001), *Immigration Controls, the Family and the Welfare State*, London: Jessica Kingsley Publishers.

Council of the European Union (2003), 'Council Directive 2003/86/EC of 22 September 2003 on the Right to Family Reunification', *Official Journal of the European Union*, 251, 3 November 2003, Brussels.

Creese, Gillian, Isabel Dyck & Arlene McLaren (1999), *Reconstituting the Family: Negotiating Immigration and Settlement*, No. 99-10, Working Paper Series, Research on Immigration and Integration in the Metropolis.
http://riim.metropolis.net/Virtual%20Library/1999/wp9910.pdf.

Curran, Sarah R. & Abigail C. Saguy (1997), 'Migration and Cultural Change: A Role for Gender *and* Social Networks?', Culture and Inequality Workshop, Princeton University.

De Jong, Gordon (2000), 'Expectations, Gender and Norms in Migration Decision-Making', *Population Studies* 54: 307-319.

Ensor, Jonathan & Amanda Shah (2005) 'The United Kingdom' in J. Niessen, J. Schibel & C. Thompson (eds.), *Current Immigration Debates in Europe: A Publication of the European Migration Dialogue*, 399-429. Brussels: Migration Policy Group.

European Observatory on the Social Situation, Demography and Family (Austrian Institute for Family Studies) (2002), 'Introduction', Annual Seminar 2002, Immigration and Family, Helsinki, Finland. http://europa.eu.int/comm/employment_social/eoss/downloads/ helsinki_2002_pressrelease.pdf.

Fonseca, Maria Lucinda, Jorge Macaísta Malheiros & Sandra Silva (2005a), 'Portugal', in J. Niessen, J. Schibel & C. Thompson (eds.), *Current Immigration Debates in Europe: A Publication of the European Migration Dialogue*, Migration Policy Group.
www.migpolgroup.com/multiattachments/3011/DocumentName/EMD_Portugal_2005.pdf.

Fonseca, Maria Lucinda, Meghann Ormond, Jorge Macaísta Malheiros, Miguel Patrício & Filipa Martins (2005b), *Reunificação familiar e imigração em Portugal*, Observatório da Imigração Estudo n°15, Lisbon: ACIME.

Gsir, Sonia, Marco Martiniello & Johan Wets (2003), 'Belgian Country Report on Immigration Management', in J. Niessen, J. Schibel & C. Thompson (eds.), EU and US

Approaches to the Management of Immigration, Migration Policy Group.
www.migpolgroup.com/multiattachments/2047/DocumentName/Belgium.pdf.

Hamilton, Kimberly, Patrick Simon & Clara Veniard (2002), 'The Challenge of French
Diversity'. www.migrationinformation.org/feature/display.cfm?ID=21.

IGC (1997), *Report on Family Reunification: Overview of Policies and Practices in IGC Participating States*. Geneva: Secretariat of the Intergovernmental Consultations on Asylum,
Refugee and Migration Policies in Europe, North America and Australia.

Inglis, Christine (2003), 'Mothers, Wives, and Workers: Australia's Migrant Women'.
www.migrationinformation.org/feature/display.cfm?ID=108.

Marinelli, Vera (2005) 'The Netherlands' in J. Niessen, J. Schibel & C. Thompson (eds.),
*Current Immigration Debates in Europe: A Publication of the European Migration Dialo-
gue*, 277-293. Brussels: Migration Policy Group.

Massey, Douglas S. (1990), 'Social Structure, Household Strategies, and the Cumulative
Causation of Migration', *Population Index* 56 (1): 3-26.

Niessen, Jan, Thomas Hudleston, Laura Citron, Andrew Geddes & Dirk Jacobs (2007),
Migrant Integration Policy Index. Brussels: British Council and Migration Policy
Group.

OECD (2003), *Trends in International Migration, Continuous Reporting System on Immigration, SOPEMI Annual Report 2002*. Paris: OECD.

OECD (2006), *International Migration Outlook, SOPEMI Annual Report 2006*. Paris:
OECD.

Oliveira, Catarina Reis & Francisco Lima Costa (2008), '"Being your own Boss": Entrepreneurship as a Lever for Migration?' in Maria Lucinda Fonseca (ed.), *Cities in Movement: Migrants and Urban Change*, 241-266. Lisbon: CEG.

Parrenas, Rhacel Salazar (2001), 'Mothering from a Distance: Emotions, Gender, and Intergenerational Relations in Filipino Transnational Families', *Feminist Studies* 27 (2):
361-390.

Satzewich, Vic (1993), 'Migrant and Immigrant Families in Canada: State Coercion and
Legal Control in the Formation of Ethnic Families', *Journal of Comparative Family Studies* 24 (3): 315-338.

Stenum, Helle (2003), 'Danish Country Report on Immigration Management', in J. Niessen, J. Schibel & C. Thompson (eds.), EU and US Approaches to the Management of
Immigration. Brussels: Migration Policy Group.
www.migpolgroup.com/multiattachments/2051/DocumentName/DenmarkMigration.pdf.

Stenum, Helle (2005), 'Denmark', in J. Niessen, J. Schibel & C. Thompson (eds.), *Current
Immigration Debates in Europe: A Publication of the European Migration Dialogue*, 95-
126. Brussels: Migration Policy Group.

Wenden, Catherine de (1999),'Le regroupement familial en Europe: quelle harmonisation
communautaire?', *Ecarts d'identité* 88: 'Droits de l'Homme à l'épreuve de l'Autre',
Mars. http://ecid.online.fr/french/numero/article/art_88.html.

5 Debating Cultural Difference: Ayaan Hirsi Ali on Islam and Women

Erik Snel and Femke Stock

Introduction: 'Clash of Cultures'?[1]

After the terrorist attacks on New York and Washington, D.C., on 9/11, there was an increasing tendency to interpret our world in terms of a 'clash of cultures' or civilisations, more specifically between the 'West' and the world of Islam (Snel 2003). The notion of a 'clash of civilisations' (Huntington 1996) was, in its time, very innovative. Huntington understood that the world after the fall of socialism was not essentially peaceful, as observers of international politics thought, but stressed that the main contemporary political tensions and conflicts were of an ideological nature, related to cultural or religious identities. This was a far-sighted analysis. Ten years later, international politics is indeed dominated by conflicts between the Western world and the world of Islam. Moreover, this alleged cultural clash occurs not only in international politics but also within societies in the Western world. We increasingly understand our contemporary multicultural societies in terms of homogeneous, autonomous, competing or even conflicting cultural formations, between which processes of mutual adjustment seem to be impossible.

The so-called Danish cartoon controversy in early 2006 again immensely popularised this notion of a cultural clash, but also showed the limitations of the notion. The publication of cartoons that directly linked Islam to terrorism brought about a wave of (often violent) protests all over the Muslim world. In reaction, Western newspapers and television widely debated the assumed contradiction between the West and the world of Islam: human rights and freedom of expression versus religious orthodoxy and intolerance. However, as so often happens, a clear-cut dichotomous worldview conceals more than it makes clear. First, it masks the heterogeneity in both worlds. The US government, for instance, clearly distanced itself from the cartoons saying that freedom of expression has its limits when religious feelings of others are violated. But there were also great differences in the Muslim world; between the uncontrolled outbursts of violence in some Muslim countries and the essentially peaceful protests of Muslim communities in most European countries. Secondly, and more important, the notion of

a 'clash of cultures' obscures the point that individuals do not coincide
with (alleged) 'communities' and 'cultures'. Portraying a contradiction
between 'Western' values such as freedom of speech and 'Islam' denies
the fact that individual Muslims may identify with both. As a Dutch
member of parliament of Moroccan descent put it: 'Muslims and immigrants are only seen as a collective. [The] individual is the greatest
victim, because his freedom of identity is at stake. In a false contradiction between 'civilisation and barbarism', Muslims have to choose in favour of or against their family, religion and their own threatened identity' (Azough 2006).[2]

This chapter is not another commentary on the Danish cartoon controversy, but deals more generally with the use of essentialist notions
of culture in public and political debates about migrants and multiculturalism in contemporary Europe. We focus on a specific issue, the
public debate about women and Islam, and particularly on the contributions to this debate by a former Dutch member of parliament, Ayaan
Hirsi Ali. If there is one topic suitable to be discussed in terms of dichotomous stereotypes – the West versus Islam, modernity versus pre-
modern cultures, human freedom versus tradition – it seems to be the
position of women in Islam and in Muslim communities. In the few
years that Ayaan Hirsi Ali was active in Dutch politics, she caused a
huge commotion in public and political debates in the Netherlands.
On the one hand she was celebrated as the Netherlands' most influential parliamentarian, someone with the courage to reveal the abuse of
women in Muslim communities and the crisis of multicultural society
in general. On the other she was heavily criticised by members of the
Dutch Muslim community, including the Muslim women for whom
she was fighting, for stereotyping Muslims as traditional, pre-modern,
unfriendly or even hostile towards women, etc. She began her public
career with a number of much-debated publications about the abuse of
Muslim women. In 2004 she made the film *Submission* with the Dutch
filmmaker and well-known critic of Islam, Theo van Gogh. Shortly
after the first (and last!) showing of the film on Dutch television, Van
Gogh was brutally murdered by a Muslim extremist who defended his
action on religious grounds. Hirsi Ali was also threatened and went
into hiding for several months.

Before we describe Hirsi Ali's view on the issue of women, Islam
and the family, we will outline the Dutch debate about immigrants,
Muslims and multiculturalism since the turn of the millennium in
more general terms. Hirsi Ali's critique of Muslims and multiculturalism was not unique, but fitted into a widespread anti-multiculturalist
public discourse – Grillo (2005) called it the 'backlash against diversity'
– in the Netherlands. We then analyse Hirsi Ali's public statements
about women and Islam, and end by demonstrating the (implicit) es-

sentialist or culturalist notion of culture in her work. We will argue that this essentialist or culturalist notion of culture, however popular it may be in current public debates about migration and multiculturalism, is heavily criticised and actually seen as outdated in cultural anthropology, the academic discipline long associated with the study of cultural diversity.

Radical Shifts in Dutch Debates about Immigration and Integration

Grillo (2005) pointed out the 'backlash against diversity' occurring in many European countries. In the aftermath of terrorist attacks in New York and Washington, D.C., (2001), Madrid (2003) and London (2005), there was a growing scepticism about or outspoken criticism of the idea of a *multi*cultural society. The old notion of multiculturalism as an enrichment of European societies suddenly made way for a new discourse emphasising the distinctiveness and separateness of immigrant cultures. In this new discourse, cultural differences were equated with problems, and multicultural society was perceived as a 'fiasco' (Scheffer 2000 [2003]). Grillo describes the rise of this new anti-multiculturalist discourse in the UK, France and Italy, but it is not hard to see similar arguments in recent Dutch debates about immigration and immigrant integration.

In the 1980s and 1990s, the Netherlands was internationally well known as an example of multicultural tolerance. The Netherlands not only welcomed foreign immigrants, but also urged them to retain their own cultural identities. 'Integration with preservation of culture' was the motto of Dutch policy for many years. Already in the early 1990s, however, Frits Bolkestein, subsequently EU Commissioner, gained attention as a critic of the multicultural model of Dutch ethnic minorities policies. Simultaneous with the Rushdie Affair in the UK, Bolkestein stressed the inherent incompatibility between the 'world of Islam' and the liberal principles of Western society with regard to freedom of speech, the emancipation of women and homosexuals, and so on. Bolkestein not only called for harder immigrant integration policies ('*with guts*'), but was also the first Dutch opinion leader that stressed the cultural aspects of immigrant integration (Bolkestein 1991; Ghorashi 2003; Prins 2004). Although his ideas were widely discussed, they were of little influence on the Dutch political debate at that time. The shift in public opinion began shortly after the turn of the millennium when Paul Scheffer, a prominent member of the Dutch Labour Party, published a much-debated newspaper article entitled *The Multicultural Fiasco* (Scheffer 2000 [2003]). In this article Scheffer distanced himself from the (until then predominant) optimism about multiculturalism and immigrant integration, warning of the rise of an 'ethnic under-class' in Dutch cities, but also shifted attention in the immigration de-bate from economic to cultural issues. The issue is not only poverty and unemployment of migrants: 'Beneath the surface of public life there is a sea of stories about the clash of cultures which are barely heard' (Scheffer 2003: 26).

Although Scheffer's article initially encountered mainly criticism, it is now generally seen as the start of a dramatic turnaround in the Dutch political debate about immigrants and multiculturalism. Mean-while, Pim Fortuyn already had started his unprecedented advance in Dutch politics. In the late 1990s, Fortuyn was still a rather marginal academic figure, known for his anti-immigrant and anti-Muslim col-umns in conservative journals (Pels 2003). He also wrote a book against what he saw as the threatening dominance of Muslim culture in the Netherlands (*Against the Islamification of Culture*, 1997). After 9/11, there was more attention for his radical views, and in the run-up to the 2002 national elections Fortuyn suddenly emerged as the most prominent critic of the then social-liberal government that had been in power for eight years. Although his anti-immigrant standpoint was not a major part of his political program, it was clear enough to mobilise a huge electorate. Fortuyn became famous for calling Islam 'a retarded culture',[3] and in a new book against the social-liberal government of that time he stated that Muslims could be dominant in their part of the world but that 'we' are in charge in our part of the world (Fortuyn 2002: 154). In other words, immigrants were welcome as long as they rejected their 'retarded' culture and assimilated in Dutch society. For-tuyn completely dominated the 2002 national election campaign, but was assassinated shortly before the elections. Despite his tragic death his party and other centre-right parties won the elections convincingly, ending almost a decade of Liberal and Social-Democratic government in the Netherlands. Dutch political commentators often refer to the sudden rise of Pim Fortuyn in Dutch politics as the 'citizens' revolt'. Later electoral research showed that it was mainly his anti-immigrant standpoint that attracted the electorate.[4]

After Fortuyn's death, a young woman of Somalian descent, Ayaan Hirsi Ali, became the most prominent spokesperson for the 'multicul-tural backlash' in the Netherlands. In 1992, Hirsi Ali sought and found asylum in the Netherlands after she had been married off against her will. After graduating from a Dutch university, she started to work for the scientific bureau of the Dutch Social-Democratic Party (PvdA). Dur-ing her studies she jobbed as a translator in abortion clinics and in wo-men's shelters. That is where she noticed, as she later wrote, that the shelters were 'full of Muslim women' and she became involved in the issue of their abuse. However, in her opinion her employer – the Dutch Social-Democratic Party – did not welcome her activism around this issue because the party was 'taken hostage by adherents of multi-culturalism on the one hand and Muslim conservatives on the other' (Hirsi Ali 2002c).[5] After she left the Social-Democratic Party, Hirsi Ali was elected as a member of parliament for the Dutch Liberal Party (VVD), which in fact is not liberal in the American or British sense of the word but rather conservative and libertarian (especially after the 2002 Fortuyn revolt).

In her subsequent contributions to Dutch public and political debate and in her numerous newspaper articles, Hirsi Ali was not only highly critical of the abuse of Muslim women but increasingly of Islam in general. In her view, the suppression of Muslim women is directly linked to Islam as a religion (or as a culture, she appears not to distinguish between the two). Her growing aversion to Islam led her to make some controversial statements. In 2003, for instance, she publicly called the prophet Mohammed 'a pervert' because he had married a nine-year-old girl (Aïsha).[6] When the ambassadors of Arab countries officially protested against what they defined as an insult to Islam, her new party leaders reacted that, since the Netherlands has freedom of speech, Hirsi Ali is free to say these things. One year later, in 2004, Hirsi Ali together with Theo van Gogh produced *Submission*. The film was a fierce protest against the abuse of Muslim women. The most shocking part (at least for Islamic believers) was the projection of Qur'an texts on barely covered female bodies. The murder of Van Gogh, Hirsi Ali's going into hiding, and her many public statements as a prominent member of parliament, made Hirsi Ali a well-known public figure, both inside and outside the Netherlands. In 2004, *Time Magazine* included her in 'TIME 100', its yearly list of the 100 most influential people in the world. In 2006, Hirsi Ali even unintentionally caused the fall of the Dutch cabinet in a complicated case in which the Dutch minister of immigration and integration annulled Hirsi Ali's Dutch citizenship (and thus her parliamentary status) because she misled Dutch authorities when she originally applied for asylum by giving a false name. As the Dutch parliament refused to accept this treatment of one of its members, the cabinet lost its parliamentary support.

All in all, the years 2002-2004 were an extraordinary period in Dutch politics: with incidents of political violence unknown in modern Dutch political history, with electoral landslides that undermined existing political powers and created new political majorities, and a climate of public opinion that was increasingly characterised by anti-immigrant and anti-multicultural sentiments. In this context, it is hardly astonishing that the prevailing ideas in the Netherlands about immigrants and multiculturalism changed dramatically. The unprecedented political violence in the Netherlands, new terrorist attacks by Muslim extremists elsewhere in Europe (Madrid 2003, London 2005), and the many public statements by popular figures such as Fortuyn, Hirsi Ali and many others contributed to a climate in which the contrasts between native Dutch citizens and new Muslim immigrants and their respective cultures were more and more emphasised.

This paradigmatic shift in the Dutch debate about immigrant integration can be summarised in four points (Snel 2003). In the 1980s and 1990s, the flawed integration of immigrants and 'ethnic minorities' was mainly perceived as a socio-economic phenomenon; the problem was the disadvantaged position of immigrant groups in Dutch society. After the turn of the millennium attention increasingly turned to cultural issues and the (alleged) deviant behaviour and opinions ('norms and values') of immigrants and ethnic minorities. In this new way of reasoning, not only did the perception of the nature of the problem change but also the notion of whose problem it was. In the old perspective the flawed integration process of immigrants was seen primarily as a problem to do with immigrants themselves: they were in a disadvantaged position and in need of the help of mainstream society to improve their situation. In the new perspective, the flawed integration process became a problem for society as a whole. There is a growing conviction that Dutch society cannot cope with too many immigrants, with too much cultural diversity, and especially with too much deviant or even violent behaviour on the part of immigrants (read: Muslims). The fear of Muslim terrorism, of course, immensely reinforced this notion that Dutch society as such is at stake. Finally, the new cultural perspective also implied a new direction to look for solutions. This meant not so much emancipation of immigrants by way of socio-economic improvement, but rather cultural adjustment and assimilation. It is emphasised more and more that immigrants have to respect not only Dutch law, but also the basic norms and values of Dutch society. It is in this political and ideological context that Ayaan Hirsi Ali received political prominence, both inside and outside the

Table 5.1 *Integration frames: 'disadvantage' versus 'culture'*

	Disadvantage perspective	Cultural perspective
Societal sphere?	Socio-economic	Culture (behaviour and opinions)
Kind of problem?	Disadvantage (low educational levels, weak labour market position)	Deviant behaviour, 'norms and values'
Whose problem?	Of immigrant groups	Of the whole society
Possible solution?	Emancipation (economic improvement)	Assimilation (cultural adjustment)

Netherlands, and formulated and discussed her ideas about the abuse of women in and by Islam.

Hirsi Ali on Islam, Women and the Family

Reading Hirsi Ali's prolific writings of recent years, one can distinguish three dominant themes in her work: 1) the suppression and abuse of Muslim women, 2) her critique of Islam in general and 3) the apparent inability of governmental policies to accomplish the social integration of immigrants into Dutch society. In Hirsi Ali's perception, Dutch immigrant integration policies are too soft and neglect, rather than helping to solve, the problem of immigrant integration. In line with the new dominant discourse, she frames the problem of immigrant integration primarily in cultural terms. *Integration is a cultural problem*, was the title of one of her first publications (Hirsi Ali 2002b). Here we will focus on the first issue, the position of women in Muslim families and communities, although we will see that this gradually transforms into a general critique of Islam and of the Dutch government; that it should do more 'to stop the violence'.

In her writings, Hirsi Ali deals extensively with the suppression and abuse of Muslim women. Muslim women suffer greatly restricted freedom, and they are often subjected to religiously legitimised abuse such as female circumcision, forced marriage, repudiation, and domestic violence. This goes even for well-educated Muslim girls who grew up in the Netherlands.

> After a few years the tremendous pressure of tradition, religion and group culture defeats their personal independence. They are either married off or are subjected to great pressure from the family, which forces them into an arranged marriage (...) I would call this a matter of arranged rape, which is even legislated in the Netherlands afterwards. (Hirsi Ali 2004: 61)

For Hirsi Ali, an arranged marriage equals 'arranged rape'. This forced intercourse on the wedding night is also overcharged with suspicion as to the virginity of the bride. 'It is in this scenario of distrust and violence that the children of the next generation are conceived and in which they grow up' (Hirsi Ali 2004: 13). Marriage, the constitutional act of the family, is thus highly problematic, and Hirsi Ali sees this bad start as symbolic of the entire marital relationship. Furthermore, Hirsi Ali points to the high rates of domestic violence in Muslim families and the disproportionate number of Muslim women in women's shelters. She directly links violence against Muslim women to traditional marriage patterns:

> Marriage, which is arranged by the family and takes place at a very early age, sets up the husband for a serious responsibility he did not choose, for a girl he hardly knows. All of this often leads to incomprehension, anger and inadequacy. Furthermore, if you are raised as a man with the idea that a woman may be beaten the step towards using violence proves small. Currently, abused women's shelters see a large influx of Muslim women. (Hirsi Ali 2003: 49)

Besides the extreme violence against Muslim women, such as circumcision, 'arranged rape', and domestic violence, there is also less excessive, daily violence that affects both women and their children. Hirsi Ali describes the Islamic family as promoting deceit, suppression and violence. She argues that the Muslim lifestyle almost inevitably implies distrust of women, both before and after the wedding.

> In marriage, the suspicion of the wife continues. As soon as the bride has been deflowered, the husband's anxiety assumes grave dimensions (...). The only remaining way to prevent her deceiving him is by denying her access to the outside world as much as possible. Every step outside requires his approval or companionship. This is a authority given to him by Allah. (Hirsi Ali 2004: 14)

This almost unbearable control necessarily evokes deceit.

> Children are confronted with their mother's lies on a daily basis. If she were to admit to being outside alone, her husband and mother-in-law would become angry. Lies are common, as is denial. Admitting is no option, this would lead to loss of face and possibly even violence (...) Children are taught by their mother to invent stories if they do not wish to be punished. So, lying is profitable (...) This has a disastrous effect on children raised by these women, especially the boys. (Hirsi Ali 2004: 15)

In her reflections on all the evil done to Muslim women, Hirsi Ali continuously combines and merges cultural and religious explanations. On the one hand (as already became clear in previous quotations), she argues that Islam is a 'culture and religion is hostile towards women' (Hirsi Ali 2003: 7),[7] and legitimises or even reinforces the suppression and abuse of Muslim women. On the other hand she stresses that

most Muslim women in the Netherlands originate from traditional regions in their home countries. She refers to 'the man or woman that
walks in from the Rif Mountains or the Anatolian countryside' (Hirsi
Ali 2002a: 178). This cultural explanation of the issue is best phrased
in an early article, which was written when Hirsi Ali was still employed
by the Dutch Social Democrats. Here she argues that Muslim migrants
are traditional and should be 'initiated in modernity':

> The major part of Muslims that have come to the Netherlands
> (is) from the countryside, where the tribal tradition still prevails
> (...) Their cultural background has three important characteris-
> tics. First, a hierarchical-authoritarian attitude. Secondly a patriar-
> chal family structure, in which a woman has a reproductive func-
> tion and should obey the man; if she does not obey she disgraces
> the family. The third aspect is the group-regulated mindset, in
> which the group always precedes the individual; there is strong
> social control; as well as a fervent protection of group honour,
> which makes people obsessed with avoiding disgrace. This tradi-
> tional mentality is imbued with traditional religious beliefs. (Hir-
> si Ali 2002a: 172)

Hirsi Ali particularly points out the 'mentality of honour' and the 'obsession with the maidenhead', resulting from this mentality, as a
source of much misery:

> The[8] Islam demands that you enter your marriage as a virgin.
> This dogma of virginity is safeguarded by confining girls to their
> homes and by sewing together their labia majora. Female cir-
> cumcision serves a dual purpose. The clitoris is removed in or-
> der to curtail the sexuality of the women and to guarantee their
> virginity. (Hirsi Ali 2003: 17)

Elsewhere, she argues that this obsession with the maidenhead results
in human and social catastrophes:

> A girl (...) who has lost her 'seal of being unused', can no longer
> find a marriage partner and is doomed to waste away in her par-
> ental home for the rest of her life. (...) The family then punishes
> the girl as well, a punishment that ranges from scolding to dis-
> owning or being incarcerated, it can even lead to an arranged
> marriage. In the worst case she is murdered. (Hirsi Ali 2004: 9)

On the other hand, Hirsi Ali is quick to add that these traditional cultural practices are fully incorporated and reinforced in Islam as a reli-

gion: 'These existing local customs have been expanded, strengthened and consecrated by the Islam' (Hirsi Ali 2003: 17). About female circumcision she writes:

> Muslim scholars have never rejected the practice of sewing up labia, because in the Islam, it is considered very important for women to marry as virgins. When they came in contact with tribal customs concerning sewing up women's labia, they must have thought: 'Hey, that is a great way to safeguard virginity. How marvellous!' (Hirsi Ali 2004: 29)

In other words, Islam equals obsession with virginity equals ill treatment of Muslim women. Still more, in this climate of honour, shame, and strict sexual morality, families discourage openness and discussion: 'In Muslim families there is a massive taboo on talking about contraception, abortion, and sexual violence. This taboo springs directly from our religion' (Hirsi Ali 2003: 46).

According to Hirsi Ali, the suppression of women creates problems that pervade the entire structure of Muslim family life. From the daughter whose prime task it is to preserve her virginity lest her family be dishonoured, a Muslim woman becomes the inferior wife of a designated husband. Added to the great stress on honour and shame, the sexual morality that comes with the package results in life-long suppression. Children are raised in a climate of distrust, deceit and violence that teaches girls to submit or deceive and boys to suppress. Furthermore, women often lack proper education and are thus less capable of providing their children with a good upbringing, creating a vicious circle of backwardness. Hirsi Ali is very clear about the idea that the ultimate cause of all this misery is not only the traditional cultural backgrounds from which many Muslims originate, but also the central dogmas of Islam as a religion. There are numerous quotations in her work to illustrate this conclusion:

> In plain words, Muslims reason as follows: the body of a woman arouses desire in a man. Men and woman who are not relatives in the first remove, and are not married according to the regulations of the Islam, should avoid each other altogether. This is impossible, which is why a woman has to dress in a way in which she evokes no or hardly any desire. (...) Thus, she stays at home and covers her body. This can all be found in the Qur'an and is expanded in the traditions of the prophet Mohammed. (Hirsi Ali 2004: 36)

Terrible practices are performed in the name of the Islam. Isn't it common practice for a citizen to make an effort to denounce abuses such as female circumcision and expulsion (Hirsi Ali 2003: 48).

This is the sexual morality of the Islam. A morality which is a part of pre-modern tribal societies, but which is consecrated in the Qur'an and is expanded in the traditions of the prophet. (Hirsi Ali 2004: 9)

Analysis: Essentialising Cultural Differences

In this section we will situate Hirsi Ali's argumentation about Islam and women in a theoretical context of divergent notions of culture. However, before that, some preliminary remarks are in order. First, it is not our intention to downplay the suppression and abuse of Muslim women. On the contrary, violence against women in Muslim communities is a serious problem that has been neglected for too long by tolerant (or indifferent?) multiculturalists and by the general public. It is the merit of Hirsi Ali and other female authors (Okin 1999; Wikan 2002) to bring this issue onto the public agenda. Secondly, we certainly do not doubt Hirsi Ali's courage in raising these issues. As Prins (2004: 145) observed, Muslim women have been murdered for less than Hirsi Ali is saying publicly. Also, after her associate, Theo van Gogh, was murdered and she herself was threatened, Hirsi Ali courageously continued her struggle. Thirdly, we do not criticise Hirsi Ali and others (Paul Scheffer, Paul Cliteur) for underlining the cultural aspects of immigrant integration. Their point of view is a welcome addition to more traditional perspectives stressing only the socio-economic aspects such as poverty, unemployment, etc. In a multicultural society we should be prepared to discuss issues of culture, traditional conventions, religion, and so on.

Nonetheless, as we think her writings and public utterances have to be taken seriously, they should also be examined critically. There are two reasons for a critical examination of Hirsi Ali's views about Islam and the suppression of women. First, her arguments are typical of the cultural discourse about immigrants and immigrant incorporation that increasingly prevails in current public debates. Secondly, given her extensive media exposure we can assume that Hirsi Ali's public utterances are of great influence on Dutch public opinion. Her arguments appear as a major contribution to public debate as much as being a product of the 'multicultural backlash' discourse that has gained prominence in the Netherlands in recent years. As a recent study pointed out, Hirsi Ali moved like a hurricane through recent Dutch politics (Berkeljon & Wansink 2006). Our intention in the following analysis is not to evaluate (and contest) the validity of Hirsi Ali's account of wo-men and families in Islam in light of empirical studies about Muslim families and communities. The aim of our analysis is rather to evaluate her discourse on a more fundamental level, and to deconstruct the un-derlying theoretical notions in her argumentation.

Our main point, then, is not that Hirsi Ali and others stress the cul-tural and religious aspects of immigrant integration, but that their argu-ment is grounded in an outdated and problematic 'essentialist' notion of culture and religion: 'culturalism'. Various authors have pointed out the paradoxical situation that whereas cultural issues increasingly domi-nate public and political debates about immigration and multicultural society, cultural anthropologists – the experts par excellence concerning cultural and ethnic diversity – question whether the notion of culture is useful at all. Some even argue that we should abandon the confusing notion of culture altogether.[9] Anthropologists especially oppose the out-dated culturalism that pervades public and political debates about multi-cultural society. Culturalism is not the idea that cultural issues are im-portant for our understanding of contemporary multicultural societies. It is, rather, a specific, but highly contested notion of culture and of the relationship between culture and human behaviour, related to what others have called the 'old model', the 'dominant discourse', 'cultural fundamentalism' or 'culturalistic fallacy' (Bidney 1953; Stolcke 1995; Baumann 1996; Wikan 1999; Grillo 2003; Snel 2003).

Following the Dutch anthropologist Vermeulen, we summarise this culturalist approach in four points: first, the tendency to understand cultures as homogeneous and fixed entities with sharp boundaries without paying attention to 'internal' diversity and 'external' influences; second, the tendency to reify cultures, that is to see cultures as fixed things that exist independently from their specific 'bearers', rather than as processes involving human agency and creativity; third, and as a consequence of the latter point, cultural continuity, rather than change, is depicted as the 'normal situation'; fourth, these homogeneous, rei-fied and static cultures are depicted as determining human behaviour: people do things *because* it is their culture (Vermeulen 1992, 2000; Baumann & Sunier 1995). This conception of the relationship of cul-ture and human behaviour is a 'culturalistic fallacy' (Bidney 1953). Cul-ture is not a fixed and autonomous entity, but something that is con-stantly produced and reproduced by human agency. It cannot be used to *explain* human behaviour, nor can religion. On the contrary, it is these terms – culture and religion – that need explaining, and it is from human behaviour that we get our clues.

It is not hard to see that Hirsi Ali's ideas about the family and the suppression of women in Islam are highly essentialist or culturalistic. Hirsi Ali delineates how the basic principles of Islam 'create' the suppression of and violence against women. Hostility against women may not be the nature of Muslim men, but is imposed by their culture and religion and maintained through socialization in Muslim families and communities. Hirsi Ali constantly refers to traditional cultural patterns that she sees as incorporated and 'consecrated' by Islam. In her perspective, Islam as such is hostile to women and thus directly related to excesses of religiously legitimated violence against women. More structurally, women are seen as inferior and mistrusted, a mistrust that, combined with an obsession with shame and honour, makes deceit an omnipresent factor in women's lives. This, in turn, leads to unwholesome family relations and thus affects the whole community. According to Hirsi Ali, both the inferior position of women in general, and the specific ways in which they are abused and suppressed, have their roots in Islam. That is, she describes in highly reifying terms how a perceived amalgam of traditional cultural practices and religious principles explains the everyday violence against women in Muslim families. Her culturalist way of thinking is also reflected in the fact that she writes about 'the' Islam (the use of the definite article in such cases – *de islam* – is allowed but not necessary in Dutch grammar), presenting Islam as a monolithic entity.

What then is wrong with this culturalist discourse both in general and in Hirsi Ali's case? First, culturalist thinking is generalising: it places different communities and their (alleged) cultures en bloc in opposition to each other, neglecting the diversity within the communities concerned. Culturalist discourse constantly thinks in terms of 'us' versus 'them', in the course of which newcomers and their deviant cultural patterns are generally seen as the cause of the problem.

> In other words, the 'problem' is not 'us' but 'them'. 'We' are the measure of the good life which 'they' are threatening to undermine, and this is so because 'they' are foreigners and culturally 'different'. (Stolcke 1995: 3)

Members of this 'different culture' are seen as homogeneous and differences between them are not acknowledged. Critics have often condemned Hirsi Ali for her generalising tone. Defending herself against the objection that 'the' Islam, as a monolithic thing, does not exist, she reinforces her generalisations by stating that though of course there are differences between Muslims, the things she addresses are fixed basic principles of Islam to which each Muslim is obliged to conform. Moreover, she claims that 'what all these Muslims have in common, is

the assumption that the basic principles of [the] Islam cannot be criticised, revised or contradicted in any way' (Hirsi Ali 2003: 39). Hirsi
Ali, of course, knows that not all Muslim men are the same. But confronted with the critique that she is generalising, she responds: 'Are
"they" all like that? No, of course not. But an awful lot of them are.
That explains the large numbers of migrant women in women's shelters' (Hirsi Ali 2004: 59).

Second, through reification, culture is given the status of a natural,
autonomous entity, independent of the people who actually live and
(re)produce 'it'. Religion and culture are described as actors 'doing'
things or 'holding' certain beliefs, rather than as products of human activity (Baumann 1999). This happens, for example, in the 'three characteristics of Muslim culture' quoted in the previous section. Ever since
2001, the reification of Islam has increased dramatically. Hirsi Ali as-
cribes numerous characteristics to Islam as an entity: 'This is the sexual morality of the Islam. A morality which is a part of pre-modern tribal societies, but which is consecrated in the Qur'an and is expanded
in the traditions of the prophet (Hirsi Ali 2004: 9). If culture, or religion, becomes a 'thing', it can also easily be transported: 'Muslims who
migrated to Western Europe took their persuasions with them' (Hirsi
Ali 2004: 8). This denies the anthropological insight that 'to repeat the
same statement in new circumstances is to make a new statement'
(Baumann 1999: 69). In the new post-migration context, Hirsi Ali considers it best simply to abandon one's cultural baggage: 'In fact this
means that the newcomer has to develop his identity as an individual
and that he has to distance himself from the traditional honour and
shame culture' (Hirsi Ali 2003: 79).

This statement also illustrates our third point, namely that culturalist
thinking is blind to cultural changes within immigrant communities.
Because we identify migrants so much with *our* picture of *their* cultural
traditions, we neglect those individuals who – sometimes with great
difficulty – try to withdraw from cultural practices they disapprove of,
use their cultural tools differently and find their own way in society.
We are often blind to the emancipation processes of young female
Muslims who resist suppression while being faithful to what they perceive to be their own identity and culture. A telling example of how
this works appears in recent research about marriage patterns of Turkish and Moroccan youth living in the Netherlands. Young Turkish and
Moroccan females still often find their spouses in their country of origin, but that is not a choice for tradition. On the contrary, these young
women do so because they want 'modern' life companions whereas
they perceive young men of Turkish or Moroccan descent living in the
Netherlands as too traditional (Hooghiemstra 2003; Buitelaar 2000).
Static images of 'the' Muslims or 'the' Turks, Moroccans or Somalians

living in the Netherlands deprive us of a good view of what is really going on in these communities. Hirsi Ali shows the tendency to phrase culture in terms of ever-fixed unchanging traditions, as she writes for example: 'This traditional world of thoughts is soaked with *petrified* religious ideas' (Hirsi Ali 2003: 78; our emphasis). Except for 'opting out', as she herself did, she actually sees few possibilities for change and thus for a better position of women within the context of Islam: 'If you want to do everything Allah the elevated has said, you will stay in your cage' (Hirsi Ali 2004: 21). In this way, she actually confronts Muslim women with the false choice that the Dutch MP, cited earlier, complained of, that is, a choice between either your own religion and family or the blessings of Western civilisation.

Such a generalising, reified and static view of culture soon becomes reductionist. Individuals and families are equated with their (alleged) cultural background, reduced to 'carriers of culture'. According to Wikan, this reductionist mode of thinking is applied, not to ourselves, but to immigrants.

> Immigrants are generally perceived as bereft of agency, responsibility and the ability to change or adapt to new circumstances. Hence there is little need to respect them as individuals, for they have no real individuality ... It is a sad fact of life that many immigrants are also actively reappropriating this model. But in doing so they are actually lending support to a racist model of themselves. For what is racism other than degradation of persons on the basis of inborn or ethnic characteristics? (Wikan 1999: 58)

This neglects the fact, however, that people simultaneously operate in divergent cultural contexts and construct multiple, intersecting cultural identifications. A young Moroccan-Dutch woman living in Amsterdam is not only a Moroccan, but also an urban youth, may be well educated, working or studying, spending time with her personal friends, and not intending to let anybody suppress her. In old-fashioned sociological terms, every person plays several 'roles', is confronted with various matching expectations, and has to cope with that situation in one way or the other. Recognising that people identify with the groups to which they belong is something completely different from seeing them as inescapably determined by the culture or religion of these groups. Still, this is what many of Hirsi Ali's arguments imply. When looking at Muslim individuals and their problems, she explains, for example, that especially this personal suffering 'is the *inescapable outcome* of the way the basic principles of Islam take shape at home, at school, in daily life and in the (state) media' (Hirsi Ali 2004: 43; our emphasis). Here again, this reductionism is disastrous in the case of Islam: 'A community that lives according to the precepts of Muhammed and the Qur'an inevitably becomes a pathological community' (Hirsi Ali 2004: 17).

So far we have shown that Hirsi Ali's argumentation is indeed culturalist, and what the problems of this culturalist way of thinking are. We will now turn to the consequences of her essentialist or culturalist way of thinking. Our main point is that culturalist discourse stigmatises immigrant communities. Stolcke (1995) even wonders if what she calls 'cultural fundamentalism' is not a new kind of racism (as also Wikan suggested). She argues, however, that the contemporary 'culturalist discourse of exclusion' differs from old-fashioned racism in that it phrases exclusion in terms of cultural differences deemed unbridgeable rather than in hierarchical terms of racial inferiority (Stolcke 1995: 7; Grillo 2003: 165). The problem with migrants, according to cultural fundamentalists, is not that they, as 'others', are inferior, but that their (essentialised) culture is just 'too different'. The latter fits with Hirsi Ali's position that it is not migrants themselves but their cultural and religious 'baggage' that is problematic: 'My hypothesis is that basic principles of [the] traditional Islam, supplemented by old habits of the specific ethnic group, clash with the elementary values and norms of Dutch society' (Hirsi Ali 2003: 64). Nonetheless, if Hirsi Ali should not be called 'racist' (a reproach that is often made too easily), she and other observers consistently portray immigrants, particularly those with a Muslim background, in a negative sense, thus stigmatising the immigrant communities involved. Both Hirsi Ali and Pim Fortuyn repeatedly called Muslims 'backward' or even 'retarded' (which in Dutch happens to be the same word: *achterlijk*). Muslims are portrayed as traditional, unenlightened, obsessed with shame and honour, violent against women, and so on.

The unintended consequence of these negative images is, however, that Muslim migrants tend to withdraw from Dutch society and focus more and more on their own identity – or what they perceive as their identity. Instead of promoting immigrant integration into the host society, the new discourse stresses *and creates* the differences between migrants and the dominant society. Another unintended consequence of Hirsi Ali's harsh tone and her critique of Islam in general is that it alienated her from her 'natural' audience, those suppressed Muslim women for whom she is fighting. The Dutch-Iranian anthropologist Ghorashi takes up this point more generally, saying that harsh criticism of Islam (by Hirsi Ali and other 'liberal feminists' such as Susan Okin) puts Muslim women in an impossible position. Muslim women are encouraged to change their life radically and abandon their culture and religion, but often they are unwilling and unable to do so:

In the Dutch context, provocative framing of Islam as oppressive for women has had a perverse consequence (..) Migrants feel attacked because of the negative tone in the public debates about migrants and their background. They see that their cultural and religious background has become a plaything in the hands of opinion leaders. This leads to a reaction on the part of the migrants, which then manifests itself either in a passive or in an active and, alas, often violent response. (Gorashi 2005: 34; our translation)

Conclusion

Hirsi Ali is undoubtedly one of the most controversial personalities in Dutch politics in recent years. Apart from Pim Fortuyn, she was the Dutch politician who probably received most media exposure. She used this public attention to disseminate a very powerful message about the flawed integration of non-Western immigrants in the Netherlands, and in the Western world in general. In her perception, immigrant integration is essentially a cultural and religious problem, the enormous cultural gap between many non-Western immigrants coming from traditional regions and the modernity of the Western world. With this framing of the problem she deliberately ignores the socio-economic aspects of integration (poverty, unemployment, labour market discrimination and so on). Over the years, Hirsi Ali has increasingly focused on Islam as the central problem. In her opinion, 'the basic tenets of Islam are a major obstacle to integration' (Hirsi Ali 2006b). Her argument gains much power from the fact that she herself is of Somalian descent and was raised as a Muslim. This immunises her against reproaches of being prejudiced or even racist. After all, she can claim to have first-hand knowledge of the cultural practices she condemns.

This chapter is not about Hirsi Ali as a person, but about her ideas on immigrant integration, Islam, women and the Muslim family. There are several reasons for a critical examination of Hirsi Ali's arguments. As she herself stressed after her parliamentary status was annulled in 2006, the debate must go on. Moreover, her ideas receive extensive media exposure and presumably her public utterances have considerable influence on Dutch public opinion. In addition, her arguments seem to be both a product of the cultural discourse about immigrants and immigrant integration that increasingly prevails in current public debates, and an important contribution to these debates. It is no exaggeration to say that Hirsi Ali's analysis of the 'inherent tensions' between Islam and the Western world reflects the dominant discourse about these issues, both in the Netherlands and in other European countries.

However, as we showed in this chapter, Hirsi Ali's way of argumentation is highly problematic. The problem is not so much that she puts cultural issues in the centre of the immigrant integration debate, but rather that she departs from an 'essentialist' or 'culturalist' notion of culture. In line with the theoretical debate about culturalism among anthropologists we have pointed out a number of flaws of Hirsi Ali's analysis on the position of women and the family in Islam. First of all, her argumentation is highly generalising and biased. The picture she draws of the Muslim community and Dutch society as having two opposing, internally coherent cultures emphasises the boundaries between them while neglecting internal diversity. Secondly, as many essentialists do, she seems to ignore cultural and religious change, especially within immigrant communities, and fails to see how immigrants find their own way in the host society, creating new cultural patterns that go beyond the traditional dichotomy of either assimilation or retaining cultural identity. Also, Hirsi Ali often reifies Islam and Muslim culture, presenting them as autonomous 'things' independent of human behaviour. Moreover, religion and culture are seen as determining human behaviour, while human agency is marginalised. In this reductionist view, individuals are no more than 'carriers of culture'. Immigrants seem to be caught in their alleged cultural heritage.

These theoretical flaws make for severe problems in a multicultural context such as the Netherlands. Culturalism tends to stigmatise the communities involved. Muslim cultures especially are perceived as traditional, unenlightened, obsessed with shame and honour, violent against women, and *thus* as unfit for Western civilisation. Nowadays, many Dutch citizens consider such presumptions commonsensical. This essentialist discourse, that stigmatises Muslims – and Muslim women in particular – and presents them with the false choice between their own tradition, religion and family and the 'blessings' of Western civilisation, makes it hard for migrant groups to identify with the dominant society. Rather than bringing them together, the new discourse has the unintended consequence of creating differences between migrants and the dominant society.

Ayaan Hirsi Ali's work is another example of the disturbing phenomenon that certain notions of culture (which are rejected by most cultural anthropologists) pervade contemporary public and political debates about multicultural societies, and cause progressive dis-identification between individuals perceived to belong to different cultural or religious communities. The issue at hand, the Muslim family, is portrayed as a monolithic, patriarchal institution, defined by religious precepts and focused on the total control of female sexuality. Marriage and procreation is presented as the only legitimate goal of Muslim women, who are suppressed through a reified group culture of honour and shame. This is enforced by the bad example of the prophet's polygamy and the many Qu'ranic verses sanctioning unequal family relations. According to Hirsi Ali, the vicious circle of violence, distrust, and deceit inherent in Islamic family relations does not allow for any change other than radical intervention. The family thus appears as the focal point of the manifestation and perpetuation of Muslim culture and religion.

The position of women in Muslim families does and should demand public and political attention. Police, social work and policies in general should indeed fight for Muslim women's rights – as they should for the rights of any vulnerable individual. However, fighting for women's rights not necessarily means fighting against Islam, as Hirsi Ali seems to imply. Her essentialist or culturalist discourse about the incompatibility of Islam and women's rights rather impedes than promotes the position of women in Muslim communities.

Notes

1   The authors thank Ralph Grillo (University of Sussex), Gerd Baumann (University of Amsterdam) and Ruba Salih (University of Exeter) for their helpful comments on an earlier version of this chapter. When we wrote this article, Hirsi Ali's writings were only available in Dutch. Since this time, some of her writings have been published in English (and in many other languages) as well (Hirsi Ali 2006a). Also, Hirsi Ali's impressive autobiography (2007) is now available in English. We would like to stress that Hirsi Ali in her autobiography gives a much less generalising picture of Islam (attributing 'abuses' to specific groups or individuals, not to Islam as such) than in her political writings that are cited here. Quotes from Hirsi Ali are taken from her writings in Dutch and are translated by J. Hoogkamer. We thank A. Kristoff for correcting our English.

2   In a similar way, Baumann (1996: 124) pointed out that the Rushdie Affair placed Muslims in the UK in the impossible dilemma of having to choose between Islam *or* freedom of speech. Baumann observed that many Muslims were reluctant to discuss this dilemma.

3   In an interview in *de Volkskrant* (9 February 2002), Pim Fortuyn stated: 'I do not hate Islam. I find it a retarded culture. I have travelled a lot in the world. Everywhere where the Islam rules, it is terrible' (reprinted in Wansink 2004: 291).

4   After the electoral landslide in 2002, political research tried to explain why Dutch voters chose Fortuyn's party (LPF) to such extent. It showed that LPF voters were not a specific social category ('deprived social groups' or 'losers of modernisation'). What LPF voters had in common, was not their social background but their antipathy against further migration and against multiculturalism in the Netherlands (Van der Brug 2003; Wansink 2004: 193-199).

5   Afterwards, Hirsi Ali described her switch from the Social-Democratic Party to the Dutch Liberal Party (VVD) as follows: 'because the evasive attitude of the PvdA made

me sick. That party has closed its eyes to the growing discontent in society. Women's suppression is not an issue' (Hirsi Ali 2003: 8).

6   'Measured by our Western standards, Mohammed was a pervert. A tyrant. If you don't do as he pleases, things will end up bad for you. It makes me think of all those megalomaniac dictators in the Middle East: Bin Laden, Khomeini, Saddam' (*Trouw*, 25 January 2003; our translation).

7   Hirsi Ali (2003: 7) in fact stated that 'the flawed integration to a large extent has to do with Islam as a culture and religion that is hostile towards women'.

8   In the translations of Hirsi Ali's texts we have retained the use of the definite article ('the Islam' – in Dutch *'de Islam'*) as we believe the usage reflects a certain mode of thinking. See further below.

9   Some anthropologists propose replacing 'culture' as a central concept in their discipline with variants like 'the cultural' (Keesing 1994: 309) or 'cultural sets' (Wolf 1982: 387). Others have even begun to 'write against culture' (Abu-Lughod 1991). All citations from Vermeulen (2000).

References

Abu-Lughod, L. (1991), 'Writing against Culture', in R.G. Fox (ed.), *Recapturing Anthropology. Working in the Present*, 137-162. Santa Fe, NM: School of American Research Press.

Azough, N. 'Cartoon-affaire gaat niet over cartoons' (*The Cartoon Affair Is Not about Cartoons), de Volkskrant*, 11 February 2006.

Baumann, G. (1996), *Contesting Culture. Discourses on Identity in Multi-Ethnic London.* Cambridge UK: Cambridge University Press.

Baumann, G. (1999), *The Multicultural Riddle. Rethinking Ethnic and Religious Identities.* London/New York: Routledge.

Baumann, G. & T. Sunier (1995), 'De-essentializing Ethnicity', in G. Baumann & T. Sunier (eds.), *Post-migration Ethnicity: Cohesion, Commitment, Comparison*, 1-10. Amsterdam: IMES.

Berkeljon, S. & H. Wansink (2006), *De orkaan Ayaan: verslag van een politieke carierre.* Amsterdam: Uitgeverij Augustus.

Bidney, D. (1953), *Theoretical Anthropology.* New York: Columbia University Press.

Bolkestein, F. (1991), 'De integratie van minderheden moet met lef worden aangepakt', *de Volkskrant*, 12 September 1991.

Brug, W. van der (2003), 'How the LPF Fuelled Discontent: Empirical Test of Explanations of LPF Support, *Acta Politica* 38: 89-106.

Buitelaar, M. (2000), 'Het liefst gewoon een Marokkaan? Over de partnerkeuze van hoogopgeleide vrouwen van Marokkaanse afkomst in Nederland', in K. Luyckx (ed.), *Liefst een gewoon huwelijk? Creatie en conflict in levensverhalen van jonge migrantenvrouwen*, 139- 180. Leuven: Acco.

Fortuyn, P. (1997), *Tegen de islamisering van de cultuur. Nederlandse identiteit als fundament.* Rotterdam: Speakers Academy.

Fortuyn, P. (2002), *De puinhopen van acht jaar Paars.* Rotterdam: Speakers Academy.

Ghorashi, H. (2003), 'Ayaan Hirsi Ali: Daring or Dogmatic. Debates on Multiculturalism and Emancipation in the Netherlands', *Focaal* 42: 163-169.

Ghorashi, H. (2005), 'Benauwd door de Verlichting. De "witheid" van de huidige debatten over emancipatie', *Eutopia* 10 (September): 31-38.

Grillo, R.D. (2005), *Backlash Against Diversity? Identity and Cultural Politics in European Cities. Working Paper No. 14.* Oxford. COMPAS.
www.compas.ox.ac.uk/publications/working_papers.shtml.

Grillo, R.D. (2003). 'Cultural Essentialism and Cultural Anxiety', *Anthropological Theory* 3 (2): 157-173.

Hirsi Ali, A. (2002a), 'Schurende normen. Integratie als inwijding in de moderniteit', in F. Becker et al. (eds.), *Transnationaal Nederland. Het drieëntwintigste jaarboek voor het democratisch socialisme*, 160-181. Amsterdam: WBS/Arbeiderspers.

Hirsi Ali, A. (2002b), 'Integratie is een cultureel probleem' ('*Integration is a cultural problem*'), *NRC Handelsblad*, 31 August 2002.

Hirsi Ali, A. (2002c), 'Waarom in de VVD verkies boven de PvdA' ('*Why I prefer the VVD above the PvdA*'), *NRC Handelsblad*, 31 October 2002.

Hirsi Ali, A. (2003), *De zoontjesfabriek* (*The Son Factory*). Amsterdam/Antwerpen: Uitgeverij Augustus.

Hirsi Ali, A. (2004), *De maagdenkooi* (*The Caged Virgin*). Amsterdam/Antwerpen: Uitgeverij Augustus.

Hirsi Ali, A. (2006a), *The Caged Virgin: A Muslim Woman's Cry for Reason*. London: Free Press.

Hirsi Ali, A (2006b), 'The Ostrich and the Owl: A Bird's-eye View of Europe', *Los Angeles Times*, 22 October 2006.

Hirsi Ali, A. (2007). *Infidel. My Life*. London: Simon & Schuster.

Hooghiemstra, E. (2002), *Trouwen over de grens: achtergronden van partnerkeuze van Turken en Marokkanen in Nederland*. The Hague: SCP.

Huntington, S.P. (1996), *The Clash of Civilizations and the Remaking of the World Order*. London: Simon & Schuster.

Keesing, R.M. (1994), 'Theories of Culture Revisited', in R. Borofsky (ed.), *Assessing Cultural Anthropology*, 301-312. New York: McGraw-Hill.

Okin, Susan Moller (1999), *Is Multiculturalism Bad for Women?* Princeton, NJ: Princeton University Press.

Pels, D. (2003), *De geest van Pim: Het gedachtegoed van een politieke dandy*. Amsterdam: Anthos.

Prins, B. (2004), *Voorbij de onschuld. Het debat over integratie in Nederland*. Amsterdam: Van Gennep.

Scheffer, P. (2000), 'Het multiculturele drama', *NRC Handelsblad*, 29 January 2000. Translated in 2003 as: 'The Land of Arrival', in R. Cuperus, K. Duffek & J. Kandel (eds.), *The Challenge of Diversity. European Social Democracy Facing Migration, Integration and Multiculturalism*, 23-30. Innsbruck: Studienverlag.

Snel, E. (2003), *De vermeende kloof tussen culturen*. Enschede: Twente University.

Stolcke, V. (1995), 'Talking Culture. New Boundaries, New Rhetorics of Exclusion in Europe?', *Current Anthropology* 26 (1): 1-23.

Vermeulen, H. (1992), 'De cultura. Een verhandeling over het cultuurbegrip in de studie van allochtone groepen', *Migrantenstudies* 8: 14-31.

Vermeulen, H. (2000), 'Introduction: The Role of Culture in Explanations of Social Mobility' in H. Vermeulen & J. Perlmann (eds.), *Immigrants, Schooling and Social Mobility*, 1-21. Basingstoke/London: Macmillan.

Wansink, H. (2004), *De erfenis van Fortuyn. De Nederlandse democratie na de opstand van de kiezers*. Amsterdam: Meulenhof

Wikan, U. (1999), 'Culture: A New Concept of Race', *Social Anthropology* 17 (1): 57-64.

Wikan, U. (2002), *Generous Betrayal. Politics of Culture in the New Europe*. Chicago: University of Chicago Press.

Wolf, E.R. (1982), *Europe and the People without History*. Berkeley: University of California Press.

6 Family Dynamics, Uses of Religion and Inter-Ethnic Relations within the Portuguese Cultural Ecology

Susana Bastos and José Bastos

The Relevance of Family in the Context of Inter-Ethnic Material and Moral Competition

In post-colonial Europe, immigration can be represented as a partially uncontrolled historical process that occurs in a historically organised world (Wallerstein 1973), with geo-strategic, political, economic, techno-logical, and identity hierarchies, competitions and vulnerabilities. This process of reversed colonisation (Ballard 2003), based upon, and rein-forcing, the collapse of empires, has brought once more to the fore a kind of group identity competition that was supposedly surpassed. This competition develops at a moral level, through the comparison of sev-eral types of socio-historical dynamics (gender and intergenerational re-lations, values about desired or undesirable performances and rela-tional patterns, different uses of religions, etc.), as well as at the mate-rial and political level, through processes of inter-group and interpersonal competition oriented towards obtaining a certain amount of social power, which threaten and transform established hierarchies (Leach 1954).

In this framework, different types of families, with different types of gender and intergenerational relations, making different uses of 'com-munity' connections and religiosity as a cultural asset, in different cul-tural ecologies typical of different 'receptive' countries, encounter dif-ferent types of economic and inter-ethnic opportunities and support different types of pressures to social integration and 'moral accultura-tion' or to racist marginalisation or exclusion. With their rituals, values and tensions, families and webs between families also provide a signifi-cant scenario of negotiations to maintain or change specific 'cultural' differences. The process of growing and relative emancipation of juve-niles requires never-ending decisions and negotiations about changing degrees of autonomy and responsibility in different shifting levels (edu-cational patterns, school performances, management of sexuality and violence, equilibration of intra-family and peer relations, economic needs and opportunities, etc.), which introduce instability inside families. At the same time, inter-ethnic and inter-strata comparison of duties, controls and liberties, namely in school, frequently introduces the construction of vulnerable, non-homogeneous and conflictive solutions and strategies of cultural continuity and transformation, since different and incompatible interests are at stake. Moving in different social fields, men and women, young and old, have different opportunities, powers and interests, and relate to locals at different inter-ethnic levels. Internal cultural change or continuity can be interesting to some of them and very menacing to others. The family, and the social actors who comprise it, can therefore become a focus for change (in a hegemonic or divergent direction) or for resistance to change. It may seek closure or openness, become defensive or confrontational, or try to change the dominant other's perspective.

In the present paper, our objectives are:
- To show that the arena of inter-ethnic relations in Portugal is, in many aspects, significantly different from that of many Northern European countries, namely in the fact that there is little use of and importance given to a public debate oriented towards the promotion of forms of ethic imperialism (e.g. in *Anthropology News* November 2006), a debate that contradicts relational policies of tolerance of diversity, respect for family and ethnic intimacy, avoidance of conflicts and diplomatic negotiation, usually shared by the ethnic groups who have enjoyed a long participation in the Portuguese cultural ecology;
- To de-homogenise the arena of inter-ethnic relations in Portugal by showing that, underneath a largely shared collective identity representation, which is to be read more as an identity ideal used as an imaginary point of convergence, different class and ideological segments develop different inter-family and inter-ethnic strategies;
- To demonstrate, on the basis of previous research (Bastos & Bastos 2006), that different ethnic groups in Portugal have different types of family dynamics, which form part of different types of resort to ethnically organised communities and churches, different forms of empowerment of men, women, and young people, and a culturally patterned organisation of their respective expectations, strategies, and relations, as well as different forms of using sexuality and imposing its selective repression; all these dimensions are articulated among themselves and are used in a significant form in inter-ethnic comparison with the objective of emphasising the imagined moral superiority of each group.

Three Dynamics Organising Families in a Specific Cultural Ecology

Comparative research among six ethnic groups living in the Lisbon metropolitan area[1] enabled us to trace three different types of family dynamics. We define types of 'family dynamics' as specific modes of articulation between gender relations, intergenerational relations, 'community' relations, religious/moral relations with values or personified transcendental entities (as gods and demons), and inter-ethnic relations developed through history. These types of family dynamics are often recognised by a significant part of the members of the group. However, while certain dynamics are considered as ideal and/or a source of honour, prestige and moral superiority, others exist which may be felt as true but relatively problematic and/or even as a source of shame and humiliation. Thus, a family dynamic pattern can be conscious or repressed, congruent with dominant ideals more apparent within the older generations or (apparently) deviant or contra-ideal, affirmed or denied, stable or unstable, more or less confronted with alternatives and accepted or not by the main representatives of the group values. At the same time, within a migratory context, a family dynamic pattern can be seen as congruent or conflictive with the dominant or hegemonic values accepted in the cultural ecologies of the recipient group.

These three types of family dynamics have been differentiated by socio-cultural and symbolic primacy given, in two cases, to the unity of families, based either in male domination or in the sacralisation of 'mothers' (human and divine), and in a last case, by the (covert) primacy given to the early erotic emancipation of male and female adolescents, an emancipation that opens the way to a battle between the sexes in adulthood, assuming different forms in different contexts.

The two types promoting family unity are related to, and have in common, the defence of closed communities, supported by ethnic churches[2] or a strict endo-group 'law', promoting intergenerational stratification, endogamy, arranged or negotiated marriages and an ideal of multiple or extended family.

The first type (FD 1) is oriented towards masculine primacy and the more or less violent control by the family of the sexuality of married and adolescent women. Clearly recognised and affirmed by the group as a practised ideal (with few known deviants), it is associated with 'honour', used to assert moral superiority over the dominant recipient group and reacts badly to change, since, as an ideal, it is supposed to be 'natural' and timeless. In official terms, it is an admired pattern which however tolerates a certain amount of rebellion, which the group tries to control through different strategies. In our sample, Sikhs[3] and Portuguese Gypsies present two different cultural forms of this family dynamic. Assertions like 'women must be controlled by their fathers and husbands, to defend the honour of men, families and the community', 'men always have the last word, women should just obey' or 'girls should marry early, therefore they must not study too long' strongly differentiate these groups from those with the other two types of family dynamics.

The second type (FD 2) is based on a much more ambiguous cultural dynamic, since gender idioms and religion suggest two simultaneous aspects: non-violent male 'natural' dominance, inside the community and the family, and the apparent submission of wives and young females; while at the same time, also emphasising the centrality of strong religious and sacred 'mothers', a dimension which is accepted by children, young couples and even by the husbands of those 'mothers' and a large part of male believers. Portuguese Hindus are the most prominent representatives of this dynamic, followed by Portuguese Ismailis, while Portuguese Sunnis of Indian descent stay 'betwixt and between' these two first family dynamics. Assertions like 'women are more religious than men' and 'you don't need to go to the temple to be religious', in the case of Hindus, and 'most of my friends are Portuguese', in the three cases, are strongly affirmed by them.

The third type (FD 3), developed by a significant number of Cape Verdean families of our sample, can be expressed in three different and non-congruent levels: an ideal (and semi-official) level of 'respected' male and gerontocratic primacy, recognised as dominant in the past (in communitarian spaces of the Cape Verdean Islands), which was compatible with the Catholic ideals of the Portuguese colonialists and missionaries as well as with the Cape Verdean bourgeoisie (identified with their colonisers); a more violent and eroticised form of primacy of young male adults (associated to the popular 'knife' crimes and the control of circumscribed 'popular' areas of the public space), which turns the facts of male promiscuity, Don Juanism and polygamy into non-overtly accepted elements; and, thirdly, an even less recognised strategy of emancipation of young girls, through erotic resources and assets, deviant flirtation, young pregnancies, multiple affairs and adultery. Although accompanied by an apparently very strong familial conflict (which can include vehement threats of expulsion and/or physical punishment), the first pregnancy soon turns into the acceptance of 'facts' (grandchildren are looked after by their grandmothers) and, last but not least, the emancipation of the young mother. In this new phase, the girl can give birth to a series of children of different absent young fathers. This affirmation of the erotic social capital of young females and their sexual autonomy can also continue after marriage. Matriarchal alliance between mothers (in most cases abandoned by their partners, due to divorce or male emigration) and daughters gives family leadership to middle-aged women, reinforces gender wars and contributes to produce a selective alliance between young boys and their maternal family members (or to react against this female primacy with an outburst of 'machismo' and Don Juanism). Ambivalently recognised by several Cape Verdean interlocutors, these two covert levels ('machismo' and the unnamed sexual emancipation of very young women since puberty) structure gender relations and have strong consequences at the intergenerational level. In our samples, Cape Verdeans score very low in the type of assertions that characterise the family dynamics that support the organisation of strong communities and very high in accusations of racism against the white Portuguese (but always after the Portuguese Gypsies).

Gerontocratic Male Domination

'Men always have the last word, women should just obey'

'In Gypsy Law, Lacha [shame] is almost like death'

Settled in Portugal since the sixteenth century, almost 50 per cent of the Portuguese Gypsies[4] live dispersed throughout the country. Obeying the Gypsy Law, they 'have no chiefs' and prefer to live among the 'Lords' (Senhores, signifying the Portuguese), not with other Gypsies.

In the absence of any politico-religious foundation, the protection of male honour emerges as the main identity organiser of the sub-group of Portuguese Gypsies which we labelled 'traditional'. These display non-organised forms of religion, close to the 'Portuguese popular religion' (Espírito Santo 1983), a mixture of non-practising Catholicism and cults associated with ancestral spirits, possession, prophecy and witchcraft.

This type of protection of male and extended family honour is mainly expressed in the violent defence of endogamy, female virginity, fidelity of wives and the social death of widows, making operative the ideal that a woman should belong sexually to a single man, in the period between leaving her parents' home and widowhood, which is to be 'observed' until her death, in permanent mourning (during which she is to dress in black, cut her hair off with scissors and wear a scarf over it).

At 27, I became a widow, in this state we are abandoned, we have no one, even the community looks at us in a different way, we no longer have any value in the community, and I miss having a companion ... at 27, cutting my hair and covering myself in black from head to toe, let's say it's not easy.

Education in these ideals is very asymmetrical: the virginity of daughters must be defended at all costs, even resorting to physical violence, while sons, who have much greater sexual freedom, must be kept from drug addiction, alcoholism and thievery but are encouraged to sleep with *paias* ('white' Portuguese girls). This would therefore be a tradition of 'respect', which in ancient times used to approximate Gypsies to the Portuguese in a similar morality, based upon the monitoring of modesty, honour and respect (i.e. fearful obedience of the young to the older and of women to men); a tradition of 'respect' which the Portuguese 'unduly left behind'. Gypsies therefore picture themselves as being the representatives of a moral tradition based upon respect and sexual dignity which used to characterise the society of the *Senhores* ('the Lords').

Physical violence erupts in close relations between fathers and unmarried daughters and between spouses, with 'normal' aggression of wives; but it can also emerge in marriages, between families and even clans, once marriages (often arranged marriages between cousins) are contracts of honour, which must not be broken. Once the marriage is agreed upon, the groom is not allowed to reject the bride (and maintain his honour); in exchange, parents of the bride have full responsibility for guarding her virginity until the wedding night, when it will be ritually verified by a widow (the *ajuntaora*), representative of her mother-in-law, who will keep its proof (the 'flowers') as treasure.

> They always call me for weddings, because I know about honour. It is the most important thing in the world, the most beautiful! Virginity, which is honour, is seen when I show the *pañuello*[5] where everybody may see the flowers [spots of blood] that the mother-in-law asked for, because she is the custodian of her daughter-in-law's honour, together with the other women, if any. It can be very bad when there is no virginity, then we have *lacha* [shame] for all the family, what a shame, my god! ... Nothing, nothing is as valuable as our honour ... It is almost like death, if there is *lacha* ... Gypsies still nurture great hate, which leads certain families to have *contrários* ['opposites']. For example, if a girl cheated, it would result in a lot of serious problems ... I had to escape to Mozambique because someone wanted to kill me, my husband and one of my sons, it's such disgrace, you can never be safe, always on the run ... This would also happen if a widow were to remarry, she'd make 'opposites' ... I don't want to change. I will not change, it would be a disappointment. Thank God, I'm 100 per cent Gypsy! (Widow, near her sixties)

Despite this, the bride – in agreement with her parents – has the right to break off the contract, reject her perspective groom (*dar cabaças*) and allow a new matrimonial contract to be drawn up. However, the loss of virginity, since it implies the infringement of a contract of honour, may have devastating consequences: extended families become '*contrárias*' (opposites), and the bride's family may have to run from the region and possibly even from the country (to Brazil, or Mozambique, etc.), leaving businesses and properties behind. Should any of its members be located and discovered by a member of the offended groom's family, they may be killed, thus giving rise to a cycle of deaths and 'blood feuds' which may continue for years.[6] An interpersonal conflict is therefore interpreted as a conflict between extended families and even clans (*raças*).

On the other hand, family union and cohesion also extend well beyond the nuclear family. Each child born is wanted and received not just by its parents, but by the whole extended family; if a member of the family needs help/support (for example, when they are in hospital or in jail), the extended family comes together, and systematically accompanies its member. Wherever the parents go (markets, fairs), the children will follow (frequently abandoning school), and this indicates a certain separation anxiety between parents and their offspring and an early initiation of children to adult roles. However, this strong bond with both the nuclear and extended family – which attaches little value to emancipation and the autonomy of the subject – is matched by a pattern of child socialisation that fiercely encourages omnipotence and spontaneity in the male child.

This family dynamic is highly compatible with the use of religion. Therefore, it is not possible to ignore certain effects produced by the recent segmentation of Portuguese Gypsies through processes of conversion of some thousands to an ethnic sect (namely the Church of Philadelphia, but also to 'Christ for Everybody', etc.) One of these, openly accepted by the members of the sects, is the 'Christianisation' of Gypsies, the last 'pagans' in Europe. It is marked by the end of visits to ('white' Portuguese) witches, now equated to representatives of the devil. This reduction of socially accepted 'transcendental' female power, traditionally used as an asset in inter-ethnic relations, shows that the reduction of male physical and social violence is countered by a concomitant repression of females' symbolic powers and violence.

Another effect of conversion lies in the elimination of non-Christian Gypsy habits, namely convincing men to resist the temptation of gambling, alcohol, drugs, the violent intimidation or aggression of women, drug trafficking, and especially the 'Law of Opposites' (concerning the infraction of pledges, and of debts of honour). A third – and no less important – effect is the reduction of discrimination against 'others' (*paios*,[7] 'blacks', etc.), and the 'openness' to the Portuguese 'Lords'.

> You are asking how could a Gypsy, after someone killed his mother, forgive those who did it? If a Gypsy had killed one of my sons, and I was not involved with God's business, of course, I would have to kill him, even if it took me a hundred years, and if I didn't kill him, I would kill his son, or his son's son. Tell me how such a transformation can happen to a Gypsy without such help! ... I am being open to you, we are the ones who are opening up the Gypsies to you ... we are the ones who are opening up the Gypsy community, which is very, very closed to the rest of society. (Shepherd of the Philadelphia Church)

> Religion has changed the Gypsy man very much ... The Evangelical Gypsy avoids certain places, he cannot go to certain marriages, they cannot drink, they don't drink, they only spend time with each other, those who are religious, and that's it ... They have more 'dough', are more quiet, are not mixed up with certain things, certain ways of life, they do not go here and there, they only spend time with each other. And even if we offend them, they don't pay us any attention, they forgive us ... turn their back, 'may Our Lord bless you', and leave. They see things differently, think differently. (Middle-aged man)

These processes allow the 'converted' segments to appear 'superior' to the large majority of 'traditional' Gypsies and, with less ambivalence, to stress the fact that 'they are Portuguese, but of a different religion'. The wish to put an end to 'evil' (criminal violence) and to become closer to the 'Portuguese' is central in the process of Gypsy religious conversion. However, and despite the clear desire to open up to other Portuguese, conversion to certain churches (namely, the Church of Philadelphia), strengthens – now in the name of the Christian message – the control of female virginity and the early withdrawal of pubertal girls from school, in order to avoid negative contact with *paio* young men.

'In the Sikh community, the greatest problem is that when the girls go to school here, they do not do as we wish'

The main migratory flows of Sikhs in Portugal (unofficial figures point to 5,000-7,000 people) reveal a number of patterns. The largest group has migrated directly from the Punjab to Europe since the early 1990s, especially after 1996; at the same time, a second group came from different regions of the Indian subcontinent (Jammu-Kashmir, Haryana); and a third, smaller group from other nuclei of the Sikh diaspora (namely, the UK and the US). The expensive usage of informal 'agents' frequently results in complex migratory routes, including instances of physical violence, detention and deportation.

Upon arrival, the majority becomes employed in temporary jobs in the area of construction, in the case of men, and cleaning (domestic or industrial) for the women; some men and women find work in restaurants (as kitchen helpers, or waiters). Some later succeed in opening their own business, e.g. telecommunications (shops where mobile phones are sold and charged), and restaurants and/or bars, frequently in partnership with family members or *Gujarati* Hindus.

Recently settled in Portugal, Sikhs represent an introverted and almost invisible and unknown 'community'. They come 'from India', as others in Portugal that have an Indian origin and differentiate themselves by their belonging to diverse religious communities (Hindus, Sunnis, Ismailis) or social webs (Catholic Goanese), but their 'Sikhness' becomes their main identity, supported by a specific ethno-religious communitarism and a history of inter-religious confrontation (used to construct inter-group boundaries) that makes 'Indianness' partially irrelevant for most identity purposes. But at the same time, in the Portuguese context, Sikhs also opt for a strategy of religious invisibility, while maintaining a 'modern' appearance in their public presentation.[8]

As among the Portuguese Gypsies, the insistence upon the fact that the honour of men (*izzat*), vulnerable and needing constant confirmation, depends on the sexual, matrimonial and family behaviour of the women they are related to is maximised in the worldview of our Sikh interlocutors. Female transgression of certain rules brings 'shame upon her', 'ruins the name of the family' and, according to a number of accounts, in certain contexts may result in forms of violence against the woman.

Izzat also re-emerges when Sikhs speak about the relations between Portuguese men and women in general. The main interpretation is that, in Portugal, 'women boss their husbands about'. Even those who recognise that 'in India too, women call the shots', note that Sikh women reach their goals (as the Portuguese do), by way of a manner of acting and speaking which does not question or threaten the authority of their husbands ('they ask permission', 'they speak politely', etc.) The Sikh perception of intergenerational relations in the Portuguese context also tends to underline the lack of hierarchical respect on the part of the children towards their parents, but also blames the weakness of the latter as producers of authority.

What currently worries Sikh parents most is the impact that a prolonged presence in Portugal may have upon their children, and especially their daughters. 'The young ones have a new head', they say. They mean that the younger generation constructs new idioms, that they can become autonomous in relation to parental expectations and authority.

> Now, it's different for my daughter, she will stay here five or ten years, she's young, and then she will like it here, and not want ... to go back to India ... She wants to stay here. Because she will have friends here, that's the reason. The wife always wants to stay close to the husband, the daughter doesn't. If she stays a long time, then she will not like being with her father. Now I have been here ten years, my daughter she has studied here for ten years, and if I go to France, she will not want to go to France, she will say: 'I studied here, I speak Portuguese, I want to stay here'. So I still have to think about how I'm going to do this, will I leave the daughter here, or send her to study in Britain, or to study there, in India ... because Portuguese is not my *language* [in English in the original] ... My language is Indian and English. Maybe she studies in England, then she goes to India, and she speaks to everybody in English. Now, if she studied here for ten years, when she goes there to India, she cannot speak to anyone. Because no one speaks Portuguese. When she is of school age, five, six, or seven years, I send her to India, and she will stay there at a boarding house ... To India, to study, in New Delhi or Chandigar. Chandigar is a good city. It has many... it is a *discipline* [in English in the original], it has a good *discipline* [in English in the original], good schools. Studying there is very good, the wife will stay here close to me, and she [the daughter] will study there in Chandigar, then mother and father *will go visit* [In English in the original], to see how she is studying there. I would like her to study in India, it is much better. Because there you have... my culture is different. The culture is different, right? She stays here, she will... if she studies here, she will make friends, and all that. No, in India she cannot. She studies there, what I want, she will do it. When she goes to school here, she does not do as I wish. (Man, in his forties)

The hypotheses expressed by the parents themselves – 'if my son told me he has a Portuguese girlfriend' or 'if my daughter were to look for a friend before marrying' – show that they recognise that their off-spring could and may become autonomous subjects. This preview of the individualisation of the young is a threat to tradition, goes against religion, and offends the prestige of the family, not just in Portugal but, crucially, in the Punjab, and it may even become an obstacle to a possible return to the motherland and the very continuation of new migratory projects within the family.

However, the main source of vulnerability for Sikh identity in the migratory context resides, as we have already hinted, in the daughters' individualisation process. The continuation of their education and the development of inter-ethnic relationships encourage the orientation of the girls towards emancipation. To paraphrase the words of our interlocutor, when 'the girls go to school here, they do not do as we wish' and 'if they stay here long enough ... they do not want to live with their parents-in-law in India or go with their husbands to any other country'. That is, they do not merely threaten the power of men upon women, but also the male migratory narrative that 'what's most important to a Sikh woman is not that she likes to live in Portugal, France, Britain or America, it is just that she likes her husband and stays close to him'.

The Secret Power of Mothers

'In our community, women are more religious than men'

Hindus, but also Sunnis and Ismaili interlocutors of Indo-Mozambican origin, represent the second type of family dynamics, in which male dominance is attenuated by the powers attributed to women, in the role of mothers.

During the second half of the nineteenth century, the forefathers of these groups (mainly originating from Kutch, Khatiawar and Surat, in Gujarat, and also coming from Diu and Daman, in the former Portuguese State of India) migrated to Mozambique. Their main strategies for professional insertion lay in trade between the interior regions and urban centres (*cantineiro*[9] commerce) and – especially after the 1930s – in high-street commerce, while the Hindu castes of Diu, masons mostly, found employment in the construction industry. A small number of Hindu and Muslim families also took advantage of the economic boom of the 1960s to expand their activities to the industrial sector (Bastos 2005). After the decolonisation of Mozambique, these groups underwent periods of great identity insecurity and (in significant numbers) migrated to Portugal, where they experienced a rapid and successful economic and social insertion (Bastos 1990; Malheiros 1996; Bastos & Bastos 2001).

We can estimate that there are currently 9,000 to 11,000 Sunnis and 6,000 to 8,000 Ismailis of Indian origin as well as 8,000 to 10,000 Hindus living in Portugal. Portugal's integration with the European Community (in 1986), the opportunities for professional improvement and education, and the social assistance offered by the United Kingdom significantly increased the number of Portuguese Sunnis and Hindus settling in England (London, Leicester, etc.) between 1998 and 2000. Since 2001, migration continued at an even higher level thanks to the global context of economic crisis and labour market contraction, the effects of which were more marked in Portugal than in many EU countries (Bastos & Bastos 2005, 2007).

Affirming the Powers of Hindu Motherhood

'To my children, I am more than a goddess'

Among Portuguese Hindus, the 'superiority' of women in the use of religious and magical resources, and the representation of the female body itself as a privileged locus for the earthly manifestation of divine power[10] is very frequently assumed. Already in Mozambique, Hindu women learned to officiate religious performances which were traditionally carried out by male specialists in their homeland, including *havans* (e.g. those dedicated to the ancestors of their husbands, or to the Hindu mother goddesses), and took it upon themselves to transmit the basic oral texts of popular Hinduism, which included the *Satyanarayan Katha*, the *Bhagavata Gita*, and the *Ramayana*.

Apart from this ritual specialisation, they also recreated 'Little Traditions'[11] that matched the everyday forms of resistance mobilised by their Gujarati non-migrant counterparts against several local systems of dominance (Bastos 2001, 2006). Namely, some of them (of different castes and socio-economic statuses) recreated direct means of communication with the Hindu goddess through possession. Reconstructed in post-colonial Portugal, female possession interferes with virtually every relationship of the women involved: husband, family members, other people of the same or different castes, ancestors, demons, goddesses, etc. We could say that its most interesting aspect is exactly the way in which it renegotiates the taken-for-grantedness of different power relations.

> My husband forced me to have intercourse, *Mataji* [Hindu mother goddess] did not like it, and I ended up suffering ... My mother-in-law put those things into his head. Who has ever heard of a husband kneeling before his wife? But at those times, it's not me. It's the *Ma* ... One day, the wife of my husband's boss, a rich *Lohana* who owned various warehouses, called me. She had much faith in the *Ma*, and she was healed ... Only after that my mother-in-law and my sisters-in-law believed. (Hindu woman)

One of the consequences of this overlapping of female gender and symbolic power among Portuguese Hindus seems to be the neutralisation (to a certain degree) of masculine idioms which insist upon the need for male control over women, since they are supposed to derive their self-control from the intense personal bond they form with the higher powers of married or virgin divine Mothers.

Denying Stereotypes of Gender Oppression

'Muslim women are very privileged'

Indo-Mozambican Hindus and Sunnis are the first to recognise clear asymmetries between women and men among themselves; however, they frequently justify these as the consequence of cultural and religious traditions based on well-defined gender roles and assumptions that have been vital in the education of the emerging generations, to keep the latter from experiencing processes of descending social assimilation and to the preservation of community 'respect' for the family and its name. In parallel, the dissociation of religion from all acts of violence, oppression and the exploitation of women and, as a consequence, the conceptualisation of the condition of women as an issue relating to a wider social context, the attribution of certain 'excesses' (in the name of religion) to specific men, and the appeal to a universal religion against historical and cultural specificities of the Hindu and Muslim world are frequently reiterated.

> Muslim women are very privileged, despite what they say. They say Muslim women are oppressed – they're not. Firstly, in the education of their children, because most Muslim women have the privilege of staying at home and educating their children the way they see fit, a privilege many Portuguese women do not have ... Secondly, Muslim husbands give great importance to their wives, because we are the mothers of their children. We take care of the organisation of the home, and the education of children. We are the ones who prepare them to become good managers of the family business. We are very privileged, it is well worth it to be a Muslim woman. (Sunni woman)

According to the narrative of numerous female interlocutors, the control imposed by the woman's female in-laws (mother-in-law and the wives of the husband's elder brothers) upon their lives is actually stronger than the supposed power of the men in their families. This shows that any discourse which tends to pit men against women, in general requires a deeper analysis. It is not therefore surprising that a number among them define themselves as privileged in comparison to Portuguese women.

Their 'privileged' condition is also emphasised when they compare themselves with other Muslim women living in diverse European contexts, namely with their British peers, whose daily experience they know very well. Recognising in themselves religious moderation, lack of interest in arguments and factional struggles, and in the presentation of their identity as Portuguese of Muslim religion, the main criticism they direct to some of their 'sisters' relates to the ways in which some of them reconstruct, experience and enunciate their religious difference in non-Muslim contexts of migration. Other than closure upon themselves and ethno-religious sectarianism, the act of making Muslim identity visible – and, in particular, the issue of the veil (and of full-body veiling) – is a frequent theme in their comparative narratives.

> In Leicester, most girls cover their heads, especially if they live in a Muslim area. Some use the veil because of their faith, because it has a special significance to them. But there also are those who are forced by the parents to veil completely ... But these same girls get to school and they may change clothes and go around in miniskirts. There is such repression here in certain families, that's morbid and is not at all part of Islam ... I do not feel that the veil is an obligation ... I am very proud to say that I am a Muslim, but I do not need to cover my head. (Sunni, young woman)

> As I usually say, a Muslim who lives in Portugal, who has lived in Mozambique, he has Satan in his eyes, in a manner of speaking. I'll explain ... In my religion, we usually say that woman, when she ventures outside the house, she is turned into Satan, because with her sensuality she may ensnare whoever she wishes ... I need to see unveiled people ... Saying this is a sin for a Muslim like me, but it is true. And if many of us prefer life in Portugal, this is because we like to have in our eyes exactly that which each person sees. (Sunni, young woman)

Following their voices, the veil used because of the obligation/repression of family and community – which so frequently is a catalyser of identity compartmentalisations and divisions – and the veil chosen as an expression of personal faith, inscribed in a process of autonomisation from family, community, and other non-Muslim spheres, are two situations which are mostly associated with the British context. More common in Portugal, the absence of the veil is often justified as the result of a much more interiorised and intimate relation with god and religion, which does not need to be exhibited. At the same time, the rejection of full-body veiling is also articulated with a Portuguese family-based pattern of interpersonal relations that would stimulate a non-malignant intention to see, be seen and see oneself.

Exceeding Hindus and Sunnis in their identification with 'modern' and 'progressive' values, our Ismaili interlocutors (both male and female) unsurprisingly emphasise equality between men and women, recognise and accept the possibility of divorce and describe parental investment in the educational and professional evolution of their daughters as equal – or even superior – to that of their sons.

Denying the Stereotype of Intergenerational Conflict

'I like my family to be happy and proud of me'

Young Sunni and Hindu people tend to accept the moral and religious authority of their families; however, they justify their acceptance in the idiom of love, the fear of losing parental love, and the emotional idioms of 'feeling proud of' and 'avoiding disappointing'. This indicates significant transformations in the affective structure of their families, in particular the alteration of the emotional model characterised by asceticism, distance and divesting of feelings, which was dominant, even in the recent past, between parents and their children.

> In our community, we don't have those terrible clashes between parents and children. Parents always exert quite a lot of pressure, especially on daughters, but after all the behaviour of the children is good thanks to the parents, isn't it, and the children also want their parents to feel happy and proud of them. (Sunni young man)

> I may very well be here and behave just like a Portuguese, have all the habits, even my way of eating, dress, speech, but then I can go to my community and eat with my hands, have the conversations I do with them, dress in a different way, have a more respectful behaviour towards the elders and especially towards men ... You're with your uncles and you cover your belly and do not wear spaghetti straps and tell them you agree with whatever they say, and then you change completely, because you do not actually agree, you just act that way temporarily. I'm there, with my aunts who say that their children may go to school, but no way may they have white friends, they're not compatible, and then I

have lots of friends. Being comfortable with both situations, without creating any conflict with the family, while remaining myself, may require some management effort, but it does not confuse me ... Marrying a non-Muslim, no, no, I know what my family wishes, so I will have to give in. (Sunni young woman)

My parents have no idea that I smoke, that I drink alcoholic drinks and eat pork, even though I do try to avoid it ... They also don't know that I have already had a boyfriend, who wasn't Is-maili. Why disappoint them? My mother may be more accepting, but for my father it would be very frustrating, having a daughter married to someone of a different religion, it would never work. (Ismaili young woman)

These young people do not picture themselves as rebels, but they do reveal that they consider themselves different in comparison to older generations in a number of ways. They display a more individualised, thoughtful and critical exploration of religion, they select 'what is or isn't essential' in their religious practice, in the production of different interpretations of religious 'authority', in their involvement with religious models which may be unlike (or even opposed to) those of their families and of most of their communities, in the significant freedom (internal and external) to compartmentalise (to a greater or lesser extent) their lives, in the transformation of some of the most conservative values of their parents into strategic arguments to promote their self-emancipation and, in particular, in their production and usage of idioms (comprehensible and matched by their non-Muslim and non-Hindu peers, teachers, etc.) which enable them to live their religious 'difference' in the Portuguese public space.

Erotic Competition and Teenage Motherhood: Mother-Daughter Complicities

Unlike Sikhs, 'traditional' Gypsies, Sunnis and Hindus of Indo-Mozambican origin, 'traditional' Cape Verdeans, with their Christian-inspired popular religiosity and a lack of congregational organisation, do not organise their social relations around the joint articulation of male domination upon young women and male gerontocracy. On the contrary, our fieldwork brings to light a rapid ascension to adulthood through early sexual activity and pregnancy (itself accepted, albeit in an ambivalent fashion).

This process is ritualised in three phases: early clandestine sexual experiences, shared among the post-pubertal strata; the coming to the fore of the 'fact' of pregnancy, met with violent reactions by the elders (the father, if there is one at home; the mother, in female-centred homes), with physical punishment of the young girl (and, in certain cases, the attempt to force a marriage with the young 'father'); and thirdly, family reconciliation, whereby the parental role is performed by the elder generation and the young girl is freed openly to take on her sexual freedom, which tends to lead her to a series of new partners and new pregnancies, without the constitution of stable relationships.

These trends (based in the adult fatalistic perception that 'young people just want to have sex, and don't think of the consequences') result in relatively high percentages of single mothers, possibly with children of different fathers, who may be looked after by their grandmothers who function as substitute mothers. What is relevant in this ritualised 'crisis' process is that the elders continue to manifest public indignation and to produce physical punishment 'as if' they didn't expect the sequence, thus exempting the older generation from an impending 'accusation' of inability to control their youngsters and incorrect performance of their 'duties'.

> Africans don't speak of such things with their children ... there is a taboo in the house. Kids speak with their friends outside, but not with their parents, No. Who is going to tackle such a conversation with their parents? ... If anyone said that they needed money to buy a condom, or the pill, it would be a disgrace in the house, because it means the child already has a boyfriend, that the child is no longer a virgin!

> In the neighbourhood, there are many young women who at fourteen already have children, they just show up pregnant and we don't know who the fathers are. Usually, it is always the woman who is branded. I think that young people just want to have sex, and don't think of the consequences. They do it and take no precautions, they end up pregnant and know that the parents will be angry, but will not kick them out. There's young people who have children and don't care about them, they know that the grandmother will take care of them. I know of a woman who has around twelve grandchildren in her house, of various children.

> Look, there's always casual affairs, the problem is that, if it's a man who is married and goes with another woman, he will be called a 'stud', and he accepts the label, he's a *malhão* [stallion, stud], while if it's a woman cheating on a man, we all know the name everybody will call her, don't we?

In this context, adolescent sexuality is widespread; virginity and mono-gamy are not highly prized. Socialisation, in the lowest strata, is pro-cessed in peer groups who occupy, and in certain cases control, the public space of social housing estates or slums, marking it and the sur-rounding spaces with their gang activities: graffiti, music (rap, hip-hop, etc.) and dances, in rupture with the traditional Cape Verdean culture of their parents (Cidra 2002). These adolescent cultural productions, in line with North American pop culture, spread by the media and by interaction in schools, match the process of changing relations between generations and genders, emancipating girls and adolescents in gener-al from the 'authority' and educational pressure of teachers and par-ents. At the same time, they give to these young Cape Verdeans a cer-tain prestige and a generational leadership, in certain Portuguese social segments, as the producers, promoters or cultural importers of graffiti, rap, suggestive dances (such as *funaná*), expressive revolt and 'a philo-sophy of pleasure, freedom and the good life' in the present.

This form of Cape Verdean adolescence is compatible with, and gives voice to, one of two processes wrestling for the space of family rela-tions in Portugal; the other is a much more traditional one, based upon intergenerational authority and respect for parents and teachers, the defence of the 'unity' of families and the reproduction, with contextual variants, or promotion of social integration, acceptance by 'society at large', and affluence, through the primacy of school and professional performances over expressive performances based upon erotic charis-ma, revolt, and sexual performances.

On the other hand, this third type of family dynamic puts mothers at the service of their daughters in families where the place of the male is uncertain or unstable. Based on the alliance of women, it contributes to increasing their identity security and prominence in the education of emerging generations (who however also receive much of their edu-cation from peers and on the street); but it also seems to have conse-quences on the organisation of couples and the family dynamics of subsequent generations. It thus causes feelings of masculine inferior-ity, which are then mobilised, in a reactive vicious circle, to strengthen male individualism and macho posturing.

> Well, in Cape Verde, culture still is a bit chauvinist, isn't it? So the men in Cape Verde have that tradition, they have their wife, and then they have some other women outside the marriage, and many children outside their marriage, I don't know if it's a question of tradition ... because this aspect of the Cape Verdean man is very prominent. Here in Portugal, I don't know if it's so visible, this kind of polygamy ... In Cape Verde, people, in this in-

stance men, set up three or four families, have many children, and this is basically accepted by the Cape Verdean society.

Based on a study by one of our Cape Verdean students (the title of which translates as *Women Who Laugh, Men Who Cry*), we can state that this type of gender war that defeats traditional male dominance is more openly present and apparent in the American diaspora. There, with the support of 'matriarchal' North American cultural ecology (Mead 1948, Erikson 1950), Cape Verdean married women actively seek legal protection and divorce; profiting from the vulnerability induced in the male identity by the 'typical' triad of Don Juanism, polygamy, and violence, these women end up 'laughing' at the affliction of their defeated ex-husbands who lose houses, children, and a significant percentage of their income to support their ex-wives and their new centrality in family life (Gibau 2002).

A result of hyphenated and hybrid identities, more open to a mixed sexuality and hybridisation, this third family dynamic is sometimes modified through the integration of Cape Verdean immigrants in non-ethnic churches which strengthen the role of the masculine figure, the sacred nature of the bond of matrimony, the stability of the monogamous family, as well as the religious control of sexuality within the family.

> Those who were born here are integrated since their childhood in kindergarten, nursery school, or primary school, and then in state schools, and end up learning more of the Portuguese culture. Now we try to transmit to them the values that our parents transmitted to us, and they are the deepest values of our motherland, such as the value of family, respect for the elders, the grandparents, and the new generation has an idea of the nuclear family, its father, mother, and children, while back home we have an idea of the extended family, grandparents, uncles, cousins, etc. These are the values that perhaps our Cape Verdean people are attempting to transmit to this second generation, which is somewhat different, but that comes from the times we live in. (Male, Catholic activist)

> Family is sacrosanct, untouchable, no one should mess with family and the preservation of the home, because family is a divine institution, it was created by God ... no man in his right mind will ever take any decision that may threaten the stability of his family. And that includes adultery. Adultery means to go looking for another woman. That can lead to the destruction of all you built. It takes years to build a happy home, but it takes minutes

to destroy it. Notice that I am speaking of adultery, because it is one of the things that most destroys a home, but there are also drink, drugs, which are other weapons which destroy the home. Adultery begins with an improper look at the woman of another man, or at the man of another woman. (Male, member of the Church of the Nazarene)

Any responsible father is concerned with the future of his son ... Now I am more at rest and peaceful, because my worry was that my daughters could have university diplomas so that they may have worthy employment and not live off the salary of the man they would have later, because a young woman with a university diploma and her own job, if she finds a partner and things do not go well, she will not stay with him and ruin her life. As regrettably I see many women with two or three children at their breast and no proper job to support themselves and their families. (Male, Evangelical church)

However, according to this religious strategy, what is at stake is not the violent control of wives and daughters or the control of male violence; on the contrary, the objective is the libidinal self-control of men, and, in parallel, of women, in the name of the 'will of God'.

From Ethnic Family Dynamics to the Portuguese Cultural Ecology

Those acquainted with the moral debates upon divergent family dynamics in North Europe, who expect the same climate in Portugal, would be disappointed: the dominant pattern of contact with immigrant family dynamics is to adopt a traditional position of juxtaposition without interference. 'Live and let live' could be the motto of this attitude. Invisibility and ignorance of others' 'private' life can, in this context, be also seen as a form of 'respect' for privacy.

The Portuguese, in general, react more to violence than to different patterns of sexuality, gender and intergenerational relations. Therefore, the most pejorative imagery about ethnic groups, present in collective representations of the 'problematic' second generations of African origin living in shantytowns, emphasises juvenile 'delinquency' (fights, robberies, etc.), drug addiction and trafficking. As well as sharing with youths of African origin their alleged connection to drug trafficking (Cunha 2001),[12] Portuguese Gypsies are also perceived as 'aggressive' and 'untrustworthy', and also as 'dangerous' while acting 'unified' (against non-Gypsies). The supposed family cohesion of Gypsies, linked to the illegal activities of some of them, and their relations with non-Gypsies (in markets, hospitals, courts, prisons, etc.), seem to be strongly related to their being perceived as 'aggressive'. It is in a similar sense, that is, as a form of violence, that the question of female genital mutilation has sporadically been featured in the Portuguese media (since certain strata of Guinean Muslims still mutilate their young daughters, in Lisbon or Bissau) but without the same effects.

Similarly, the insignificant crime rate registered among young Portuguese Muslims and Hindus of Indian origin (and their model behaviour in the public space, namely in Portuguese schools) contributes to the construction of their image as people who are 'peaceful', 'hard-working', 'respectful' of the law and of valued public patterns which partially converge with the national image of the 'honest' Portuguese. A positive image that is also related to the crucial role played by Sunni, Ismaili and Hindu elites in the social and economic integration of their communities (Tiesler 2000; Vakil 2004) and mainly to the ways in which those Muslims and Hindus live and communicate their religious 'difference' in public contexts: as 'moderate' believers, largely uninterested in 'factional rivalries' and 'critical of all type of fundamentalisms, religious sectarianisms and radicalisms' (Bastos & Bastos 2006). In this dimension, it is important to point out that Portugal was not affected by the turning of the tide against diversity which has spread across Europe after 9/11. The relation between the (new) Islamic presence in Portugal and Portuguese society did not result either in tension and conflict, or in controversial discourses in the Portuguese public arena, unlike what has happened in other European countries.

AIDS and teenage pregnancies in the case of second generations of African origin, male aggression against young and older women who have broken Gypsy Law, and the relatively high number of deaths resulting from inter-family conflicts are not unknown among certain strata of the Portuguese population. But the Portuguese continue to be ruled by the popular saying *entre marido e mulher, não metas a colher* ('do not interfere between husband and wife'). It is indeed symptomatic that the most radical 'ethical' reaction in inter-ethnic relations has recently been conducted by a web of female academics in social sciences, not against an ethnic group settled in Portugal but against a limited number of wandering Gypsies from Romania, detonated by the fact that young mothers beg in central Lisbon with babies at their breast or sleeping in their arms, a strategy also well known from poor or addicted Portuguese female beggars. With one difference: by repackaging existing, traditional fears of Gypsies (see Bastos, Ibarrola-Armendariz, Sardinha, Westin, & Will 2006; Bastos 2007) in new ethical preoccupations, without any proof young Roma women have been accused of being 'fake mothers' using kidnapped and abused children who should be taken from them by the Portuguese police and child protection services.

On the other hand, the defence of female virginity and certain forms of class endogamy, and what amount to arranged marriages, are not infrequent within the higher strata of Portuguese Catholic elites with aristocratic identifications or ideals (Pedroso de Lima 2003). The prevalence of 'mothers' – associated with an emphasis on the sacred character and benevolence of Our Lady of Heaven, the Virgin Mary (one of the most common names in Portugal, even for males) and which favours the link between the (sacred) Mother and their sons and daughters – continues to be dominant in several bourgeois and rural strata that support the permanent reference to Portugal as a Catholic country. However, covert polygamy, Don Juanism and male promiscuity, gender confrontation, or young unmarried mothers living with the support of their mothers are also present in the lowest strata of the population of rural and suburban Portugal. Until the democratic revolution of 1974, the legal designation of 'son of an unknown father' was banal, even though direct reference to it could be considered an offence to the honour of son and mother (treated as a 'whore'). And in rural Portugal, those young 'abandoned' mothers were accepted and helped by the local population. Social values such as piety and 'respect' (the desire to not be offensive to others) were more relevant than repressive Catholic moralism.

During the twentieth century, a cluster of dimensions has been emphasised by social scientists to justify the creation of a cultural space characterised by practical tolerance of diversity regarding inter-ethnic relations and diverse family dynamics:

i) a special type of education of children, soft and warm, prolonging childhood, basically conducted by women,[13] scarcely interested in the consolidation of character and non-adapted to the 'new organisation of the world' (Poinsard 1911; Lourenço 1978), producing in men a typical 'femininity' (Descamps 1935), that will be defined as a mixture of high need of affiliation associated with a low need for power and positive orientation to others (McClelland 1961), situating the Portuguese at extreme distance from Spaniards (Bastos 2000, 2002);

ii) collectivism (that is, the primacy of solidarity based in familial values extended to neighbours, communities and compatriots) and 'femininity', with low differentiation of sexual roles (Hofstede 1984);

iii) the prevalence of a pacifist stance (Bastos 2000), based upon a 'feministic'/Christian worldview, associated in the press and popular conversation with the *brandos costumes* (soft customs) as well as with the 'accommodating ways' of the Portuguese, ambivalently invoked; but also

iv) an anarchic individualism, which makes the Portuguese react to any kind of organisation of their lives (Dias 1953), accompanied by a soft verbal moralism and acceptance of deviant choices as 'human' (since 'everybody has their weaknesses');

v) and last but not least, the dislike of politics and the systematic denigration of politicians, as well as the quasi-absence of a dynamic civil society looking for militant 'advanced' causes (Marques & Santos 2004).

In return, generations of inter-ethnic conviviality with this 'pacific' cultural ecology seems to create in their former colonial subjects 'Portuguese' ethnic variants that are also characterised by policies of respect, fewer displays of moral, cultural or political dichotomisation, a softened fundamentalism, low active civic participation of immigrants (Albuquerque & Teixeira 2005), political disinterest and the absence of a confrontational stance.[14]

Identifying with their former colonisers (Bastos & Bastos 2005, 2007), Hindus and Muslims who lived for decades in Mozambique and Portugal and in recent years migrate to the UK insist on recognising a characteristic Portuguese cultural ecology, proposing to assume abroad new forms of inter-ethnic sociability that goes beyond politics of arrogance, social parallelism and religious sectarianism.

Mozambican and Portuguese Hindus are very unlike the ones from Kenya, Tanzania, and Uganda. We lived many years with the Portuguese, they with the British... The Mozambicans got many things from the Portuguese, they were still Hindus but also Portuguese, more authentic, more open. The Hindus from the Kenya, Tanzania, and Uganda are more like the British. They may be very nice upfront, but you never know what they're feeling inside. They call us *portuguesiá*, and as a joke, we call them the *londrinos* (Londoners). (Portuguese Hindu in London; Bastos & Bastos 2005: 87)

If I could go back, I would still choose Mozambique. The friendship of the Portuguese was very different from that of the British. The British were pure rulers. In Mozambique, many Portuguese and Indians had personal relationships ... And these differences are still noticeable today. The British in general are more reserved, more rigid. You always have to be thinking in the

words you are going to use, even among Muslims. The Portuguese however are more sociable, more transparent and they like
to joke around. Look, there is a word to sum it all up. The Portuguese, be they Catholics, Muslims, or Hindus, are more familiar.
(Portuguese Muslim in Leicester; Bastos & Bastos 2007: 274)

We are trying to organise a Portuguese club ... for Catholics, Hindus, Muslims, atheists, it doesn't matter ... We are going to get
women and men together in the same room, serve some olives,
cod cakes, Portuguese cheese, *samosas*, and shrimp, and we already contacted some boys who are going to sing *fado*. Imams
here forbid music, but we are going to have music, they insist
on the separation of men and women, but we are going to get
everyone together at the same table. Against religious sectarianism, we are going to get together Catholics, Hindus and Muslims. We are going to mix, to show people here, Muslims or not,
that we have a different way of life. And we are going to speak
Portuguese. (Portuguese Muslim in Leicester; Bastos & Bastos
2007: 278)

Concluding Remarks

Despite this practical tolerance of diversity, insertion within the Portuguese context seems to be particularly threatening to the first family
pattern (FD 1). In particular, mixed and prolonged schooling requires
new forms of family and community control upon the sexuality of
young girls, and new strategies to guarantee endogamy and/or virginity, as is the case of Sikhs –who can send their virgins back to India –
or that of Portuguese Gypsies – who in recent years have been promoting even earlier marriages, intentional school abandonment at puberty,
religious conversion to a 'Gypsy Church' and the reinforcement of processes of antagonistic acculturation (Devereux 1985).
    More akin to the Portuguese cultural ecology, FD 2, protected by the
closure of religiously driven ethnic communities, and the resulting enhanced control of its youngsters, which facilitates concentration upon
studying, endogamy and familial economies, supports a slow affluent
integration partially based on cultural juxtaposition (which some interpret incorrectly as 'ghettoisation'). The success of this form of social insertion leads to the perception, detected in a number of Portuguese
authorities, that a non-institutionalised 'multiculturalist' tolerance respectful of difference is the correct manner in which to respond to the
diversity of family dynamics, thereby treated as a private dimension of
those communities. At the same time, institutionalised 'multicultural-

ism' or political participation, at least within the groups we studied, is not one of the main claims of the communities themselves.

Despite a certain success of the third type of family dynamics among Portuguese adolescents, in schools, due to the lack of community organisation and greater openness to an earlier and uncontrolled mixed sexuality and hybridisation, young African culture in Portugal, represented in this study by Cape Verdeans, is often tainted by perceptions of (juvenile) violence and criminality, a stigma which the Portuguese media still feed. Lower classes of Portuguese, recently migrated from rural areas, with affluent expectations, compete for scarce material and identity resources with the segments of migrant groups of African origin with a descending social insertion. Both share employment in construction and domestic cleaning and compete for the attribution of council houses from the State. Those migrants therefore become dangerous competitors, a situation which stimulates the emergence of a degree of verbal and behavioural racism, especially when an economic crisis is felt (as is currently happening).

Due to the already mentioned Portuguese cultural ecology, such direct and subtle racism in Portugal has not been politically supported by a xenophobic extreme right, given the pressure of cultural ideals which defend idealised identity images of pacifism, family-based civility, non-arrogance, tolerance and inter-ethnic openness (Bastos 2000, 2002). However, these images tend to conceal processes of non-institutionalised forms of racialisation and marginalisation, which are relatively invisible to dominant public opinion and scarcely controlled by governments, courts of law or movements within 'civil society'.

Notes

[1] Carried out in 2004 and 2005, the comparative research focused on the articulation of family dynamics, the use of religious resources and inter-ethnicity in the Lisbon metropolitan area in Portugal. Our methods included a first phase of research, during which five families in each of six main ethnic groups living in Portugal (selected in order to obtain a maximum degree of heterogeneity) were studied with the classic methods of social and cultural anthropology. In the second phase, to increase comparability, we constructed an attitudinal questionnaire (comprising 183 items, mostly directly derived from our fieldwork), which was then administered to 40 subjects from each sub-group (Bastos & Bastos 2006). In this paper, we will mainly use the results of the first phase of research. Ethnic or ethno-religious groups studied were: Sikhs; Ismailis (*Khojas*); Sunnis of Indian origin (dominant in the Central Mosque of Lisbon); Hindus; Gypsies and Cape Verdeans. Gypsies were segmented in Traditional Gypsies (with non-organized religiosity) and in Evangelical Gypsies, associated to the Philadelphia Church (Gypsy Church). Cape Verdeans were segmented in members of the Nazarene Church, of an Evangelical Church, as

practising Catholics and as Traditional Cape Verdeans (with non-organised religiosity). Unless otherwise specified all quotations are from people we interviewed.

2   In this context, we define ethnic churches as churches locally oriented to mono-ethnicity or, in the case of Muslims of Afro-Indian origin, oriented both to the control of the church and its use not only as a place of worship but also as a place of intracultural meeting.

3   The only ethnic group in our sample having no previous contact with the Portuguese cultural ecology, since the other three Asian 'communities' has come mainly from Mozambique, after decolonisation.

4   The Portuguese constitution forbids the counting of subgroups ethnically or religiously defined, and also the organisation of religious or ethnic parties, trying to evade social discrimination of minorities. Different authors calculate their number between 20,000 and 80,000, but the widely accepted figure is approximately 50,000.

5   'Pañuello' literally refers in Spanish to the little white handkerchief used to receive the first blood (the 'flowers') of a young virgin in the ritual of the ajuntamiento (the central part of the Gypsy marriage ritual, when the control of the virginity and the subsequent deflowering of the bride is done by the ajuntaora, an old woman specialised in performing this specific ritual by using her finger enveloped in the pañuello). Portuguese Gypsies speak in Portuguese with a mix of some Spanish and Romani words associated with rituals and those values associated to the Gypsy Law.

6   The 'feud' system of private vengeance (that characterises Finnish and Portuguese Gypsies and also British Romanichels) is opposed by Acton, Caffrey and Mundy (2001: 91) to the 'tribunal' system of the kris (as in the case of Vlach Roma), as two ideal types of Gypsy organisation.

7   Paios (or gadjes) is the current Romani name given by Portuguese Gypsies to the 'white' Europeans, also called senhores (Lords) in more direct and respectful relations.

8   The Portuguese frequently mistake Sikhs for Mozambican 'Indians', who have a strongly positive shared representation, and are therefore not the target of negative public opinion. It is however worth pointing out an exception. Many Hindus describe Sikhs as potential 'threats' to the honour of young Hindu women, and to the respect associated with the name of their families. According to several interlocutors, Sikh immigrants without stay permits not infrequently resort to a strategy of persistent seduction of young Hindu women (or to marriages of convenience with non-Indian women) in the attempt to facilitate their legalisation process in Portugal.

9   The business of the cantineiro included the acquisition and transport of various types of products (peanuts, cashews, cotton, corn, etc.) harvested by the natives to the towns. Locally, cantineiros also sold capulanas – the traditional cloth – and other textiles, basic foodstuffs, 'colonial' wine and other basic goods (kerosene, pots and pans, hammers, nails, knives, etc.)

10 Many informants recall that, in Portugal (as well as in Mozambique), the people into whom 'the goddess and the spirits of the pitru [ancestors] descend' are mainly women. Most men explain this by stating that 'the ladies are more religious, purer than men'. On their part, most Hindu women emphasised the superhuman aspect: 'we cannot do anything for Her to come or not to come. It is only Mataji [general name of the Hindu mother goddess] who may decide'.

11 The notion of 'Little Traditions' is evoked in this paper (in inverted commas) to emphasise that women's expressive traditions are often described as 'lower' than scriptural Hinduism, at least by certain Brahmanised sectors of the Hindu diaspora.

12 And with young autochthones represented as a minority of deviants.

13 The relevance of strong familial relationships as a parameter that induces differences between the 'South' and the 'North' appears in recent UNESCO research about the

'quality of life of children' in the central states of the world system. In peripheral countries, in five of the six parameters (associated with material life), the Portuguese appear in second place in what concerns the quality of 'familial relationships', after Italians; Germany is in 13th place, Poland (predominantly Catholic) in 14th, Austria (also mainly Catholic) in 16th, Canada in 18th, the US in 20th and the UK is in the opposite extreme (21st) (*Diário de Notícias*, 14 February 2007). This ranking strongly correlates with the ranking of Hofstede (1991) based on four factors that explain the variance of the answers to an attitudinal questionnaire. Differences in the 'quality of familial relationships' result less from the divide between Catholics and others; instead they seem to be related to the divide between male dominance ('masculinity', associated with 'individualism' and a competitive and hierarchical worldview with 'winners' and 'losers', linked with an ideal of victory as a dominant social value) and the relevance of the affective and 'pacific' role of women in relation with men and children inside the family and inside communities, producing a 'sentimental' pattern of tolerance, generosity and spontaneous sociability, associated with 'femininity' and an ideal of happiness (J. Bastos 2000; J. Bastos & S. Bastos 2000).

14   Portugal is considered one of the most advanced European countries in terms of the politics of integration, after Sweden (British Council & Migration Policy Group 2007).

References

Acton, T., S. Caffrey & G. Mundy (2001), 'Theorising Gypsy Law', in W.O. Weinrauch (ed.), *Gypsy Law, Romani Legal Traditions and Cultures*, 88-100. Berkeley: California University Press.

Albuquerque, R. & A. Teixeira (2005), *Active Civic Participation of Immigrants in Portugal. Country Report prepared for the European Research Project*. POLITIS: Oldenburg. www.uni-oldenburg.de/politis-europe.

Ballard, R. (2003), '*Migrations in Europe*', Conference Paper, FCSH/CEMME, Lisbon.

Bastos, J. (2000), *Portugal Europeu, Representações identitárias dos portugueses*. Oeiras: Celta.

Bastos, J. (2002), 'Portugal in Europe: The Inter-national Identity Strategies of the Portuguese', in L. Beltrán, J. Maestro & L. Salo-Lee (eds.), *The Idea of Europe as Viewed from Two European Peripheries: The Nordic Countries and the Iberian Peninsula*, 223-247. Alcala: Alcala University Press.

Bastos, J. (2006), '"Nós dizemos que eles são como nós precisamos que sejam para nos vermos como nos vemos": vicissitudes identitárias nas relações interétnicas', *Revista da Faculdade de Ciências Sociais e Humanas* 18: 83-111. Lisbon: Edições Colibri/FCSH.

Bastos, J. (2007) 'Que futuro tem Portugal para os portugueses ciganos?', in Mirna Montenegro, edit., *Ciganos e cidadania(s)*, 61-96. Setúbal: ICE / ACIME.

Bastos, J. & S. Bastos (1999), *Portugal Multicultural. Situação e estratégias identitárias das Minorias Étnicas*. Lisbon: Fim de Século.

Bastos, J. & S. Bastos (2000), '"Quanto mais modesto mais português": contribuição para o reequacionamento da antropologia urbana à luz da antropologia dos processos identitários', in S. Bastos (ed.), 'Antropologia urbana', *Ethnologia* 9-11: 13-49. Lisbon: FCSH & Cosmos.

Bastos, J. & S. Bastos (forthcoming) 'What Are We Talking About When We Talk About Identities?', in Bastos, J., Dahinden, J., Gois, P. & C. Westin (eds.), *Identity Processes and Strategies in Inter-Ethnic Europe*. Amsterdam: Amsterdam University Press.

Bastos, J., A. Ibarrola-Armendariz, J. Sardinha, C. Westin, & G. Will (2006), 'Identity, Ethnicity, Representation and Discrimination', in Penninx, R., M. Berger & K. Kraal (eds.), *The Dynamics of Migration and Settlement in Europe:. A State of the Art*, 201-232. Amsterdam: IMISCOE Joint Studies/Amsterdam University Press.

Bastos, J., A. Correia & E. Rodrigues (2007), *Sintrenses ciganos*. Sintra: CMS.

Bastos, S. (1990), *A Comunidade Hindu da Quinta da Holandesa. Um Estudo Antropológico sobre a Organização Sócio-Espacial da Casa*. Lisbon: LNEC / ITECS.

Bastos, S. (2005a), 'Indian Transnationalisms in Colonial and Postcolonial Mozambique', in V. Bilger & Kraler, A. (eds.), *African Migrations: Historical Perspectives and Contemporary Dynamics* (thematic issue), *Vienna Journal of African Studies*, 8: 277-306.

Bastos, S. (2005b), 'Hierarchical Alterity is a Mere Illusion: Some Reflections on the Creative Power of Women's Expressive Traditions in the Portuguese-speaking Hindu Diaspora', *Lusotopie* XII (1-2): 109-123. Paris: Brill.

Bastos, S. & J. Bastos (2001), *De Moçambique a Portugal. Reinterpretações identitárias do Hinduísmo em viagem*, Lisbon: Fundação Oriente.

Bastos, S. & J. Bastos (2005), 'Our Colonisers Were Better Than Yours'. Identity Debates in Greater London', *Journal of Ethnic and Migration Studies* 31 (1): 79-98.

Bastos, S. & J. Bastos (eds.) (2006) *Filhos diferentes de deuses diferentes. Manejos da religião em processos de inserção social diferenciada: uma abordagem estrutural dinâmica*. Lisbon: Observatório da Imigração /ACIME.

Bastos, S. & J. Bastos (2007) '"The Blood of a Muslim is Worthless, After All": Identity Debates between Portuguese and British Sunnis in Leicester', in *Lusotopie*, XIV, 1: 271-285, Paris: Brill.

British Council & Migration Policy Group (2007). *Migrant Integration Policy Index*. Brussels: British Council & Migration Policy Group.

Cidra, R. (2002), '"Ser Real": O *rap* na construção de identidades, na Área Metropolitana de Lisboa', in J. Bastos (ed.), 'Antropologia dos Processos identitários' (thematic issue), *Ethnologia* (12-14): 189-222. Lisbon: FCSH & Fim de Século.

Cunha, M. I. (2001), *Entre o bairro e a prisão*. Lisbon: Fim de Século.

Descamps, P. (1935), *Le Portugal, la vie sociale actuelle*, Paris : Firmin-Didot.

Devereux, G. (1985) *Éthnopsychanalyse complémentariste*, Paris: Flammarion.

Dias, J. (1953), 'Os elementos fundamentais da cultura portuguesa', in A. Marchant (ed.), *Atas do 1º Colóquio Internacional de Estudos Luso-brasileiros*, 51-65. Nashville: The Vanderbilt University Press.

Erikson, E. H. (1972) [1950, 1965], *Childhood and Society*. Harmondsworth: Penguin.

Espírito Santo, M. (1983) *A religião popular portuguesa*, Lisbon: A Regra do Jogo.

Gibau, E. (2002) *Homens que choram, mulheres que riem: os cabo-verdianos de Newark, USA*, tese de licenciatura em Antropologia, Lisbon: FCSH; mimeo.

Hofstede, G. (1991), *Cultures and Organizations – Software of the Mind*. London: McGraw-Hill Book Company.

Leach, E.R. (1954), *Political Systems of Highland Burma*. London: Bell.

Lourenço, E. (1978), *O Labirinto da Saudade. Psicanálise Mítica do Destino Português*, Lisbon: Dom Quixote, 3rd edition.

Malheiros, J. (1996), *Imigrantes na região de Lisboa – os Anos da Mudança. Imigração e Processo de Integração das Comunidades de Origem Indiana*. Lisbon: Colibri.

Marques, M.M. and Rui Santos (2004). 'Top-down and Bottom-up Reconsidered: The Dynamics of Immigrant Participation in Local Civil Society', in R. Penninx, K. Kraal, M. Martiniello, & S. Vertovec (eds.), *Citizenship in European Cities. Immigrants, Local Politics and Integration Policies: Diversity and Convergence in European Cities*, 107-126. Aldershot: Ashgate.

McClelland, D. (1961), *The Achieving Society*. New York: D. V. Nostrand Company, Inc.

Mead, M. (1948), *Male and Female*. New York: William Morris & Comp.

Pedroso de Lima, Maria Antónia (2003) *Grandes famílias, Grandes Empresas*, Lisbon: Dom Quixote.

Poinsard, L. (1911). *Le Portugal inconnu*. Paris: Bureau de la Science Sociale.

Rodrigues, D. & A. P. Santos (2000), 'Being an Evangelical Gypsy: Religiosity in a Small Gypsy Community in Portugal', in Rodrigues, D. & Del Rio, P. (eds.), *The Religious Phenomenon: An Inter-disciplinary Approach*, 51-56. Madrid: Fundación Infancia y Aprendizage.

Tiesler, N. (2000), 'Muçulmanos na Margem: a nova presença islâmica em Portugal', *Sociologia, Problemas e Práticas*, 34: 117-144.

Vakil, A. (2004), 'Do Outro ao Diverso. Islão e Muçulmanos em Portugal: História, Discursos, Identidades', *Revista Lusófona de Ciência das Religiões* III (5-6): 283-312.

Wallerstein, I. (1974), *The Modern World-System*. New York: Academic Press.

7 The Dream of Family: Muslim Migrants in Austria[1]

Anna Stepien

Introduction

'Luxury is family and time', said recently Fiona Swarovski, a prominent Austrian and heiress of the Swarovski Crystal empire. The dream of a family – by which I mean the longing for community, safety, acceptance and support realised through the family – can take different forms, but is common to many people, independent of their culture, tradition, religion or nationality. The family is valued, is in fashion, maybe even more than ever before, seen as a constant part in an inconstant world, imagined as a secure haven in an insecure, changing and globalised environment.

This chapter investigates Muslim migrant families in Austria and their dream of a family. Their views on the family are shaped in their countries of origin, and in the country of immigration as idealised images from their childhood or youth. Families are cherished in the new home country as part of a cultural heritage. Consequently they are idealised, by contrast with what is an imagined (but not really known) representation of 'Austrian' families. The same is true of Austrian representations of Muslim families. In these representations imagination plays a greater part than reality.

Muslim families are at the centre of much current interest due to their increasing numbers and presupposed 'otherness', in which religion plays an important role. Most of the present studies of Muslim family relations, however, concentrate on such issues as the status of women, on arranged (or forced) marriages, or on female genital mutilation and honour killings (neither of which are of Islamic origin). Few investigate the Muslim family in the round, as a social unit, its evolution and internal and external interactions with mainstream society, especially in the context of migration and integration. Generally, there has been a tendency to approach the subject from other points of view such as legal status, situation in the labour market, or from the standpoint of integration policies. Even when discussing integration the emphasis has been on individuals rather than on families, or on specific family members – wives, children, etc.

There is a particular need for studies from the perspective of immigrant families in Europe, and in this chapter, I focus on the life of
Muslim migrants, and seek to contribute to a better understanding of
their family values, principally through the voices of a limited number
of Muslim respondents in Austria (see appendix at end of this chapter).
The main goal is to highlight the consequences of the migrant's views
about family for the integration process and future strategies. In particular, I want to show how the dream of a family of Muslims evolves
and is shaped through migration. I argue that this dream is not so
much connected to religious views as to the solitude, the lack of extended family, and familiar cultural surroundings, all accompanying
the migration process. I claim that the contrast between 'Muslim' and
'Austrian' families, even if backed by religion, evolves in its specific
form first in exile, when experiencing migration. In the process, Muslim families are idealised and their image reshaped. As a consequence,
they are often pictured as in-between, neither belonging to the changing situation in the country of origin but neither are they felt to be 'at
home' in the new country of destination. Additionally, Muslim migrants often do not have much contact with 'ordinary' Austrian families
and find it difficult to make any comparison in this regard. Austria,
with its long tradition of recognition of Islam and the Islamic faith
community on the one hand, and restricted migration policy on the
other, reinforces this specific picture, wherein the return project becomes part of the dream of a family.

By any measure, immigration is one of the most stressful events a
person can undergo. Most critically, immigration removes individuals
from many of their relationships and predictable contexts – extended
families and friends, community ties, jobs, living situations, customs
and often language. Immigrants are stripped of many of their sustaining social relationships, as well as of their roles which provide them
with culturally scripted notions of how they fit into the world. Without
a sense of competence, control and belonging, they may feel marginalised. Disappointed aspirations and dreams, when coupled with a hostile reception in a new environment, may lead to feelings of distrust,
suspicion and anger. The repercussions of the responses at an individual level are felt within the family. Migration creates particular pressures on the family system and can even have destabilising effects.
Migration often creates changes within the structure of the family; former family leaders may be 'demoted' and the nature of gender relationships may shift. Immigrant families may try to keep their traditional
social and sex role norms as a defence against the strong pressure to
acculturate.

I seek to illustrate these points as follows. Firstly, I describe the overall situation of Muslims and the recognition of Islam in Austria. Sec-

ondly, I discuss official and unofficial views on the subject of the family in Islam. I then analyse opinions on the family generated on the
basis of my interviews with Muslim immigrants in Austria, explaining
which particular aspects of 'Muslim' and 'Austrian' families are contrasted. Lastly, I discuss the relation between family, migration and religion and their influence on each other.

Muslims in Austria

According to the last census conducted in 2001, 339,000 Muslims live
in Austria, and constitute 4.2 per cent of the total population. Their
main countries of origin are: Turkey (36.3 per cent), Austria (28.3 per
cent), Bosnia and Herzegovina (19.1 per cent), Serbia and Montenegro
(6.4 per cent) and Macedonia (3.2 per cent). Some 28 per cent of Muslims have Austrian citizenship. There are around 200 prayer centres in
the country. The character of Islam in Austria has been shaped by the
historic encounter of the Austro-Hungarian Empire with the neigh-
bouring Muslim world. In 1878, Austria officially incorporated the former Turkish provinces of Bosnia and Herzegovina. The general recognition of Islam according to the *Hanafi* rite[2] was confirmed, and in
some points expanded, by the Law of Recognition of Islam in 1912.
This law was crucial for the Muslims' later appeal for official recognition, in 1979, of the Islamic Faith Community in Austria (*Islamische
Glaubensgemeinschaft in Österreich*) as a legal, public and corporate body
representing officially the interests of Muslims. In 1988 the Constitutional Court cancelled the definition 'according to the *Hanafi* rite' and
extended official recognition of Islam to all Muslims. The status of
publicly recognised religion obliges the Republic of Austria to safeguard the practice of the religion in general, to allow the teaching of
the faith in public schools and to fund teachers appointed by the religious community. Moreover, publicly recognised religious bodies are
entitled to set up their own schools and teacher-training colleges,
which should follow the curriculum set by law for public schools.

In public discussions, this particular legal status of Islam in Austria
is often presented as a role model for other European countries as it facilitates the integration of Muslims into Austrian society, and because
of its strong legal position it creates a platform for common discussions on the same level with other religious or state institutions. Nevertheless, there is a debate in Austria, as in other European countries, on
the development of 'parallel societies' (see Ballard, Hagelund *supra*). In
a survey conducted in September 2004 about the difficulties of adapt-
ing to Austrian lifestyle and rules, 31 per cent of those questioned mentioned Turks[3] in this connection. Austria is not a traditional country of

immigration and for a long time has not perceived itself as such. Its immigration and integration policies and policymaking process still reflect that ambivalence. Austria does not have a real tradition of the legal regulation of integration. The 'Integration Agreement' of 2002 can be seen as the first such measure, and there is no specific law covering diverse integration measures, with a broad spectrum extending beyond language courses and courses for illiterate persons.[4] Between 2003 and 2005, the integration debate in Austria focused on perceived failures. At the federal level, there has been much talk about 'the integration deficit of immigrants' as set out in the revised Aliens Law, 2002. The main emphasis was on obligatory language courses. In the debate on naturalisation, integration is of vital importance, but is understood in terms of possessing a stable income, having a good command of German and having 'assimilated' to the 'Austrian way of life' (König & Perchinig 2005).

After 9/11, as in other European countries, there was increasing attention to Muslim communities, especially from a security perspective, with conferences (including imams' conferences in 2003 and 2006), meetings and diverse workshops organised by various institutions. There was also a negative side to this interest. Election campaigns in 1999, 2002, 2005 and 2006 saw an increasing use of xenophobic and Islamophobic speech by the FPÖ (Austrian Freedom Party) and the BZÖ (Union of the Future of Austria). For example, one of the election campaign posters of the FPÖ proclaimed *'Pummerin statt Muezzin'* ('Pummerin – the name of the bell on the tower of St. Stephen Cathedral in Vienna – instead of muezzin': 'Rather hear the bell ringing than the muezzin ranting'). Currently, posters feature *'Dahaam statt Islam'* ('At home instead of Islam'). There was also a controversial study (BM. I/SIAK 2006) commissioned by the ministry of interior, and an official statement by the Austrian minister of the interior (Liese Prokop from the Conservative Party, ÖVP) that 45 per cent of Muslims in Austria were not willing to integrate and this fact was considered a 'time bomb'. Also in January 2008 a statement by Elke Winter, the main candidate of the FPÖ for the municipal government in Graz, thought offensive to the Prophet Muhammad, provoked a new debate on Muslims in Austria and met with a strong critique from other parties and eventually the FPÖ itself. This revealed a recurrent tendency to use anti-Muslim statements on the part of right-wing parties during election campaigns. Not without controversy for the migrant family issue was also a decree of the minister of social affairs, Ursula Haubner (BZÖ), concerning restrictions on children's allowance and social aid for migrant families in 2006. After strong criticism from the other political parties as well as the Austrian president, Heinz Fischer, the decree was 'softened' by Liese Prokop by issuing a new regulation.

Unfortunately, for various reasons Austria still appears to be a country of transition or of immigrants' broken dreams rather than a place to make a new home. After 9/11, there was a debate in many countries of Western Europe about migrants living 'parallel lives' or in 'parallel worlds' which also took place in Austria. The form this debate has taken has seemed from the outset misguided and irrelevant. The polarisation of ethnic communities and ethnic families in European towns and cities has a complex background. On the one hand, there are certainly people who may prefer to live close to people with a similar ethnic background, and what is wrong with that? On the other hand, many of them would probably move, if they could afford it. However, the educational, work-related, legal and financial framework does not facilitate such changes.

The Family in Islam

In Islamic thought the family is perceived as the highest social unit and the core of society. However, the concept of family itself has been continuously changing. In the Muslim migrants' countries of origin similar transformations are taking place as in European countries, where the structure and size of a family is substantially the product of the wider economy and social structure of the country, and the interaction between various family members and the construction and reconstruction of their roles. These are both external and internal changes, and debates taking place both inside and outside Islam which influence the concept of family, and the identity of its members. There is thus a continuous process of construction in time and space.

Islam emphasises family formation as a crucial responsibility of couples. Family relations are specified in Islamic jurisprudence to achieve the welfare and useful life of its members. The rights of children in particular have been stressed as future builders of society and upholders (and defenders) of the faith (Rahim 1992: 1). Islam is not only a religion of worship, but also a social system, a culture and civilisation. Islam has a pervasive social character and tends to consider the family as something absolutely good and almost sacred. Besides providing tranquillity and mutual support and understanding between husband and wife, the obvious function of a family is to provide a culturally and legally acceptable way of satisfying the sexual instinct, as well as to raise children as the new generation. It is within the family system that Muslims acquire their religious training, develop their moral character, establish close social relationships and sustain loyalty both to the family and to society at large. The support system in the family (financial, social and emotional) is paramount in establishing the peace of mind and security needed for life. This is particularly important for the socially dependent members, namely children, the elderly, the single adults (especially females), as well as the sick and handicapped. The family in Islam includes both the nuclear (husband, wife and their children) and extended varieties by caring for all the relatives (ahl). The husband and wife are the principals of family formation. Their relationship in marriage is described in the Qur'an as incorporating the major qualities: love (passion, friendship, companionship) on the one hand, and mercy (understanding, tolerance, forgiveness) on the other within the overall objective of tranquillity. The Sura 30: 21 is frequently quoted to describe one of the purposes of family life. It starts by referring to the unity of origin of husband and wife, which is a confirmation of equality and a basis for harmony between them. There can be no better expression of the relationship between two human beings living together in blessed marital bondage. Such a relationship is so highly valued that Allah made it among His signs (Sura 7: 189). Marriage is fundamental to family formation in Islam. Parents are held responsible for the social, cultural and moral training of children as well as for their physical welfare and health care. In return, parents (especially mothers) are held in great esteem and should receive respect and tender loving care from their children. As they grow old and fail to support themselves, the children should provide shelter and adequate financial support for their parents in addition to continuing social support. Ageing, sick or handicapped parents should never be abandoned; this is the built-in social security system in Islamic society.

Especially for women, both their life course and their everyday life are, it is argued, wholly determined by what sort of family they have and what happens to the family. A woman is completely happy, it is said, if she is married and her husband supplies the household with what is necessary, and they have children together. The advancement of the next generations gives meaning to family life and the parents' endeavours. The present and everyday life lies with the family as a community; the future lies with happier children (Dahl 1997: 48-49).

Thus the family has a special place in Islam and in the Islamic world. In Islam the family is the only group based on kinship that is recognised. In practice the family was the instrument wherewith the first Muslim community was founded in Medina. The family institution made it possible to organise a society of believers (al-umma), thus breaking away from the pre-Islamic society that was based on a tribal system. Three stages are distinguished in the description of Islamic law. First, the comprehensive character and far-reaching significance of Islam in Muslim life are pointed out – how Islam embodies religion, morals, law and justice all in one, thus constituting collective identity and loyalty in the Islamic world. Next, it is emphasised how the law is embedded in the very heart of Islam, and finally, how family law is at the centre of the law. This is a significant chain leading to an understanding of identity, politics and practical everyday life – the connection between religion, law, and the family.

The message of the Qur'an is that women, as believers, are equal members of *al-umma* – the Muslim community – and that God weighs women's and men's actions on an equal scale as regards entry to Paradise. As legal persons, women themselves received through Islam the right to own property, the right to inherit, and the right to dispose of their property independently. But the commandments concerning these matters are themselves discriminatory. Most of them are rules of family law. Traditionally, family law is the central part of the law, because the family is the unit on which the Muslim community is based. If families do not function properly, the community will not function. It is therefore necessary to protect the family and its supporters.

While great power politics and Western colonialism encroached on the Arab-Muslim world throughout the nineteenth century and imposed on the legal system of individual countries an extensive modernisation on the Western model, family law was not touched. Thus, Egypt, for example, experienced an almost dramatic secularisation of the law, but family law according to Islamic legal principles of the sharia[5] was left intact. It was considered of minor importance by the great powers and at the same time sacred to Arabic-Muslim considerations. In this way sharia survived in family law, both substantively and procedurally, and the rules of family law, as they were formulated from the seventh to the ninth century, still fundamentally apply. In this respect, the colonial powers achieved only a geographical dominion and economic exploitation, leaving the Islamic faith and its collective concept of personality and identity unscathed. Thus Arab women were promoted to the historic and unexpected role of guardians of the old traditions and the collective identity. However, times are also changing in this respect. Modern society is on a collision course with tradition; in the meeting of modernity and tradition old forms are being given new contents, as is the case when young educated Muslim women deliberately take to wearing the veil. Nowadays, work cannot be imposed on one sex by the other, in family life, as in other areas of societal life; it is by negotiations between the parties involved that the foundation for organisation, sustainability and viability of the family must be created.

Muslim Immigrants' Views on the 'Family'

Interviews[6] conducted with Muslim immigrants in Austria revealed the very high value placed on the family, though such views are perhaps as much connected to traditional views of family, which may be strengthened in the migration context, as specifically to religion. The opinions below present a wide spectrum of the role and the function of family nowadays.

Samira: There is no substitute for family, with time you may find some friends but they will never be the same as family to you. I have not had any problems finding a friend here as I have lived in a dormitory and study here.
Family is very important to me; it is an immense support, especially if one is abroad. I could never give up my religion and would not accept it if somebody spoke wrongly about my father.

Ahmed: There is no substitute for family, what happens there doesn't happen anywhere else. I do not have any friends here – some colleagues, but not friends. It is not easy, people are closed to any contacts, but if you manage it, then you can have a really good friendship with them. Anyway you always hear the question, 'why are you here?' And how can one ask like this? A real friend wants you to stay in the place he lives in. And when I hear on the bus or tram what people are saying about foreigners ... then you wonder how can you make any friends here? I would like very much to have a good friend here, but already at the beginning there is a dividing wall present.
The family is the core of society, whatever the religion you may have. The most important thing is that there is harmony in the family and everybody contributes to it. To me, the family means cohesion and bonds, where all try to understand each other. If it happens, there is also harmony in society. I would never give up my religion. I would be quite a different man without religion; I do not allow myself many mistakes if I am religious. It is also important that a family has a common goal. A family without a common goal cannot be a family.

Fatos: A friend cannot replace a family here; if I do not have any friends here it will not disturb me. From a friend you cannot have the same as from the family. From your own family you have everything; they will do everything they can for you.
For me, the family is everything that is in my life. It has

never changed. For the family I will do everything, really
everything.

Aishe: The family means to me that I can marry and have a happy marriage, to bring up children, to share. It means mutual support, life partnership, an extended family, where
we share the same religion and can celebrate our festivities. One would feel alone without a family. If you have
any problems you receive the strongest support from your
family, but still, first is religion, and you have to ask it before you ask your family.

One should not, however, forget alternative or what are sometimes
called 'progressive' voices in relation to the subject of the Muslim family today. Contemporary Muslim families are undergoing change, becoming less extended, with more women educated and gainfully employed. It is difficult to say that arranged marriages are declining, but
the age of marriage is rising; modern contraceptives are slowly becoming more prevalent in certain communities. However, the family remains the constitutive point of reference for everyone. At the same
time, the modern epoch is characterised by the will for independence,
freedom and individualism. Daily life today, however, makes things increasingly difficult: couples are separating; break-ups are multiplying
and imbalances increasing (Ramadan 2001: 36). The Islamic point of
reference is opposed to this splintering process. If modernity can only
be obtained at this price, then, in the opinion of Tariq Ramadan, we
should understand why the Qur'an and the *Sunna* reject the actualisa-
tion of such modernisation. Similarly, if the whole world is caught in
this process, being ashamed to refer to the family, then Muslims, wherever they are, should remind others of its importance, its meaning and
its finality (Ramadan 2001: 37). For Ramadan, the family is very important as it constitutes the human being as such. To ask mankind to be
without family is tantamount to asking an orphan to give birth to his
or her own parents and the Islamic point of view requires exactly the
opposite attitude (Ramadan 2001: 37).

Nowadays progressive voices related to Muslim family issues and
Muslim family law are especially present in the current debates on
feminism, gender and women's rights in Islam. One such progressive
voice is presented by Kecia Ali. Her chapter on 'Progressive Muslims
and Islamic Jurisprudence: The Necessity for Critical Engagement with
Marriage and Divorce Law' describes the difficult relationship that progressive Muslims have with Islamic law, as discussions on Islamic law
today tend to reflect only different degrees of conservatism and fundamentalism (Ali 2005: 163). She stresses the fact that, for those living in

the Muslim world, negotiation with Islamic law as it is enforced through personal status codes is a practical necessity. However, Muslims who live in the West encounter Islamic law only to the extent that those living in the Muslim world choose to apply it in their personal dealings. For many it is especially present in family matters. Paradoxically for progressive Muslims, this is the arena where traditional Islamic law is thought to be most conservative (Ali 2005: 163). In Ali's opinion these are the neo-conservatives who are the most prominent fraction in debates over the proper legal and social rights of Muslim women today. Their views are represented in publications and conferences of Muslims also in the West. They support the continued enforcement of law as developed by jurists during the classical period and, in this transformed form, by legislatures in Muslim nations (Ali 2005: 173). The author stresses the need for a thorough exploration and analysis of traditional jurisprudence as the role of human agency in the creation of these laws is evidenced by the diversity of legal views on it. Concerning marriage law, Ali shows that the result of such exploration and analysis will be a closer – but still only human, and therefore fallible – approximation of divinely revealed sharia than what currently exists (Ali 2005: 183).

'Muslim' and 'Austrian' Families Contrasted

Discussions on the Muslim family in Austria among migrant families and within Austrian public discourse are mostly dependent on and reflect political debates and the accompanying legal regulations. They are, as Erel describes discourses on Turkish families in Germany, 'contradictory, complex and multifaceted' (Erel 2002: 128), and changing over time. These debates mostly converge around a racialised dichotomy of modernity versus tradition and individual versus community. Austria is seen as a modern society, characterised by individualisation, the fragmentation of stable relationships and forms of belonging, increasingly rapid change and the pluralisation of cultural options, as well as a sharpening of social inequalities and a decline in economic opportunity (cf. Heitmeyer et al. 1997). The nuclear family is one of the central social institutions challenged by modernisation (Beck & Beck-Gernsheim 1995). However, these challenges can also be seen to have positive aspects such as an increasing realisation of democratic and egalitarian family relations (cf. Giddens 1992). Within such discussions of the modernisation of family relations, migrant families' experiences are not considered and are tacitly assumed as residues of tradition. Thus, Muslim (Turkish) families are contrasted with the modern Austrian family as the embodiment of tradition in the sense of patriarchal gender relations, continuity and stability. Public discourses on the Muslim (Turkish) family are sketched by the dichotomy of modern Austrian versus traditional Turkish, where gender and family relations are critically evaluated. The specific definition of modernity here is of particular importance.

My respondents found it difficult to compare their family with the 'ordinary' Austrian family, as, with the exception of Samira, they have not had or have not maintained any contact with Austrian families. Moreover, they were critical about the changes in their countries of origin where families and familial relations are becoming increasingly similar to those found in Europe. They stressed once again the immense influence of the lack of an extended family on their daily routine.

Fatos: It is like day and night, you cannot compare ... I do not think I would decide again to come here, but there was war, I could not study, I could do nothing. I think if I lived there I would have 70 per cent less stress. Close to the family, it would be different. And here the life is 'cold', you have nobody to walk around with, you cannot simply visit your relatives, speak to somebody, organise a trip. You can do this only with your wife and child. The moment I cross the border I feel different, like a human being. It is so different in my country. I think it is all about family, in a family you are simply as you are and do not 'disturb' anybody.

Interesting remarks were made by my respondents on the internal relations in the family and particularly the position of children in the family, perceived from the comparative perspective.

Aishe: In the Austrian family children leave the parents' home when they are eighteen years old. In Islam parents care for their children to get them into their own family, marriage. The children want more freedom here.

Samira: I think there is more confidence in our families than here, but it can depend on the economic problems and stress, which many Iranian families now have. The women can in most cases study here, but they are limited in their choice concerning their future husband and family. There is also too much value put on someone's appearance, you have to show what jewellery you have, etc., but my mother was not like that. She put more value on our education. But still, I did not feel comfortable there.

Fatos: I think they [Austrians] live well, they do everything they
             want. They look more for themselves, what they want, and
             if they have an opportunity they take it. We are different.
             Even if one does not have so much he thinks about chil-
             dren, to do something for them, so that they have a house
             later on. Here it is different. When you are eighteen you
             leave the parents' house. Parents here certainly do not
             think that much about their children. It is only important
             that you go to school, and then they finance it, books and
             clothes. Also the relation between parents and children is
             not that warm, they do not do that much for each other.

At the same time, some informants expressed a willingness to sacrifice
lives and aspirations for the sake of children, while others reflected on
the changing realities of family relations both in Austria and in countries of origin.

Rabia: Of course it is better to live there, with the whole family.
             But we want to stay here, for our children. Here they have
             more possibilities; they can learn foreign languages, etce-
             tera.

Ahmed: In Austrian families persons are less connected to each
             other than in Egyptian families. Children are taught their
             faith by their parents, as this is their task and obligation.
             But Austrian children are more independent. In the Egyp-
             tian family parents are more caring about their children,
             are more attentive. There is more cooperation. It is easier
             to live. The daily routine is different; one is not chained to
             his job. Here I fear losing my job. Here you have to ask
             the grandparents to look after the children, in Egypt it is
             clear. Similarly, here partners pay separately for them-
             selves; in Egypt it would be shameful to do so. Also when
             your neighbour is paying you a visit, you let him in; here
             you speak at the door. There is maybe more respect with
             regard to the parents and elderly as well, but it is also
             changing.

Ahmed: I am aware of the fact that the life there and generation
             [in Egypt] also changed. Both partners have to work now
             for the family upkeep. Until I graduated I lived with my
             parents; my mother was always at home. But now it has
             also changed in many families.

Fatos: The life there is, however, not the same as before. When I came here, I had a specific mentality and it did not change, I stayed with this mentality, whereas people there went with time and changed. It is not as before, kids are taking drugs, are smoking, the same here. But I stayed with this other mentality, which does not exist there anymore, but I cannot change it.

Lastly, when asked about feeling at home in Austria, some of the interviewees mentioned returning to their (or their parents) country of origin. Returning home is seen as a way of escaping stress in the family, job, education and feelings of insecurity. The return project gives a new motivation. It is legitimated by the family of origin and the tradition of family cohesion and solidarity. The nostalgia for family members is also a sign that in difficult times the family is particularly needed.

Fatos: I do not feel at home here at all. Sometimes I cannot understand these people at all. How they can do some of the things they do, for example leaving their family with children? It is not normal. But somehow, later my child will be probably similar to them. I cannot say they are bad; everybody has their own direction in life, their own life. They do everything they can in their lives. My family would live certainly better in my country of origin; my wife could go to the garden with a child, or to visit any of our relatives. They have also more free time than people here. And here, she spends the whole time at home. In my home country you do not have to pay rent. Here you have to work for it, then you have little spare time ... and the circle closes itself. I am going to build a house there one day, when my child is an adult; I will go back there, for myself. But my child will probably stay here. As I already said, I would never say that this is my country. I would not say that, in spite of the facts about how bad the future can become in my country. It is like that because I was there till I was nineteen, my childhood was there and I cannot change myself.

Family, Migration and Religion

Migration is a family project that encompasses several generations in real or imagined space. It is a break in the biography. Since the official end of labour migration in 1974, the integration of immigrant populations has become an irreversible fact, particularly as a result of policies on family reunification. These have contributed to the recomposition of 'Muslim' families in Europe and the continent's noticeable increase in family size (Cesari 2005: 1). Over the past two decades, family-linked migration developed into the most important form of legal migration within the European Union. Family plays a decisive and very important role in the migration process, even if this contribution is not that visible in some cases. The study of families as transnational phenomena requires the processes of globalisation to be considered from the level of everyday life and the perspective of civil society, and the focus on the construction of families themselves under diasporic conditions, how they shape and are shaped by movement, separation and reunion. The voices of my respondents mirror various aspects of this process.

In contrast to what are seen as individualised and fragmented Western societies, Islam emphasises the group and community. Three of five injunctions of Islam – prayers, fasting and haj – are directly related to group activity and participation. The Muslim is rarely alone, because the emphasis on the group in the Muslim family is still relatively strong. As Necla Kelek (2005) in her book *Die fremde Braut* (*Foreign Bride*) observes, in the Muslim family 'one finally belongs not to himself, but to the family, the *Umma* which owns one's respect' (Kelek 2005: 236). Most Muslim immigrants come from countries with types of individual-group interactions which differ from those of their host countries (see Ballard *supra*). Gretty M. Mirdal (2000), in her chapter on 'The Construction of Muslim Identities in Contemporary Europe', uses the terms 'cultures of relatedness' and 'cultures of separation', coined by the Turkish social psychologist Kagitcibasi (1996). In her opinion, Muslims in contemporary Europe have their roots in 'cultures of relatedness'. For them, adjusting to a Western lifestyle means not only a change toward (post)modernity, urbanity and globality, but also toward a 'culture of separateness', which requires autonomy and independence and in turn, changes in family and child rearing patterns (Mirdal 2000: 38).

The voices of my informants support this opinion.

Samira: I had a real home, I did not have to bother about money, and I had a certain security, good 'company' around me, and always some kind of attention from part of my family. I had more possibilities than here and a better standard of

life, family and relatives to pay a visit to. I was never alone
there and here I am almost always alone. And this is a big
difference. The first two years were very difficult for me; I
had to take on all responsibility myself, which I was not
used to before, to learn a language. Here in the beginning
I was very cautious about contact with other people as I
knew that there are big differences between us. Partly I
was afraid of those situations, but not any more now.

Ahmed: I have never had to make any special arrangements with
my relatives or friends, I just visited them. I had much
more time than here. In Austria it is different, you have
very little time for your family, friends, but maybe that has
also changed in Egypt ... For me it was an enormous
change between my life there and here, now.

Fatos: Here, everybody looks out for himself, minds his own interests and business. Then I behave similarly, distantly.
When somebody needs help I will help him of course, but
it is somehow cold. Later on, when you need something,
the other person does nothing for you, there are such people. It is really difficult to find a friend here, a good one
and then to keep him. It is like that because everybody
has to work and looks after his own business. Ok, you can
speak with him on the telephone. I have a good friend
here, but we do not see each other often and this is a
minus. However, I also have to have time for my child.

Furthermore, Mirdal points out that the ties with the father, and the
difficulties of using the father as an identification figure, constitute
some of the problems that have been extensively dealt with in relation
to second and third generation immigrants of Islamic origin (Mirdal
2000: 38). Cases of anti-social behaviour and difficulties in socialisation have been blamed on the weakness of the father as a positive identification model (Mirdal 2000: 38). However, this is probably more a
general phenomenon in contemporary individualistically orientated societies than one that is specific to migrant communities.

Another interesting aspect is that, despite the often-idealised recollections of the extended family based on vacations in the country of origin, immigrants are ready to sacrifice extended family and neighbourhoods for a better socio-economic situation.

Rabia's husband:
It was a great time these three months; we visited all of

our family, one after the other. There is more family life
there; you do more things together like picnics, excur-
sions. Here people sit and watch the television, everybody
in his own flat. We would stay there, but the socio-economic situation here is much better.

Fatos: My family would certainly live better in my country of origin. My wife has to stay the whole day at home whereas
in Kosovo she could go into the garden outside, or go visit
an aunt. Even here if you have any aunt here, it is not the
same as there. Here she has also no time and has her
own family to take care of. There in Kosovo they have
more time and leisure, you do not have to pay for your
flat, but it is difficult to find a job.

An important issue is that of gender differentiation.

Fatos: I think in my country a woman has more respect for a
man. But now it has probably also changed. Here it's like:
'You do this, so I have to do this for you'.

Within migrant communities, women may face different problems
from men in the migration and integration process. On the level of social contacts there is a dramatic change for them from the way of life
in the village to that within ones' four walls. Furthermore, the traditional subordination of women is likely to be challenged in the migration process. One fact that Fatos did not mention here is that he does
not allow his wife to leave the house without his permission or without
the company of his brother. As he explained to me, he wants to protect
her in this way, but also puts obstacles in her way so she will not meet
another man. His family's honour as well as his honour depends upon
the behaviour of his wife or any other female in his family. She cannot
take German language courses or work. However, due to the need to
earn more money for the family, he thought she could work some
hours as a cleaning lady in a private house. This would not alter her
isolated position, only exchange one form of isolation for another. Muslim women and immigrant women in general show more openness to
accommodate themselves, but still, in many cases, they are hindered
by their men in this process.

Idealisation of the family and the dream of family – not necessarily
the same thing – have already been the subject of research by Düzgün
Firat (1996). He demonstrates that it is mostly parents with a strong
orientation to the country of origin who idealise the society of origin.
Isolated from developments there, they base their views on what their

country was like when they left (Firat 1996: 59). This idealisation is connected to isolation and disadvantages in various spheres of life, not only in the host country, but also in the country of origin. This fact, among others, influences their decision to stay in the host country. On the macro level, the dream of family and its idealisation is closely involved with the process of building a new identity in new, changed surroundings. Significantly, the home represents the central place where parents preserve the collective memory. It is the sacred and symbolic place within which identification is constructed. At the same time, it is the place for conflict and exchange between generations interacting with different spatial-temporal points of view, where external and internal practices come together in a hybrid space (Bracalenti & Benini 2005: 68).

Conclusion

The key issue of this chapter is the dream of family and idealisation of family, its expression, role, and evolution among Muslim immigrants in Austria. In particular, the chapter has asked about the consequences of this dream for the Muslim immigrants' integration process and their future strategies. Through the narratives of Muslim migrants regarding family matters, the chapter documented three major outcomes.

Firstly, it draws attention to dichotomies in the public discourse in Austria towards Muslim immigrants. On the one hand, they enjoy already established and already traditionally constituted recognition, on the other hand they are also immigrants and even if they were born in Austria, are still perceived and treated as such, which does not really make them feel welcome and at home. Thus, despite official recognition, at the same time they experience exclusion and face racist populist political statements and posters in everyday life (such as those of the FPÖ or BZÖ), or exclusionist legal regulations. This further influences the possibilities of contact and exchange with 'Austrian' families, giving a lot of space to create and maintain mutual concepts which do not always meet with the given reality. This imagined space consequently feeds, and is fed by, amongst other things, the idea of family as the mainstay of life. Thus, the Muslim family with its values and rules of universal and also imaginative character is accorded high priority.

Secondly, the idealisation of the family assumes a particular form at a particular time, which in this case is in the context of the migration experience. Whereas less attention would be paid to the family in the country of origin, it gains a particular importance in exile, where life may be lived through recollection and memory, and the variously formed recollections take on a very selective character.

Thirdly, this specific situation, when not really accepted, has an important consequence for the integration process with all its complexity. 'We' encompasses the family and the nostalgia for it and, together with it, its specific religious and ethnic features, the dream of existing, missed and future family, the dream of the idealised past. Many Muslim immigrants come from societies where, at the time of their migration, the traditional view of family issues was predominant. However, as they also observe, it has changed and what they are celebrating is an imagined picture. Notably, the dream of a family is at the same time a dream of acceptance, freedom in its broad meaning, safety and socio-economic prosperity, for which, in a way, family and its values are even sacrificed. Luxury is family and time, but family with limited possibilities and perspectives is no luxury at all.

Appendix

Notes on interviewees cited in the chapter (all names have been changed):

Ahmed: 43, originally from Egypt, has lived in Austria for sixteen years and has Austrian citizenship, is married to a woman of Polish origin and has a six-year-old child. He came to Austria after finishing his studies in law in Cairo to visit his cousin and stayed here. His diploma was officially recognised at the faculty of law at the University of Vienna, and he later finished the law practice at court. After three years of searching for a job in his profession, he started to work in a pizzeria. His wife works part-time in a bakery. He has a cousin in Vienna.

Fatos: 27, originally from Kosovo, has lived in Austria for seven years and has applied for Austrian citizenship. He is married to a woman who is also from Kosovo, and has a one-year-old child. He came to Austria as a refugee during the beginning of the war in Kosovo. He graduated from secondary school and wanted to study at the university in Vienna. The pressure to work for the family and the university administrative requirements hampered him in his goal to study. He works as an electrician, together with his brother and cousin, who also live in Vienna. His wife comes from a village next to his, and came to Vienna two years ago, after their marriage in Kosovo. She does not work.

Samira: 34, originally from Iran, has lived in Austria for eleven years. She does not have Austrian citizenship and is not married. She finished her medical studies in Vienna where she is now completing her PhD studies. She came to Vienna for the purpose of studying. When she came to Vienna, her older brother was already here, her younger brother also came to study in Vienna two years earlier. She is involved in one of the projects at the university but does not have a permanent job.

Aishe: 25, was born in Austria and has Austrian citizenship; her parents are from Turkey (her father came to Austria as a guest worker at the beginning of 1980s), and she lives in Austria. She is married to a man with a Turkish background and has a two-year-old child. Her parents, three sisters and two brothers also live in Vienna. She is a teacher at the Islamic secondary school in Vienna. Her husband works for a small private company. Her sister and her friend also participated in the interview.

Rabia: 27, originally from Turkey, came to Austria three years ago after her marriage in Turkey. She has Austrian citizenship and is expecting her second baby. She does not work. Apart from her husband, she does not have any relatives in Austria. Her husband has lived in Austria for ten years. He came to Austria as textile merchant and stayed for economic reasons. His parents are no longer alive, and his only brother lives in France.

Notes

1   I am very grateful to Ralph Grillo for his comments on this chapter and the persons I interviewed for their time, openness and interest. The following references have been especially valuable for formulating the material discussed in this chapter: Abdo-Tubi (1987), Bauman (2003), Bhabha (1990), Bryceson and Vuorela (2002), Farnández de la Hoz (2002), Furher and Uslucan (2005), Michalski (2006) and Safi (2005).

2   One of the four Sunni schools of law (*Maliki, Hanabali, Hanafi, Shafei*).

3   Institut für Markt- und Sozialanalysen (IMAS International), Survey: *Die Formel des Zuwandererproblems*, No. 17, September 2004.

4   The 'Integration Agreement' is part of the Aliens Law of 2002 and was the first instrument on the federal level demanding substantial action from authorities and immigrants. It is a compulsory contract, which has to be signed and fulfilled by the concerned alien. Other supportive measures described in § 51 have a voluntary character. Prior to the 'Integration Agreement' of 2002 there were no effective legally regulated integration measures. They were mentioned for the first time in the 'Residence Law' of 1992 as so-called 'integration facilities', and in the Aliens Act of 1997 in the form of measures for promoting integration, though they did not have an effective legally regulated character.

5   'Sharia' refers to religious law. Tariq Ramadan (2001: 31 ff.) presents the sharia as follows: on the basis of the root of the word, it means 'the way' ('the path leading to the source') and it outlines a global conception of creation, existence, and death and the way of life it entails, stemming from a normative reading and an understanding

of scriptural sources. It determines 'how to be a Muslim'. For scholars and jurists, it is the corpus of general principles of Islamic law extracted from its two fundamental sources, the Qur'an and the *Sunna*, but also using the other sources.

6   The material deployed in this chapter is derived from narrative interviews with five Muslim immigrants of first and second generation in Austria. These were mostly contacted through my networks or are my friends. Interviews took place mostly in their houses and lasted around one to two hours. Additionally, this work is partly based on 34 expert interviews conducted in 2004-2006 in Austria, Germany, and the UK with Muslim and non-Muslim scholars, leaders of various organisations, politicians and clergy.

References

Abdo-Tubi, N. (1987), *Family, Women and Social Change in the Middle East: The Palestinian Case*. Toronto: Canadian Scholars' Press.

Ali, K. (2005), 'Progressive Muslims and Islamic Jurisprudence: The Necessity for Critical Engagement with Marriage and Divorce Law', in O. Safi, (ed.), *Progressive Muslims: On Justice, Gender and Pluralism*, 163-189. Oxford: Oneworld.

Bauman, Z. (2003), *Liquid Love: On the Fragility of Human Bonds*. Cambridge: Polity Press.

Beck, U. & E. Beck-Gernsheim (1995), *The Normal Chaos of Love*, Cambridge: Polity Press.

Bhabha, H. (1990), 'The Other Question: Difference, Discrimination and the Discourse of Colonialism', in R. Ferguson (ed.), *Out There: Marginalization and Contemporary Cultures*, 71-87. New York: New Museum of Contemporary Art.

BM.I/SIAK (2006), *Perspektiven und Herausforderungen in der Integration muslimischen Mitbürgern in Österreich*. Vienna: Bundesministeriums für Inneres. www.bmi.gv.at/publikationen, accessed 8 January 2008.

Bracalenti R. & M. Benini (2005), 'The Role of Families in the Migrant Integration Process', in J. Pflegerl & S. Trnka (eds.), *Migration and the Family in the European Union*, 59-80. ÖIF Schriften, Heft 13, Vienna: Das Österreichische Institut für Familienforschung.

Bryceson, D. & U. Vuorela (eds.) (2002), *The Transnational Family: New European Frontiers and Global Networks*. Oxford: Berg.

Cesari, J. (2005), 'Introduction', in J. Cesari & S. McLoughlin (eds.), *European Muslims and the Secular State*, 1-7. Aldershot: Ashgate.

Dahl, T. S. (1997), *The Muslim Family: A Study of Women's Rights in Islam*. Oslo: Scandinavian University Press.

Dassetto, F. (ed.) (2000), *Islamic Words: Individuals, Societies and Discourse in Contemporary European Islam*. Paris: Maisonneuve et Larose.

Erel, U. (2002), 'Reconceptualizing Motherhood: Experiences of Migrant Women from Turkey Living in Germany', in D. Bryceson & U. Vuorela (eds.), *The Transnational Family: New European Frontiers and Global Networks*, 127-46. Oxford: Berg.

Fernández de la Hoz, P. (2002), *Migrantenfamilie und Intergration in den EU Mitgliedstaaten*. Bericht der Europäischen Beobachtungsstelle zur sozialen Situation Nr.10, Demographie und Familie, Vienna: Österreichisches Institut für Familienforschung (Austrian Institute for Family Studies).

Firat, D. (1996), *Die Migration als Belastungsfaktor türkischer Familien*. Dissertation. Hamburg: Verlag Dr. Kovać.

Fuhrer, U. & H.-H. Uslucan (eds.) (2005), *Familie, Akkulturation und Erziehung: Migration zwischen Eigen- und Fremdkultur*. Stuttgart: Verlag W. Kohlhammer.

Giddens, A. (1992), *The Transformation of Intimacy: Sexuality, Love and Eroticism in Modern Societies*. Cambridge: Polity Press.

Heitmeyer, W. et al. (1997), *Verlockender Fundamentalismus*. Frankfurt: Suhrkamp.

Institut für Markt- und Sozialanalysen [IMAS International Survey] (2004), *Die Formel des Zuwandererproblems*, No.17, September 2004.

Kagitcibasi, C. (1996), *Family and Human Development Across Cultures: A View from the Other Side*. Hillsdale, NJ: Lawrence Erlbaum Associates Publishers.

Kelek, N. (2005), *Die fremde Braut. Ein Bericht aus dem Inneren des türkischen Lebens in Deutschland*. Cologne: Kiepenheuer & Witsch.

König, K. and B. Perchinig (2005), 'Austria', in J. Niessen, Y. Schibel & C. Thompson (eds.), *Current Immigration Debates in Europe: A Publication of the European Migration Dialogue*. Brussels/Warsaw: Migration Policy Group.

Michalski, K. (ed.) (2006), *Religion in the New Europe*. Budapest/New York: CEU Press.

Mirdal, G. M. (2000), 'The Construction of Muslim Identities in Contemporary Europe', in F. Dassetto, (ed.), Islamic *Words: Individuals, Societies and Discourse in Contemporary European Islam*, 35-48. Paris: Maisonneuve et Larose.

Pflegerl, J & S. Trnka (eds.) (2005), *Migration and the Family in the European Union*. ÖIF Schriften, Heft 13, Vienna: Das Österreichische Institut für Familienforschung. www.oif.ac.at/aktuell/sr_13_migration_family_eu.pdf; accessed 16 April 2007.

Rahim, O. A. (1991), *Family Planning in the Legacy of Islam*. London and New York: Routledge.

Ramadan, T. (2001), *Islam, the West and the Challenges of Modernity*. Markfield: The Islamic Foundation.

8 Who Cares? 'External', 'Internal' and 'Mediator' Debates about South Asian Elders' Needs

Kanwal Mand

Introduction

> People are living longer and that doesn't mean that if people are living longer they are happy and healthy, they are not. That's the main thing ... Care ... is it the family's responsibility, or the land, or should the country take responsibility? (An outreach worker for Ekta, a voluntary group, London, 19 March 2004)

> I don't think that the Asian community like us to be involved. They're very independent people and look after their own people. They usually have some family and feel reluctant to accept services from outside the family. (Social worker, quoted in Department of Health publication 1998: 31)

This chapter explores how 'external' debates, notably in the public sphere which, as Grillo *supra* notes, often reflect migrants' imagined cultural practices, interact with 'internal' debates that occur within migrant families. Several authors draw attention to the impact of external debates in the form of policies on South Asian families in Britain in the arena of care and service provision (Boneham 1989; Forbat 2004; Katbamna et al. 2004). South Asian families are often positioned in public discourses as 'looking after their own', and this, it is argued, contributes to the low take-up of services by Asian elders and the misrecognition of their actual care needs (Forbat 2004; Harper & Levin 2003). Such assumptions about families fail to recognise that they are undergoing change arising from a variety of factors related to the migration process and the development cycle of households (Mand 2004), and it is in these contexts that internal discussions and negotiations about who cares, and for whom, occur. Through a focus on the elderly, this chapter illustrates how external discourses in the form of policies construct South Asian families in a guise that marginalises the experiences of the elderly who may need care beyond the family. At the same time debates within families concerning who should care for the elderly are apparent and, more often than not, stress idealised situations based on gender models which denote specific family members to care for the elderly (Gardner 2002).

Alongside public discourses and internal debates within South Asian families there is a third voice, that of voluntary organisations, and this chapter will draw attention to the role of such organisations working in the 'community'. In particular this chapter explores the role played by the Ekta project, an assisted charity, which caters for the needs of elderly South Asian men and women and their carers in East London. Ekta stands for 'oneness', and members of the Ekta project are drawn from different South Asian groups.[1] Although such organisations play an important role in the welfare of elderly migrants and their carers, their significance for migrant families has been largely ignored. This chapter shows that such organisations go beyond providing practical support (Mand 2006), and that they mediate debates and discourses occurring in the public sphere and internally in migrant families.

While this chapter draws attention to three sets of voices – those within public discourse, notably in national policies, those among members of minority ethnic families, and those in Ekta – it is important to bear in mind that these are not homogenous. For example, family members can maintain different positions, which may vary according to generation and gender, and as we shall see public discourses can be contradictory (Forbat 2004). Furthermore, although an element of ethnic division exists, for example, between a 'white' public sphere and minority ethnic families, this is not always the case: staff working in the local authority, for instance, are drawn from minority groups. The ethnic makeup of Ekta does not necessarily correspond with a South Asian background, although the majority of staff and volunteers are of South Asian heritage. The position Ekta occupies also testifies to the complexity of differing agendas within these three sets of voices: Ekta acts on behalf of families and the public sphere while at the same time maintaining an agenda that is necessary for the organisation to be recognised by the local authority and funding bodies.

Changes in the Composition of South Asian Migrant Families

The 2001 census revealed an increase in the number of elderly British residents of South Asian origin in the UK (Burholt 2004). The growth in numbers of the elderly reflects a wider trend of an ageing population in Europe and has obvious ramifications for the provision of state welfare in countries like Britain. In this context, representations of South Asian families as self-sufficient units and culturally bound to look after their own, which figure in public debates, are undoubtedly of concern, as they fail to account for the changes occurring within such families.

It is the first generation of South Asian migrants who arrived in Britain in response to labour shortages during the 1960s who make up the category, predominantly, of elderly Asians. However, a great deal of variety exists within and between South Asian families both in terms of age profile and composition of families. For example, 33 per cent of Pakistani families and 42 per cent of Bangladeshi families are likely to have four or more children (Beishon et al. 1998: 88). The composition of migrant families is also influenced by a variety of factors including their migration histories and the extent to which transnational links are maintained. These in turn are affected by policies regulating migration in different geographic places and in some cases older links between sending and receiving contexts such as those established under colonialism (Mand 2004). Furthermore, we cannot speak of the composition of South Asian families in any general sense as migrants' movements between and across places are intimately related to state policies. State policies such as immigration regulations and legislation have played a profound role in defining families and thus the entry and subsequent residence of migrants in the UK.

It is important to bear in mind that immigration policies target and affect entry and residence at a variety of levels. A key illustration of this process was the Primary Purpose Rule, installed during the 1980s by the Conservative Government, that challenged the legitimacy of arranged marriages and implied that male spouses or fiancés seeking to join partners were 'bogus' and simply attempting to gain entry into the UK. However, this particular rule came under attack from the European Court as it discriminated on 'the basis of sex ... [by] stricter immigration controls for men than for women' (Sachdeva 1993: 93, Menski 1999). Significantly for the elderly, entry into Britain is subject to demonstrating that there are no carers at the point of departure. Furthermore, immigration rules stipulate that entry into Britain to join families is feasible only if the potential entree can demonstrate that their stay would not entail recourse to public funds. The sponsorship forms that migrant families have to provide contain stipulations that there are sufficient material resources as well as accommodation. Gardner's work on Bangladeshi elders in London, and their carers who are often women, draws attention to immigration policies as re-inscribing gender roles and creating hierarchical relations between people and places. In doing so she argues that cultural norms about gender roles are 'exacerbated by the British state. Immigration procedures mean that women's entry into the UK is dependent upon whether they are wives or mothers' (Gardner 2000: 131). At the same time, there is an internally held ideal, within Bangladeshi families, that women are carers and therefore being a carer is central to Bangladeshi women's self-perception of being good women (Gardner 2000: 130-131).

'They Look after Their Own' versus 'We Look after Our Own'

Research indicates that elderly ethnic minority migrants are less likely to use the social services on offer from the local council and other non-profit organisations 'because social work has operated in exclusionary ways ... [and] since South Asians families are expected to look after older persons themselves, they are unlikely to approach social services (Bowes & Dar 2000: 306). In her 1989 study of Sikh elders, Boneham points to several prevailing myths surrounding the experiences of being an elderly member of an ethnic minority living in Britain. For instance, she highlights the perception that all elderly South Asian migrants seek to return to their homelands. Whilst there existed a 'myth of return' (Anwar 1979), recent research on transnational ties has illustrated that migrant families utilise a variety of ways of maintaining relations with their point of origin, which may or may not involve literal returns, and that this process engages family members differently not least due to gender and generational norms (Gardner 1995; Mand 2004).

Although the literature on change within South Asian families in Britain is growing, this has tended to focus on intergenerational negotiations in the context of marriages (Prinja 1999, Shaw 2000), while changes in family organisation arising from marital or geographic separation and/or divorce are rarely taken into account significantly in public discourses (Mand 2005). Hence, certain aspects of change become incorporated in the public discourse on South Asian families at the expense of others. For example, the myth relating to South Asian families as caring for their elders and less likely to require the services of the state in terms of care continues in spite of changes. However, there is a need for services and care homes for elderly Asians. In the London borough of Newham, and in other areas beyond London, state-sponsored residential care homes do exist that house within them specific ethnically aligned units, for example the Green Gate residential home in East London has an Asian unit, where the elderly can reside on a permanent and/or on short-term basis. Short-term residence can be appropriate if an elder is in a 'crisis' and vulnerable or if family members have gone on holiday. Such residential homes are in addition to gender-specific assisted care homes in the area where women and men reside with a day warden in attendance. One home I studied housed twelve elderly women ranging in age from their mid-50s to 80s, and the longest period that one resident had been there was for thirteen years. In some cases women, returned 'home' to their families for weekends while in others, no contact was maintained.

In the sub-continent too, Palriwala (1994) notes anxieties existing with regards to care for the elderly, notably in urban contexts and she draws attention to these being related to new economic and demographic pressures affecting families. In addition migration plays a key role for the experiences of the elderly who are left behind or who travel in order to be cared for by relatives living abroad (Mand 2004). Meanwhile, there are ideals and norms about becoming older in South Asia and these are often referred to elderly migrants in the UK. For example, elderly South Asian women are said to take on fewer domestic responsibilities in their old age, although my observations in the UK highlighted that being part of a migrant household meant that elderly women are active in the household, for example, caring for the grandchildren, doing housework and cooking. Nonetheless, the elderly can and often are constructed within families as a 'burden' or 'backward' with regards to the familial life and expectations in the UK. At the same time, immigration policies construct elderly migrants seeking to join family in the UK as simply needing care and hence a drain on the state's resources rather than as providers of care to British families.

As mentioned earlier, public discourses about migrant families are not homogenous, as was illustrated in two policy statements issued by the Department of Health in the late 1990s. The *National Strategy for Carers* (Department of Health 1999) attempted to provide an 'inclusive approach' whereby carers of and within families are also supported by statutory services. Forbat's analysis (2004) draws attention to a general underlying assumption in the policy 'that caring is a voluntary component of family life' and argues that it 'position[s] people from minoritized ethnic backgrounds, ... stereotypically ... to care out of culturally determined norms of family obligations' (Forbat 2004: 315). However, the ways in which policy positions minority families are not fixed; an earlier policy had expressly sought to question stereotypical understandings of ethnic minorities. *They Look After Their Own Don't They?* (Department of Health 1998: 3-5) drew attention to the 'significant disadvantage' experienced by ethnic minorities in spite of some good practice owing to the 'ethnocentric nature of service provision'. Particular issues are raised in this publication relating to staff assumptions of 'they look after their own', and the document is critical of staff for not taking into account the 'complex nature of care giving, gender and employment changes affecting the first and second generation families' (Department of Health 1998: 31). Some of the discussion on language further illuminates the ways in which public discourse is not in itself homogeneous. For example, the document highlights that staff may take 'shortcuts' by using relatives as interpreters, and this it found to be unsatisfactory. Whereas one social worker is quoted as finding the use of relatives to be time saving since family members know the situation and they are known to the elderly person, another is quoted as finding the practice of using interpreters from the family a potential impediment (Department of Health 1998: 28-29).

Some writers have criticised assumptions such as 'they look after their own' as a form, albeit unconscious and unwitting, of 'cultural racism'. Cultural racism implies that ideas about cultural practices are essentialised and seen to be deterministic of behaviour. The recognition of cultural racism draws attention to the changing ways in which racism is expressed and experienced which has been to move away from a biological and physiological signifiers towards practices and values based on 'culture' (Forbat 2004; Song 2003). While the significance of race in understanding public discourse and debate for the experiences of minority ethnic elders remains pivotal (Bowes & Dar 2000), discourses about the family are often framed around essentialised ideas about the culture of a particular migrant group. However, Song (2003) shows that distinctions are made between migrant groups: for example, Asians may be represented along the lines of ethnicity, where the emphasis is on cultural practice, while other migrant groups (she gives the example of African Americans) may be represented along racial lines. Hence, looking at how public discourse frames South Asian families necessitates a comparison with other migrant groups present within the nation-state. For example, as Reynolds (2004) notes, Asians are constructed through such cultural practices as arranged marriages and multi-generational households, whilst Afro-Caribbeans tend to be associated with 'problems' of criminality and familial breakdown. Additionally, Reynolds has highlighted the way in which the Black (Afro-Caribbean) family in Britain is stereotyped as being female headed, despite there being variations within Caribbean cultures, and that this (mis)represents them as being against the norm of two-parent families (Reynolds 2002).

Meanwhile, a more general criticism of the British welfare policy of 'care in the community'[2] is that it fails to take into account the politics of community care and the allocation of resources within and between different community groups. Nonetheless, an underlying premise of the 1990 National Health Service and Community Care Act was a move away from institutional provision towards communal care, without accounting for the diversity of familial and communal relationships and how these link with norms and practices involving care and the ways in which these alter over the life course and over time (Horden & Smith 1998).

Despite the existence of public discourses and the shape these take in terms of policies that affect families, we cannot assume these discourses set the agenda for the ways in which migrant families live their lives in Britain. For example, Baumann (1996) illustrates how, in a multi-ethnic suburb in West London (Southall), dominant discourses, notably those of the state, do indeed have a strong impact on 'demotic' (everyday) discourses present within migrant communities and voiced by individuals. At the same time, he shows that these dominant discourses are only partially incorporated by ethnic communities. Following Baumann, it is worth exploring how public discourses and internal debates construct the family and how these overlap, before moving on to the role of intermediary organisations like Ekta.

Who should care for the elderly, why, and how are common questions linking public discourses and debates within migrant families. From an external perspective 'caring for their own' relates to the perception of South Asians having a different morality from the 'Western' family in which the focus is less on the individual and more on the collectivity (see Ballard *supra*). The debates within families are similar to those occurring in the public sphere, in so far as they too are framed in cultural norms and traditions that are imagined or idealised. This is particularly the case with families of North Indian origin who traditionally stress obligations and reciprocity, though these vary according to a member's stage in life and gender. An idealised scenario is for elderly parents to be cared for by sons and their wives in the context of multigenerational households (Vatuk 1990). The absence of such care can result in 'shame' for the elderly family member and the wider kin group. However, it is worth noting that there are many elderly family members who are not cared for by their children and in many cases it is others or extended kin who take on this role. During fieldwork in Goa, I found that nuns in convents are looking after many elderly Catholic Goans whilst their children were working in Middle-Eastern countries or had settled in the West. Furthermore, it is important to stress gender in the context of care, whereby although ideals state that it is sons who care for their elderly parents, research indicates that in fact it is daughters who play a key role (Chen 2001). Significantly in the British context these ideals are being remembered and/or imagined by elders as most of them had migrated prior to their parents becoming elderly. At the same time a critical appraisal of the relationship between gender and the provision of care either on a voluntary basis or through more formal means is often marginal in both internal and public debates (see McKie et al. 2004).

Furthermore, with respect to the morality of care and its provision both internal debates and public discourses present an image of the family as a solid unit, unaffected by processes of social change. As such the family is simply seen as a site of support. Feminist scholars, however, have drawn attention to the family as being a site of support and *oppression* and one that inherently makes demands on members on the basis of gender ideals and generational norms (Moore 1988; Palriwala 1994). This leads us to another similarity between external and internal debates. South Asian elders are constructed as being in need, and unable to engage with the modern lifestyles that characterise British society. The elderly are seen as the maintainers of tradition and as refusing to let go of 'homeland' practices, which in turn negates the active role that they play in maintaining families (Gardner 2002; Mand 2004).

Caring for Asian Elders and Their Carers: Ekta, a Community-Based Organisation

Formed in 1987, Ekta was initially established because of the 'unmet needs' of South Asian migrant families particularly the elderly and their carers. Previously, it was the Ethnic Minority Unit, made up of several organisations, which was responsible for the 'needs' of *all* migrants in the London borough of Newham. A survey, commissioned by the unit and entitled 'The unmet needs of ethnic elders'[3] established that there was a severe lack of services and that take-up of available services was noticeably low in the case of ethnic minorities. The survey into the 'unmet needs of ethnic elders' identified the needs of all ethnic minorities living in Newham regardless of race, religion, age and gender. The key conclusion, according to Ramesh Verma (the founder and current Chief Executive Officer of Ekta), who undertook the original survey, 'very clearly [stated] that they [ethnic minorities] needed services. The question was not that they did *not* need services but they needed them *badly*' (interview with Ramesh Verma, CEO Ekta, 22 June 2004).

This initial report drew attention to the general ways in which the needs of the ethnic minorities were being ignored. There were difficulties, as Verma explained, in providing a uniform service for all ethnic minorities regardless of gender, generation and culture. The perceived limitations in providing a general service resulted in Ekta forming a distinctive organisation and becoming an assisted charity concerned specifically with South Asian elders and their carers. Interviews and discussions with Verma about her original survey drew attention to specific issues that hindered South Asian elders taking up services on offer from local council welfare services. In the main these related to poor training in cultural awareness, including the assumption that South Asian families take care of their own, the lack of interpreters and/or staff who could speak to the elderly, and the vulnerability of elderly men and women to mental and financial abuse from within the family. Research conducted in Canada on elder abuse similarly shows that migrant elders are less likely to point out that they are being neglected or abused owing to generational attitudes, particularly the notion that the family is an appropriate source for help and care, as well as the notion that the elderly drain resources from the country owing to their perceived 'neediness' (Harbison & Morrow 1998).

The move towards catering specifically for Asian elderly migrants and their carers is significant given the multicultural context within which families are located in London. It aligns the community group along a pan-ethnic basis denoting migrants from the sub-continent. The splintering of groups such as Ekta is significant owing to the ethnic diversity in this borough of London (Newham), where alongside South Asians there are sizeable Somali, Turkish and Afro-Caribbean populations and, more recently, a growing number of Eastern European migrants. At the same time, the establishment of Ekta along the lines of difference from other minority groups with specific cultural 'needs' reflects a broader tendency to celebrate diversity and illustrates the initiatives taken on at local and national levels in the bid to promote multiculturalism.

Tables 8.1, 8.2, and 8.3 give information regarding the ethnic and religious composition of the borough and indicate the place of birth of residents. It is worth remembering that the census data from 2001 do not capture the recent arrival of Eastern Europeans into the area.

Currently, Ekta is made up of approximately 30 volunteers and five paid staff including outreach workers. At the last count there were over a hundred elderly members registered with Ekta and these include elderly men and women drawn from different South Asian groups such as Pakistani and Bangladeshi Muslims, Gujaratis, Sikhs and Indian Christians. Despite a long waiting list of members, translatable as a need for the organisation, funds are in short supply, resulting in the loss of paid staff and the rejection of members. Funding is sought through various means including national and local government grants as well as individual initiatives. Ekta was shortlisted for a charity award in 2006 and it was stated by Ramesh Verma that 'service provision for Asian elders in Newham was not religiously and culturally appropriate

Table 8.1 *Ethnic identity (principal groups), Newham Borough, 2001 (%)*

White	39.4
Black African	13.1
Indian	12.1
Bangladeshi	8.8

Source: Census 2001, www.statistics.gov.uk/census2001/profiles/00BB-A.asp#ethnic (accessed March 2007)

Table 8.2 *Religious affiliation, Newham Borough, 2001 (%)*

Christian	46.8
Muslim	24.3
Hindu	6.9
Sikh	2.8
Buddhist	0.7
Jewish	0.2
Other	0.3
None/Not stated	18.0

Source: ibid.

Table 8.3 *Place of birth, Newham Borough, 2001 (%)*

UK	61.8
Other EU	2.6
Outside EU	35.6

Source: ibid.

[and therefore] nobody was making use of it', hence the need for the Ekta project. When shortlisted for an award, the CEO of Ekta is recorded as stating that the organisation is 'not about providing special services but providing equal services that people can use'.[4] Despite the CEO moving away from the notion of 'special services' for Asians, research by the council indicates that Ekta is an important source of support and information for South Asian minorities in the London borough. For example, a local council survey monitoring language use in the borough asked Punjabi-speaking respondents what sources of support they used. Eighty-one per cent cited voluntary organisations of which 56 per cent named Ekta (representing 46 per cent of the whole sample). When Punjabi speakers were asked where they would go for help, advice or support, 40 per cent said they would go specifically to the Ekta Project, or the Trinity Centre (which houses the Project), 22 per cent to other local service or community centres. A quarter (23 per cent) said they would ask their friends, family and neighbours. Two or three respondents each mentioned their doctor, the council offices or town hall, and the Citizen's Advice Bureau or similar centre.[5]

Alongside a befriending scheme for elderly migrants, Ekta organises weekly get-togethers, a swimming club, walking groups and artistic projects, for example, a play that raised awareness of breast cancer – in rehearsal during fieldwork following the success of an earlier endeavour when women performed a play representing their migration experience. During my period of fieldwork several activities were organised for the women, taking them outside the immediate vicinity. We took a trip, very much like that represented in Gurinder Chadha's film *Bhaji on the Beach*, although this time it was Eastbourne and not Blackpool. One of the key reasons women sought to be part of Ekta was the isolation and loneliness that they experienced whether living alone or with their families. For women who live on their own, council support workers are central in ensuring that they are able to carry out domestic tasks such as cleaning and laundry. The warden and local council staff that come to the residence in order to perform domestic tasks care for those living in sheltered accommodation, and the local council provides a minibus for women to go shopping on a weekly basis. Shopping trips are also organised by Ekta although in the main Ekta provides its members with the facility to get together weekly, attend their swimming classes and other organised activities.

In addition to undertaking day trips with the elderly women, I attended a weekly women's group where the majority of women were Sikh or Gujarati, and on average aged around 60 years old, with one woman in her mid-80s. Several meetings took place on a weekly basis for men and women and members attended the one closest to their place of residence. A large majority of the women arrived at the community centre on the minibus arranged by Ekta and at all times were accompanied by volunteers who were Asian. The women's living arrangements differed; some lived on their own in council flats or sheltered accommodation, others with their husbands and in two cases with married sons and grandchildren. The borough has several residences specifically inhabited by Asian men and women, respectively, while there is one larger unit that houses both men and women in sheltered accommodation with varying degrees of 'independence'. This is not to say that these women maintained no links with family members, rather arrangements were often made involving sleep-overs with family members over weekends, during ritual occasions when more elaborate visiting occurred, and when women in the household travelled to the sub-continent to visit kin there. The perception that children are not there for the elderly, emotionally and/or physically, was repeated to me by many of the women. In some cases the women adopted a particular pragmatism, as they stressed the difficulties of living with children while for others living away from children had improved their social relationships. In rare cases, women were totally isolated from familial networks though this tended to be restricted to cases where there had been severe physical and mental abuse or abandonment.

Bridging the Internal and External Debates: The Role of Community Organisations

There is no doubt that the organisation of South Asian families is changing in the British context as it is in the sub-continent. Furthermore, in the space of the community centre I encountered the need to look beyond the family for the support of South Asian elders (Mand 2006). In this sense Ekta as an organisation acts as a stand-in family. When I asked one elderly woman about her contribution of stories to the *yaada* (remembrances) project, involving members telling their stories about their migration from Punjab, she spoke of the need to collect stories as being of benefit to the elders stating: 'there is no one to hear our stories and its very important and very near to our heart. Children have no time to ... we try to revive them [oral narratives] in the form of drama, poetry, dance and plays'.

On the one hand the above quote illustrates changes in intergenerational relations as experienced by this elderly woman. On the other, as a result of changes, stories are told beyond the family, first to Ekta staff, but later they are retold in the form of public performances. The *yaada* project was turned into a play in partnership with local sixth form students (i.e. age sixteen plus) with the assistance of a playwright, and subsequently performed at the sixth form centre. Therefore the support that comes from Ekta fulfils the desire to be cared for in spite of the perceived unavailability of family members and offers an opportunity for intergenerational contact. A focus on organisations like Ekta draws attention to a space wherein internal idealised perceptions are re-considered in the light of actual lived experiences for some elderly migrants, and through the performances are presented to a wider public sphere.

Other ways in which Ekta acts as a mediator includes providing information to the elderly about their pension rights, specific health issues like being aware of diabetes and the Asian diet, as well as housing matters. Ekta arranges for experts in various fields to come and speak to the members at their meetings. The elderly pass on such information to their family members (if they live with them), although the main concern for Ekta is for the elders to know their rights and entitlements. For example, during the course of fieldwork a representative of the council came to talk to the elderly about their right to claim disability and/or pension benefits, especially if they were also widowed. Moreover, a key role is played by the organisation in educating other service providers involved in the care of elderly migrants. For example, the elder abuse awareness training organised by Ekta is attended by members of the social services and by staff from care homes as well as health workers. Ekta's role is prominent, given the recognition of migrant's needs being 'unmet' and the lack of recognition in debates in the public sphere concerning changes taking place within South Asian families, notably in areas like elderly abuse. To this end, campaigns were launched by the organisation to draw attention to abuse occurring within families and the necessity for those external care providers to look beyond the stereotypes. Financial abuse is one of the key issues that Ekta sought to tackle, and volunteers and staff are trained to be vigilant.

> If you know that somebody is getting £180 a week [through benefits and pension] but yet the person's coat is falling apart and she has no money in her pocket and can't pay for her tea, then you wonder why.

The exposure of elder abuse occurring within South Asian families is resisted from within the Asian community. As the trainer explained, there is hesitancy in acknowledging the occurrence of elder abuse. She recounted some of the reactions on her training in elder abuse awareness from 'the community'.

> Our own Asian people [who] said 'don't say that because white people will think' ... And I said that is what I am trying to say! ... [they said] 'It looks *besharam* (shameless) that you are telling us that it happens, this happens in the Asian community and there are white people listening there'.

A tension exists between the representation of an ideal South Asian family that cares for one another, coming from the wider community, and the sensitive issue of abuse within families raised by Ekta. Interestingly the exposure of issues such as abuse in families is perceived as a betrayal, the public sphere associated with 'white people listening'.

Additionally, Ekta seeks to represent elderly members drawn from the different Asian groups in a culturally sensitive manner, given that the original survey undertaken by Verma indicated a lack of cultural awareness regarding 'values' held within the Asian community, for example, the idea of *sharam* (shame), which may result in an elder not speaking about their negative familial experiences given the ideal and status associated with becoming elderly and being cared for by family members. At the same time, Ekta wishes to move away from stereotypes that are held within the Asian communities, for example, daughters-in-law who are often expected to be carers and the elderly person in need (i.e. mother-in-law) as being pitted against one another. This was illustrated to me in the following quote from the founder, speaking first in the voice of an observer and then in the role of an elderly abused women.

> These ladies ... they think maybe it's their fault and maybe I
> didn't bring up my son ... I have done something wrong in my
> past life and, after I die, they are going to take this money away
> anyway ...

Switching now to speak about the types of intervention, she commented:

> [We] visit the family first because we work with carers as well
> [we ask the carer] ... we know how stressful it is and will you tell
> us what is the problem ... looking after your mother-in-law or
> father-in-law? Tell us and we can support you ... so we start work-
> ing [with the carer/ family] taking mother-in-law to the centre to
> a centre for two hours a week or so she [carer] gets a break.

Organisations such as Ekta provide invaluable aid to elderly men and
women and yet at the same time operate according to an ethos that
seeks to challenge cultural essentialism from the top down as well as
at the grass roots level. They can be interpreted as holding an intermediate position, whereby they are involved in a form of translation between one voice (the public) and the internal voice (of migrant families). This position is, however, a difficult one to straddle as they
seek to promote the well-being of the elderly and their carers while at
the same time being vigilant, despite opposition from the community
at large, of the abuse that can and does occur within South Asian families. At the same time, Ekta recognises the onus placed on women
in caring for family members while also having resources to deal with
the pressures that are associated with caring and inter-family dynamics
that come from the organisation's staff make-up.

   In the context of changing familial organisation, there have emerged
new ways of relating, notably through the utilisation of support networks beyond the family. This in turn means that groups like Ekta become important actors in the lives of migrant families, hitherto ignored
in the accounts of migrant familial life. Nonetheless, Ekta as an organisation holds a complex position as it maintains a secular ethos owing
to the diversity of its member's religious identities. Although all major
religious festivals are celebrated within the different groups at the level
of dance and food, clear limits are placed. The celebration of religious
occasions is divorced from any sermons or specific religious practices.
The religious aspects are split off from the festivities, and sometimes
these are collapsed together. For example, during *diwali*, the festival of
lights, the weekly group members (women) danced the *giddha* (Punjabi
folk dance) and *dandiya* (Gujarati folk dance), but although *diwali* is
celebrated by both Punjabi and Hindus the women were not allowed to

recount devotional tales or songs. Women objected to the distinction between religion and events like *Eid* (Muslim) or *Baskahi* (Sikh). In fact, when elderly Ekta members raised specific political and/or religious issues or practices within the groups they were severely reprimanded by volunteers and outreach workers. The reasoning behind such secularism is to ensure harmonious gatherings. As one outreach worker explained:

> We don't bring the religious bit you know? But that's where all the problems starts ... 'My religion is better than yours' or 'This is what happened'. It is bound to cause problems. So no religion and the same thing with politics. We don't want to know what has happened in Pakistan or in India or Sri Lanka ... No, keep it out! So I tell my members that look, our women can't read and write anyway which is good in one way but men, yeah, they do and they used to bring newspapers in their back pocket and say 'Oh Pakistan this has happened and India has done this and this'. So about ten years ago we said 'No!' 'I don't want to see any paper here. You have six and a half days so read as many papers as you want'.

Ekta as an organisation needs also to be located in the context of British debates about multiculturalism and difference. Organisations like Ekta mediate between the external and the internal. Although members of Ekta hold different religious and regional identities, as an organisation there are certain ideological ways of operating and aims that underlie Ekta's approach. By maintaining a position of being secular and multicultural, wherein cultural diversity is celebrated at a particular level (without the religious aspects), Ekta is different from other religious community groups. Besides a commitment to being secular, Ekta is also committed to denouncing the negative as well as the positive aspects of South Asian families, and at this level speaks out against the wider community. Hence, conflicts arise because of the political and social messages that the organisation seeks to establish and its views on the social injustices experienced by migrants on the basis of gender and generation. Whilst we can interpret Ekta as taking on the caring practices ideally performed by family members there are nonetheless boundaries that the organisation sets. For example in insisting that religion and politics be kept outside the meetings, Ekta promotes a view of multiculturalism (akin to that of the State) wherein more palatable differences (such as festivals) are promoted whilst others (notably religious) are curtailed.

Conclusion

The strategies and practices that South Asian families incorporate with regard to care for the elderly are influenced by a variety of factors including the household's stage in the development cycle, the migration process, transnational networks and so on, and these are further informed by voices in the public sphere and internally within families. There is some degree of overlap between public and internal voices linked to particular moral and/or ideological positions. It is interesting to note that neither internal nor external discourses are homogeneous, rather, they can and often do contradict each other, as is revealed when looking at the 1999 and 1998 Department of Health initiatives. The growing number of elderly migrants in the UK coupled with the lack of appropriate services and the low take-up of those that exist by migrants is clearly of concern to service providers and community organisations. This chapter has raised a third voice, that of a community-based organisation, Ekta, which can be seen to mediate between the two perspectives and plays an essential role in ensuring the well-being of the elderly and their carers whilst also educating other service providers. The chapter has drawn attention to the significance of such a perspective, which hitherto remains marginal in the account of migrant families.

Yet the role that Ekta plays is shifting and contextual, depending on audience. For example in relation to wider service providers, Ekta acts as an educator of Asian practices and speaks on behalf of the elders. At the same time the context of these elderly women's lives presents a very different picture to the stereotypical depiction of South Asian families as being self-sufficient units. In the absence of familial support Ekta acts like a family member, one that has time to listen and undertake the process of developing understanding between family members. Nonetheless, Ekta can and does speak against the community and in some cases its members. Furthermore, Ekta maintains its own ideological position; it seeks to represent all Asian cultures and refutes any specific religious affiliation. This differs from members' own wishes but affords organisations like Ekta a legitimacy because they are not are religiously aligned. In this sense, Ekta adopts the State's discourse on multiculturalism, by accepting and celebrating difference and diversity in certain spheres whilst religious differences are minimised through a secular stance.

Acknowledgements

The research on which this chapter was based was funded by an Economic and Social Research Council award (M570255001), and was part of the 'Families & Social Capital ESRC Research Group' at London South Bank University. I thank Ralph Grillo for his editorial comments.

Notes

1 See www.multikulti.org.uk/agencies/bengali/london/17586; accessed December 2007.
2 The National Health Service and Community Care Act (1990) sought to enable aging people or those affected by disability to live independently within the community and be cared for by the community.
3 An 'in-house' report was produced in the late 1980s following this survey undertaken by Ramesh Verma (the founder of Ekta).
4 www.charityawards.co.uk/previous/2001/winners/research; accessed August 2006.
5 www.languageshop.org.uk/language%20summaries/Punjabi%20Summary.htm; accessed December 2007.

References

Anwar, M. (1979), *The Myth of Return: Pakistanis in Britain*. London: Heinemann Educational.
Baumann, G. (1996), *Contested Cultures: Discourses of Identity in Multi-Ethnic London*. Cambridge: Cambridge University Press.
Beishon, S., T. Modood & S. Virdee (1998), *Ethnic Minority Families*. London: Policy Studies Institute.
Boneham, M.A. (1989), 'Ageing and Ethnicity in Britain: The Case Study of Elderly Sikh Women in a Midlands Town', *New Community* 15 (3): 447-459.
Bowes, A.M & N.S. Dar (2000), 'Researching Social Care for Minority Ethnic Older People: Implications of some Scottish Research', *British Journal of Social Work* 30: 305-321.
Burholt, V. (2004), 'Transnationalism, Economic Transfers and Families' Ties: Intercontinental Contacts of Older Gujaratis, Punjabis and Sylhetis in Birmingham with Families Abroad, *Ethnic and Racial Studies* 27 (5): 800-829.
Chen, M.A. (2001), *Perpetual Mourning. Widowhood in Rural India*. New Delhi: Oxford University Press.
Department of Health (1998), *'They look after their own don't they?' Inspections of Community Care Services for Black and Ethnic Minority Older People*. www.dh.gov.uk/PublicationsAndStatistics/Publications/PublicationsInspectionReports/PublicationsInspectionReportsArticle/fs/en?CONTENT_ID=4008284&chk=X6h3hC; accessed February 2007.
Department of Health (1999), *Caring about Carers: A National Strategy for Carers*. www.dh.gov.uk/PublicationsAndStatistics/Publications/PublicationsPolicyAndGuidance/PublicationsPolicyAndGuidanceArticle/fs/en?CONTENT_ID=4006522&chk=yySBZ/1999; accessed February 2007.

Forbat, L. (2004), 'The Care and Abuse of Minoritized Groups: The Role of Statutory Services', *Critical Policy* 24 (3): 312-331.

Gardner, K. (1995), *Global migrants, Local Lives: Travel and Transformation in Rural Bangladesh*. Oxford: Clarendon Press.

Gardner, K. (2002), *Age, Narrative, Migration. The Life Course and Life Histories of Bengali Elders in London*. Oxford: Berg.

Harper, S & S. Levin (2003), *Changing Families as Societies Age: Care, independence and ethnicity*. Working Paper Number WP503. Oxford. Oxford Institute of Aging.

Harbison, J & M. Morrow (1998), 'Re-examining the Social Construction of "Elder Abuse and Neglect": A Canadian Perspective', *Ageing and Society* 18: 691-711.

Horden, P & R.M. Smith (1998), *The Locus of Care: Families, Communities and the Provision of Welfare since Antiquity*. London: Routledge.

Katbamna, S, W. Ahmed, B.A. Bhakta, R. Barker & G. Parker (2004), 'Do They Look after their Own? Informal Support for South Asian Carers', *Health and Social Care in the Community* 12 (5): 398-406.

McKie, L, S. Bowlby & S. Gregory (2004), 'Starting Well: Gender, Care and Health in the Family Context', *Sociology* 38 (3): 593-612.

Mand, K. (2004), Gendered *Places, Transnational Lives: Sikh Women in Tanzania, Britain and Indian Punjab*. University of Sussex: Unpublished DPhil Thesis.

Mand, K. (2005), 'Marriage and Migration at the End Stages', *Indian Journal of Gender Studies. Special issue: Marriage and Migration in Asia* 12 (2 &3): 407-425.

Mand, K. (2006), 'Friendship and Elderly South Asian Women', in *Community, Work and Family. Special Issue: Families, Minority Ethnic Communities and Social Capital* 9 (3): 309-323.

Menski, W. (1999), 'South Asian Women in Britain: Family Integrity and the Primary Purpose Rule', in R. Barot, H. Bradley & S. Fenton (eds.), *Ethnicity, Gender and Social Change*, 81-98. London: Macmillan Press.

Moore, H. (1988), *Feminism and Anthropology*. London: Routledge.

Palriwala, R. (1994), *Changing Kinship, Family, and Gender Relations in South Asia. Processes, Trends, Issues*. Leiden: Women and Autonomy Centre (VENA).

Prinja, S. (1999), *With a View to Marriage: Hindu Gujaratis in London*. London School of Economics: Unpublished DPhil Thesis.

Reynolds, T (2002), 'Analyzing the Black Family', in A. Carling, S. Duncan & R. Edwards (eds.), *Analyzing Families*, 69-76. London: Routledge.

Reynolds, T. (2004), *Caribbean Families, Social Capital and Young People's Diasporic Identities*. Families and Social Capital ESRC Research Group Working Paper Series, Number 12. London: South Bank University.

Sachdeva, Sanjiv (1993). *The Primary Purpose Rule in British Immigration Law*. Stoke-on-Trent: Trentham Books and School of Oriental & African Studies.

Shaw, A. (2000), *Kinship and Continuity: Pakistani Families in Britain*. London: Routledge.

Song, M. (2003), *Choosing Ethnic Identity*. London: Polity Press.

Vatuk, S. (1990). 'To be a Burden on Others: Dependency Anxiety amongst the Elderly in India', in O. Lynch (ed.), *Divine Passions: The Social Construction of Emotion in India*, 64-88. Berkley: University of California Press.

9 Italian Families in Switzerland: Sites of Belonging or 'Golden Cages'? Perceptions and Discourses inside and outside the Migrant Family

Susanne Wessendorf

Introduction

> We celebrate every birthday together and then we are all together at grandma's place, and we also celebrate Christmas there ... the family *is* the most important, you know, among the Swiss I notice, I ask them, 'When did you move out of your parents' place?' and they say 'At 17'. Then I ask 'Why?' And they say: 'Because my parents restricted me', the Swiss just take the step, they leave and have no more connection to the parents, it's really different ... For me it's really the most important ... to have a family that works, to see each other, it's a pleasure, isn't it?

Luca, whose views are cited above, is a second-generation Italian born in the German part of Switzerland in 1972. His parents had migrated from Sicily in the early 1960s. He grew up in an extended network of kin and was raised by his parents and his grandmother, together with his cousins. This large network of relatives provided him with social and emotional stability during his childhood and adolescence, and spending time with his cousins and his uncle of the same age group strengthened his association and identification with other Italians. His relatives were not only family, but also peers with whom he could share many interests during adolescence. Luca is proud of what he sees as his 'typical Italian family' characterised by frequent contact with parents and siblings, big family gatherings and a strong sense of support within the family. The family is not just an important element of his everyday life, but through notions of what he sees as 'the typical Italian family' he also asserts his Italianness. By pointing to his Swiss peers' disconnection from their family, he emphasises the difference between himself and the majority society, and distances himself from the Swiss.

In contrast, Antonio experienced his family as a 'golden cage'. According to him, Italian families 'always meddle with your businesses'.

He was born in Naples and came to Switzerland at the age of two. He revolted against his parents' expectations of upward social mobility and against their wish for him to marry an Italian woman. Today, he does not have many Italian friends in Switzerland and pities his sister who is married to an 'oppressive Italian husband' and perfectly fits into his parents' expectations. He finds Italian families hypocritical: 'On the surface, everything is perfect, but underneath, things explode'.

This chapter discusses how such different positions and competing discourses regarding the family came about in the context of Italian migration to Switzerland. Furthermore, it describes how these competing positions among migrants and their children themselves are not reflected in public discourse, where, rather, Italian family relations are somewhat idealised. The first part of this chapter focuses on the different discourses among Italians themselves. It illustrates the emergence of both a 'dominant', essentialist discourse about the family among Italians, and a more differentiated, 'demotic' discourse. Baumann (1996) uses the concepts of dominant and demotic discourses to refer to the ways in which both migrants and non-migrants describe people of different origins. The dominant discourse is characterised by notions of cultural homogeneity, while the demotic discourse is based on more differentiated self-definitions of 'culture' and 'community'. In the present case, the dominant discourse is distinguished by the celebration of *la famiglia* as the ultimate site of 'Italian culture'. This celebration of the family resulted from the separation of family members over extended periods of time during the initial years of migration to Switzerland. Similar reifications of the Italian family have been shown to be instrumental in the expression of ethnic identity in other contexts, too, for example in accounts of Italians in Britain (Fortier 2000) and among Italians in the United States (Boscia-Mulè 1999). In contrast to this dominant discourse of the ideal family, the demotic discourse about the family among Italians in Switzerland was primarily developed by members of the second generation. It is characterised by a more critical stance towards the family, grounded in a critique of, for example, the parents' gender ideologies and their expectations of close relations with kin.

The second part of the chapter describes how, despite the existence of contrasting discourses about the family among Italians themselves, the public discourse about Italian families in Switzerland does not reflect these different attitudes, but idealises Italian families. Although Italian migrants were stigmatised during the early years of their migration, this stigmatisation was not based on negative images of their family or gender relations, but on what was perceived to be improper behaviour in public space. These categories of stigmatisation applied to Italians stand in stark contrast to those applied to migrants who came to Switzerland later, such as Muslims. In contrast to Italians, these newer migrants have been stigmatised on the grounds of their family and gender relations. The last part of the chapter discusses these different categories of judgement applied to migrants from various origins.[1]

Southern Italian Labour Migration to Switzerland and the Emergence of Translocal Families

Italian post-war migration was part of European labour migration with hundreds of thousands of southern and south-eastern Europeans moving to north-western Europe to help build the booming post-war economy. From 1946 until 1975, about 2.5 million Italians migrated to Switzerland.[2] Most of them returned to Italy because of seasonal work contracts, but by 1970, approximately half a million Italians lived in Switzerland. Due to return migration, numbers declined to about 300,000 by 2001 (Niederberger 2003). For a total population of seven million inhabitants in Switzerland, this is a considerable number.

The original plan of most migrants was to buy a house and some land in Italy and return within five years. However, many did not manage to do so due to a lack of jobs in Italy and because they wanted their children to finish school in Switzerland. Since most migrants dreamed of returning, and because of short-term residency permits during the first years of their migration, they frequently travelled back and forth between Switzerland and Italy. They spent every summer holiday and sometimes Christmas in Italy, and developed lively translocal relations. These connections to the homeland were translocal rather than transnational because Italian migrants travelled back and forth between the village of origin and the place of settlement in Switzerland and felt a strong relation to these two places rather than the respective nation-states. This 'translocal social field' (Glick Schiller 2003) formed the context in which their children grew up.

Second-generation Italians in Switzerland, the children of Italian migrants who were born in Switzerland or came to Switzerland before primary school, number approximately 211,000 and they are the biggest second-generation group in the country. They grew up during a time of economic and political uncertainty. Particularly from the 1950s to the 1970s, conditions in Switzerland were harsh in terms of discrimination on the housing and the job markets, and migrants experienced economic hardship and political instability because of short-term residency permits (Braun 1970; Niederberger 2003).

Many Italian families in Switzerland were 'incomplete', with one or both parents living apart from their children for extended periods of time. This was due to restrictive laws of family reunion, a lack of childcare facilities in Switzerland, translocal obligations towards kin in Italy and the dream of returning. Although the family was important in the southern Italian context already prior to emigration, these conditions of migration strengthened family ties even more and had an important impact on the cultural perceptions of the family among migrants. The factors which led to the separation of Italian families and the strengthening of family ties are summarised in the following section.

Factors Leading to Separation and Farewell

Only in 1960 did Swiss laws of family reunion allow Italian labour migrants to bring their families after three uninterrupted years of residence in Switzerland (in 1964 reduced to eighteen months of residence). Therefore, many migrants had to endure a long separation from their children. During the 1970s, 45 per cent of Italian women in Switzerland lived apart from their children for extended periods of time. In many accounts, Italian migrants describe the separation from small children and the breakup of their families as a very difficult experience. In fact, many migrants illegally brought their children to Switzerland. During the 1970s, 10,000 to 15,000 children were illegally living in Switzerland, hidden in migrants' apartments (Meyer-Sabino 2003).

In addition to the difficulties of family reunification, there was a lack of childcare facilities. Many mothers could therefore not do wage labour and stayed in Italy with the children, while their husbands worked in Switzerland. Others migrated to Switzerland and found childcare places in Swiss families who kept their children during the week. They therefore only saw their children during the weekends. Yet other migrants left their children in Italy to be looked after by close relatives, and only took them to Switzerland once they realised that they would or could not return to Italy in the near future. Similarly, some migrants sent their children to boarding schools in the north of Italy to have them closer. The intention was to have the children educated in the Italian system in order to facilitate the return to Italy, but to be able to visit them regularly, at least once a month. When the parents realised that they would not return to Italy as soon as they had originally planned, they took their children to Switzerland.

Thus, in addition to restrictive laws of family reunion and a lack of childcare facilities in Switzerland, the parents' wish of returning had a large impact on the children's translocal upbringing and led to extended periods of separation. Some children were sent back and forth between Italy and Switzerland during their childhoods. Others spent the first part of their childhood in Italy and were then, at the age of about ten or as adolescents, taken to Switzerland. The former were called the *via vai kids* (the back and forth kids), the latter the *ricongiunti* (the reunited) (Meyer-Sabino 2003). Both the *via vai kids* and the *ricongiunti* had major difficulties with integration once they settled in Switzerland for good. Not only did they have difficulties with language acquisition and integration into the education system, but they also suffered from separation from kin in Italy. In fact, pedagogical and psychological studies undertaken in the 1980s showed that the longer Italian children lived apart from their families, the worse they did in school (Gurny et al. 1984). Similarly, those children who grew up as 'commuters' or whose parents were absent for extended periods of time suffered from the many separation experiences and a lack of continuous and reliable emotional ties, which resulted in difficulties in school and professional careers. Members of the second generation who grew up under these circumstances have been shown to be more likely to suffer from depression and drug abuse (Meyer-Sabino 2003).[3]

The majority of children, however, grew up in Switzerland together with their parents. These children only went to Italy for holidays and grew up in a context of 'holiday translocalism'. Nevertheless, they experienced separation from their parents, for example because of their parents' translocal obligations towards kin in Italy. Women particularly, but also men, travelled to Italy to look after their elderly parents and sometimes had to stay for extended periods. The efforts the parents' translocal lives required were often mutually exclusive with investing in their children. They found themselves faced with the dilemma of looking after their children, earning enough money to build a future in Italy and caring for elderly parents in Italy. Migrant women's translocal caring work and the stretching of kin responsibilities across space has been illustrated in various recent studies on transnational families, e.g. among Italians in the UK (Zontini 2004) and Moroccans in Italy (Salih 2003); see also Baldassar *infra*.

Thus, experiences of separation formed an integral part of migrants' and their children's everyday lives. For example, at the end of each holiday was the moment of farewell from relatives and friends. Members of the second generation have vivid memories of these farewells, and they particularly remember how much their parents suffered when leaving Italy. Antonietta describes how she used to feel when she left the southern Italian region of Apulia after the long summer holidays:

'When I left I always felt a bit bad. And I remember how, when we were preparing to leave, the relatives came to greet us, and everybody was crying, it seemed like a funeral each time, a tragedy! When we went away, I remember that each time the grandparents cried, that they (the parents) went to greet everybody, *mamma mia*, it really was a tragedy, I will always remember how everybody cried, the parents, and even us'.

This 'tragedy' of farewell left strong impressions of what it means for a family to live apart. In light of these separations, many Italian migrants created an ideal image of the family, united and rooted in one place.

The Family as Translocal Site of Ethnic Reification

The disruption of the families led to 'being united' (*essere uniti*) becoming a key symbol among Italian migrants in Switzerland. In fact, in a study on Italian women in Switzerland undertaken during the 1980s, Allemann-Ghionda and Meyer-Sabino (1992) speak of the emergence of a 'myth of the Italian family', fostered by Italian migrants themselves. They explain this as result of the many separations from kin. This has been confirmed in my own research. 'Being united' as an important element of family life, emphasised time and again and often experienced during the holidays in Italy, is a crucial element of most first-generation Italians' everyday lives in Switzerland, and has evolved into part of a dominant discourse about Italianness among Italian migrants. Importantly, *essere uniti* has broader connotations than simply being together physically. Rather, it implies a sense of standing up for each other no matter what. The migration project, which was understood as an undertaking of the whole family, no matter who had to stay behind and for how long families lived apart, strengthened these notions of unitedness and mutual support, particularly among the first generation. Hence, rather than taking the family for granted through continuous day-to-day interaction, Italians, like many other migrants with transnational families (see Bryceson & Vuorela 2002) constructed their ideas of the family and its emotional and economic importance more deliberately.

The second generation experienced this emphasis on family ties with particular intensity during the yearly holidays in Italy. The family was central all through their stay in Italy, and much of the holiday time was spent with visits to close or distant relatives, eating together being the central focus of the day. These visits were undertaken with mixed feelings of obligation and enjoyment. On the one hand, the *tour de famille* was a considerable investment of holiday time, on the other, being part of a big family was a highly enjoyable and sociable break from a more individualised lifestyle in Switzerland that was centred on work.

While relatives in Italy warmly welcomed their emigrant kin and included them in their world as part of them, they also expected certain degrees of conformity and behaviour which they deemed as proper.

These expectations were especially related to gender relations, and young women in particular had to adapt to the local expectations in order to maintain the family reputation (Wessendorf 2007a). Furthermore, experience with Italian kin in Italy was sometimes characterised by feelings of exclusion, for example when migrants and their children were called *Svizzerotti* ('Swiss', jokingly but also a bit condescending) by family members. Being called 'Swiss' by one's own relatives is an example of the symbolic power of notions of the family in regard to who belongs and who does not. It shows how, especially in the context of migration, the family is not only a genealogical fact based on blood and kinship, but also an imagined community (Bryceson & Vuorela 2002). Inclusion within the family in Italy, put into practice during the migrants' vacation through the exchange of invitations, visits and particularly food, is crucial in regard to the second generation's perceptions of the family. It can lead to particularly strong translocal connections among the second generation, or, as a result of feeling excluded from the family in Italy, to the disconnection from Italy altogether.

In the Swiss context, the imagined (and mystified) family served as an ideological construct to demonstrate ethnic particularity and difference. Hence, while there emerged a 'myth of the Italian family', rooted in the concrete experience of loss and separation, the 'united Italian family' also evolved as a marker of ethnic assertion in confrontation with the majority society and other migrant groups. Luca's statement at the beginning of this chapter illustrates this reification of ethnicity through notions of the family. A similar process has been observed by Purkayastha (2005) who shows how, among South Asians in the United States, parents often present the emphasis on family support among South Asians as a unique characteristic of South Asian cultures to their children.

However, 'familism',[4] the overarching importance of the family and the role of the family as primary fundamental social unit, can be more than just an ideological package. In her research among Italian migrants in the US, Boscia-Mulè (1999: 34) illustrates that particularly among working-class Italian families with a low socio-economic status, familism is 'a coping strategy by which ethnic families counterbalance cultural and structural marginality'.

> The 'sense of family' is the yardstick by which my respondents compare themselves to the 'Americani', and construct a self-image of moral superiority and rationalize social distance. It is also a measure of comparison and judgment among ethnic families, a powerful mechanism of cultural control. (Boscia-Mulè 1999: 34-35)

Similar to the Italian Americans described by Boscia-Mulè, familism among Italian migrants in Switzerland is not just a 'cultural precondition', but also a consequence of the harsh conditions migrants met during the first years of their migration, characterised by low wages, high costs of living and high aims in terms of financial betterment and return to Italy (Soom Ammann forthcoming). Today, however, Italians are structurally well integrated in Switzerland, their children are economically established, and they can rely on social security provided by the state. Nevertheless, strong family relations and frequent contact with children continue to be important among many Italians. This unity of the family fulfils the first-generation migrants' wish for continuity, and it symbolises that their migration and the many sacrifices that came with it were worth it. When first-generation migrants talk about their lives, the family plays a major role as a happy and secure space.

This unity of the family is also expressed in the everyday relationships between the first and the second generation. Many second-generation Italians who participated in my research have daily contact with their parents, either by telephone or visiting them, and some of them talk to their mothers over the phone several times a day. According to Juhasz and Mey (2003), many members of the second generation are empathetic of their parents' lives and the sacrifices that came with migration and therefore feel morally obliged to help and support their parents and be in frequent contact. Taking care of each other within families, being in frequent contact and providing support is therefore the norm in many Italian families in Switzerland.

However, the experiences of the second generation with the 'united family' are not only characterised by mutual support and reciprocity, but also by pressures to conform. The following section discusses how some members of the second generation find the fine balance between care and control difficult to negotiate in everyday life. While this is a general characteristic of family relations in European societies, among Italians in Switzerland with the family as idealised social unit for the first generation, the line between care and control appears to be thinner and more fragile and therefore more difficult to deal with.

The Family as 'Golden Cage'

Although second-generation Italian adults in Switzerland mostly appreciate their families, adolescence was a time when especially the daughters experienced the family as restrictive rather than supportive. The life histories of second-generation Italians show that when relationships within families are examined more closely, the family evolves into a site where care is closely interlinked with control, and rights are tied to obligations.

The idealisation of the family among Italian migrants and, as I will show later in the chapter, in public discourse, somewhat obscures the conflicts which took place in families during many second-generation Italians' adolescences. Such conflicts have often been described as inter-generational and cultural conflicts between parents who hold on to their traditions, and adolescents who want to break out of the rigid control of their parents. Although such explanations bear the danger of creating essentialist categories of 'the traditional migrant family', in Italian families many such conflicts took place (Allemann-Ghionda & Meyer-Sabino 1992). Disagreements between parents and children mainly evolved around issues of control in the realm of gender relations, sexual orientation, obligations towards kin and ideas of care and responsibilities within the family.

At the time of Italian migration to Switzerland, southern Italian families were characterised by patriarchal family structures with strict gender roles, compulsory heterosexuality and a considerable responsibility for kin relations. These family ideologies have been described as an 'honour and shame complex' in the social sciences, and much of the anthropological research on Italian families has focused on honour and shame, described as a gender-based division of labour and morality.[5] Honour is a kind of prestige in which individuals and families are involved and which is based on the performance of male control over female chastity to defend one's family's reputation. Honour and shame have been described on a local level as individual and familial struggles for reputation, status and position (Davis 1969), but also from a sociohistorical perspective as a result of resistance against the State's and the Church's control over family affairs and resources (Schneider & Schneider 1971). The categories of honour and shame have been criticised as essentialist cultural categories that served the simplified homogenisation of the Mediterranean as 'cultural space'. However, they do play an important role in southern Italian family relations and gender ideologies (Kertzer & Saller 1991). These ideologies are characterised by a double standard where

> female infidelity is considered a grave insult to men and a serious threat to family stability. At the same time however, it is expected of a 'normal', 'healthy' man that he will take every opportunity for sex that presents itself, and his self-image ... will thereby be enhanced. (Baldassar 1999: 11)

Many Italian women in both southern Italy and in Switzerland question this double standard and complain about the restrictions and social control exercised on women.

Despite such complaints, not just the men, but also the women are often the guardians of this morality (Baldassar 1999), and in both Italy and among Italians in Switzerland, southern Italian mothers raise their daughters with considerably different standards than their sons. This reproduction of gender inequalities is related to pressures of conformity in the wider social context, and the fear of social exclusion because of 'immoral behaviour' (Baldassar 1999; Boscia-Mulè 1999; Goddard 1987). During the adolescence of the second generation, the tightness of Italian social networks in Switzerland played an important role in complying with cultural norms within the family because of the public implications such private behaviour can have. In this context, 'family responsibilities take on an almost formal quality of rights and duties owed to one another by virtue of common membership in a reputation-bearing social unit' (Berkowitz 1984: 84). Thus, the concern for an honourable image of the family was one of the main reasons why cultural norms, even if questioned and criticised on an individual level, were reproduced and sometimes reinforced within Italian families in Switzerland. Since the reputation of a family is to a high degree defined through the proper behaviour of both the mother and the daughters, they were subject to particularly high expectations of conformity.

For example, until the late 1980s, when the second-generation women who participated in this research (born in the 1960s and early 1970s) were teenagers, most southern Italian parents did not let their daughters spend time outside the house, except maybe on Saturday or Sunday afternoons. Some daughters negotiated a bit of freedom by going out with their older brothers who were expected to look after them, or by supposedly spending time at a female friends' house 'to do homework', but instead going to a Sunday afternoon dance club where they met their peers.

The restrictions imposed on daughters were not limited to adolescence, but women recounted that up until the age of twenty or even 22, they had to fight and argue to be allowed to go out and spend time with friends. Maria, born in 1971, is a typical example of this:

> Susanne Wessendorf (SW): Did you grow up differently to your brother?
>
> Maria: Yes yes, I am still the woman, he could go out, I had to stay at home, he could do whatever he wanted, he could go to concerts, to the stadium, but me, concerts at the stadium? Forget it!

SW: Neither with him?

Maria: But he didn't take me with him! Sometimes he did, sometimes he didn't. But you see, I couldn't do what I wanted, you had certain timetables.

SW: Did you object to this?

Maria: Yes, a lot, but you see, resisting is hard, it's hard, that's why I left home at 23. I always wanted my freedom ... I couldn't hold back, but you weren't free. When you had a boyfriend, forget it ... I wasn't even allowed to sleep at a girlfriend's place, not even at twenty or 22, forget it.

Maria is one of many among daughters of Italian migrants with similar experiences of restrictions. As with many other women, Maria's wish to move out of her parents' home is linked to the wish for more freedom to spend time outside the house, with friends and peers, and to build up relationships outside the family. But parents often had clear-cut expectations of a woman's life course which involved marriage at a young age, and certainly not living outside the family before marriage.

The young women dealt with restrictions in many different ways. Some put up with it because they did not have the courage to rebel or because they were surrounded by other (mostly Italian) girls who did not have any greater freedom. Others suffered greatly from the limitations and tried to break out of the tight family regulations. This sometimes led to the break-up of families and the disconnection of daughters from co-ethnics (Wessendorf 2007b). Maria's example shows how difficult it can be to resist parents' expectations and restrictions, and in fact, many women only found the strength to move out of their parents' house when they were in their twenties and when they had gained a certain degree of economic stability and personal independence.

Although the significance of women's private behaviour is more important for the family reputation than that of men, conflicts in families did not only take place between daughters and parents. Second-generation Italian men, too, complain about the amount of control exercised by their parents and about expectations of frequent contact, obligations of care and compulsory heterosexuality. As mentioned at the beginning of this chapter, one of my informants called the family a 'golden cage' where on the surface, everything seems harmonious, but in reality, relationships are conflictual. He felt pressured to conform to his parents' expectations of social upward mobility. Rather than getting a white-collar job, he would have preferred to become a car mechanic.

Importantly, such conflicts helped some parents to change their own attitudes, especially in the realm of gender relations, and to rethink their perceptions of gender-related behaviour. Therefore, over time, and as the second generation grew older, family conflicts were mostly resolved, and both parents and children managed to find compromises between their diverging views of individuality, family obligations and gender ideologies.

Gender-related conflicts in migrant families are currently subject to much public debate in regard to migrants from various backgrounds, especially those of Muslim origin. However, in regard to Italians in Switzerland, family conflicts have not been part of the public discourse. Rather, Italian families have been, and continue to be, portrayed as happy units of solidarity and loyalty. Thus, the critical voices within the families, or, in other words, the demotic discourse, do not form part of this public discourse. However, during the early years of their migration, Italians were ascribed negative stereotypes on other realms, particularly regarding behaviour in public space, order and hygiene.

From Discrimination to the Celebration of Italian Migration

From the 1950s until the 1970s, many Swiss perceived Italian migration to Switzerland as threatening the integrity of 'Swiss culture', and in various civil protests against immigration, terms such as 'over-foreignisation' (*Überfremdung*) and metaphors such as 'the boat is full' were used to emphasise that Switzerland could not accept more migrants. At a time when nearly 50 per cent of the overall migrant population in Switzerland was Italian, these fears were concretely directed at Italian migrants. In newspaper articles, anti-immigrant leaflets and in public speeches, they were described as knife-wielding criminals, seducers of Swiss women, spaghetti-munchers and lazy slackers who did nothing but hang around at railway stations. Italians were seen as different on the grounds of their darker skin and darker hair, physical features that set them apart from the majority society and served to stigmatise them as inferior. But rather than being described in racial terms as the Italians and Irish were in nineteenth-century Britain (e.g. as 'white negroes'; Fortier 2000), they were ethnicised as sources of degeneracy in public debates about hygiene, street noise and decency. Similarly, in her study of Italians in the UK, Fortier shows how during the early years of Italian immigration in the nineteenth and early twentieth centuries, dirt was used as 'the key metaphor in substantiating the boundaries of inclusion/exclusion' (Fortier 2000: 20).

Importantly, this stigmatisation of things interpreted as 'typically Italian' such as noisiness and a lack of orderliness were not reflected in the Swiss' attitudes toward Italian migrants' family relations. Sociological studies undertaken in the 1960s show that despite the many negative stereotypes ascribed to Italians in the realm of public behaviour and cleanliness – issues which were often described as a threat to the integrity of 'Swiss culture' – many Swiss valued Italian families positively, seeing them as cohesive and harmonious units (Braun 1970; Stolz 2001). As I show further below, this positive view of Italian families has persisted until today.

With time, the stigmatisation of Italian migrants regarding issues such as cleanliness and behaviour in public space, paralleled by much discrimination on the housing and the labour market, decreased for several reasons. With economic growth during the post-war period, Italy became the ideal holiday destination for Swiss middle-class families, and from the 1970s, more and more Swiss could afford to go on holiday in Italy. This contributed to Italy's rise in popularity among the Swiss and the increasing acceptance of Italians in Switzerland. Moreover, the arrival of migrants from other parts of the world who were perceived as more different contributed to the acceptance of Italians as part of the Swiss 'imagined community' (Anderson 1983). By distancing themselves from migrants of different origins, Italians played their part in becoming 'more Swiss' than other migrants (Wimmer 2004).

Socio-economic conditions during the time of Italian migration also facilitated this rising image of Italians. Italians came to Switzerland at a time when jobs were easily available and public institutions such as schools could handle a minority of children who needed support in terms of language learning. Italians and their children managed to integrate on a structural and educational level thanks to the availability of jobs and apprenticeships, but also thanks to their high ambitions in terms of upward mobility (Bolzman et al. 2003; Juhasz & Mey 2003). The structural integration into the labour market of both first- and second-generation Italians has led to the disappearance of Italian migrants in the kind of public discourse which problematises migration. Instead, Italians are idealised as the good migrants who have made it. Today, they are the 'model minority'.[6] In exhibitions, books and radio programmes, Italians are presented as an historical example of migration and its possible outcome which is generally assessed as positive, despite the many hardships Italians were confronted with (i.e. Bachmann 2003; Cangemi & Von Aarburg 2004; Halter 2003).[7] Family histories and the experiences of different generations of migrants play an important role in this portrayal of Italian migration to Switzerland and are at the centre of many such accounts.

The general impression transferred by these public representations of Italian migration history is that Italians are now an integral part of

Swiss society. This image is created independent of the actual social integration of Italians, especially the first-generation migrants. In fact, many Italians continue to lead separate lives from the Swiss and from other minority groups, and the involvement of the first generation in Swiss social networks, associations or clubs is still very limited. Furthermore, many first-generation Italians in the German part of Switzerland have not yet learnt the local language and only manage to get by, after 30 to 40 years in the country (in Francophone areas Italians found it easier to learn the language). They primarily socialise with other Italians, be it relatives or friends. Similarly, some members of the second generation also mainly socialise with other second-generation Italians.

Despite this rather limited social integration of the first generation and among some members of the second generation, Italians in Switzerland are perceived to be well integrated and are described as 'the good migrants'. A sociological study about the Swiss public perceptions of migrants in the city of Zurich, undertaken in 1969 and repeated in 1995, shows how among the Swiss, the stigmatisation of Italians during the 1960s changed not only into the acceptance, but into a particular appreciation of Italians as part of Swiss society in 1995 (Stolz 2001). Also in today's public discourse, there is a notion of 'what would Switzerland be without the lovely, warm-hearted Italians'. Newspaper articles talk about the 'Mediterraneanisation of Switzerland', about 'How we [the Swiss] became little Italians', about Italians as 'our favourite foreigners', and about Switzerland as a country full of 'Italophiles' (Blickenstorfer 2002; di Falco 2003). Among members of the Swiss urban middle classes, attributes of what they see as Italian lifestyle such as good food or fashion have become a symbol of what enjoyable life is about (Wimmer 2004). *Italianità*, Italianness, is hip, and it is now described as part of Swiss culture, with Italian food as an integral part of Swiss national food (di Falco 2003), rather like Chicken Tikka in the UK. A journalist describes this Mediterraneanisation as follows:

> Swiss children are currently most often called Laura and Luca. Their parents consume more and more Prosecco, Mozzarella and olive oil and are enthusiastic about football. They play beach volleyball, plant palms on their balconies, and annoy street cleaners with rubbish, and neighbours with noisiness at night: Switzerland is becoming Mediterranean. (Blickenstorfer 2002)

The special appreciation of things Italian among many Swiss, particularly in the realm of lifestyle choices, food and fashion, stands in stark contrast to the public criticism of Italian migrants' lifestyles during the

1960s and 70s. This transformation of stereotypes ascribed to Italians, from being a threat to 'Swiss culture' to becoming an integral part of it, was, however, paralleled by continuities regarding the perception of Italian family relations among many Swiss. As mentioned above, studies have shown that already during the early years of Italian immigration, family relations among Italian migrants were seen as positive and harmonious, and this image has persisted until today (Braun 1970; Stolz 2001).

This positive image of Italian families stands in stark contrast to the image ascribed to the families of migrants from other origins in various media reports. Families of Muslim background are in particular described as rigidly traditionalist, especially in the realm of gender and inter-generational relations. Such gender-related cultural categories are often used to construct Muslims as too different to become part of the host society. In contrast, Italians were rarely criticised for their family and gender relations despite the existence of similar gender-related conflicts within their families. Rather, their family relations were and continue to be idealised both among many Italians themselves and in public discourse. The reason for such differing discourses applied to Italians as opposed to Muslim migrants might lie in the dramatic sanctions against the breaking of gender rules believed to characterise some Muslim migrants, such as, for example, honour killings. Such instances have led to essentialist discourse in the media about their patriarchal and rigid gender relations described as 'traditionalist', 'sexist' and 'fundamentalist' (see, for example, Der Blick (2006), Meyer (2005)). Among Italians, in contrast, the sanctions against the breaking of gender-related rules were usually confined to the families themselves. They were therefore not discussed in public discourse, even if physical violence was sometimes involved. The same holds true for conflicts within Swiss families where instances of domestic violence against women are often left uncovered.

The contrast between the public discourse about Muslim families as opposed to Italian families shows how different criteria and categories are used in the discursive inclusion or exclusion of migrants of different origins and during different times. Family relations are a particularly powerful category with which some migrants are idealised as warm-hearted people who contribute to the good of the majority society, while others are essentialised as violent and oppressive. This kind of argument covers the variations of family relations among migrants of the same regional and religious origin. Moreover, the category of the family as discursive instrument of inclusion and exclusion exemplifies that migrants are predominantly judged and categorised along ethnic and religious lines rather than other categorical differentiations such as class and educational, or urban and rural backgrounds. This holds true for both the idealisation of migrants like Italians, and the stigmatisation of those of other origins.

Conclusion

During the early years of their migration after the Second World War, Italian migrants in Switzerland suffered greatly from the restrictive laws of family reunion and the many separations from family members. This led to a certain idealisation of the Italian family among many migrants, and to a dominant discourse based on the construction of 'the united family' as typically Italian. While this idealisation of the family has been questioned by the descendants of Italian migrants themselves, public discourse in Switzerland idealises Italian families.

However, Italian migrants have been subject to much stigmatisation in other realms. During the 1950s and 1960s, 'cultural differences' between Italians and Swiss were perceived to be a hindrance to integration, and Italians were stigmatised because of what was seen to be inappropriate behaviour in public space. Today, these stigmatisations have disappeared and Italians are seen to positively contribute to 'Swiss culture' with their Mediterranean lifestyles. In this process, the previous stigmatisation of Italians has been replaced by the stigmatisation of other migrants, particularly those of Muslim origin. As opposed to the earlier categories of stigmatisation against Italians, the family plays an important role in the depiction of Muslims as unable to integrate into Swiss society. The focus thereby lies on what are described as rigid and traditionalist gender relations, an outcome of much public critique of the sanctions against the breaking of gender rules among some Muslims, such as, for example, honour killings or 'forced marriages'. While, as a result of such practices, gender relations among Muslims become a matter of a public debate which centres on essentialist notions of Muslim religious ideologies, family-related issues remain in the private realm in relation to other migrants such as Italians, even if similar conflicts occur.

The family is a powerful category that can serve both the discursive construction of cultural differences in negative terms, and the idealisation of other 'cultures'. The example of Italian migrants is interesting from a historical point of view because it shows how public perceptions and discourses about migrants change over time and how different criteria of inclusion and exclusion are used during different times and for migrants of different origins. By taking an historical in-depth look at past migrations and processes of settlement, this chapter has described the elasticity and changeability of perceptions about 'culture' and 'cultural difference' in public discourse. Furthermore, the chapter has illustrated the different discourses which exist among migrants themselves, and how these discourses change over time and between the generations. Such discourses can be both dominant and based on essentialist categories of cultural unity, and demotic, influenced by a variety of ideas about culture, community and belonging. Hence, the dominant, essentialist discourse can be found both in the realm of the public discourse transferred by the media, and among migrants themselves who sometimes create such a discourse in reaction to difficult economic, political and social circumstances. By creating idealised notions of 'community' or 'the family', they counter the insecurities brought about by migration, attempting to create a continuity of the social values and cultural practices with which they were most familiar.

Because of Italian migrants' long-term settlement process and their conscious engagement with their migration history, Italians in Switzerland are a particularly interesting example to unpack these different levels of dominant discourses, both the public one and that prevailing among migrants themselves, and to juxtapose these with the demotic discourse which is most often expressed by members of the second generation who have diverging and sometimes contradictory views of what is seen to be 'the typical Italian family'.

Acknowledgments

I would like to thank the participants of this research. Many thanks to Steven Vertovec and Ellie Vasta for support and advice through the course of this project and to Karen Lüdtke and Eva Soom Ammann for their comments. Thanks also to the Swiss National Science Foundation, the Janggen-Poehn Stiftung, the Freiwillige Akademische Gesellschaft, the International Federation of Women Graduates, the University of Oxford Scatchered European fund, the Institute of Social and Cultural Anthropology, University of Oxford, and St. Antony's College, University of Oxford, for funding support.

Notes

1   The material presented here draws on qualitative ethnographic research carried out in the German part of Switzerland as well as in southern Italy during one year. Along with participant observation, 58 life history interviews were undertaken with descendants of second-generation Italians who are between 25 and 40 years old. Twenty-three of the interviewees had migrated to their parents' village of origin in southern Italy (see Wessendorf 2007a). In this paper, I focus on those second-generation Italians who stayed in Switzerland.

2 The vast majority of post-war labour migrants came from the very south of Italy and migrated to the German- and French-speaking parts of Switzerland, a distance of approximately 1,500 kilometres. Although the southern part of Switzerland is Italian speaking, southern Italians were seen as culturally different from the Swiss.

3 Heroin addiction, especially, has been shown to be a problem among second-generation Italians in Switzerland. The reasons for this are manifold and cannot only be explained by experiences of separation or by the migration background, although these certainly play an important role (conversation with Nella Sempio and Mara Hermann-Aita, Multikulturelle Suchtberatungsstelle Basel [Multicultural Drug Addiction Outreach Centre] (MUSUB), Switzerland.

4 Southern Italian 'familism' has been a recurrent theme in anthropological studies of southern Italy and Italian diasporic communities. See, for example, Banfield (1958), Ginsborg (1990) and Silverman (1968), and John Davis's critique of the concept (1970).

5 The principal anthropological studies of the honour and shame complex in Southern Italy include Davis (1969), Goddard (1987) and Schneider and Schneider (1971). For a critical examination of the concept and a historical overview of anthropology's use of it, see Giordano (2002). The honour and shame complex has been criticised as one of the major analytic tools through which Mediterranean societies have been exoticised (e.g. Driessen 2002; Greverus et al. 2002).

6 Similar processes have been observed in other contexts, for example among Italians in the US who 'became white' over time (Foner 2000).

7 For examples see: www.limmatverlag.ch, www.da-und-fort.ch, www.italiazurigo.ch and www.dolcelingua.ch.

References

Allemann-Ghionda, C.& G. Meyer-Sabino (1992), *Donne italiane in Svizzera*. Basel: Fondazione Ecap.

Anderson, B. R. (1983), *Imagined Communities: Reflections on the Origin and Spread of Nationalism*. London: Verso.

Bachmann, D. (2003), *Il lungo addio: una storia fotografica sull'emigrazione italiana in Svizzera dopo la guerra – Der lange Abschied: 138 Fotografien zur italienischen Emigration in die Schweiz nach 1945*. Zurich: Limmat Verlag.

Baldassar, L. (1999), 'Marias and Marriage: Ethnicity, Gender and Sexuality among Italo-Australian Youth in Perth', *Journal of Sociology* 35 (1): 1-22.

Banfield, E. C. (1958), *The Moral Basis of a Backward Society*. Chicago: Free Press.

Baumann, G. (1996), *Contesting Culture: Discourses of Identity in Multi-Ethnic London*. Cambridge: Cambridge University Press.

Berkowitz, S. G. (1984), 'Familism, Kinship and Sex Roles in Southern Italy: Contradictory Ideals and Real Contradictions', *Anthropological Quarterly* 57 (2): 83-92.

Blickenstorfer, D. (2002),' Locker wie Latinos. Essen und Feiern, Erotik und Freude: Mediterranes Lebensgefühl erobert die Schweiz'. In *Facts*, Vol. 31, December.

Bolzman, C., R. Fibbi & M. Vial (2003), *Secondas – Secondos. Le processus d'intégration des jeunes adultes issus de la migration espagnole et italienne en Suisse*. Zurich: Seismo.

Boscia-Mulè, P. (1999), *Authentic Ethnicities: The Interaction of Ideology, Gender Power, and Class in the Italian-American Experience*. Westport, Connecticut, London: Greenwood Press.

Braun, R. (1970), *Soziokulturelle Probleme italienischer Migranten in der Schweiz*. Erlenbach-Zurich: Eugen Rentsch.

Bryceson, D. F.& U. Vuorela (2002), 'Transnational Families in the Twenty-first Century', in D. F. Bryceson & U. Vuorela (eds.), *The Transnational Family: New European Frontiers and Global Networks*, 3-30. Oxford: Berg.

Cangemi, F.& D. von Aarburg (2004), *Eigentlich wollten wir nicht lange bleiben. Si pensava di restare poco. 12 Geschichten aus der Emigration. 12 storie d'emigrazione.* Zurich: Frenetic.

Davis, J. A. (1969), 'Honour and Politics in Pisticci', *Proceedings of the Royal Anthropological Institute 1969*: 69-81.

Davis, J.A. (1970) 'Morals and Backwardness', *Comparative Studies in Society and History*, 12 (3): 340-353.

Der Blick (2006), 'Türkin vom eigenen Vater und Mann bedroht', in *Der Blick*, 22 May 2006.

Di Falco, D. (2003), 'Ausstellungsrezension: Il lungo addio', in *Der Bund* (Bern), 23 July 2003.

Driessen, H. (2002), 'People, Boundaries and the Anthropologist's Mediterranean', *Anthropological Journal on European Cultures* 10: 11-24.

Foner, N. (2000), *From Ellis Island to JFK: New York's Two Great Waves of Immigration.* New Haven: Yale University Press; Russell Sage Foundation.

Fortier, A.-M. (2000), *Migrant Belongings: Memory, Space, Identity.* Oxford: Berg.

Ginsborg, P. (1990), *A History of Contemporary Italy: Society and Politics, 1943-1988.* Harmondsworth: Penguin.

Giordano, C. (2002), 'Mediterranean Honour Reconsidered', *Anthropological Journal on European Cultures* 10: 39-58.

Glick Schiller, N. (2003), 'The Centrality of Ethnography in the Study of Transnational Migration. Seeing the Wetland Instead of the Swamp', in C. Brettell & J.F. Hollifield, (eds.), *Migration Theory: Talking across Disciplines*, 99-128. New York: Routledge.

Goddard, V. (1987), 'Honour and Shame: The Control of Women's Sexuality and Group Identity in Naples', in P. Caplan, (ed.), *The Cultural Construction of Sexuality*, 166-193. London: Tavistock.

Greverus, I.-M., R. Römhild & G. Welz (2002), 'Reworking the Past, Shaping the Present, Considering the Future: An Introduction to the Two Issues of "The Mediterraneans"', *Anthropological Journal on European Cultures* 10: 1-10.

Gurny R., P. Cassée, H.P. Hauser & A. Meyer (2004), *Karrieren und Sackgassen: Wegen ins Berufsleben junger Schweizer und Italiener in der Stadt Zürich.* Diessenhofen: Ruegger.

Halter, E., (ed.) (2003), *Das Jahrhundert der Italiener in der Schweiz.* Zurich: Offizin.

Juhasz, A. & E. Mey (2003), *Die zweite Generation: Etablierte oder Aussenseiter? Biographien von Jugendlichen ausländischer Herkunft.* Wiesbaden: Westdeutscher Verlag.

Kertzer, D. I. & R. P. Saller, (eds.) (1991), *The Family in Italy: From Antiquity to the Present.* New Haven: Yale University Press.

Meyer, F. A. (2005), *Wir sind so frei. In* Der Blick, 17 December 2005.

Meyer-Sabino, G. (2003), 'Frauen in der Emigration', in E. Halter, (ed.), *Das Jahrhundert der Italiener in der Schweiz*, 203-219. Zurich: Offizin.

Niederberger, J. M. (2003), 'Die Integrationspolitik der Schweiz nach dem zweiten Weltkrieg', in E. Halter, (ed.), *Das Jahrhundert der Italiener in der Schweiz*, 93-107. Zurich: Offizin.

Purkayastha, B. (2005), *Negotiating Ethnicity. Second-Generation South Asian Americans Traverse a Transnational World.* New Brunswick: Rutgers University Press.

Salih, R. (2003), *Gender in Transnationalism: Home, Longing and Belonging among Moroccan Migrant Women.* London: Routledge.

Schneider, J.& P. Schneider (1971), 'Of Vigilance and Virgins', *Ethnology* 10 (1): 1-24.

Silverman, S. F. (1968), 'Agricultural Organization, Social Structure, and Values in Italy: Amoral Familism Reconsidered', *American Anthropologist* 70 (1): 1-20.

Soom Ammann, E. (forthcoming), *'Noi che abbiamo fatto una vita qua'* – *Biographien pensionierter italienischer Paare in der Schweiz*, PhD thesis, University of Berne, Switzerland.

Stolz, J. (2001), 'Einstellungen zu Ausländern und Ausländerinnen 1969 und 1995: eine Replikationsstudie', in H.-J. Hoffmann-Nowotny, (ed.), *Das Fremde in der Schweiz: Ergebnisse soziologischer Forschung*, 33-73. Zurich: Seismo.

Wessendorf, S. (2007a), '"Roots-Migrants": "Transnationalism" and "Return" among Second-generation Italians in Switzerland', *Journal of Ethnic and Migration Studies* 33 (7):1083-1102.

Wessendorf, S. (2007b), 'Who Do You Hang Out With? Peer Group Association and Cultural Assertion among Second-Generation Italians in Switzerland', in T. Geisen & C. Riegel (eds.), *Jugend, Zugehörigkeit und Migration: Subjektpositionierung im Kontext von Jugendkultur, Ethnizitäts- und Geschlechterkonstruktionen*, 111-127. Wiesbaden: VS Verlag.

Wimmer, A. (2004), 'Does Ethnicity Matter? Everyday Group Formation in Three Swiss Immigrant Neighbourhoods', *Ethnic and Racial Studies* 27 (1): 1-36.

Zontini, E. (2004), *Italian Families and Social Capital: Rituals and the Provision of Care in British-Italian Transnational Families*, Working Paper No. 6, Families & Social Capital ESRC Research Group. London: South Bank University.

10 Dealing with 'That Thing': Female Circumcision and Sierra Leonean Refugee Girls in the UK

Radha Rajkotia

Introduction

Criminalisation of female circumcision combined with heightened media attention in the West has meant that it has come to be seen as a universal wrong within the public sphere (Walley 2002). Specific laws prohibiting the practice exist in Australia, Belgium, Canada, Norway, Sweden, the United Kingdom and the United States, while general criminal and/or child protection laws have been applied to female circumcision in Denmark, France, Germany, the Netherlands and New Zealand (Rahman & Toubia 2000). All of these countries have large immigrant communities and have been compelled to address female circumcision as it is seen as a threat not only to the 'victims' of the practice, but also the cultural integrity of the individual countries (Dembour 2001).

In 1999 the largest ever case against female circumcision was made as French courts convicted Hawa Greou, an *exciseuse* (woman who performs circumcisions) from Mali, of 'voluntary bodily injury causing mutilation or permanent disability' against a girl who had been circumcised at the age of eight. Through the course of the investigation dozens of girls were found to have been through the hands of Greou, and their parents were consequently also brought to trial. Although France does not have specific laws pertaining to female circumcision, action was taken under general criminal law. Greou was found guilty of circumcision of 48 girls.[1] A total of 23 mothers and three fathers received prison or suspended prison sentences. The initial complainant's mother was sentenced to two years' imprisonment (Reproductive Freedom News 1999; Dembour 2001).

The movement towards the criminalisation of female circumcision, however, is not a new phenomenon, nor is the resistance that it has met from those still involved in the practice. Colonial administrations and missionaries enacted laws against female circumcision in Kenya, Sudan and Burkina Faso as early as the early 1900s. These attempts were unsuccessful and protest grew over foreign intervention in the population's tribal and cultural affairs. Jomo Kenyatta, later president of Kenya, in his ethnography of Kikuyu people and society, *Facing Mount Kenya* (1965 [1938]), provided detailed descriptions of the practice of male and female circumcision, and the significance behind it. He also argued that Africans themselves should be encouraged to discuss and decide for themselves a position vis-à-vis circumcision, through education and scientific enquiry (1965 [1938]: 148). Governments in Egypt and Sudan later attempted to enforce their own bans on female circumcision in the 1940s but these were also unsuccessful as awareness-raising campaigns, failing to sensitise people to the new laws, and so little change was either promoted or registered (Rahman & Toubia 2000). In Kenya, an officially sanctioned council of male leaders in the Meru District banned the practice of clitoral excisions in 1956. Adolescent girls met this ban with defiance and responded by beginning a movement of circumcising themselves and each other, claiming that not only would they fight to maintain their own culture but they would defend the status of their generation in the eyes of an increasingly oppressive government (Thomas 2000).

International conferences held during the United Nations Decade for Women (1975-1985) laid the foundations of contemporary discourses on female circumcision. A review of these discourses suggests that they are based on a combination of the different interactions between those striving to eliminate, and those striving to defend, the practice as witnessed through the historical snapshots instanced above. What has also developed, however, is another set of reflexive discourses which look at the broader interplay between arguments posed on both sides of the issue.

The literature on female circumcision (or genital mutilation, depending on which side the author is placed) reflects not only the historical foundations of the arguments but also emphasises the breadth and depth of discussion of the subject. Broadly speaking there are the two camps within the current debate on female circumcision. Within the camp of proponents there are African authors arguing in defence of cultural tradition (Ahmadu 2000) alongside Western cultural relativists arguing for women's autonomy in defending and defining their own bodily integrity (Manderson 2004). The literature produced by authors and activists opposing circumcision is much more extensive (Dirie 1998; Dorkenoo 1994; Hosken 1979; Lightfoot-Klein 1989; Koso-Thomas 1987; Toubia 1993; Walker 1992; Walker & Parmar 1993). Here, women of all ethnic origins and religions come together to protest against female circumcision on the basis that it violates women's human rights and fundamental freedoms. Although there is recognition that its practice also represents another fundamental right, the right to freedom of cultural life, this is placed in secondary position.

Rahman and Toubia, for example, write:

> In the context of human rights associated with culture, the criti-
> cal inquiry for FC/FGM (female circumcision or female genital
> mutilation) is to assess whether this particular cultural practice
> infringes upon other human rights. Determining which cultural
> practices should be respected and preserved and which are unac-
> ceptable infringements upon human rights and fundamental
> freedoms is a complex task that must always be approached with
> caution. However, *given that FC/FGM has been regarded by the in-
> ternational community as gender discrimination and an act of vio-
> lence against women, this procedure should be regarded as an act that
> violates women's human rights. The right to participate in cultural
> life does not protect this practice.* (2000: 32; emphasis added)

The argument here is a simple one but as such it does not provide us
with any concrete justification for this ranking of rights. In essence it
leads us back to the colonial perspectives of the early 1900s, when 'outsiders' were unable to comprehend or accept such an alien and barbaric practice (Kenyatta 1965 [1938]). On the other hand, a number of
authors have called for the voices of those most directly affected to be
heard, and have drawn attention to the negative effects on women of
international campaigns to eradicate the practice (Abusharaf 2001;
Gruenbaum 2001; Manderson 2004; Schweder 2000; Walley 2002).
Scheper-Hughes takes this argument further still by proposing that
any 'outside attention' that this issue receives, positive or negative, may
do more harm than good (1991: 27).

The purpose of this chapter is not to argue the legitimacy of either
internal or external representations of female circumcision, nor is it to
advocate for the use of internal or external arguments in general.
Rather this chapter will propose an argument to bridge the gap between these two perspectives. By exploring the meaning of female circumcision within the Sierra Leonean cultural institution of *Bondo* or
secret society, and the relationships between teenage girls and *Bondo* in
Sierra Leone and England, this chapter will highlight the transformation of this cultural institution as it undergoes both migration and adolescent development. I argue that *Bondo* is central to girls' identities as
women in the context of Sierra Leone, and Sierra Leoneans in the context of England. As they move from Sierra Leone to England, the significance of *Bondo* therefore transforms.

Similarly, I suggest that *Bondo* takes on new meaning as girls grow
through adolescence. The affiliation to *Bondo* that is central to their
identities as women and Sierra Leoneans when they are young adolescents loses significance as they enter late adolescence and adulthood.

For girls in Sierra Leone, however, the ability to diverge from the group is limited so that they are unable to express independent ideas and perspectives toward both circumcision and *Bondo*. Girls in England on the other hand are able to express their individual opinions and assume independent positions as the significance of *Bondo* transforms and they find the freedom to express themselves.

The material presented in this chapter is based on in-depth interviews conducted between 2004 and 2005 in Freetown, Sierra Leone and the south-east of England. Interviews were conducted with a total of 43 girls in Sierra Leone and nineteen girls who had migrated from Sierra Leone to England in the five years preceding the interview. In both countries, girls participating in the research were aged between fourteen and 25 years. Of the nineteen girls interviewed in England, five had arrived in the country unaccompanied and were now living independently in the county of Sussex (south of London). The remaining fifteen had migrated with family members and were now living in London. The latter (aged between fourteen and sixteen) were much more closely associated with the larger Sierra Leonean community in London while the former (aged over sixteen years) maintained visibly weaker ties. This was partly a product of choice but also of proximity.

The following section explores both the context and meaning underlying female circumcision in Sierra Leone and documents girls' perceptions and experiences, thereby providing a framework in which refugee girls' perspectives can be understood.

Bondo in Sierra Leone

Initiation into *Bondo,* the secret society for women, is said to be the most significant period of a Sierra Leonean woman's life.[2] It is the time during which a girl crosses the threshold into womanhood, learning what her role as a woman means in terms of marriage, family and community. Traditionally, girls are initiated into *Bondo* when they are about fourteen or fifteen years old. Boys of the same age are initiated into the equivalent male secret society, *Poro*. During the process of initiation, girls are taken into the secret *Bondo bush* for anything ranging from a few days to a few weeks. *Bondo bush* areas are customarily found on the outskirts of inhabited rural areas and are considered sacred. Consequently only those who have been initiated may enter these areas.[3]

Girl initiates are taught how to complete domestic chores properly as well as how to carry themselves in an appropriate way for their new standing. They are supervised and taught by more senior members of the society and consequently undertake chores for them also. Rituals are performed, inducting girls into their new positions in relation to the secret society, their community and the spirit world (Ferme 2001: 208). One of these rituals is circumcision, during which the initiate's clitoris is 'excised'. The World Health Organisation recognises four types of genital cutting: clitoridectomy, excision, infibulation and a fourth 'unclassified' type, which includes practices such as piercing, pricking, stretching and burning. Type II genital 'excision' is most commonly practiced in Sierra Leone. This process involves 'excision of the clitoris with partial or total excision of the labia minora'. [4] To undergo circumcision a girl must be a virgin and will be checked by senior members of the society before any cutting takes place.

Completion of initiation into *Bondo* is marked with a procession of the new initiates re-entering their villages or local communities. It is at this time that they display their new status as women and they celebrate this by wearing new clothes that their families have bought for them. The process of initiation unites members and provides them with a sense of social affiliation on the basis of their status as women. They may come together and practice their rituals in an environment that is constructed and ruled by them, without the interference of men or social structures that apply outside of the *Bondo bush*. It is a period during which they are able to leave their homes for anything from three of four days at a time, without permission of their husbands and return without fear of reproach. The authority of husbands is, at that time, subjugated to that of the secret society ritual.

The authority that *Soweis*, the leaders of the secret societies, hold is not only recognised within the matriarchies that they govern, but also by broader Sierra Leonean society. This has led to the existence of dual power structures: matriarchy and patriarchy. The two systems exist harmoniously side by side, aware of each other's authority and therefore striving to avoid threat. As much as a husband will know better than to interfere with his wife attending a *Bondo* initiation, she will know better than to apply the freedoms and status that she has enjoyed in the *Bondo bush* to her everyday life. Walter Goldschmidt's fieldwork with the Ugandan Sebei in the 1960s revealed similar patterns of social organisation (Goldschmidt 1976). He proposed that:

> excision enhanced women's status by binding them together as a group in possession of ritual secrets revealed through initiation; men respected and feared these secrets, thereby offering women greater leverage in male/female interactions. (Walley 2002: 27)

In talking about *Bondo* and initiation, however, an important distinction is drawn between *Bondo*, as an institution and cultural tradition, and the act of circumcision. Politicians and a large proportion of the

Sierra Leonean population are sympathetic to the institution of *Bondo* and its broader significance as a rite of passage for girls entering womanhood. However, the issue of circumcision is often left either unaddressed or completely avoided in public discourse. There is no legislation prohibiting female circumcision, nor are there practical initiatives in place to refine the ritual. The bulk of advocacy and sensitisation work is done by non-government organisations, national and international. The main thrust of these campaigns is geared toward eliminating circumcision as part of the initiation process, or at the very least allowing girls to reach eighteen before choosing for themselves whether they would like to be circumcised or not.

Bondo in Britain

Of the nineteen girls interviewed in London and Sussex, eleven had been initiated. Eight of these eleven were in the age fourteen to sixteen range. The mean age of initiation was six years, with the majority of girls (seven) being initiated between five and six years. The youngest age of initiation was one year and the oldest was thirteen. All of them had been initiated in Sierra Leone and they had no knowledge of *Bondo* initiations occurring in England.

The reasons girls offered for why they had or had not wanted to be initiated follow very similar lines as those given by the girls in Freetown. However, because most refugee girls in England were so young when they were initiated their memories of the event are somewhat obscured. None of the girls knew that they were going. Four of them did not know anything about it at all, and have very little recollection of it; others recalled going with older sisters, or cousins. Amidst their somewhat hazy memories what often stood out was their sense of fear. For example, Sebatu went because her sisters were going. She remembers screaming and that they had a party afterwards – that's all. Rachel, explained that she went with her aunty and cousins, but when she went in she was scared because she saw the 'knives and things' (from interview notes). Two girls who did not want to be initiated had run away from home because they were being forced into going to the *Bondo* *bush*. They are now living in England and their forced initiation has formed part of their applications for asylum.

Are They Happy That They Went?

Given that so many of the girls were so young when they were initiated, the perspectives that they now hold (having been or not been initiated) provide a greater insight into how they *themselves* feel about *Bondo*. They were much more able to elucidate their own experiences and the rationales behind their own positions when asked whether they were happy about their initiation/ non-initiation status. Table 10.1 summarises the reasons they gave.

The phrases in italics highlight reasons that were given by both girls in Freetown and England. 'Becoming part of something' features highly in both settings, being cited six times and eight times in Freetown and England, respectively. Closer examination of the 'something' that girls in both setting allude to highlights significant differences. In Freetown, girls who talked about the importance of becoming part of something described wanting to be recognised as 'women' by other women. They explained that other women did not treat them in the same way as girls who had been initiated because they would not be 'real' women, and that being initiated meant that they could go into the *Bondo bush* when friends initiated their daughters. They would not have to worry about being excluded. The reasons are therefore very closely linked to their status as 'women' and inclusion on the basis of 'womanhood'.

The inclusion which girls in England refer to is different in its nature. Of the eight girls who related initiation to 'being a part of something', four highlighted that all of their family (in some cases male and female) had been initiated and so they would not want to be left out. The remaining four all pointed to *Bondo* as part of their tradition or culture, which they needed to adhere to in order to remain 'Sierra Leonean'.

> Dora was initiated when she was five years old. She doesn't remember it happening but remembers first finding out about it when her [Sierra Leonean] friends were talking about it. She then asked her mum about it and found out that she too had been initiated. She thinks that it is a good thing because all of her family has been initiated (including the boys); all her [Sierra Leonean] friends have also been and they are happy about it too so she

Table 10.1 *Reasons girls are happy or unhappy about being initiated or left uninitiated*

Reason	Number of times cited
It means you become part of something	8
Don't really know what it is for	3
It doesn't really make a difference	3
It affects your sexual pleasure	1
The church advises against it	1
Have had education that advises against it	1
Don't like society traditions	1

doesn't mind. She wouldn't want that thing 'dangling' there anyway. She sometimes talks about it with her Sierra Leonean
friends, and also sometimes her Nigerian friends – 'they do
something similar but it's disgusting because they make you eat
it!'

She wouldn't talk about it with white people because she would
have to smack (hit) them. They wouldn't understand and they
would look down their noses at her. They think they are so smart
and so perfect at everything – she hates the way they talk to people. (Notes from interview with Dora, aged fourteen)

Dora perceives her initiation as instrumental in binding her ties both
with her family and her friends. Although she is willing to share in
her 'African' identity by talking about it with other African friends, she
also uses it to set herself apart from other Africans by denouncing their
practice as inferior. All the while, however she condemns 'white people'
for 'not understanding' her own cultural practice. She therefore not
only uses *Bondo* as a means of identifying herself as a Sierra Leonean
alongside her family and friends, but simultaneously uses it to differentiate herself from non-Sierra Leoneans.

Although many girls, in a similar fashion to Dora, embraced *Bondo*
as a symbol of their Sierra Leonean identity, others criticised it as such.
Yema (aged fifteen) left Freetown when she was eight years old to join
her mother who was living in England. Her departure from Sierra
Leone was sudden and she was consequently not initiated before she
left. All of the female members of her family had been initiated and
her granny still wants Yema to return to Sierra Leone so that she may
be initiated. Yema is determined that she will not go to *Bondo*:

it's rubbish tribe business that someone started and now everyone follows. They say it's supposed to stop you from having sex
but all my aunties had it and they all got pregnant early so I
think it's rubbish.

Yema's reaction to *Bondo* displayed characteristics that were rarely seen
in the perspectives of girls in Freetown. Having learnt what the purpose of *Bondo* was, she explored its significance in terms of people she
knows and then *independently* came to her own conclusion as to
whether she would accept the rationale given by those around her. Her
disapproval of the process of initiation was not based on teachings
from her school, church or family, but rather stemmed from a personal
assessment that she has made on the basis of her own observations.

Yema was not the only girl from the England sample to have come to her own conclusions about *Bondo*. Fatu, now aged nineteen, had been initiated when she was five years old. She stated clearly that she 'hated' *Bondo*. Although she has no recollection of her own initiation experience, she has witnessed many other girls' initiations since and she knows the 'blood and pain' of the *Bondo* bush all too well.

> The people don't tell you though! When you go into the *Bondo* bush they tell you that you when you go out you must not tell anyone about what has happened because they don't want those little girls to know. They tell you that if you talk about it at all then your stomach will grow and swell, and then you will die. Even those small girls don't know what is happening to them! All the women in the family will arrange it and then the mother and aunty will say, 'come and drop me so-so place' and it is only when you get there that you see all these people and they grab you.

> I was scared to even talk about it with anyone – it was only when I came here and saw the other girls talking that I realised that they [women in *Bondo* bush] had lied. These girls were talking about it openly and they didn't die. These girls had already come here and knew that what those women were saying were lies – it was only me who didn't believe it. They fill you with fear so that you never want to talk to anyone, but now I'm not afraid anymore. Now I will tell anyone who asks about it!

> It is not like in this country where people tell you what they are doing all the time – there, they don't tell you and then they do these things to you. If those girls could choose, they wouldn't do it – they just don't know what is going to happen to them. No one would choose to harm their own body like that!

Despite 'hating' *Bondo*, Fatu was unable to express this to anyone while she was in Sierra Leone for fear of death. She perceived secrecy and trickery as instrumental in sustaining the practice of *Bondo* and only truly recognised the possibility of choice on arrival in England.

As will be discussed later, choice only prevails for those girls who are against *Bondo* as law restricts its practice and public discourse condemns it. Of the total of nineteen girls, twelve stated that they would not want their daughters to be initiated and one said that she would definitely want her to be initiated. The remaining six all indicated that they would want to initiate their daughters if their daughters expressed

a wish to do so. Their choice was limited however, and they acknowledged that they may not be able to carry out their daughters' wishes.

Bondo and Identity

As Christine Walley points out, much of the literature on female circumcision is posed either in terms of cultural relativism or what she
refers to as 'politically informed outrage.' Although female circumcision has received significant attention, Walley argues that anthropological accounts of female circumcision have limited themselves to descrip-
tive accounts of the practices, which do not consider the possible
'transformation' of such practices either across places, or through time.
The danger, she claims, is that this leads to a deepening divide between
'other' cultures in which female circumcision is practised, and Western
cultures in which it is challenged (Walley 2002: 32).

The perspectives Sierra Leonean girls have of *Bondo* transform both
through migration and as they grow older. Younger girls, in the fourteen to sixteen age range, in both Sierra Leone and England, are preoccupied with securing group membership and claiming part of the
group identity through *Bondo*. By affiliating with a group, girls are able
to 'self-categorise' and self-compare.[5] The concept of 'self-categorising'
stems from sociological theories of identity formation in which adolescents seek to form opinions that coincide with those of people who are
important to them. Cottrell (1996) suggests that once adolescents have
self-categorised themselves, they are then able to compare themselves
to members of the in- and out-group. By aligning themselves with several groups they are able to self-compare the different 'selves' they have
created through their various affiliations (Cottrell 1996: 11). These affiliations are generally based on 'visible and socially categorised markers [such] as gender, race, accent, language, class, religion and nationality' (Rumbaut 1994: 754). The extent of self-comparison does not stay
constant throughout adolescence. Early adolescence is more greatly
marked with social comparison and normative standards whereas late
adolescence brings together internalised standards and personalised beliefs (Harter 1993: 356). This is evident in Cottrell's study of high
school students in Australia, where he notes that students become less
focused on defining crowd types as they move into late adolescence.
Rather, they look to the future and to possibilities beyond adolescent
categories, which they have used previously. As the students graduate
from school, they also 'graduate' from an experimental and disjointed
sense of self, into one which is more integrated (Cottrell 1996: 41).

Young Sierra Leonean girls in England and Sierra Leone do not seek
membership of the same kinds of groups, however, and, consequently,

the ways in which they experience and perceive them is different. Girls in Sierra Leone perceive *Bondo* as necessary to their admission into 'womanhood.' Their fear of 'cusses' and insults is central to both their desire to be initiated and their satisfaction at having been initiated. Although this is in many ways equal to expressing an aspiration of being part of a group, it emphasises a greater concern about the consequence of *not* being part of a group. Exclusion carries far greater consequence than the lost benefits of inclusion. Girls of the same age group in England, conversely, are more concerned with securing *inclusion* in the collective that represents their identity as Sierra Leoneans, than in their membership of 'womanhood.' Their focus is directed at guaranteeing their ethnic identity through *Bondo*.

This difference in focus seems fitting when the risks of exclusion (for girls of all ages) are assessed; for girls in England, there is the risk of damage to their identity as Sierra Leoneans; for girls in Sierra Leone, the risk of possible damage to their identity as *women*. For girls in England, there are viable alternatives which they may adopt in terms of their ethnic identity. Girls like Yema, who referred to *Bondo* as 'rubbish tribe-business', can offset the risk of diminishing her Sierra Leonean identity by rejecting *Bondo* by compensating in another way (for instance, maintaining language), or by eschewing her Sierra Leonean identity and instead defining her identity as 'African', or 'black-British'. Girls in Sierra Leone, however, are left with little choice if they damage their identity as women. They risk losing an aspect of their identity, which they cannot easily substitute with anything else. As such, the ability of girls in the two contexts to *choose* whether to align themselves to this group is widely divergent.

Furthermore, it is difficult for girls in Sierra Leone independently to internalise beliefs that they may have in opposition to *Bondo*. Girls of all ages in Sierra Leone who oppose *Bondo* tend to do so on the basis of church instruction or concerns raised through reproductive health classes. Walley points out that it is difficult to assess whether when girls 'parrot' the opinions they have heard, they are doing so because they genuinely believe them or because they are expressing them in front of a particular audience. She argues that girls from the Sabaot ethnic group in Kikhome, Kenya, represented different aspects of their perspectives depending on their audience, and that this was not as much a deception or a desire to please, as a display of the different opinions that the girls held, both consciously and subconsciously (Walley 2002: 25).

While this may be true of the girls I interviewed in Sierra Leone, I would argue that their 'parroting' of the arguments they learnt from church or sexual health classes can also be attributed to their need for social affiliation. Due to the difficulty a girl faces in standing in opposition to *Bondo* and the risk that she takes in doing so alone, it is easier for her to align herself with a group that can *collectively* stand in opposition. This is not to suggest that girls are being disingenuous in their reference to religion or reproductive health concerns as reasons for opposing *Bondo*, rather it is to highlight the significance of group membership in supporting girls' perspectives and, to a large degree, protecting them from the risks which they may face as individuals. As such, the 'graduation' to which Cottrell refers does not occur for girls in Sierra Leone. They are not able to extract themselves from the alliances and affiliations which they have used to give them status and integrate the different perspectives which they have gained into a 'harmonised self.'

There is no expectation that girls in Sierra Leone should come to independent decisions regarding *Bondo*. Independent decisions against *Bondo* are often treated as a sign of immaturity and families' only means of dealing with such immaturity is through initiation. Even in the cases where girls align themselves with church perspectives on *Bondo*, there is no guarantee that this will hold up before older female relatives or community members.

> Priscilla was initiated when she was thirteen years old. She wanted to be initiated because she was told that otherwise she would not be able to have children and men would not want her. She also wanted to get new clothes.

> Priscilla is a devout born-again Christian and now feels terrible that she has been initiated into *Bondo* as it is a blood covenant with the devil. It is not in the Bible and is 'devil-business'. Being initiated is the greatest sin she has ever committed and she knows that she will never be able to repent enough to be absolved. It makes her very sad when she thinks about it now, and she often wonders how her life would be different if she had not been initiated.

> I asked Priscilla whether she would want her daughter to be initiated. 'No!' she exclaimed. After a moment she added, 'unless my mother-in-law wants me to go and then I can't say no.' (Notes from interview with Priscilla, aged 25)

So, the question is then what changes for girls when they leave Sierra Leone and arrive in England? What change occurs to allow them to express, as Fatu so clearly did, a perspective which is not based on group affiliation?

As discussed earlier, membership of *Bondo* represents very different things for girls in Sierra Leone and girls in England. When girls migrate from Sierra Leone to England, *Bondo* transforms from a representation of their womanhood, to a representation of their ethnic or national identity. The choices that are available to them in terms of affiliation increase and the consequences of their choices are not as damaging. There is little risk of them being denied their status as women and the status which is derived through *Bondo* in Sierra Leone is not recognised as such by broader British society. The distance that migration produces between girls and where *Bondo* is practiced enables them both to explore other perspectives and maintain them on an individual and personalised level. The older girls in England have little contact with Sierra Leonean adults and their social networks are largely made up of Sierra Leonean and African girls and boys in their same age range. Only one of the girls maintained contact with family or other adults in Sierra Leone. The pressure for them to conform to societal norms from Sierra Leone is therefore only felt through their peers. As Fatu highlighted, girls discuss *Bondo* together and share their personal experiences. They are able to express opinions which they may have previously hidden, and may feel secure in the knowledge that any desire they have for their daughters not to be initiated will be respected. Importantly, however there is also the opportunity for them to express any positive ideas that they have about *Bondo* without fear of being ridiculed or condemned, despite being in the minority. The need for group affiliation and approval diminishes.

Keniston (1965) proposed that social identity is formed through a combination of agency, freedom of choice and commitment (cited in Stevens 2002: 63). Inasmuch as *Bondo* represents an important component of social identity formation in Sierra Leone, the extent to which girls are able to approach it with freedom of choice and agency is limited. What is available to them is commitment. In England, transformation of *Bondo*, the limited interaction that older girls have with older Sierra Leoneans and the distance between all girls and the place in which initiations occur, provide girls with greater agency and freedom of choice. They are able to commit to choices which they make independently.

An important distinction that must be made, however, is that migration enables girls to *express* perspectives which have previously been silenced; it does not *produce* new perspectives. The observations, on which Fatu and other girls' conclusions were based, had been made in Sierra Leone, but they had not had the freedom to express them until in England. For two girls, running away from home was their only form of expression.

Despite England providing the opportunity for freedom of expression for girls who have been initiated and are now unhappy about it, law and public discourse prevent girls who advocate *Bondo* from expressing their opinions freely. All of the girls in the fourteen to sixteen age range stated that if anyone, they would talk to other Sierra Leoneans or Africans about *Bondo*. White people or other non-Africans would either not understand, or would judge them negatively. For young people in this early period of adolescence, self-categorisation and self-comparison are achieved self-consciously (Stevens 2002: 64). Perception that a belief on the basis of ethnicity or culture will be met with hostility from the majority population may lead to either, as in the case of most young girls, concealment of the particular belief, or, as in Dora's case, concealment and a hostile counter-reaction.

However, Sierra Leonean girls in England are aware not only of public perceptions of their cultural practices but of the legal implications also.

> Aminata went to *Bondo* when she was a baby. She doesn't remember it and although she was forced, she is now happy that she went. She has a friend who didn't go and she really suffers. She is always unsatisfied and chasing after so many men. She is so unhappy that she is now saving money so that she can go to Africa and have her clitoris removed. Aminata doesn't think it has really affected her sexual pleasure because she still has some feeling there and she is pleased that she has something that is so important in her culture.

> She doesn't want to send her daughter to *Bondo* because she will be put in prison here. But if her daughter really wants to go, if she finds out from friends and says that she really wants to go, then Aminata will agree and have to go to prison. 'I will just tell them [the authorities] that my daughter wanted to go, what can I do?'
> (Notes from interview with Aminata, aged 21)

The UK first introduced legislation specifically focusing on female circumcision in 1985 with the Female Genital Mutilation Act.[6] This Act stipulated that 'a person is guilty of an offence if he excises, infibulates or otherwise mutilates the whole or any part of a girl's labia majora, labia minora or clitoris'. This does not include procedures which are undertaken in order to preserve the mental or physical health of the female, nor does it apply to procedures undertaken at the time when a female gives birth. Individuals authorised to perform these procedures include registered medical practitioners, midwives and those in training for either of these fields. In 2003, the Act was extended to criminalise extra-territorial operations, stating that it is an offence to assist a girl in being mutilated overseas (UNICEF 2005). The maximum penalty for this offence was also increased from five years to fourteen years' imprisonment (Female Genital Mutilation Act 2003). The government extended the legislation to incorporate extra-territorial operations in response to growing concern about a legal loophole which allowed parents who were taking their daughters overseas for operations to escape prosecution.

Whilst being in favour of *Bondo* as a symbol of her culture and wanting to fulfil her daughters' wishes, Aminata was also clearly aware of the legal consequences she would face in England. Girls in the fourteen to sixteen age range also cited 'being in England' as a reason it would be more difficult to initiate their daughters, even though they would want to follow their daughters' wishes. The legal and public discourse condemning female circumcision cause girls to adjust their behaviour in terms of performing future initiations.[7] They also mean that girls conceal their opinions or experiences from non-Africans. At a stretch, they might share such opinions or experiences with other Africans (although in both cases, this is much more likely to be the case for girls who are proponents of the practice).

Conclusion

Social identity is developed through a process of self-categorisation, self-comparison and integration of the 'possible selves' into a harmonised, individual identity. This process, however is predicated on agency and freedom of choice – two requirements that are not easily accessible to girls in Sierra Leone. The association of circumcision with 'womanhood' combined with the fear of insults and secrecy surrounding *Bondo,* mean that young adolescent girls are eager to be both included and protected within the collective identity that *Bondo* offers. In England, young adolescents are preoccupied with solidifying their collective sense of ethnic identity and see *Bondo* as instrumental in defining themselves against other Africans, and mainstream British society.

As girls in Sierra Leone grow older, they reflect on their own experiences and the experiences of others. Lack of choice and limited agency, however mean that it is difficult for them to maintain independent opinions on *Bondo;* rather, they continue to align themselves with groups (either old or new) with whom they may share perspectives. This pattern is not so much attributable to a lack of consideration on the part of the girls as it is symptomatic of the lack of choice and freedom of expression available to them in Sierra Leone.

This chapter has argued that migration enables girls to express personal beliefs which had previously been silenced or ignored in Sierra Leone. As group affiliation becomes less important, girls are put less at risk when presenting and acting upon personal and individual perspectives. For these girls, as they progress through adolescence they become less self-conscious about their opinions and are able to find a position on the internal-external spectrum, which suits them independently.

An important component of the findings relates to choice. Not only is it instrumental in allowing adolescents to explore and determine their own identities, it is also crucial in allowing us to better understand female circumcision. As seen from the experiences of girls in Sierra Leone, lack of choice can lead to a subjugation of personal beliefs and an inability to express or act on individual convictions. However, some girls in the UK face a similar lack of choice and limited freedom of expression.

Girls who are happy about having been circumcised are limited in their ability to express this due to the hostile legal and social discourses that are prolific in the UK. Kimmel and Weiner point out that 'minority youth' are often able to advance smoothly in their processes of identity formation if they have been able to develop a strong sense of ethnic identity in an environment that fosters an appreciation of cultural diversity (1995: 413). Public discourse surrounding female circumcision in the UK does little to promote cultural sensitivity, the result of which can be seen in the experiences of the younger adolescents who would at least, hide their own experiences or at most develop aggressive behaviours toward the white, mainstream society. Another study exploring the perspectives of this group as they move into late adolescence would be useful in examining the impact on their identities of their own concealment and the hostile public discourse.

Nonetheless, I would argue that the findings presented in this chapter point to a broader argument about female circumcision and choice. Girls frequently referred to choice, or the absence of choice, as being pivotal to their experiences of female circumcision. Furthermore, a number of girls determined that despite their own beliefs, they would want their daughters to have the choice as to whether they were initiated or not. Each of the girl's accounts drew on individual perspectives, which although not always expressed as such, were particular to their own experiences.

The findings have also shown, however, that girls in the early stages of adolescence are preoccupied with group affiliation and that this plays a major role in influencing their choices. As they pass into stages of late adolescence, it is possible that the beliefs which they had held so strongly, and that had been closely associated with membership of a particular group, will have waned. I would argue therefore that choice around female circumcision is both necessary and important because it strongly contributes to girls' processes of identity formation. I would not suggest that girls should choose whether or not to be initiated before turning eighteen, as the findings have shown that their perspectives change as their individual identities develop further. However, I do believe that a more open environment in which girls can approach *Bondo* and female circumcision – in England as well as in Sierra Leone – will enable to make them choices that will inevitably be better fitting for their individual identities: both as Sierra Leoneans and as girls.

Notes

1   news.bbc.co.uk/1/hi/world/europe/281026.stm, 17 February 1999.
2   Secret societies are referred to differently by the various ethnic groups; *Bondo* and *Sande* are the most commonly used names and are derived from Temne and Mende roots, respectively.
3   Due to the lack of security in the countryside during the recent conflict in Sierra Leone, large numbers of internally displaced people arrived in the capital, Freetown, and were forced to carry out their traditional practices in this new setting. In addition to this, families based in Freetown were keen to protect the initiation prospects of their daughters, now threatened by widespread rape and sexual violence. Campaigns by secret society leaders encouraged parents to initiate their daughters whilst they still could. This resulted in increasing reports of initiations being carried out in Freetown. Since the end of the conflict, reports of initiations taking place in Freetown persist but with lesser frequency. It is unclear to what extent these urban initiations occur.
4   www.who.int/mediacentre/factsheets/fs241/en.
5   I did not ask girls how they self-categorised themselves as I was less interested in obtaining a 'tick-box' style definition of their identity, and more interested in exploring their identity through the different issues discussed.
6   www.opsi.gov.uk/acts/acts2003/20030031.htm#1.
7   Given the difficulty in implementing the Female Mutilation Act 2003, and the lack of prosecutions in the UK since the first legislation was passed in 1985, it is conceivable that girls like Aminata may choose to return to Sierra Leone to initiate their daughters. Although present, the risk of prosecution in the UK is slight (for a discussion of European implementation of female genital mutilation legislation, see Dembour (2001)).

References

Abusharaf, R. (2000), 'Revisiting Feminist Discourses on Infibulation: Responses from Sudanese Feminists', in B. Shell-Duncan & Y. Hernlund (eds.), *Female 'Circumcision' in Africa: Culture, Controversy and Change*, 151-166. Boulder: Lynne Reinner Publishers.

Ahmadu, (2000), 'Rites and Wrongs: An Insider/ Outsider Reflects on Power and Exci-
    sion', in B. Shell-Duncan & Y. Hernlund (eds.), *Female 'Circumcision' in Africa: Cul-
    ture, Controversy and Change*, 283-212. Boulder: Lynne Reinner Publishers.
BBC News (1999), *Woman on Trial in Paris for Female Genital Mutilation*, 2 February
    1999. http://news.bbc.co.uk/1/hi/world/europe/270396.stm.
Cottrell, J. (1996), *Social Networks and Social Influences in Adolescence*. London: Routledge.
Dembour, M. (2001), 'Following the Movement of a Pendulum: Between Universalism
    and Relativism', in J. Cowan, R. Wilson, & M. Dembour (eds.), *Culture and Rights*, 56-
    79. Cambridge: Cambridge University Press.
Dirie, W. (1998), *Desert Flower: The Extraordinary Journey of a Desert Nomad*. New York,
    William Morrow.
Dorkenoo, E. (1994), *Cutting the Rose: Female Genital Mutilation, the Practice and its Preven-
    tion*. London: Minority Rights Publications.
Ferme, M. (2001), *The Underneath of Things: Violence, History, and the Everyday in Sierra
    Leone*. Berkeley: University of California Press.
Gruenbaum, E. (2001), *The Female Circumcision Controversy: An Anthropological Perspective*.
    Philadelphia: University of Pennsylvania Press.
Harter, S. (1993), 'Stress, Coping and Adaptation', in S.S. Feldman & G. Elliott (eds.), *At
    the Threshold: The Developing Adolescent*, 352-387. Cambridge: Harvard University
    Press.
Hosken, F. (1979), *The Hosken Report: Genital and Sexual Mutilation of Females*. Lexington,
    Mass.: Women's International Network News.
Keniston, K. (1965), *The Uncommitted: Alienated Youth in American Society*. New York: Har-
    court, Brace, & World, Inc.
Kenyatta, J. (1965 [1938]), *Facing Mount Kenya*. New York: Vintage Books.
Kimmel, D. & Weiner, I. (1995), *Adolescence: A Developmental Transition*. New Jersey: John
    Wiley & Sons, Inc.
Koso-Thomas, O. (1987), *Circumcision of Women: A Strategy for Eradication*. London: Zed
    Books.
Lightfoot-Klein, H. (1989), *Prisoners of Ritual: An Odyssey into Female Genital Circumcision
    in Africa*. New York: Haworth Press
Little, K. (1967), *The Mende of Sierra Leone: A West African People in Transition*. London:
    Routledge.
Manderson, L. (2004), 'Tensions Between Cultural Diversity and Human Rights', *Interna-
    tional Feminist Journal of Politics* 6 (2): 285-307.
Obermeyer, C.M. (1995), 'A Cross-Cultural Perspective on Reproductive Rights', *Human
    Rights Quarterly* 17: 366-381.
Rahman, A. & Toubia, N. (2000), *Female Genital Mutilation: A Guide to Laws and Policies
    Worldwide*. London: Zed Books.
Reproductive Freedom News (1999), *African Women Struggling Against Female Genital Mu-
    tilation*, Reproductive Freedom News VIII (4), Centre for Reproductive Rights, April
    1999. http://crlp.org/rfn_99_04.html.
Rumbaut, R. (1994), '"The Crucible Within": Ethnic Identity, Self-Esteem, and Segmented
    Assimilation Among Children of Immigrants', *International Migration Review* 28 (4):
    748-794.
Scheper-Hughes, N. (1991), 'Virgin Territory: The Male Discovery of the Clitoris', *Medical
    Anthropology Quarterly* 5(1): 25-28.
Schweder, R. (2000) 'What about "Female Genital Mutilation"? And Why Understanding
    Culture Matters in the First Place', *Daedalus* 129 (4): 209-233.
Stevens, J. (2002), *Smart and Sassy: The Strengths of Inner-City Black Girls*. New York: Ox-
    ford University Press.
Tajfel, H. (1978), *Differentiation between Social Groups*. San Diego: Academic Press.

Thomas, L. (2000), '"Ngaitana (I will circumcise myself)": Lessons from Colonial Campaigns to Ban Excision in Meru, Kenya', in B. Shell-Duncan & Y. Hernlund (eds.), *Female "Circumcision" in Africa: Culture, Controversy and Change*, 129-150. Boulder: Lynne Reinner Publishers.

Toubia, N. (1993), *Female Genital Mutilation: A Call for Global Action*. New York: Women Ink.

UNICEF (2005), *UNICEF UK Position Statement*, 19 October 2005. www.unicef.org.uk/unicefuk/policies/policy_detail.asp?policy=12.

Walley, C. (2002), 'Searching for "Voices": Feminism, Anthropology, and the Global Debate over Female Genital Operations', in S. James & C. Robertson (eds.), *Genital Cutting and Transnational Sisterhood: Disputing U.S. Polemics*, 17-53. Urbana/Chicago: University of Illinois Press.

Walker, A. (1992) *Possessing the Secret of Joy*. New York: Harcourt Brace Jovanovich.

Walker, A. & Parmar, P. (1993), *Warrior Marks : Female Genital Mutilation and the Sexual Blinding of Women*. New York: Harcourt Brace.

World Health Organisation (2000), *Female Genital Mutilation, Factsheet No. 241*. www.who.int/mediacentre/factsheets/fs241/en.

11 Socio-Cultural Dynamics in Intermarriage in Spain: Beyond Simplistic Notions of Hybridity[1]

Dan Rodríguez-García

Introduction: Immigration and Mixed Marriages in Catalonia, Spain

One of the less researched but fundamental aspects of the settlement and accommodation of immigrants in receiving countries is the relationship between migration and life course, particularly with respect to family and household dynamics in migration and marriage and family formation in the host country. This relationship includes processes of endogamy and exogamy (i.e. marrying within/outside one's own group), an aspect crucial to understanding processes of interethnic relations and social incorporation in plural societies.

Spain is the country in the European Union that has undergone the greatest increase in international immigration in the last few years, in 2006 receiving nearly 45 per cent of all immigrants arriving in the EU. The *Padrón* (the Municipal Register Data which includes both registrants with and without legally documented residence), as of 1 January 2006, reported 4,144,166 foreign residents living in Spain, representing 9.3 per cent of the total population (INE 2007a). With the increase in international immigration and the permanent settlement of immigrants in Spain in recent years, mixed marriages[2] and the formation of multi-local, transcultural, and transnational families are growing realities. Data provided by INE (2007b) for 2006 recorded that 24,412 Spanish nationals married foreigners –11.5 per cent of total marriages (211,818) – an increase of 6 per cent over 2001 figures.

Catalonia is the most populated autonomous region in Spain and the autonomous community with the largest number of foreigners: the *Padrón*, as of 1 January 2006, recorded 913,757 resident foreigners living in Catalonia, representing 12.8 per cent of the total Catalonian population (INE 2007a). According to data provided by IDESCAT (2007) for 2005, the proportion of mixed marriages between people of Spanish nationality and those of foreign nationality was 14.8 per cent (4,590 of the total 31,140 marriages). In comparison to data for 2001, there has been an increase of 8.4 per cent. Spanish men accounted for 62.9 per cent of those involved in mixed marriages in Catalonia, and they married Latin Americans (50.1 per cent), chiefly Colombians, followed by European women of the non-European Economic Area (19.1 per cent), mostly Eastern Europeans. Spanish women in Catalonia who married a foreigner represented 37 per cent of the total, and their choice of foreign partners was more equally distributed among different nationalities: Latin Americans (35.1 per cent), mostly Argentinian; Africans (20.2 per cent), chiefly Moroccans; and citizens of the European Union (20.6 per cent), mainly Italian.

Since the early 1980s, West Africa – mainly the Gambia and Senegal – has become an increasingly significant source of immigration to Spain, to the extent that at present, these two groups are the major sub-Saharan nationalities living in Spain, where they have a particular concentration in Catalonia. At the end of 2005, they accounted for 80 per cent of the total sub-Saharan immigration to Catalonia (23,414 in total; 13,130 Gambian and 10,284 Senegalese) and 70 per cent of the number living in Spain overall. Most Senegalese and Gambians living in Catalonia marry people of their own nationality. However, in recent years, there has been an increase of mixed marriages, mostly between Senegalese or Gambian men and Spanish women, and a rise in the formation of transnational and transcultural Senegalese- and Gambian-Spanish families in Catalonia. The processes of intermarriage among Senegambians in Catalonia will herein be the focus of this paper.

The Senegambian case is useful for evaluating the effectiveness of mixed unions as a 'straight-line' assimilationist strategy. The 'straight-line' assimilation perspective, widely adopted by anthropologists, sociologists, and demographers since the 1950s (Banton 1955; Gordon 1964), has argued for assimilation as a 'single final destination' (Todd 1994). In this context, endogamy has been interpreted as a 'traditional behaviour,' an 'act of defensive structuring,' or an 'anti-integratory' element that limits pluri-ethnic integration and maintains differences – as opposed to exogamy, which causes them to disappear (Coleman 1994). Métissage has frequently been used as a synonym for a society without differences, as traditionally, exogamy has been treated as one of the direct indicators of the integration or assimilation of the immigrant population, presupposing that it implies the absence of ethnic and racial prejudices and that it is the last step in a series of cultural and structural assimilations. Senegalese and Gambian populations, in general, have significant differences, such as their phenotype and religion, from dominant Spanish society. For this reason, exploring the dynamics that occur within the intermarriages of this particular group elucidates the accuracy or limitations of mixed marriage as a vehicle for assimilation and also calls into question the meaning of culture itself. The intent of this paper is to show the highly complex and multifaceted nature of processes of interculturalism, in which change and retention, hybridity and segregation, globalisation and localisation, are reversible and complementary, rather than competing.

Marriage Patterns among Senegalese and Gambian Immigrants in Catalonia

Most Senegalese and Gambians living in Catalonia marry people of their own nationality. Of those who do intermarry, however, men are more likely to form exogamous unions than Senegambian women. The reasons for both of these trends are preferential, normative, and structural.

First, marriage trends within this community are explained by the traditional pattern of male migration (with subsequent reunion with the wife in the home country) and by the goal of temporary migration (with return and investment in the place of origin of the financial and/ or educational capital obtained abroad). Most of the Senegalese and Gambians living in Catalonia are young males who emigrate from rural origins with the objective of improving their living standards. As economic migrants, they take on the most precarious jobs in agriculture, construction, services and manufacturing, while supporting a large, diversified underground economy as well as incipient ethnic and transnational businesses. Despite working in unskilled jobs, a number have high educational attainments. Initially, the intention of most of those who migrate to Catalonia is temporary migration with the aim of obtaining resources to be invested in their country of origin. The family sees the emigrant son as a saviour: life insurance for parents in countries where the population lives on very slender means. In this sense, immigrating to Europe has become a sort of 'rite of passage' for the youth. While they are awaiting sufficient resources to go back, however, return is often delayed indefinitely, turning these temporary migrants into 'permanent' immigrants. As explained by one of the interviewees:[3]

What you want is to be rich; that's the dream inside your head: you want to go back richer than your father, you understand? But what happens? You spend years here, years, years. You want to be rich in order to go back, and you'll never be rich! ... You always want to have twice as much, but it never comes! And one year goes by, and then another. And the years go by and you don't even notice! (Sherif, a 37-year-old Gambian man married to a Spanish woman, with whom he has three children)

Secondly, endogamy is an element of group cohesion and of reference within the Senegambian family organisation; it is the basic means and the principle vehicle for the transmission of the values and cultural codes of the society of origin, to which return is intended. For these structural reasons, Senegalese and Gambian men are more exogamous than their female counterparts.

Thirdly, religious factors play a significant role in the marriage choices of the Senegambian population, the vast majority of whom are Muslim. While marrying within the common religion is the preference and norm, Islam permits Muslim men to marry Muslim, Jewish, or Christian women, while Muslim women are not permitted to marry non-Muslims, as the children of these unions are considered *kafir*, or lost to Islam.

Finally, the tendency for both Senegambian men and women to marry endogamously can be partly attributed to the host society's negative attitudes towards 'miscegenation', which are based on a set of stereotypes concerning immigrants who come from poor countries (who are perceived as delinquents or opportunists), as well as to the prejudices of the predominantly 'Caucasian' host society towards non-white skin colour:[4]

> I arrived here and hear 'nigger', 'coloured' ... So then, I thought, 'If I marry a white Spanish woman, I may get in trouble!' You can always find someone who loves you, but what about her environs? Depending on the family, who knows what would happen. So, to avoid all this ... the less trouble the better. Nobody likes being in a discotheque with a white woman and people saying things. (Amar, 33-year-old Senegalese man married to a Senegalese woman)

> Some people think that women that get involved with us are those who cannot find a person who loves them; they might be considered prostitutes. (Lamine, a 40-year-old Senegalese man, married to a Spanish woman, with whom he has one child)

> There is a lot of racism. They say, 'How can this black man have that house?' ... Society does not admit mixed couples, even if they say they do. I lost most of my friends; I know they dislike me because I am with a black person, as if it said 'AIDS' or 'drug pusher'. (Ángela, a 37-year-old Spanish woman, cohabiting with a Gambian man, with whom she has a five-year-old daughter)

However, as previously mentioned, mixed marriages are a growing reality also among African origin populations, largely as a consequence of unforeseen 'permanent' settlement. As explained by Sherif, a 37-year-old Senegambian man married to a Spanish woman, with whom he has three children,

> I didn't intend to get married here. When I came, I planned to come and work, make some money, and then go back to see my mother and look after her. ... Then time goes by, until you meet someone and then you talk and so on and, well, here we are. ... There [Gambia], they always look for a wife for you so you can get married, when you're a kid, without you knowing. And you come here to make some money and then go back and then give the money to her family, and then talk to her and get to know her, and then if you can, you get married. ... For me it was like I won the lottery.

Data from the research sample further suggest that most Senegalese and Gambian men who form mixed unions are either single or have previous relationships that have not been formalised; they also have socio-economic resources and contacts abroad (chain migration) prior to emigration. Mixed unions tend to be homogamous (both spouses share similar socio-economic status) or, at least, hypergamous (i.e. 'marrying up') for the Senegalese or Gambian spouse. Within this latter context, so-called 'marriages of convenience', in which the reason for the union is to reduce the period established by law for the acquisition of nationality, are possible. Currently, in Spain, nationality through residence is obtained after a period of ten years. This period is reduced to five years for those who qualify as asylum seekers or refugees and to two years if the applicants are nationals of Latin American countries, Andorra, the Philippines, or Equatorial Guinea, or if the applicants are Sephardic. Nationality through residence is obtained after one year by – among other cases – those who at the time of application have been married to a Spanish citizen for a year and are not legally or de facto separated. Some of the interviewees in Catalonia justify marriages of convenience as a means of becoming legal in the host country, in order thereby to improve access to resources and social mobility. Strictly speaking, however, marriages of convenience are not common among the Senegalese and Gambians living in Catalonia and are more common among immigrants from Eastern Europe, Russia, and Latin America, especially Cuba.

The Dynamics of Hybridity: Socio-Cultural Change and Retention, Conflict and Accommodation

My research with Senegalese and Gambians in Catalonia involved in mixed unions did not show a direct relationship between intermarrying and 'straight-line' assimilation. Instead, I have found that the context of union formation and the dynamics of mixed unions present a particularly active and complex socio-cultural hybrid space. All of the unions demonstrate varying degrees of negotiation between the host culture and the immigrant culture; some practices are maintained and others, perhaps more conflictive, are not. For instance, food traditions of the country of origin are often maintained. As explained by Mercè, a 32-year-old Spanish woman married to a Gambian man with whom she has two children:

> We eat everything, but we make a lot dishes from there [the Gambia], such as rice with peanut sauce, couscous, and so, instead of paella [traditional Catalan rice dish], we make that at least twice a week. And my children are so happy! The day I make rice, they go like, 'Wow, I want rice!' My husband taught me how to make the peanut sauce ... the first week we married! [laughing] And every time I cook it better.

However, other discrepancies between socio-cultural models of the immigrant country and of the host country may generate greater conflict, such as a clash between the independence of the Western way of life and the model of African family solidarity (i.e. economic help for the family in the country of origin and mutual help between fellow-countrymen in the host society).

> Most of those that leave the Gambia have the support of the whole family: your mother, your father, your brothers help you to leave; they give you money, they give you all their support, they prepare the way for you; and then you owe the family! You've got a responsibility to the family. If you come here and in two or three years you've forgotten that, you're just not like your family anymore: the relationship has been broken... In mixed couples, there's conflict over that. (Alagey, a 46-year-old Gambian man, married to a Gambian woman, with whom he has five children)

> *Mbay:* Me, if someone rings the doorbell, I go to open the door. ... I can't live without people! If anything happens to me today, people will come today! If they let you leave Africa, you get the money together and send it back to Africa, right?

Juana: I'm not saying anything about that. But what I will tell you is that there are many that say they're your friends when you've got something; if you've got nothing, they see you in the street and don't even say hello.

Mbay: You've seen my house – there's tons of people; when it's time to eat, everyone!

Juana: That's why we're the way we are.

(Mbay, a 50-year-old Senegalese man, and Juana, a 43-year-old Spanish woman, married and with four children)

There are, nevertheless, contradictions among Senegalese and Gambians themselves between an overt discourse of solidarity and a covert discourse of autonomy and individuality. Furthermore, conflict does not always arise and, in any case, is lessened if there is flexibility and negotiation on the part of both spouses:

Samba: We used to think, when you come here to Europe, you marry a white woman, you forget your family. ... I say, 'Well, if I marry someone who is a *Fula* like me, then I'll go on helping my family; if I get me a white woman, maybe she won't let me help my family'. But it was the other way round: everything I want, I send it to my family; and even if we've not got anything, she helps me find something to send it there. So I say, 'Look, what people said isn't true!'

Ángela: There are *morenos* [Senegalese and Gambians] that only live for their family over there and they forget what they've got here; and there are people that even though they're with a white woman, they shouldn't think that we're not going to help.

(Samba, a 40-year-old Gambian man, and Ángela, a 37-year-old Spanish woman, cohabitants with one daughter)

For example, suddenly five friends turn up without having phoned, right? And my wife could get mad, for example. *Mais* [But], there in Senegal, never! That's our custom. ... *Mais* here, it's very difficult. I understand it because it's the education you get from when you're a kid. If you show up and we're eating, you have to eat. Here all that's more closed up; *mais* I understand. Here, I've learnt a lot. It's tough, because I've got my culture; she's got her culture, too. There are things I don't understand about marriage here; but I do it because you have to respect other people's culture. She's respected my culture, too: first, she became a Muslim, that's something, isn't it? [So] I've got to respect her too. There are some things that are very hard, but I try. (Malick, a 42-year-old Senegalese man, married to a Spanish woman, with whom he has one child)

Hence, differences do not always make for insurmountable obstacles. Rather, where negotiation and mutual accommodation of differences occur, cultural practices are transformed and re-invented by the social actors themselves, giving rise to very diverse responses. As Sulayman-Sa, a 52-year-old Gambian man married to a Spanish woman, with whom he has three children, explains, being clear from the beginning is the way to avoid problems in the future:

I don't have to pretend to be another person. This leads to many conflicts among mixed marriages. ... We are from different cultures, so we have to manage it well, always saying the truth. I said to my wife, from the beginning, 'I am Muslim, and I do not eat pork'; I said that very clear! 'I do not drink alcohol'. But others keep these things hidden, and then the second generation turns up, that is, their children. They are probably going to be raised by your mother-in-law, and you might find your mother-in-law feeding your children ham; so the fight starts: 'Why are you giving pork to my children!' But tell her before, so she and all the family knows, idiot! You can eat ham, I'll have a sardine! And I have problems with nobody.

Another source of conflict is different models of gender relations – that is, conflict between the separation of sexual roles and the trend towards the equality of roles. As Abdul explains:

Women here [Spain] are different than there [Senegal]. For example, in Senegal you have your wife, but you leave the house and come back whenever you want; no problem. ... There, men bring the money home, so they do not have to stay at home all the time; they are always out. But here it is different: you and your wife both work. So all the expenses ... all this is different. ... Here there are limits; there, there are no limits [laughter]. (Abdul, a 32-year-old Senegalese married to a Spanish woman, with whom he has one child)

The context in which these dynamics of conflict and accommodation most obviously take place is in the upbringing of children, specifically in the intergenerational transmission of values and socio-cultural models. In general, the parents try to preserve and transmit their respective values, with some degree of flexibility. Senegalese and Gambian parents resign themselves to the idea of their children 'losing their culture of origin' and understand that children, particularly those born and/or brought up in Catalonia, live in another context, with different values and points of reference. On the one hand, Senegalese and Gambian parents encourage their children to adopt modern ways of doing things, since these skills may help them acquire a good education and employment opportunities. On the other hand, they may feel threatened by their children – especially their daughters – becoming 'too Westernised' in their behaviour in areas such as choice of friendships, sexuality, and drinking. The contrasting socio-cultural background that Senegalese and Gambian parents want to transmit to their children has to do with values and customs linked to traditional family dynamics and the affiliation to Islam. As this attempt at transmission of culture occurs in a context in which Islam is looked down on socially, it is difficult for immigrants' children – who, like all children, seek acceptance by the majority group – to openly identify themselves as Muslims and as the children of immigrants. As explained by an interviewee:

> They are like chameleons until they're sufficiently sure to be able to show it in public. And the fact is that it's really hard to be continually justifying a choice that isn't normal, that people look down on. Here, in countries like Spain, with not many resources, where you can't provide them with a clear alternative, those kids are at risk of being marginalised. (Maryam, a 44-year-old Spanish woman who converted to Islam and who is married to a Senegalese man, with whom she has two children)

Social rejection of the children because of phenotype leads to similarly adverse reactions. For example:

> My daughter says she doesn't want to be black; she says she's 'white coffee', and I tell her, 'You're like your Dad'. And she says, 'No, Dad is black; I'm white coffee'; and she says, 'Couldn't he be more white?' I don't know why she says that ... (Ángela, a 37-year-old Spanish woman, cohabiting with a Gambian man, with whom she has a 5-year-old daughter)

Some of the Senegalese and Gambians interviewed argue that the main obstacle to the transmission of socio-cultural values in mixed couples is the fact that the children spend more time with the Spanish mother than with the Senegalese or Gambian father:

> There's a problem, because there are lots that just don't control it ... because, in the first place, hey, the kids just don't know their Dad's culture! They were born here, everything they know is here, nothing else. [They know] very little of the Gambia, and they don't respect it, they don't. Theirs is basically 90 per cent their mother's culture, nothing else. ... There's a clash of cultures: the father wants them to go one way, the mother another, and then. ... The kids are a bit rebellious in the family, you know, and then it's pretty difficult, pretty hard. (Alagey, a 46-year-old Gambian man married to a Gambian woman, with whom he has five children)

These difficulties, together with the fact that the values the Senegalese and Gambian fathers want to transmit to their children may come into conflict with the values of their Spanish wives (hierarchy based on age and the separation of sexual roles versus more equality in intergenerational dealings and the trend towards the equality of sexual roles) may lead to the break-up of the couple. As explained by Lamine, a 40-year-old Senegalese man living in Catalonia since 1985, divorced from a Spanish woman who did not convert to Islam and remarried to a Spanish woman who did:

> The first marriage didn't last long. Because after the girl was born ... while she's my responsibility, she has to know where her Dad is from. Why is Dad different from Mum? Why has Dad got that culture and gets up for Ramadan? Those things my kids have got to know; if not, their culture gets lost! And the girls are here. ... *Donc* everything they learn here, that's Spanish culture, that's not their Dad's culture. ... Because she [his ex-wife] said, 'You change or we're through'. I told her, 'I'm not changing, you decide' ... For her, the girl is Spanish and her mother is Spanish and so she doesn't have to learn anything about African culture. Well, I don't see it that way. ... Here [with his current wife], it's very different from before. She doesn't have ideas like that; she's shown she doesn't mind.

The break-up of mixed couples because of conflicts over gender relations or the raising of children tends to be accompanied by a process of cultural revitalisation. This may result in the formation of a new endogamous union, one which is justified in terms of cultural-religious similarities. As explained by Aliu, a 56-year-old Gambian man living in Catalonia since the early 1990s, divorced from a Spanish woman – with whom he has an adolescent son – and remarried to a much younger Gambian woman:

> Respect for your parents ... that's very important. Here, it's very different, it's like equals. ... Disobedience, it's not something that we like. We come from a different education. ... And the kids that are born here have other customs. ... I put up with a lot [in his marriage to his Spanish ex-wife] because we're different, with different customs. We're accustomed to obedience, to obeying the husband, and not to saying, 'Bring me that', and she says, 'You get it!' [In the Gambia], the woman is born educated for obedience in marriage; it's not discrimination, it's the way of life we have. The woman is boss of the house. Her happiness, the success of her children, depend on the harmony she has with her husband.

Some would argue that this revitalisation is not generated by a cultural-religious issue, but by the desire to maintain certain social privileges. As Malang, a 43-year-old Senegalese man married to a Senegalese woman, with whom he has two children, explains:

> For me, those are the false ones; it's the false ones that do it. Because Muslim religion, those that practise it, they don't practise it because they believe in God. ... Me, I see couples here that, like in Africa, I've seen friends that got married and then went, because the Muslim religion is always an instrument for keeping the woman in her place and the man on top. And those people, they do it because then it breeds that mentality in the woman: a woman is like that, with him on top.

In fact, in the cases analysed, the formation of an endogamous union following the breakdown of a mixed union was motivated in greater part by the desire for the social differentiation of gender roles than it was by the desire to share an affiliation with Islam or a common country of birth.

These examples alert us to the fact that the gender conflicts that occur in mixed unions are sometimes due to a particular interpretation of culture, rather than the culture itself; that is, culture does not manifest itself as an essential, fixed, singular, and determining set of values and customs. Some Spanish women who divorce from Senegalese or

Gambian man choose, in fact, to maintain the Islam faith they have adopted. As one interviewee explains:

> When I went to the Mosque in Barcelona, to take classes and so on, there are Spanish girls married to African men who got divorced, but wanted to keep on following Islam, so then ... (Pilar, a 32-year-old Spanish woman who converted to Islam and is married to and has one daughter with a Senegalese man)

Within the context of gender relations, perhaps the most contentious practice that Senegalese or Gambian immigrants might seek to maintain is female circumcision, a traditional practice in Senegal and the Gambia and an illegal practice in Spain (I have explored this issue in depth in a previous publication, Rodríguez-García 2002b). Among the Senegalese and Gambian population living in Catalonia, the majority, in fact, reject female circumcision. In all the cases of mixed couples (i.e. comprised of Senegalese and Gambian men and Spanish women) interviewed, among whom a greater discontinuity of female circumcision is to be expected than in endogamous marriages, both partners rejected circumcising their daughters (actually or potentially), considering it a harmful, antiquated practice and a sign of a lack of integration into the host society. At the same time, all of the men and some of the women approved of male circumcision, which is considered a religious precept to be maintained and/or a practice that is beneficial for health (hygiene). Nevertheless, the Spanish wives tended to say that they would only have their male offspring circumcised if it were medically necessary. These viewpoints are illustrated in the following conversation between Falla, a 37-year-old Gambian man, and Imma, a 36-year-old Spanish woman, a married couple with five children:

Falla: The boys, yes; it's part of my religion: if they are not... circumcised, they're not allowed to go inside a mosque, because they're not sacred; they're not... clean. With women, it's that I don't want them to do it.

Imma: It's not a question of religion. It's a question of... of the submission of the woman; as a punishment.

Falla: No, for me, just for Omar [referring to his younger child, and only boy] we're thinking of...

Imma: Well, you've been thinking of it; I've not been.

Falla: [half-joking] Well, we're going to have trouble there...!

Imma: If he doesn't need it, then no. But, anyway, [smiling] it's not going to be a cause for separation, eh...? Well... we will come to some agreement.

Falla: Look, Jimmy [a friend of Falla's] in Mataró [a city close to Barcelona], you know him? He had it done to his son, and so what?

Imma: Like all of them; they've all been doing it ... I've asked the doctor, and he says, 'Well, for the time being the kid doesn't... He's fine'.

Falla: But I see that he's carrying dirt around; that's what I've always thought.

Imma: And how many kids die having that done, because they cut off the prepuce because they haven't got skin to cut off?

Falla: No, no, it's something the doctors do.

Imma: Doctors? It was a witch-doctor that cut yours off!

Falla: No, a witch-doctor, no. I had it done naturally: they cut it naturally. Then they put natural things on so that it heals. Witch-doctoring, no; they say that that's better. You have to go down to the beach, ten minutes there. Then they put leaves on [laughing]. That's the most horrible thing there is! I'll have it done to my son, but at the doctor's, not natural like that; at the doctor's it just takes a minute and that's that.

Imma: If he wants to do it because he's convinced of his religion, and thinks it's a sign of purity... well.

Another Senegalese interviewee explained:

The majority, those that have black African wives like themselves, some are doing things as if they were living there [in Africa]. Here, it's going to happen; in the future it's going to be like what happened in France. In France the children have now started to stand up for their rights; one has reported her parents, for trying to have her as if she were... living there. The daughters don't agree with it. I don't; I'm integrated and my kids are going to be integrated. (Lamine, a 40-year-old Senegalese man married to a 32-year-old Spanish woman who converted to Islam, with whom he has one daughter)

These views regarding circumcision are also held by many endoga-mous couples, who resist family pressure from the country of origin in order not to have their daughters circumcised:

I take my kid [to be circumcised] here [in Catalonia] to the doc-tor's. He's eight. My daughter, no; my daughter, no [lowering her voice] [...] In my country they do, but my daughters here, no, be-cause I bring her young. [My parents] want to do it, but I don't like it [lowering voice even further]. I don't like it [...] My hus-band doesn't want it either. The boy, yes; the girl, not. (Khadi, a 27-year-old Senegalese woman married to a 45-year-old Senega-lese man, with whom she has three children, one daughter and two sons)

I'm not doing it to my daughters. Because it's not a religious thing and... I just don't see it. With the boy, yes, I'm absolutely convinced, but not with my daughters. I've asked our ministers lots of questions about this, asking them if it's a religious thing that's got to be fulfilled one hundred percent and they said no; it's a question of personal taste, and doesn't affect the woman at all. And then, from a sanitary point of view, it's not hygienic, and so I'm not convinced. [My wife] thinks the same; she sees it quite clear now, we've talked about it [...] And when they went to the Gambia, I told them that 'Look, when you get there, my mother or your parents are going to say to take them [to be cir-cumcised]. Say no'. We agreed and she went with the girls on holiday. When they suggested it, she said, 'No, my husband doesn't want it, that's why'. And so they didn't do it. I think it's a question of educating people that... that it doesn't make sense. The boys, yes; because they say it's cleaner, so as not to catch ill-nesses and things. I'll take all of my boys to the hospital to have it done. (Alagey, a 46-year-old Gambian man married to a 42-year-old Gambian woman with whom he has five children, two daughters and three sons)

In cases where female circumcision is maintained among Senegalese and Gambian residents in Catalonia, this decision is linked to their transmigratory project and to the idea of return to the country of origin because female circumcision, even in African countries in which it is prohibited by law, plays a fundamental role in the integration of females into society (see Rajkotia, this volume). However, as immigrants acquire full civil rights as citizens (i.e. employment, housing, schooling, health care, etc.), and as female circumcision is dissociated from its social functions and meanings (i.e. the requisite for attaining marriageable status, with the related goal of forming a home and a family), it is to be expected that there will be changes. We should bear in mind, nevertheless, that these changes may also include transformations and/or re-creations in the host society (e.g. processes of neo-traditionalism, such as the option of having circumcision carried out in hospitals under the appropriate medical conditions, using anaesthesia and sterilised equipment, including post-operative care, etc.).

When examining the issue of cultural change and cultural maintenance among Senegalese- and Gambian-Spanish families living in Catalonia, it is significant to note that most of the people whom I interviewed conveyed the importance of their transnational situation. Senegalese and Gambians living in Catalonia tend to live in a situation of transnationalism, in which there is a constant flow of contacts, goods, and information between the society of origin and the society of immigration. For some of the interviewees, the situation of transmigration means not belonging anywhere: they feel that they belong *neither* here *nor* there. The reality is that transnationalism involves dealing with multiple localisations and cultural backgrounds (here *and* there). For mixed couples with children born and/or brought up in Catalonia, the long-term project might be transnational residency. What is most common is to show children the two realities and to let them choose:

> If one day I get lucky, my dream is to go with her [his wife] to my country. I don't mean so as to stay there; but if we were retired: here for a while, there for a while. Of course, the difference is, um ... we've lived our lives here now, and having lived here, my children are half from here. So my dream is for them to know both places. (Sulayman, 52-year-old Gambian man married to a Spanish woman, with whom he has three children)

> [My children] I don't know; they're getting older now, they are grown up. ... And when they were kids, they tended to do what ... they followed their Dad; and what they know and everything comes more from their Dad than from me. But he never stopped me showing them my things. ... Because we've never tried ... I mean: 'you've got to be this or that'. We've taught them and now it's up to them to choose what they want; when they're grown up, let them choose what they want. (Gloria, a 52-year-old Spanish woman married to a Gambian man, with whom she has three children)

Mercé: You try to go to the [African] parties, so the kids can see
             something of his culture and all.

SulaymanGe:
             Traditions and all that, it gets lost with the parents. If you
             don't show them the way, you don't tell them what there
             is, of course it gets lost. Of course, they are in another cul-
             ture that is different from yours; so you have to fight to
             show them the way, tell them about it. And from time to
             time, when you can, you bring them there [to the Gambia]
             so they see it. I don't mean so that they stay, but you can
             be there for a month or two on holiday so that they see
             the family, get to know them too.

             (Mercé, a 37-year-old Spanish woman, and SulaymanGe, a 43-
             year-old Gambian man, married, with two children)

A priority for the majority of mixed couples is that the children be educated in Catalonia, as that will provide them with greater resources for
social mobility. Work and health conditions in Senegambia are also
considered to be problematic by Spanish spouses.

       For me, the most important thing is public health. ... I would go
       [to the Gambia] blindly, provided that the public health system
       would be more. ... In fact, we were about to go! We haven't yet
       because we thought, 'Now this one [their 13-year-old daughter]
       with diabetes' – it's scary to go there. And also the education is-
       sue. (Imma, a 36-year-old Spanish woman married to Gambian
       man, with whom she has five children)

The Senegalese and Gambian spouses in mixed unions, however, tend
to reiterate their desire to 'leave the door open' to future transnational
residency for their children or even to the possibility of permanent
emigration. These views are expressed in the following conversation
between a married couple: Lamine, a 40-year-old Senegalese man who
has lived in Catalonia since 1985, and Pilar, a 32-year-old Spanish woman; they have one child together.

Pilar: Studying, for the future, all that has to be here.

Lamine: I'm not going to send my kid to study there when I'm not
             there ... at least until he's grown up; and then ... [laugh-
             ing] if he wants to go and live in Miami or in. ... When
             he's grown up, it won't be my responsibility; he can live

> where he wants. I'm free, I decided to live here because I
> wanted to. He'll live where he wants and do what he
> wants; I just want to give him every opportunity, which I
> didn't have when I was a kid.

The children themselves, born and/or brought up in Catalonia, rarely fulfil the expectations of their parents. They tend to identify themselves primarily as Catalan or Spanish.[5] But they may also accommodate multi-positional senses of belonging. Moreover, a stronger sense of connection to the country of origin of their Senegalese or Gambian parents may occur amongst children in families that face economic and social difficulties. As well, while children may appreciate the educational opportunities available in Spain, they may be more closely connected with the other society of origin if they are able to enjoy privileges of ethnic community attachment. These ideas are conveyed by Jeuru, a 41-year-old Gambian man who arrived in Spain in 1977, and Maria José, a 37-year-old Spanish woman – a married couple who have three teenage children and live in a precarious socio-economic situation in a small, isolated rural village in Catalonia:

Jeuru: I tell them, 'Here, if you want to work for the government, it's very difficult; but in the Gambia, with your surname. ... I phone my uncle, who works in the government, and that's it!' [When their eldest son is asked if he wants to go to the Gambia, he responds, while looking at a map of the country, 'Of course I want to go!']

Mª José: If it wasn't because of the circumstances, we wouldn't be here. It's not that we don't want to go to the Gambia, rather the opposite.

Racism, xenophobia, and marginalisation – and in general the hostility of the surrounding environment – can also contribute to processes of ethnic resilience among immigrants and their descendants. This tendency may be linked to the desire to seek better opportunities beyond Spain, including the possibility of emigrating to their country of origin, or to that of their immigrant parents to form a family there, or of migrating elsewhere. Likewise, Andall's (2002) analysis of young African-Italians in Milan, for example, suggests that racism and discrimination can contribute to ethnic revitalisation and to the articulation of a desire to seek better opportunities beyond Italy.

In general, the degree of socio-cultural change and retention depends on several factors: marginalisation, the individual's migration project and life goals, transnational and community ties, the socio-eco-

nomic situation, etc. Notably, I have observed cases in which socio-economic precariousness does coincide with greater retention of the original cultural practices and others in which people who even on improving their socio-economic status – and are therefore living in a situation
of greater stability – show tendencies towards cultural revitalisation.

Concluding Remarks

By analysing the growing reality of unions between people of different
national and/or ethnic and cultural backgrounds, I have argued that
mixed unions present a particularly active and complex socio-cultural
hybrid space – an 'in-between space' (Bhabha 1994: 1) or 'diasporic
space' (Brah 1996: 195, 208) – that encompasses both the local and the
global (Geanâ 1997; Meyer & Gestchiere 1999) and in which the differences and identities of ethnic origin, class, and gender intersect and
are contested.

I have found that cultural links, both with 'here' and 'there', are integral to the identity formation of transnational families. The acts of intermarrying and of bringing up children in Senegalese- and Gambian-
Spanish households require the family to deal with multiple localisations, a process that involves accommodating multicultural senses of
belonging and integrating cultural aspects from the different origins of
the family members: food, language, religion, ethnicity, gender roles,
values and norms, and so forth.

The experiences of the descendants of immigrants and visible minorities, moreover, challenge the perceptions of 'race', origin, nation, and
gender and underscore the need for highlighting complex affiliations
based on multi-ethnicities and transnationalities (Ifekwunigwe 1999;
Mahtani 2002; see also Modood 2003). The behaviour and identity processes of the descendants of immigrants are neither static nor singular,
but rather are constantly negotiated and are multi-directional and segmented (Varro 1995; Zhou 1997; Suárez-Orozco & Suárez-Orozco
2001; see also Portes & Zhou 1993, 1994; Kim & Hurh 1993). The evidence that arose from my research, supported by findings from earlier
studies, reveals that it might, in fact, be important for the children of
immigrants to maintain 'multi-cultural competencies' in order for
them to successfully adapt, not only to avoid the development of
anomic personalities but also to take full advantage of the opportunities available (for 'Mexican-immigrants' and 'Mexican-Americans' in
the United States see, for example, Suárez-Orozco & Suárez-Orozco
2001: 7-9, 60-61).

Further, in line with other studies (Noiriel 1996; Kalmijn 1998; Breger & Hill 1998; Fu 2001), this research highlights the importance of

social factors specifically in shaping patterns of endogamy and exogamy and in affecting the dynamics of living together and the raising of mixed-union children. Although the conflicts that arise are often seen in terms of a 'cultural incompatibility' – which can lead to a 'clash of civilisations' discourse – these conflicts are due more often to socio-economic, situational, and personal factors than to cultural differences, or at least are due to a combination of factors. This reality points to the need for an argument to counter culturalist discourses, which emphasise the essentialisation of culture (Werbner & Modood 1997). Such a counter-argument can be applied, for example, to the culturalisation of gender conflicts, as has been pointed out in earlier studies (see, for example, Lauth Bacas 2002: 10). In general, reductionist notions of culture need to be avoided: on the one hand, it would not be true to say that culture (i.e. origin, ethnic affiliations, etc.) is so multidimensional and fluid that it does not exist (Grillo et al. 2000); however, on the other hand, the notion that culture or origin is something essential, fixed, singular, and determining, is an equally flawed perspective. What proves to be the case more often than not is that social actors as active subjects, rather than cultures as whole, hardened, fixed entities, are important protagonists in processes of socio-cultural transmission and adaptation.

Finally, this article has argued against a naïve interpretation of processes of hybridity; a critique is offered of the aptness of traditional views and judgements regarding practices of exogamy and endogamy. One should not make a priori assumptions about the moral or social value of endogamy or exogamy. Exogamy should not necessarily be equated with assimilation, nor should it be prescribed as the recipe for social harmony and cohesion. Similarly, the fear of endogamy as a sign of ghettoisation and lack of integration is not necessarily justified. What is ultimately crucial to fostering social integration (versus social exclusion) in the host society are the rights of citizenship – civil, political, and social: access to social and economic resources such as education, health care, employment, housing, participation in political life, and the right to family reunification.

Mixed marriages and transnational families are, in general, an under-researched topic. This paper raises a number of questions that call for further comparative research to be carried out in different European countries amongst different immigrant groups; this research must take into account differences in origin, socio-economic profile, generation, and structural organisation. In particular, the analysis of intergenerational dynamics and the negotiation of multiple identities as a result of culturally or ethnically diverse family backgrounds warrant special attention, as these topics have important social and political implications.[6] Some questions to address are: How do patterns of endogamy and exogamy vary between migrant groups in different countries? Are some groups more likely to 'marry out'? If so, which factors (location, language, religion, ethnicity, education, etc.) play a more important role in shaping those patterns? What are the political discourses and social constraints affecting that reality? What is the relationship between patterns of endogamy and exogamy and socio-economic stratification and mobility? How do the second generation experience transnationalism and ethnic identity processes? Finally, what types of differences are there between the second, '1.5', and third generations as well as between men and women?

Notes

1   This article is based on a programme of research with multi-sited fieldwork conducted between 1994 and 2002 in Catalonia, the United Kingdom, and the Gambia (Rodríguez-García 2002a, 2004, 2006a). This research incorporated both ethnographic and quantitative methods. Qualitative research was based on participant observation and included interviews with representatives of several immigrant associations and of local administration. A total of 53 interviews (22 thematic and 31 semi-structured in-depth interviews) were conducted, recorded, and transcribed. Quantitative research in Catalonia included a survey of a non-probability (quota and snowball) sample of 251 individuals, of whom 184 (73 per cent) were Senegalese or Gambians (58.7 per cent were men and 41.3 per cent women). The questionnaire contained 51 variables and collected information about the individual and his or her unions. It included place of birth, age, year of arrival, legal situation, religion, ethnic group, marital status, number and type of all unions, offspring, education level, place of residence, occupation, salary, etc. In addition, the research included census data analysis, with two main sources: the Census of Population of Spain 1991 and the Statistics of Population of Catalonia 1996.

2   I will be using the terms 'intermarriage' and 'mixed marriage' as equivalents for 'bi-national marriage', since these terms are commonly used in the European and American literature on migration and ethnic relations. However, it bears mentioning that these notions (and terms of hybridity, etc.) are contested concepts, especially in their meanings as social constructs; my lack of specific reference to such contestation does not imply that the terms are unproblematic or naturalised: see, for example, Root (1996: 7-14); Ifekwunigwe (1999: 17-22); Phoenix and Owen (2000: 73, 92); Tizard and Phoenix (2002: 7-12, 50-52); Rodríguez-García (2002a: 171-83); Rodríguez-García & Freedman (2006). See also Olumide (2002).

3   I have translated all interviews, quotations, and conversations into English. Although in many cases, my informants spoke imperfect Spanish, Catalan, or English, I have not tried to render their imperfections into perfect English. In the quote references, I will be using 'Senegalese', 'Gambian' or 'Spanish' to refer to country of birth.

4   Several studies in Spain confirm these negative attitudes towards mixed marriages involving immigrants and visible minorities, especially immigrants of African origin and gypsies (the historical internal 'others'); see, for example, Calvo Buezas (2000: 74-75, 186-187). The huge outbreak of racial discrimination in the neighbourhood of Ca n'Anglada (in the province of Barcelona) in 1999, when Moroccan-Spanish couples experienced particularly harsh judgment, can also be mentioned here (see Rodríguez 1999).

5   Similarly, Tizard and Phoenix (2002: 131-136) found little 'loyalty' to African-Caribbean or African origins amongst children of mixed parentage in Britain.
6   I have explored some of these topics in postdoctoral research conducted in Canada between 2004 and 2005 on patterns of marriage among ethnic groups (see Rodríguez-García 2007, 2006b, 2006c).

References

Andall, J. (2002), 'Second-generation Attitude? African-Italians in Milan', *Journal of Ethnic and Migration Studies* 28 (3): 389-407.
Banton, M. (1955), *The Coloured Quarter: Negro Immigrants in an English City*. London: Jonathan Cape.
Bhabha, H. K. (1994), *The Location of Culture*. London: Routledge.
Brah, A. (1996), *Cartographies of Diaspora. Contesting Identities*. London: Routledge.
Breger, R. & R. Hill (1998), 'Introducing Mixed Marriages', in R. Breger & R. Hill (eds.), *Cross-Cultural Marriage. Identity and Choice*, 1-32. Oxford: Berg.
Calvo Buezas, T. (2000), *Inmigración y Racismo. Así sienten los jóvenes del siglo XXI*. Madrid: Cauce.
Coleman, D. A. (1994), 'Trends in Fertility and Intermarriage among Immigrant Populations in Western Europe as Measures of Integration', *Journal of Biosocial Science* 26 (1): 107-136.
Fu, V. K. (2001), 'Racial Intermarriage Pairings', *Demography* 38 (2): 147-159.
Geanâ, G. (1997), 'Ethnicity and Globalisation. Outline of a Complementarist Conceptualisation', *Social Anthropology* 5 (2): 197-209.
Gordon, M. (1964) *Assimilation in American Life: The Role of Race, Religion, and National Origins*. New York: Oxford University Press.
Grillo, R. D., B. Riccio, B. & R. Salih (2000), *Here or There? Contrasting Experiences of Transnationalism: Moroccans and Senegalese in Italy*. Brighton: University of Sussex, Centre for Culture, Development and Environment.
IDESCAT (Catalan Institute of Statistics) (2007), *Moviment natural de la població 2005, Nota de premsa: La nupcialitat a Catalunya l'any 2005*, Press release, 19 January 2007. www.idescat.net/cat/idescat/serveis/premsa/NPmatrim2005.pdf.
Ifekwunigwe, J. (1999), *Scattered Belongings: Cultural Paradoxes of 'Race', Nation and Gender*. London: Routledge.
INE (National Institute of Statistics) (2007a), *Padrón Municipal de Población*. www.ine.es.
INE (National Institute of Statistics) (2007b), *Movimiento Natural de la Población 2006. Datos provisionales: Matrimonios de extranjeros*. www.ine.es.
Kalmijn, M. (1998), 'Intermarriage and Homogamy: Causes, Patterns and Trends', *Annual Review of Sociology* 24: 395-421.
Kim, K. C. & W. M. Hurh (1993), 'Beyond Assimilation and Pluralism: Syncretic Sociocultural Adaptation of Korean Immigrants in the US', *Ethnic and Racial Studies* 14 (4): 696-712.
Lauth Bacas, J. (2002), *Cross-Border Marriages and the Formation of Transnational Families: A Case Study of Greek-German Couples in Athens*. Oxford: University of Oxford. www.transcomm.ox.ac.uk/working%20papers/WPTC-02-10%20Bacas.pdf.
Mahtani, M. (2002), *Interrogating the Hyphen-Nation: Canadian Multicultural Policy and 'Mixed Race' Identities*. Toronto: CERIS Working Paper No. 20, October 2002.
Meyer, B. & P. Gestchiere (eds.) (1999), *Globalization and Identity: Dialectics of Flow and Closure*. Oxford: Blackwell.

Modood, T. (2003), 'New Forms of Britishness: Post-immigration Ethnicity and Hybridity in Britain', in R. Sackmann, B. Peters & T. Faist (eds.), *Identity and Integration. Migrants in Western Europe*, 77-90. Aldershot: Ashgate.

Noiriel, G. (1996), *The French Melting Pot. Immigration, Citizenship and National Identity*. Minneapolis and London: University of Minessota Press.

Olumide, J. (2002), *Raiding the Gene Pool. The Social Construction of Mixed Race*. London: Pluto Press.

Phoenix, A. & C. Owen (2000), 'From Miscegenation to Hybridity: Mixed Relationships and Mixed Parentage in Profile', in A. Brah & A. Coombes (eds.), *Hybridity and its Discontents: Politics, Science, Culture*, 72-95. London: Routledge.

Portes, A. & M. Zhou (1993), 'The New Second Generation: Segmented Assimilation and its Variants among Post-1965 Immigrant Youth', *The Annals* 530: 74-96.

Rodríguez, F. (1999), 'Miedo en Ca n'Anglada: Más incidentes racistas en Terrassa, donde los magrebíes no salen de sus casas', *La Vanguardia*, Web Edition, 16 July 1999.

Rodríguez-García, D. & J. Freedman (2006) 'Exploring the Meaning of Intermarriage', in *Love Across Cultures*, The SIETAR Europa Magazine, Issue 2, September 2006.

Rodríguez-García, D. (2002a), *Endogamy, Exogamy and Interethnic Relations. An Analysis of the Processes of Mate Choice and Family Formation among Senegalese and Gambian Immigrants in Catalonia, Spain* (in Spanish). Barcelona: Universitat Autònoma de Barcelona, unpublished PhD thesis. www.tdx.cesca.es/TDCat-0223103-184400.

Rodríguez-García, D. (2002b), 'Female Genital Mutilation among Senegambian Immigrants in Africa and Catalonia, Spain: The Debate Between Cultural Relativism and Universalism' (in Spanish), in A. González Echevarría & J. L. Molina (coords.), *Abriendo surcos en la tierra. Investigación básica y aplicada en la UAB*, 79-102. Bellaterra: Universitat Autònoma de Barcelona; Servei de Publicacions.

Rodríguez-García, D. (2004), *Inmigración y mestizaje hoy: Formación de matrimonios mixtos y familias transnacionales de población africana en Cataluña* (Immigration and Hybridity Today. The Formation of Mixed Marriages and Transnational Families of African Migrants in Catalonia, Spain). Barcelona: Servei de Publicacions de la Universitat Autonoma de Barcelona (awarded publication).

Rodríguez-García, D. (2006a), 'Mixed Marriages and Transnational Families in the Intercultural Context: A Case Study of African-Spanish Couples in Catalonia, Spain', *Journal of Ethnic and Migration Studies* 32 (3): 403-433.

Rodríguez-García, D. (2006b), 'Socio-ethnic and Institutional Factors in Patterns of Marriage in Toronto, Canada: Contesting the Horizontal Mosaic', paper presented at the annual meeting of the American Sociological Association, Montreal, 11-14 August 2006.

Rodríguez-García, D. (2006c), 'Marriage Patterns and Discourses of Segregation and Assimilation Amongst Ethnic Groups: The Case of Chinese Ethnic Communities in Toronto, Canada', paper presented at the annual meeting of the North American Chinese Sociologists Association, Montreal, 10 August 2006.

Rodríguez-García, D. (2007), 'Intermarriage Patterns and Socio-ethnic Stratification among Ethnic Groups in Toronto'. *CERIS Working Paper* No. 60. Toronto: Joint Centre of Excellence for Research on Immigration and Settlement.

Root, M. (ed.) (1996), *The Multiracial Experience: Racial Borders as the New Frontier*. London: Sage.

Suárez-Orozco, C. & M. Suárez-Orozco (2001), *Children of Immigration*. Cambridge: Harvard University Press.

Tizard, B. & A. Phoenix (2002), *Black, White or Mixed Race? Race and Racism in the Lives of Young People of Mixed Parentage*. London: Routledge.

Todd, E. (1994), *Le Destin des Immigrés. Assimilation et ségrégation dans les démocraties occidentales*. Paris: Seuil.

Varro, G. (1995), *Les Couples Mixtes et Leurs Enfants en France et en Allemagne*. Paris: Armand Colin.
Werbner, P. & T. Modood (eds.) (1997), *Debating Cultural Hybridity. Multicultural Identity and the Politics of Anti-Racism*. London: Zed Books.
Zhou, M. (1997), 'Segmented Assimilation: Issues, Controversies, and Recent Research on the New Second Generation', *International Migration Review* 31 (4): 975-1008.

12   Debating Culture across Distance: Transnational Families and the Obligation to Care[1]

Loretta Baldassar

Introduction

This chapter explores some of the transnational dimensions of debates within and about families, in particular the way kin who are separated by distance and national borders construct and negotiate cultural notions of obligation about aged care.[2] I argue that debates about migration and caregiving concerning transnational families, both internal (at the micro level of everyday practice) and external (at the generally more meso and macro levels of policy and service provision), must be understood not as an attribute of individuals or families alone, but as a function of relationships between agents and social institutions within and across both home and host settings. In other words, a focus on transnational caregiving shifts attention from the behaviour of individuals to the pattern of relations between people, social units and institutions. In this way, internal debates concerning migration and care within the transnational domestic sphere (Gardner & Grillo 2002) provide a link between micro, meso and macro levels of analysis locating the practices of individuals and families in the context of local and transnational communities and states.

This examination of migration, family, culture and caregiving is explored ethnographically using case studies of transnational families comprising ageing parents from Italy, New Zealand and Afghanistan (the latter living in transit in Iran) and their adult migrant children living in Perth, Western Australia, the most (geographically) isolated capital city in the world. While these countries, aside from Italy, might appear to have only limited relevance to a volume exploring immigrant families in Europe, the practices and processes of transnational caregiving that are documented are pertinent to the global care chains (Yeates 2004, 2005) which are increasing in scope and complexity and which affect all areas of the world, not least Europe with its increasing immigration. Furthermore, the examples not only represent the traditional focus on migratory relationships between developed and developing nations but also the much less common focus on migration between developed nations (Brijnath forthcoming 2008). Hence, the discussion involves an analysis of both formal and informal care provision, including the development of social capital, in local, national and transnational contexts. The emergent patterns are pertinent to Europe with its diversity of socio-cultural groups, forms of migrant interaction and the multifarious discourses of power that help define them, including state legislation, transnational agreements, access to resources and historical context. While the examples are not all European, the approach of linking the micro-levels of people's lives to the macro structures that influence them is arguably of great relevance to one of the key aims of this volume: understanding the tensions surrounding family, community and nation so evident in Europe today.

The 'transnational family' in this context is best understood, following Grillo (*supra*), as an 'iconic cultural, social and ideological "site"'. Under examination here are the interrelations between the family as 'moral order', albeit one that is socially constructed and contested through internal debates, and the external debates and constraints that impact upon the institution of 'the family' and its members, in particular those relating to the provision of aged care and the associated notions of obligation to provide such care. The processes of transnational caregiving are negotiated at the intersections of individual choice within what might be called micro patterns of kinship and obligation as well as within the more formal structures and infrastructures (or absence of them) of relevant services, technologies and resources at macro-state and meso-community levels. A key question to arise from this discussion is the interconnectedness of these 'levels', how much influence they exert on each other, how they are influenced by transnational family contexts and what particular mix of support they in combination provide.

Distant Care across Borders

Transnational caregiving is primarily characterised by varying degrees and forms of communication and interaction. The most common ways people exchange emotional and practical care across distance is by regular telephone calls, faxes and letters and, more recently, email and mobile phone text messages. Financial assistance is also often exchanged. In addition, visits between migrants and kin are important avenues for caregiving and are the only way of delivering 'hands-on' personal care.

There is an argument for considering transnational families as people practicing caregiving in deterritorialised contexts. As Bryceson and Vuorela (2002: 10) argue: 'One may be born into a family and a nation, but the sense of membership can be a matter of choice and negotiation'. On the other hand, all migrants and their transnational family members are located in particular places at particular times and their caregiving practices are variously affected by this 'territorialisation'. Transnational carers must negotiate the expectations and regulations of (at least) two nation-states, often including the complicated 'borders' created by language and culture. It is in accounting for this particular nexus between agency and structural constrains that the notion of internal and external debates about obligations to exchange care in transnational families is pertinent.

Baldassar, Baldock and Wilding (2007) argue that all family caregiving is mediated by a dialectic comprising the capacity (ability, opportunity), the culturally informed sense of obligation and the negotiated family commitments of individual members to provide care within specific family networks. As there are few transnational structures designed specifically to facilitate transnational caregiving (e.g. reciprocal health care agreements and access to dual citizenship), these practices are largely organised by the structures of kinship and community, in particular the sense of obligation to engage in reciprocal care exchanges. Notions of obligation are debated within families as well as more broadly within communities, both local and national, and are influenced by and in turn influence existing and historical patterns of social structures and service provision in the countries of relevance. Blackman, Brodhurst and Convery (2001: 3), for example, argue that the values and structures of diverse welfare regimes predispose societies towards particular configurations of social care for older people. This multifaceted approach to understanding caregiving resonates with Schuller, Baron and Field (2000: 20) who, drawing on Bott (1957), argue that family and social networks are best conceptualised as social systems rather than as aggregations of individuals each with their own psyches, and these social systems should be understood in terms of their place in external social systems. Networks (in this Bottian sense) mediate between the personal and the structural and are to be understood in their own right (Schuller et al. 2000: 21). Similarly, Chamberlayne and King (2000: 3) emphasise what they call 'the contextualised dynamics of caring' and distinguish between 'the private level of personal and family situations, the social level of informal networks, and the public level of structures and resources', which correspond broadly to micro, meso and macro levels of analysis.

Macro factors which influence transnational caregiving include access to telecommunication infrastructures, travel visas and health insurance, the social and migration policies governing settlement and immigrant integration including welfare services and employment, and state provision of aged-care services in both home and host countries. Meso factors include the community and voluntary associations that support (or impede) practices of transnational caregiving, the relevance of networks of co-nationals over time, and the trajectories of 'community' settlement. Micro factors refer to family and personal histories and life cycles, including the changing ways in which migration is understood. All these levels are informed by cultural notions of appropriate care which influence kin relations as well as community and state provisions (and vice versa).

One concept that is often employed to identify the links between networks of exchange that mediate between individuals, communities and states, is social capital. Chamberlayne and King (2000: 9), for example, employ Putnam's (1993: 167) definition of social capital 'as the capacity to mobilise support and resources in the informal sphere, based on norms of reciprocity and networks of civic engagement'. Similarly Loizos (2000) defines social capital as social networks, shared values, and emergent trust. The following section presents some of the heartfelt internal debates about aged care that are played out within transnational families. These debates might be summarised as centring around notions of obligation to give and receive care. The relationship between notions of obligation and the production of social capital is examined as they are played out through particular configurations of micro, meso and macro practices of transnational caregiving in three migrant and homeland settings.

Debating Cultures of Care

Afghan Refugee Case Study

Mina and her husband, Seyyad, who migrated to Perth in the 1990s, were born and lived in Kabul where they owned a fruit and vegetable shop.[3] Neither have any formal educational qualifications. They fled Afghanistan in the mid-1980s with their children and many of Seyyad's relatives to Pakistan where they lived for four years. In Pakistan, Seyyad was the main breadwinner for his large extended family. He could only find heavy physical work and life was very difficult. In their third year in Pakistan, Sayyed's father died. Seyyad's brother travelled to Pakistan for the funeral from Perth where he had been accepted as a refugee. According to Mina:

> He came from Australia and saw for himself how bad our situation was. When he was back in Australia, he sent us some money monthly. Then he sent us a sponsorship form to migrate to Australia ... After [several months] our refugee application was accepted. It was supposed to be a happy occasion ... But I felt immediately very sad ... I thought I would be very far away from

my parents if I go to Australia ... I had not seen my parents for
four years ... Having your own family members close by is a different feeling. My husband had his mother, four brothers and
their wives and his sisters. My husband was very happy with the
news but I said to him that I should first write a letter to my parents and ask for their opinion and advice ... They answered me,
'Don't hesitate and just go to Australia. Our country Afghanistan
is still full of trouble and you better not think of going back' ...
My parents wanted me to accept the offer and so we came to
Australia.

Mina explained that she had no idea what Australia was like. The couple
were eventually offered a state housing commission home for people on
low incomes. Although Mina had a number of her husband's relatives
living in the same suburb whom she met regularly, she felt that they did
not replace her own relatives, who would have offered her more support
and compassion. Mina's parents and six brothers live in Iran and her
only sister lives in Afghanistan. Mina worries about her family constantly. Her father is unwell and unable to care for himself. Her mother
also has health problems. They live with their sons who manage to get
day labour occasionally. Afghan refugees have no formal entitlements in
Iran (Strand, Suhrke, & Harpviken 2004). They are not permitted
health benefits and must pay up-front fees for medical care. Many do
not have valid work visas and are forced to accept exploitative work conditions. They do not have access to public schools and private schools
are prohibitively expensive; consequently many Afghan children do not
attend school. They are generally not well accepted by Iranians and are
often forced to pay exorbitant rental rates making overcrowding and
poor living conditions common. In addition, their future in Iran is uncertain and many anticipate being forcefully repatriated to Afghanistan.
    Mina's parents and brothers contacted her soon after she arrived in
Perth: 'they told us about their situation and how desperate they were
and requested money'. Seyyad interrupted his wife to explain:

    You know we have our own family and children to take care of in
    Australia. We have a lot of expenses ourselves. Australia is also
    getting more and more expensive. We are in a situation where
    we are not able to support other family members.

The distribution of meagre funds is a common dispute between Afghan couples. Men generally want to spend money on their families as
it is the duty of sons to care for their parents. Mina manages to phone
her family once a month but is not able to send them any money, a situation which weighs heavily on her.

During the interview, Mina introduced her eldest daughter (sixteen years of age) who was recently engaged to her (eighteen-year-old) cousin (Seyyad's sister's son). Mina was particularly delighted with the amount of help she received with the engagement ceremony from the local Afghan community, most of whom also came from Kabul. She likes the groom very much and since the event, her in-laws have been nicer to her: 'Now my husband's family likes me more than before'.

Mina was happy for Zahra (the interviewer) to visit and interview her family in Iran and entrusted her with several gifts to give them including velvet fabric, children's toys and a video of her daughter's engagement. Gifts are commonly exchanged via travellers, particularly as the postal services are not always reliable. Without Seyyad's knowledge, Mina also gave Zahra some Australian dollars (saved from her housekeeping budget) to give to her mother so that she could buy a gold ring for her granddaughter's engagement. Gold is traditionally gifted to brides from their families. Mina knew that her parents would want to buy such a gift but would not be able to afford it.

Mina's family in Iran were living in a two-bedroom half-built house. Zahra was invited into the front room where they sat on large cushions. Mina's father explained that they did not want to waste money on furniture when they might be sent back to Afghanistan any time. Mina's mother began by lamenting 'What kind of world is this, having only two daughters and none of them living with me?' Their rent is relatively cheap but the house is in bad condition and a long way from the city and day labour: 'It is not a good place for us to live, but what can we do?' Mina has attempted to sponsor her parents twice with no luck. The whole family has temporary visas which they must pay to renew every three months. Zahra met Mina's mother again at a bazaar where she bought a gold ring for her granddaughter which Zahra brought back to Australia. Mina's mother is pleased her daughter is living in Australia but she misses her. Mina was able to visit them three years ago and they are all waiting for her next visit. They hope that if one of their sons gets married she will come for the wedding ceremony.

The Afghan sample is comprised of people from ten families who arrived in Perth in different periods and who have different ethnic and religious backgrounds. Refugees, like Mina and Seyyad, from the early waves of forced migration are a mixture of professionals and labourers from large cities in Afghanistan and belong to the ethnic groups of Tajik and Pashtun. They generally arrived under the auspices of the UN Special Humanitarian Program and have lived in Australia between nine and fifteen years. Notwithstanding this length of time, most have not been able to gain employment commensurate with their level of expertise and education. Some of these families, like Seyyad's, were able

to gain entry into Australia as an extended family, including siblings
with their spouses and married children.[4]

Parents and other relatives of the Australian-based Afghan refugees
are themselves also refugees. Zahra was only able to interview parents
and other members of extended families who live as refugees in Iran,
about two-thirds of whom had been there for many years. Several Afghan refugees living in Australia have parents, siblings and other relatives scattered throughout other countries including Pakistan and India, and many have applied from these countries for refugee status in
Europe and America. Extended networks of these refugee families are
'plurinational', stretching between various countries, rather than
mainly between home and host countries, as is the case of the majority
of migrants in the study.

At the micro level, the Afghan refugees in the sample have restricted
capacity (agency and resources) but a great sense of obligation to provide transnational care. This includes 'survivor guilt' as well as a felt
obligation to support parents which many describe as 'cultural'. At the
macro level, refugees experience the greatest state impediments, having no rights and few services, including often no passport. Their limited ability to afford and access communication technologies in Australia is mirrored by the relative absence of these technologies among
their family in Iran. At the meso level, families and communities have
extensive transnational ties that operate across borders to provide traditional caring practices, for example, through financial support, finding
marriage partners, providing sponsorship and by visiting. Women, particularly those who are not formally educated, often rely on kin to negotiate social and public activities (Kamalkhani 2004).

To some extent, the community attempts to fill these kin roles.
Mina's story reveals how marriage arrangements can bolster family
and community networks of support. Through the betrothal of her
daughter to her husband's nephew, Mina's position in the extended family was further consolidated and she felt more secure in these family
networks. Peter Loizos (2000: 126) develops this line of argument
further, showing how refugees who would appear to lose everything,
rarely lose their kin and network relations:

> Because although refugees very often lose their economic and
> material capital, they rarely lose nearly as much of their human
> and social capital ... It is ... their characteristics as 'social capital-
> ists', which assist significantly in the issue of their longer-term
> adjustment, and government policies which ignore or disrupt
> such processes inflict additional penalties upon them.

Loizos (2000: 141) is careful to point out that social capital can never substitute for basic economic support and concludes that while 'social capital is a useful reminder that there is more to life than market or Marxist economics ... we should [not] forget the priorities of economic life'. In Loizos' sense, social capital is pertinent to the notion of obligation. The dire economic circumstances of the Afghan refugees results in keen expressions of caregiving obligation as refugee families regularly restrict their own meagre subsistence in order to be able to support family abroad (one man mortgaged his house so that he could afford to help his parents in Iran). However, the limits of obligation and the pressures of economics are also evident. In cases where demands and obligations exceed capacity, a breakdown in networks can result as individuals attempt to shield themselves from obligations they cannot meet. One family, for example, had lost touch with their kin in Iran and were surprised when Zahra managed to locate them. They warned Zahra that although they were very keen to hear about their welfare, they had no money to give them and they knew that this would be a source of tension. This Iran-based family expressed anger that their Australian kin had 'abandoned' them and were keen to re-establish contact. They were very upset that Zahra had not been given any gifts for them.

Not surprisingly, a common complaint among Perth-based refugees was that their families (back home or in transit countries) did not understand the level of difficulty they faced in earning money. As Seyyad explained, 'They assume that we are wealthy because we live in a wealthy land'. Unsustainable obligation appears to result in a breakdown in social networks and obligation, although this may be temporary. Despite the precariousness of transnational caregiving practices, the refugee case would, in general, appear to be characterised by high individual (micro) and community (meso) support, sense of obligation and social capital in the face of limited, if any, state (macro) support.

Italian Case Study

In providing an overview of the Italian sample, the case of Sara, a recent professional migrant I first interviewed in 2000, is instructive. Sara originally came to Australia on a scholarship in 1987 with the full support of her family. She had been unhappy in her job in Italy and wanted to pursue a higher degree. Sara had no connections with the large post-war Italian-Australian community.

> Absolutely nobody, and for the first year I avoided them like ... like hell, ... Because the last thing I wanted to do was to be here for a year and speak Italian and eat spaghetti and you know, be nostalgic about Italy. I said, 'I am here, I am going to learn Eng-

lish. I am going to stick with the people I work with, if there are no Italians, who cares'.

Sara defines herself as a very different type of migrant to the earlier (1950s) Italian migrant cohort:

> For them [post-war migrants] it must have been really hard. For me it was really a piece of cake. I mean I have been back almost every year ... I had a permanent job held for me in Italy, so at anytime I could go back and that's what made it really clear that this was a choice ... also because my parents had the economical capacity of coming here whenever they liked.

Her parents were initially delighted that Sara had the opportunity to study in Australia: 'They thought I would see something new, then come back'. But when Sara successfully applied for permanent residency, her parents were 'devastated' and 'their attitude changed dramatically'.

> As soon as they learned that I was going to stay, every subsequent visit ... they described what they saw here in derogatory terms ... I guess they missed me ... I remember saying, 'I am thirty and I am not coming back, this is it, I am staying' ... Their attitude is still ... 'We don't understand your choice, we don't think it is a good place to live'.

These debates about migration, settlement and where to live involved Sara's extended family.

> I remember clearly one visit ... during Christmas ... being questioned by a bunch of relatives, not just my parents. In fact, I think that my parents instigated the whole thing, and I was questioned quite harshly. You know, people saying, 'What the hell are you doing there?'

Sara confided that part of her motivation to emigrate was to be free of the restrictions her family imposed on her.

Sara was pregnant with her first child at the time of interview and she explained that the tensions about her migration have in some ways been increased by the arrival of her baby:

> I think they were delighted that I am pregnant ... I have been teasing them and saying, 'Oh you are happy only because you wanted to be grandparents'. And they were saying, 'Well we are

not bloody grandparents because, you know, we don't live there and ... we are going to hardly see this grandchild'.

Sara's parents wanted to visit for the birth and on the advice of a colleague Sara suggested they come a few weeks later to avoid the increased stress of house guests. This attempt to balance her needs with those of her parents left Sara feeling 'very guilty': 'I cannot keep them away, in fact I am feeling already guilty, I am saying maybe I should let them come for the birth'. Despite these tensions, Sara wants her parents to migrate to Australia or to visit and stay in their own place for six months each year. Her parents' refusal to consider this option upsets Sara.

The guilt that Sara feels about not being able to provide adequate support for her parents as they age is something which concerns her parents. For example, they have attempted to hide any episodes of serious illness from both Sara and their other (local) daughter in Italy. Unlike in the refugee sample, this type of secrecy appears to be a common response to dealing with illness in transnational migrant families in which homeland kin have access to adequate health care (see Baldassar 2007b). Sara explains:

> They didn't tell me [about Mum's serious illness], because they didn't want to worry me. It is scary for me ... I don't have an option ... I mean they managed to keep it hidden from my sister! They tricked her completely, my Mum was in hospital with a very serious heart condition, and my sister would ring them up and ... say, 'Where is Mum?', and my Dad would say, 'oh she is ... with the next door neighbour, I will get her to call you'. So then ... She'd ring from the hospital ... So they tricked her, and we got so upset ... so angry because [we] felt that [we were] being excluded and all that.

Sara's parents explained that they chose to hide the hospital stay from their daughters so as not to worry them. 'Given the large distance, she cannot possibility help so what is the point to worry her? Therefore, we decided that we should also not tell [our local daughter], because it is not fair to worry her either, just because she lives nearby'.

The potential future aged-care needs of Sara's parents fills the whole family with dread. Sara's parents can afford to pay for a full-time live-in carer if needed. This care arrangement is preferred over residential care in Italy, although the most preferred option is being cared for by family (Blackman et al. 2001), a scenario Sara and her sister are not sure they can provide:

I guess [it will be] a disaster ... because it would fall all back on my sister, and that is a worry that I have. If that happens, ... there is no way that I could go back and care for them. I guess that I would have to ...visit ... Nursing homes exist, but we have had two grandmothers dying with us, and the Italian philosophy and attitude is that if the relative needs care, you care for them ... Well, I would feel guilty. Because I feel ... they have cared for me and I should care for them. I feel that's why they lived all their lives – for their children.

Despite the constant internal family debates and the lack of 'license to leave' afforded to Sara by her parents, they continue to maintain very close contact with daily email exchanges, weekly phone calls and regular visits. Sara describes this level of 'staying in touch' as the only way she can assuage her sense of having disappointed her parents. Recently she bought her parents a computer and taught them how to use email: 'That's been what relieved me of the guilt, actually, I was feeling so guilty that they were lonely, they were missing me, and I had left them and all that and then I gave them the gift of communication'.

I have argued elsewhere (Baldassar 2007a) that it is useful to differentiate separate cohorts of Italian migrants in Australia. The most numerous cohort is also the oldest, having arrived in the decades immediately following the war. I describe these immigrants as proletarian 'communal-oriented' migrants. They initially had limited capacity to practice transnational caregiving in terms of access to time, finances and resources, but in recent years this capacity has increased significantly (and for some people matches the regular and frequent transnational communication exchanges of the most recent arrivals). Through their significant remittances, the act of migration itself was a form of family and community caregiving for the post-war group. They enjoyed 'license to leave' because their migrations were sanctioned by their families, communities and nation as the only means to a viable future. In contrast, the more recent migrants, like Sara, are professional and business people and can be defined as more 'individual-oriented' (Blackman 2000). Unlike the post-war group, these migrants tend to have greater difficulty negotiating both license to leave and to settle. Many of their parents (like Sara's) are mortified at their decision to live in Australia. As a consequence, they experience tensions, often manifesting as a strong sense of guilt, associated with their decision to leave Italy.

These two cohorts differ mostly at the meso level. The post-war group have formed strong communities of support, including formal clubs and associations, often along regional and provincial or even town-based lines. This community formation is partly a response to the

historical hostilities of the general population, which resulted in residential and occupational segregation, and partly a result of migration
chains and networks stemming from *paese* and province. This meso level of organisation includes and extends to transnational networks. For
example, when a post-war migrant's parent dies in Italy, it is not un-
common for the community to participate in a kind of 'virtual funeral'.
A mass is organised for the deceased and is attended by the migrant's
family as well as townspeople, co-regionals and fellow club members,
even if they are from other regions in Italy. When a migrant's kinsper-
son visits from Italy, they are often invited out by this same wider circle
of friends and associates. Similarly, when these migrants visit Italy, they
often engage in a 'postal run' delivering letters and well wishes to the
kin of fellow migrants in Australia, even if this means travelling considerable distances and into other provinces and regions (Baldassar 2001:
37). This cohort continues to be heavily homeland-focused, despite the
considerable passage of time, because the greater capacity to stay in
touch brought about by the growth in personal wealth and communication technologies appears to have increased the obligation to participate
in transnational family caregiving exchanges (see Wilding 2006).

The more recent, professional migrants tend not to be connected to
the post-war group and do not identify along ethnic, town, regional,
provincial or national lines but rather draw their social identities and
friendships from their professions or work places. As a result, they are
much less likely to rely on social networks at the level of community
through, for example, formal clubs and associations. However, many
have formed informal friendships and associations with other recent
Italian migrants with whom they may socialise and exchange support.

There are less evident differences between the two cohorts at the micro level, particularly in terms of cultural notions of obligation. All interviewees defined being a 'good child' in cultural (and national) terms,
a representative comment being, 'For Italians, being a good child
means caring for your parents and not putting them in a home'.[5] Both
cohorts must negotiate a similar set of (contemporary) macro issues.
There are currently limited state provisions for aged care in Italy. Care
services have historically been built around a tradition of church and
family support, and this history informs the cultural obligation and
practices of family care. Notwithstanding recent developments to improve the provision of aged-care services in all sectors (Trifiletti 1998),
for many migrants in both cohorts there is a strong sense of family
shame associated with the use of institutional care, which is popularly
characterised as 'locking' the elderly away. Older, more traditionally
minded, parents are generally emphatically hostile to these institutions
(Blackman et al. 2001). This view is reflected in the common practice
in Italy of the elderly living out their final years in the homes of one of

their (Italy-based) children. These preferences and practices increase the pressure on migrants, particularly women, to visit in order that they might provide assistance with that care.

There is evidence that younger, relatively affluent and more mobile parents, like those of most of the recent migrants, have a more philosophical outlook on their older age. While most, like Sara's parents, have themselves nursed their own parents in their own homes, they are unsure whether their children will be able to do the same for them. A number indicated fatalistically that their children might place them in a nursing home, 'when their time came', although all fervently hoped this would not be the case. Elsewhere, I have discussed how older Italians desire a close relationship with their families, especially children and grandchildren, such that their perceptions about their health and well-being have been found to be associated with how close they feel they are to their children (Baldassar forthcoming 2008; see also MacKinnon & Nelli 1996: 74).

Like the refugee sample, both cohorts in the Italian sample seem to indicate strong family (micro) levels of social capital, characterised by a pronounced sense of obligation to care for ageing parents on the part of migrant children as well as a clear preference to be cared for by family expressed by parents. The post-war migrant cohort have more developed community (meso) networks of support due to the limited amount of state (macro) support services available in both the home and host settings in the post-war period. The recent migrant cohort reveals a comparative lack of community (meso) levels of support due to a combination of less difficult integration (they do not experience social exclusion), better English language skills and professional employment as well as the gradual increase in state-provided aged-care services and an increased ability of both parents and migrants to afford to purchase care support. Despite the relatively increased level of state support available today, migrants and parents alike (in both cohorts) experience a great deal of tension, characterised by feelings of guilt and concern associated with choosing state services over the more traditional practices of family and community care.

New Zealand Case Study

The New Zealand sample and, in particular, the case of Tom, who migrated to Perth in the 1970s, provides something of a contrast to Sara's, Mina's and Seyyad's notions of obligation.[6] Tom's parents originally migrated from the United Kingdom and have been living in New Zealand for over 60 years. They have several children, most of whom live quite local to their parent's house. One lives in Europe and Tom lives in Perth. The parents are very elderly and in failing health.

The father is quite incapacitated and is prone to depression. The mother has had a series of illnesses that have required hospitalisation. Until recently they had one son living with them, but he had a falling out with his father and moved out. A daughter who lives close by gives the daily care support, in part, that this son provided. However, this daughter has limited time and, to use her words, 'emotional energy' to care for her parents as she has small children and a physically dependent family member.

The parents are adamant that they do not want to move out of their house. At the time of interview, the parents were managing their daily lives with a variety of home care support services including the preparation of evening meals and assistance with showering several times a week and a cleaner twice a week. The daughter assisted with shopping trips, hospital and doctor's appointments and trips to the swimming pool. She also received frequent phone calls from her mother and provided extensive emotional support. Her husband often visited her father, particularly when he was in 'one of his really bad moods', to help diffuse tensions. The other local children visited from time to time but, according to the local daughter, none could be relied upon to provide regular daily help. The sons had worked together to make the house more liveable, installing railing along the walls, a gate at the top of the stairs and a new shower. Despite all these forms of support, it was clear that the elderly couple were struggling to meet the challenges of daily life. Several times in the interview they stated that they did not expect their children to provide any further assistance.

> Father: You have to allow for [the fact that] our children all have their own family and their own occupations. We can't expect a tremendous amount and we don't ... we keep in the front of our minds that we left our parents when we were coming over here and we were unable to give any support to them ... I think the main factor is that we brought our children up to stand on their own feet, to run their own lives ... if we could help them, we would. But other than that, we didn't expect them to wait upon us hand and foot and we accepted the fact that they are independent.

> Mother: We've never looked on children as insurances [for our] old age.

> Father: So we can't expect their help ... even though we are ... [pause, did not finish sentence]

Tom explained that his parents were happy about his decision to leave New Zealand on a travelling holiday to Europe when he was 21: 'They were enthusiastic and encouraging and supportive about it'. In fact, his parents commented that Tom was a lot older than his siblings were (most had been sixteen or seventeen) to 'make the move away'. Like many of the New Zealanders interviewed, Tom's sister described his move to Australia (over thirty years ago) as 'not really a migration'.

> New Zealanders and Australians tend to just travel backwards and forwards willy-nilly ... You sort of think Australia, it's close ... so I feel he's not far away really and I relate it to some of my other (local) brothers who I don't see for months and months.

Although he actually lives thousands of miles away, Tom is known in the family as the one who is 'closest' to his parents and siblings. Distance is not perceived as a great barrier to 'staying in touch'. A trained counsellor, Tom provides much appreciated emotional support to his parents and sister and now that his parents are ageing he tries to visit at least once every year. His sister explained:

> [my parents] look to him as a counsellor ... They enjoy his conversation ... He ...counsels my father through some of his moods and he does the same with Mum. When he visits he ... give[s] them a lot of time and energy.

Tom sets aside time each week to phone his parents. He and his sister also support each other emotionally by email. His sister finds this form of communication ideal.

> The last [email] I wrote to him ... was like an update ... I don't [want him to] feel that he's obliged to ... give me input or counsel or whatever. If he feels that he wants to ... then that's fine and that's open.

Tom's sister reflected on the freedom that distance provides Tom in his caregiving.

> When you're away as he is away, he can control how much input he has and how much he receives ... I can't really because I'm so close ... Maybe that's part of his appeal ... Distance makes the heart grow fonder.

Tom, his sister and parents all commented on how the parents wanted to be independent in their own homes. When asked if they were satisfied with their level of independence, the father replied, 'we have no choice, we have to be'. The parents' expectation that their children would also be independent, 'that's the way we brought them up', together with their expressed view that they 'don't have a right to complain' because they did not assist their own aging parents appears to justify for them the level of support they now receive. In addition, all of these family members report being very happy with the government subsidised services provided. However, Tom and his parents did feel that it was unjust that these services are legally meant to cease if there is a visitor staying in the house. Tom explained that he did not want the services to clean and cook for him, just to continue for his parents so that he did not need to take on these duties and could concentrate on 'just being there for them and having time to really talk'. For their part, Tom and his sister did not mention any feelings of guilt about the amount of care they provided. In fact, it was quite the opposite. Tom's sister talked about her need to 'withdraw support' in order to 'look after' herself and her family. She was very clear that 'her family's needs came first'. Tom talked about how his parents must be responsible for their decision to continue living alone.

> So you want to live on your own? It means you got to do your shopping, it means you got to get yourself where you want to go. If swimming is important, that they take themselves ... so those kinds of things have to be either reintroduced or let go of.

Ten migrants and their families in New Zealand are included in the study. Reflecting broader migration patterns (Wood 1980), the migrants are all relatively young and mostly male, having settled in Perth either for love or work opportunities. Given the youthfulness of this sample, most of the parents in New Zealand are in good health making much of the discussion about transnational aged care speculative. While Tom's parents represent a small minority in the sample who receive regular care assistance, they are also representative of a common pattern of aged care across New Zealand, which could be described as assisted home-care. Ashton (2000) reports that almost all respondents in a 1996 survey over the age of 65 and living in private dwellings indicated they were able to access the facilities they required.

New Zealand has a national program of elderly long-term health care which is means-tested but provided free to those who cannot afford to pay (Merlis 2000). Even so, state-provided care tends to be seen as a supplement to family and community care. Family members are expected to provide most day-to-day caregiving needs with only minimal state assistance until or unless this is not possible (Opie 1992; Uttley 1995; Ng & McCreanor 1999). Defining the limits of possibility is, of

course, a relative measure such that Tom and his sister, in their particular contexts of caregiving, arguably appear to view obligation to provide aged care in a more limited manner than either Sara or Mina and
Seyyad. For example, Tom and his parents seem to make a clear distinction between emotional and personal care, preferring to leave the
latter to state funded service providers. In contrast, Sara and Mina and
their respective parents expect (and arguably prefer) family, not service
providers, to give personal care.

In comparison with the refugee and Italian samples, the New Zeal-
and respondents generally exhibit a greater degree of individualism on
the part of both migrants and parents. At the macro level there is a far
more comprehensive state aged-care support system including extensive home care and institutional services. At the micro level, families
are generally willing and happy to rely on state services, particularly if
this enables parents to remain in their own homes. Similarly, there appears to be a relatively limited level of meso, community network involvement except for those state services designed to assist with home
care.

Some Reflections from the Data

The negotiations, capacities and obligations of transnational caregiving
reflect the particular combination of micro, meso and macro factors
and the resulting levels of social capital. Caregiving is exchanged according to 'negotiated commitments', within which context the providers and recipients of care understand their relationships to each other
and to others (see Finch & Mason 1993). Factors which are considered
in these negotiations include stage in family life cycle, history of relationships and individual skills and experiences. For example, although
Tom's parents had access to several local children, it was expected and
accepted that Tom would provide the bulk of the emotional and moral
support because of his significant counselling skills. His local sister,
who might normally be expected to deliver most of this kind of care because of her gender, was partly exempted due to her considerable (nuclear) family commitments, which included the care of a disabled dependent. The relatively limited care Tom's parents received from their
children was sustainable because of the high levels of care support provided by the state.

In transnational contexts, negotiated commitments are often highly
influenced by the particular histories of family relationships as they are
played out over migration histories in specific contexts of care. So, for
example, whether migrants are given 'license to leave' by their parents
and kin may have a significant impact on the tenor of relationships as

well as the level and type of support provided (see Baldassar 2007a). Tom's move to Australia was hardly perceived as a migration and rather than create impediments to caregiving, this distance appeared in some ways to enhance his ability to provide focused and substantial emotional and moral support. In contrast, the obvious tensions associated with her decision to settle in Australia tended to exacerbate Sara's feelings of guilt about not being able to provide the care (including access to their grandchild) that her parents wanted. Sara's anguish was in no small measure fuelled by the limited aged-care services available in Italy, as well as the general perception that care should be provided by family. Different again was Mina's experience. Although she would have liked to have lived closer to her parents to care for them as is expected of daughters, they fully supported her move to Australia in the hope that she could have a better life. And while Mina would have liked to provide them with more financial support, her parents understood that her husband's obligations to his own family took precedence, even though this absence of support significantly diminished their quality of life.

Similarly, myriad factors impact on 'capacity' to engage in family caregiving exchanges including having the skill, physical and mental health, finances, time and resources. Transnational caregiving practice is further influenced by migration policy and visa restrictions, international relations between home and host countries, welfare services and infrastructure, and access to travel and telecommunication technologies. Tom and his parents, as New Zealanders, can travel freely between the two countries whenever and for as long as they wish and they have access to government-funded medical care in both places. Sara and her parents can easily afford the visitor visas required and as Italians they have access to free basic medical support in both countries under formal reciprocal agreements. In stark contrast, the refugees, depending on their visa status, may not be able to travel outside their country of residence without jeopardising their refugee status and they may not have any rights to medical help in Australia. In addition, many, like Mina's family, have to pay for all their medical care in Iran. When these refugees do scrape together enough funds to pay for a visit they may have great difficulty obtaining a visa because certain categories of person, including Afghani women over 60 (like Mina's mother), are on the Department of Immigration's high risk list of applicants who are likely to overstay their visitor's visa. Australia's high-risk list is similar to lists maintained in EU countries; people from African, Asian and Middle Eastern countries are singled out for specific scrutiny.[7]

Sense of obligation has a significant impact on the practice of all forms of caregiving, with people making decisions about how to organise their resources, mobility and time in order to accommodate obligations to care. As has already been noted, in transnational contexts, sense of obligation to care is bound up with levels (private, communal and institutional) of care support available to parents in the homeland. Elsewhere (Baldassar, Wilding & Baldock 2007) we have reported that our research found an overwhelming desire, on the part of elderly people, for independence as an ideal in old age and preferably throughout the remainder of their lives, regardless of cultural background or country of origin. However, ideas about independence and ageing are culturally constructed and reflect contextualised dynamics of caregiving, which in turn influence notions of obligation to provide and receive care. There are also apparent differences in perceptions about what are considered to be 'preferred' care scenarios. These notions of independence, preferred care and obligation are influenced by a combination of micro, meso and macro factors including historical patterns of care, the structural constraints on that care, as well as family circumstance, including the specificities of kin relations.

Unlike their New Zealand (and Dutch) counterparts for example, refugee and Italian parents in the study are less likely to define independence in old age as a state that does not require assistance from family (see Baldock 2003). Relying on state aged-care services is perceived by most Italian parents as not being adequately cared for by family, and in many cases there are no adequate state services to depend on. The refugee parents in Iran are even more dependent on family for aged care given the complete lack of services available to them at all levels, yet most parents are relieved that their children can migrate to Australia and so escape a life of deprivation in Iran, even if this means they are left without adequate care support.

Conclusions

Comparing nation of birth sample groups, as I have been doing in this paper, treads the tricky ground of collapsing the important analytical distinction between the organisational features of the state, on the one hand, and the ideological processes of nation-building on the other (Blanc, Basch & Glick Schiller 1995: 685). I have attempted to eschew 'methodological nationalism', the false assumption that particular cultural traits or processes are 'unitary and organically related to, and fixed within, [geographic] territories' (Wimmer & Glick Schiller 2002: 305) by highlighting significant differences within each national group and by acknowledging their social construction in specific contexts (Eriksen 1991: 127). Following Chamberlayne and King's (2000: 5) argument, patterns of informal networks, including family networks, are

in many ways a response to public regimes: 'when structural determi-
nants produce consequences for identities, everyday strategies and social relationships, then a cultural pattern has emerged, particularly if it
has an enduring and reproducible character'. Despite the current emphasis in the literature on transnationalism as de-territorialising processes, the case studies here show that the nation-state remains a co-
gent means of understanding the caregiving exchanges of transnational
families. People's constructions of their national, ethnic and cultural
identities inform their sense of obligation to care and the care practices
they choose to engage in. Equally importantly, nation-states provide the
borders, replete with rules and regulations, which shape the caregiving
practices that cross and are contained by them.

The remittance practices of the refugee sample and the practice of
extended return visits by Italian migrants to provide personal care to
parents partly reflects the limited possibilities for institutional care in
the relevant home and transit countries as well as the cultural expectation that these forms of care be provided within the family. Are these
examples of low state service provision creating the context for highly
developed meso and micro networks? Maloney, Smith and Stoker
(2000: 33), following current arguments about the nature of 'governance', argue that the state has a substantial role in creating the conditions for social capital: 'Social capital can thus be seen to focus attention on the dynamics of state institutions'. The refugee and Italian case
studies suggest that states can create the conditions for social capital
by not providing a service, (which is probably not what Maloney et al.
had in mind). Similarly, recent neo-liberal policies in aged care which
aim to bolster family and community networks in order to decrease, or
at least defer, state institutionalisation have often resulted in increased
pressure on families, particularly women, to provide care, and have
been critiqued as a form of welfare retrenchment (Ackers 1999: 73;
Blackman et al. 2001: 199; Chamberlayne & King 2000: 9).

At the same time, Blackman et al. (2001: 147) identify 'signs of a
shift in social attitudes from family obligation and responsibility to individual responsibility and citizenship rights'. Evidence of this shift is
especially clear in the Italian case study as traditional notions of family
obligation are being challenged by rapid changes in employment, gender and family relations. The consequences for aged care can be grim
particularly if adequate state and community services are not in place.
An enduring image from my fieldwork is of lonely and barely adequately cared for elderly struggling to maintain their health, and in particular, their morale. Equally enduring is the image of the hectic and
demanding schedules of their children as they struggle to cope with
the various demands on their time, including those of their aging parents.

This is not to suggest that familism or communalism is preferable to individualism or vice versa. Blackman et al. (2001: 165) point out that 'all systems have strengths and weaknesses, and the possibilities for reform lie in building on the strengths and tackling the weaknesses'. For example, elderly people in familistic cultures (like Italy) may prefer to live apart from their children but have no option, citing the apparent ideal of 'intimacy at a distance' for elderly in countries that do offer adequate services (Blackman et al. 2001: 160). On the other hand, adequate services may still leave elderly people feeling socially excluded as the case of Tom's parents suggests. What seems to be clear from our study is that the absence of state structures at the transnational level places a greater onus on families to negotiate appropriate care at the micro and meso levels. The post-war Italians enjoy a high level of social capital at the micro level as do the more recent migrants. However, the older cohort has the additional benefit of well developed meso community structures, largely entirely voluntary and organised for Italian migrants by Italian migrants. These types of structures have been identified by Blackman et al. (2001: 188) as particularly important examples of preventative services promoting social interaction, both among older people and with the wider community. Historical patterns in the common arrangement of care in the home-country, closely related to the level and provision of relevant services provided by the state, and reflected in culturally constructed notions of independence and preferred arrangements of care, have a significant impact on the experience of caring of the distant (transnational) care-giver.

Notes

1   An early version of aspects of this paper was presented at the symposium, 'Sociability and its Discontents: Civil Society, Social Capital, and their Alternatives in European and Australian Society', in August 2005, convened by Dr. Nicholas Eckstein, Cassamarca Senior Lecturer in History, Sydney University. Many thanks to Ralph Grillo for his valuable input into this paper.

2   The ideas presented here are drawn from a larger collaborative study by Baldassar, Baldock and Wilding, funded by an Australia Research Council Grant A00000731, 'Transnational Care-giving: cross-cultural aged-care practices between Australian immigrants and their parents living abroad'. Data collection comprised approximately 200 life-history interviews and participant observation with migrants and refugees in Perth, Western Australia, and their parents abroad in Italy, the Netherlands, Ireland, Singapore, New Zealand and Iran. Details of the research and of a framework for analysing transnational caregiving between adult migrant children and their homeland-based parents have been described at length elsewhere (Baldassar, Baldock & Wilding 2007).

3   Mina and Seyyad – pseudonyms are used for all informants – were interviewed in Perth by Zahra Kamalkhani in 2004. Thanks to Zahra for her insights on this section.

4   More recent arrivals, like all refugees in Australia today, are seldom allowed entry as an extended family group unless they already have one family member with permanent residency in Australia. Among these later arrivals it is more common to find individual family members, particularly women, without their extended family.

5   Zontini (2007: 1112) and Reynolds and Zontini (2006: 21) report similar findings among Italians in Britain.

6   Tom was interviewed by Raelene Wilding in 2003. Thanks to Raelene for her guidance with this case study.

7   It is important to note that there are no applicants from Western Europe on such lists, even though, according to Australian Immigration statistics, the UK produces the highest number of people who overstay their visitor's visas than any other country.

References

Ackers, L. (1999), *Shifting Spaces: Women, Citizenship and Migration within the European Union*. Bristol: Policy Press.

Baldassar, L. (2001), *Visits Home: Migration Experiences between Italy and Australia*. Melbourne: Melbourne University Press.

Baldassar, L. (2007a), 'Transnational Families and Aged Care: The Mobility of Care and the Migrancy of Ageing', *Journal of Ethnic and Migration Studies* 33 (2): 275-297.

Baldassar, L. (2007b), 'Transnational Families and the Provision of Moral and Emotional Support: The Relationship between Truth and distance', *Identities* 14 (4): 285-409.

Baldassar, L. (forthcoming 2008), 'Missing Kin and Longing to be Together: Emotions and the Construction of Co-presence in Transnational Relationships' in Svašek, M. (eds.), Transnational Families: Emotions and Belonging, Special Issue, *Journal of Intercultural Studies*.

Baldassar, L., C. V. Baldock & R. Wilding (2007), *Families Caring Across Borders: Migration, Ageing and Transnational Caregiving*. London: Palgrave Macmillan.

Baldassar, L., R. Wilding & C. V. Baldock (2007), 'Long-distance Care-giving: Transnational Families and the Provision of Aged Care', in I. Paoletti (ed.), *Family Caregiving for Older Disabled People: Relational and Institutional Issues*, 201-227. Nova Science: New York.

Baldock, C. V. (2003), 'Long-distance Migrants and Family Support: A Dutch Case-study', *Health Sociology Review* 12 (1): 45-54.

Blackman, T. (2000) 'Defining Responsibility for Care: Approaches to the Care of Older People in Six European Countries', *International Journal of Social Welfare* 9 (3): 181-190.

Blackman, T., S. Brodhurst, S. & J. Convery (2001), *Social Care and Social Exclusion: A Comparative Study of Older People's Care in Europe*. London: Palgrave Macmillan.

Blanc, C.S., L. Basch & N. Glick Schiller (1995), 'Transnationalism, Nation-states and Culture', Current Anthropology 36 (4): 683-86.

Bott, E. (1957), *Family and Social Networks*. New York: Free Press.

Brijnath, B. (forthcoming 2008) 'Familial Bonds and Boarding Passes: Understanding Caregiving in a Transnational Context', *Identities*.

Chamberlayne, P. & A. King (2000) *Cultures of Care: Biographies of Carers in Britain and the Two Germanies*. Bristol: Policy Press.

Eriksen, T. H. (1991), 'The Cultural Contexts of Ethnic Differences', Man 26 (1): 127-144.

Finch, J & J. Mason (1993), *Negotiating Family Responsibilities*. London: Tavistock.

Gardner, K. & R. Grillo (2002), 'Transnational Households and Ritual: An Overview', *Global Networks* 2 (3): 179-190.

Kamalkhani, Z. (2004), 'Migration from Iran, Iraq and Afghanistan: Seeking Refuge and Building Lives', in R. Wilding & F. Tilbury (eds.), *A Changing People: Diverse Contributions to the State of Western Australia*, 236-251. Perth, Western Australia: Department of Premier and Cabinet.

Loizos, P. (2000), 'Are Refugees Social Capitalists?' in Baron, S., Field, J. & Schuller, T (eds.), *Social Capital: Critical Perspectives*, 124-141. Oxford/New York: Oxford University Press.

MacKinnon, V. & A. Nelli (1996), *Now We Are in Paradise, Everything is Missing*. Footscray: Department of Nursing, Victoria University of Technology.

Maloney, W. A., G. Smith & G. Stoker (2000), 'Social Capital and Associational Life', in S. Baron, J. Field & J. Schuller (eds.), *Social Capital: Critical Perspectives*, 182-196. Oxford; New York: Oxford University Press.

Merlis, M. (2000), 'Caring for the Frail Elderly: An International Review', *Health Affairs* 19 (3): 141-150.

Ng, Sik Hung & T. McCreanor (1999), 'Patterns in Discourse about Elderly People in New Zealand', *Journal of Aging Studies* 13 (4): 473-489.

Opie, A. (1992), *There's Nobody There: Community Care of Confused Older People*. Oxford University Press: Auckland.

Reynolds, T. & Zontini, E. (2006) *A Comparative Study of Care and Provision across Caribbean and Italian Transnational Families*. London: London South Bank University, Families and Social Capital ESRC Research Group Working Paper Series No. 16.

Schuller, T., S. Baron & J. Field (2000) 'Social Capital: A Review and Critique', in Baron, S., J. Field & T. Schuller (eds.), *Social Capital: Critical Perspectives*, 243-263. Oxford; New York: Oxford University Press.

Strand, A., A. Suhrke & B. Harpviken (2004), *Afghan Refugees in Iran: From Refugee Emergency to Migration Management*. Oslo: International Peace Research Institute.

Trifiletti, R. (1998), 'Restructuring Social Care in Italy', in J. Lewis (ed.), *Gender, Social Care and Welfare State Restructuring in Europe*, 175-206. Aldershot: Ashgate.

Uttley, S. (1995), 'New Zealand and Community Care for Older People: A Demographic Window of Opportunity', in T. Scharf & C. Wenger (eds.), *International Perspectives on Community Care for Older People*, 171-189, Avebury: Aldershot.

Wilding, R. (2006), 'Virtual Intimacies: Family Communications across Transnational Borders', *Global Networks* 6 (2): 125-142.

Wimmer, A. & N. Glick Schiller (2002), 'Methodological Nationalism and Beyond: Nation-state Building, Migration and the Social Sciences', *Global Networks* 2 (4): 301-334.

Wood, R. (1980) 'Causes and Consequences of Increased New Zealand Emigration: A Commentary', in I. Pool (ed.), *Trans-Tasman Migration*, 141-140, Hamilton: Population Studies Centre, University of Waikato.

Yeates, N. (2004) 'Global Care Chains: Critical Reflections and Lines of Enquiry', *International Feminist Journal of Politics* 6(3): 369-391.

Yeates, N. (2005) 'A Global Political Economy of Care', *Social Policy and Society* 4 (2): 227-234.

Zontini, E. (2007) 'Continuity and Change in Transnational Italian Families: The Caring Practices of Second-generation Women', *Journal of Ethnic and Migration Studies* 33 (7) 1103-1119.

Notes on Contributors

Loretta Baldassar is Associate Professor in Anthropology and Sociology at the University of Western Australia. She has published widely on migration, including *Families Caring across Borders: Migration, Aging and Transnational Caregiving* (with Cora Baldock and Raelene Wilding, 2007); *From Paesani to Global Italians: Veneto Migrants in Australia* (with Ros Pesman, 2005); and her award-winning book *Visits Home: Migration Experiences between Italy and Australia* (2001). She is currently editing *Transnational Intimacies* (with Donna Gabaccia), and another book on second-generation identities (with Zlatko Skrbis). She is also engaged in a community project entitled 'Italian Lives in Western Australia'.

Roger Ballard is Director of the Centre for Applied South Asian Studies at the University of Manchester. Having completed his doctorate at the University of Delhi, he returned to the UK to conduct studies of the Sikh community in Leeds and of Pakistani – and especially Kashmiri – Muslim communities in the Pennine Region. On the basis of his extensive fieldwork both in the UK and in settlers' villages of origin, he has also acted as an expert witness in legal proceedings in which South Asian settlers have become involved. In addition to publishing numerous papers in books and journals, he edited *Desh Pardesh: The South Asian Presence in Britain* (1996).

Susana Bastos is Head of the Department of Anthropology in the Faculty of Social Sciences and Humanity at the Universidade Nova de Lisboa, Co-director of Centre for the Study of Migrations and Ethnic Minorities (CEMME), and senior researcher at SociNova Migration. Her books include: *Filhos Diferentes de Deuses Diferentes* (*Different Children of Different Gods*) (2006); *De Moçambique a Portugal* (*From Mozambique to Portugal*) (2001); *Antropologia Urbana* (*Urban Anthropology*) (ed. 2001); *Portugal Multicultural* (*Multicultural Portugal*) (1999); *O Estado Novo e os seus Vadios* (*The 'New State' and Its Vagrants*) (1997); and *A Comunidade Hindu da Quinta da Holandesa* (*The Hindu Comunity at Quinta da Holandesa*) (1990).

José Bastos is Associate Professor at the Department of Anthropology in the Faculty of Social Sciences and Humanity at the Universidade Nova de Lisboa, Co-director of Centre for the Study of Migrations and Ethnic Minorities (CEMME), and senior researcher at SociNova Migration. His publications include: *Sintrenses Ciganos* (*The Gypsies of Sintra*) (2007); *Filhos Diferentes de Deuses Diferentes* (*Different Children of Different Gods*) (2006); *Antropologia dos Processos Identitários* (*Anthropology of Identity Processes*) (ed. 2002); *De Moçambique a Portugal* (*From Mozambique to Portugal*) (2001); *Portugal Europeu: Estratégias Identitárias Internacionais dos Portugueses* (*European Portugal: International Identity Strategies of the Portuguese*) (2000); and *Portugal Multicultural* (*Multicultural Portugal*) (1999).

Maria Lucinda Fonseca is Full Professor of Human Geography and Co-ordinator of the Research Unit on Migration, Cities and Minorities at the Centre for Geographical Studies at the University of Lisbon. She has worked extensively in social and urban geography and migration issues. She is co-leader of the IMISCOE Research Cluster B5 on Social Integration and Mobility, Education, Housing and Health. Recent publications include: 'Social Integration of Immigrants with Special Reference to the Local and Spatial Dimension' in *The Dynamics of International Migration and Settlement in Europe: A State of the Art* (2006) edited by R. Penninx, M. Berger and K. Kraal; 'Building Successful Urban Policy in the New Era of Migration in *Europe and Its Immigrants in the 21st Century: A New Deal or a Continuing Dialogue of the Deaf?* (2006) edited by D. Papademetriou; and *Reunificação Familiar e Imigração em Portugal* (*Family Reunification and Immigration in Portugal*) (2005).

Ralph Grillo is Emeritus Professor of Social Anthropology, University of Sussex. He is the author of *Ideologies and Institutions in Urban France: The Representation of Immigrants* (1985) and *Pluralism and the Politics of Difference: State, Culture, and Ethnicity in Comparative Perspective* (1998). He is co-editor (with Ben Soares) of *Journal of Ethnic and Migration Studies* Special Issue, 30 (5) 2004 on Islam, Transnationalism and the Public Sphere in Western Europe and co-editor (with Valentina Mazzucato) of *Journal of Ethnic and Migration Studies* Special Issue, 34 (2) 2008, on Africa<>Europe: Transnational Linkages, Multi-Sited Lives.

Anniken Hagelund is a sociologist and senior research fellow at the Fafo Institute for Labour and Social Research in Oslo, Norway. She wrote *The Importance of Being Decent: Political Discourse on Immigration in Norway, 1970-2002* (2003) and a number of articles about immigration and integration policy in Scandinavia. Recent publications include: 'Why It Is Bad to be Kind: Educating Refugees to Life in the Welfare

State. A Case Study from Norway' in *Social Policy and Administration*, 39 (6) 2005 and 'A Matter of Decency? The Progress Party in Norwegian Immigration Politics' in *Journal of Ethnic and Migration Studies* 29 (1) 2003.

Kanwal Mand completed her Ph.D. at the University of Sussex in 2004 and worked as a research fellow at the Families and Social Capital ESRC Research Group of London South Bank University. She is currently working on an AHRC-funded project entitled 'Home & Away: Experiences and Representations of South Asian Children'. Her publications include: 'Gender, Ethnicity and Social Relations in the Narratives of Elderly Sikh Men and Women' in *Ethnic and Racial Studies* 29 (6) 2006; 'Friendship and Elderly South Asian Women' in *Community, Work and Family* 9 (3) 2005; and 'Marriage and Migration at the End Stages' in *Indian Journal of Gender Studies* 12 (2-3).

Meghann Ormond is a Ph.D. candidate in cultural and health geographies at the University of St Andrews in the UK. Prior to this, she worked with Maria Lucinda Fonseca at the University of Lisbon's Centro de Estudos Geográficos, conducted research on family migration and urban social exclusion, facilitated the coordination of IMISCOE Cluster B5 on Social Integration and Mobility, Education, Housing and Health and formed part of the 2006 International Metropolis Conference Executive Secretariat. Author and co-author of pieces on international migration, consumption, media and health, she has studied and worked in the US, Canada, Morocco, Belgium, Portugal, the UK and Malaysia.

Radha Rajkotia completed her D.Phil. from the University of Sussex in 2007. Her research and professional work has centred on refugee education, livelihoods, sexuality and gender-based violence, with particular focus on adolescent refugees. She has worked for the Refugee Council and Asphaleia in the UK, and is currently working for the International Rescue Committee as a Youth and Livelihoods Technical Advisor for West Africa. She is based in Freetown, Sierra Leone.

Dan Rodríguez-García is Professor of Social and Cultural Anthropology and a member of the Migration Research Group (GRM) at the Autonomous University of Barcelona. He has conducted research in the Gambia, London, Catalonia and Toronto, with an emphasis on international and transatlantic comparison. His research interests include interethnic relations and models of socio-cultural accommodation, socio-ethnic stratification, intermarriage and transnational families, and ethnic identity processes and intergenerational relations. Recent publications include: *Immigration and Hybridity Today* (*Inmigración y Mestizaje Hoy*, 2004); 'Mixed Marriages and Transnational Families in the Intercultural Context' (*Journal of Ethnic and Migration Studies* 32 (3) 2006); 'Intermarriage Patterns and Socio-Ethnic Stratification among Ethnic Groups in Toronto' (*CERIS Working Paper Series* 60, 2007); and 'Immigration and Models of Incorporation: Contexts, Key Issues, and Future Tendencies', in *Policies and Models of Incorporation, a Transatlantic Perspective: Canada, Germany, France and the Netherlands* (CIDOB Foundation 2007).

Erik Snel studied sociology in Utrecht and is now affiliated with the Department of Sociology at Erasmus University Rotterdam. From 2002 until 2005, he was also affiliated with Twente University in the Netherlands as Professor of Intercultural Policy-Making. His earlier research interests include poverty, migration and immigrant integration, urban development, and urban policies in general. A recent publication is 'Transnational Involvement and Social Integration' (with Godfried Engbersen and Arjen Leerkes) in *Global Networks* 6 (3) 2006.

Anna Stepien graduated in 2000 in European studies at the Faculty of Law in Poznan and is a Ph.D. candidate in political science at the University of Vienna. She is writing her dissertation about the evolution of Islam in Europe based on examples in Austria, Germany and the UK. She has been involved in several research projects with the EUMC (FRA), ICMPD, Austrian Academy of Sciences and Caritas Austria. Her main research interests concern European migration and integration policies, empowerment of migrants and minorities, multicultural education and the evolution and institutionalisation of Islam in Europe. Her publications include: 'Discrimination and Exclusion of Migrants and Minorities in the Field of Employment in the 15 Member States of the European Union' (with M. Jandl and A. Kraler, 2003), 'Muslims in Europe – Unity in Diversity' (2005) and 'Islamic Religious Instruction in Austria: Integrating New Generations of Muslims through Religion?' in the forthcoming book *Educating for Migrant Integration – Integrating Migration into Education: European and North American Comparisons* edited by H. Schissler, P. Triadafilopoulos and R. Ohliger.

Femke Stock graduated in religious studies from the University of Groningen, specialising in Islam and Muslims in Western Europe. Her current Ph.D. research at the same university focuses on issues of home, belonging and identity among descendants of Turkish and Moroccan migrants in the Netherlands.

Susanne Wessendorf obtained her Ph.D. in social anthropology at the University of Oxford. She has a Masters of Philosophy from the University of Basel in social anthropology, European anthropology and linguistics. Her doctoral research focused on second-generation Italians in Switzerland and the interrelationship of integration and transnationalism. Her recent publications are: '"Roots-Migrants": Transnationalism and "Return" among Second-Generation Italians in Switzerland' in *Journal of Ethnic and Migration Studies* 33 (7) 2007 and 'Sushi-Eating Secondos and Casual Latinos: Political Movements and the Emergence of a Latino Counter-Culture among Second-Generation Italians in Switzerland' in *Journal of Intercultural Studies* 28 (3) 2007. She is currently engaged in a post-doctoral project at the Max Planck Institute for the Study of Religious and Ethnic Diversity in Göttingen, investigating patterns of 'super-diversity' in a London neighbourhood.

Index

IMISCOE Reports

Rainer Bauböck, Ed.
Migration and Citizenship: Legal Status, Rights and Political Participation
2006 (ISBN 978 90 5356 888 0)

Michael Jandl, Ed.
Innovative Concepts for Alternative Migration Policies:
Ten Innovative Approaches to the Challenges of Migration in the 21st Century
2007 (ISBN 978 90 5356 990 0)

IMISCOE Dissertations

Panos Arion Hatziprokopiou
Globalisation, Migration and Socio-Economic Change in Contemporary
Greece: Processes of Social Incorporation of Balkan Immigrants in
Thessaloniki
2006 (ISBN 978 90 5356 873 6)

Floris Vermeulen
The Immigrant Organising Process: Turkish Organisations in Amsterdam
and Berlin and Surinamese Organisations in Amsterdam, 1960-2000
2006 (ISBN 978 90 5356 875 0)

Anastasia Christou
Narratives of Place, Culture and Identity:
Second-Generation Greek-Americans Return 'Home'
2006 (ISBN 978 90 5356 878 1)

Katja Rušinović
Dynamic Entrepreneurship:
First and Second-Generation Immigrant Entrepreneurs in Dutch Cities
2006 (ISBN 978 90 5356 972 6)

Ilse van Liempt
Navigating Borders: Inside Perspectives on the Process of Human Smuggling
into the Netherlands
2007 (ISBN 978 90 5356 930 6)

Myriam Cherti
Paradoxes of Social Capital:
A Multi-Generational Study of Moroccans in London
2008 (ISBN 978 90 5356 032 7)

Marc Helbling
*Practising Citizenship and Heterogeneous Nationhood:
Naturalisations in Swiss Municipalities*
2008 (ISBN 978 90 8964 034 5)